REFORMING ANTITRUST

Industrial consolidation, digital platforms, and changing political views have spurred debate about the interplay between public and private power in the United States and have created a bipartisan appetite for potential antitrust reform that would mark the most profound shift in US competition policy in the past half-century. While neo-Brandeisians call for a reawakening of antitrust in the form of a return to structuralism and a concomitant rejection of economic analysis founded on competitive effects, proponents of the status quo look on this state of affairs with alarm. Scrutinizing the latest evidence, Alan J. Devlin finds a middle ground. US antitrust laws warrant revision, he argues, but with far more nuance than current debates suggest. He offers a new vision of antitrust reform, achieved by refining our enforcement policies and jettisoning an unwarranted obsession with minimizing errors of economic analysis.

Alan J. Devlin is a partner with Latham & Watkins LLP and was Acting Deputy Director of the FTC's Bureau of Competition. He is also Adjunct Professor at Georgetown University Law Center. His publications include Antitrust & Patent Law, Principles of Law & Economics, and over thirty articles published at Stanford, Harvard, Yale, Berkeley, Northwestern, and elsewhere.

Reforming Antitrust

ALAN J. DEVLIN

Georgetown University

CAMBRIDGE
UNIVERSITY PRESS

University Printing House, Cambridge CB2 8BS, United Kingdom

One Liberty Plaza, 20th Floor, New York, NY 10006, USA

477 Williamstown Road, Port Melbourne, VIC 3207, Australia

314–321, 3rd Floor, Plot 3, Splendor Forum, Jasola District Centre, New Delhi – 110025, India

103 Penang Road, #05–06/07, Visioncrest Commercial, Singapore 238467

Cambridge University Press is part of the University of Cambridge.

It furthers the University's mission by disseminating knowledge in the pursuit of education, learning, and research at the highest international levels of excellence.

www.cambridge.org
Information on this title: www.cambridge.org/9781316518342
DOI: 10.1017/9781009000260

© Alan J. Devlin 2021

This publication is in copyright. Subject to statutory exception and to the provisions of relevant collective licensing agreements, no reproduction of any part may take place without the written permission of Cambridge University Press.

First published 2021

A catalogue record for this publication is available from the British Library.

Library of Congress Cataloging-in-Publication Data
NAMES: Devlin, Alan (Alan James), author.
TITLE: Reforming antitrust / Alan J. Devlin, Georgetown University, Washington DC.
DESCRIPTION: Cambridge, United Kingdom ; New York, NY : Cambridge University Press, 2021. | Includes index.
IDENTIFIERS: LCCN 2021024996 (print) | LCCN 2021024997 (ebook) | ISBN 9781316518342 (hardback) | ISBN 9781009000260 (ebook)
SUBJECTS: LCSH: Antitrust law. | Competition, Unfair. | Law reform. | BISAC: LAW / Antitrust | LAW / Antitrust
CLASSIFICATION: LCC K3850 .D48 2021 (print) | LCC K3850 (ebook) | DDC 343.07/21–dc23
LC record available at https://lccn.loc.gov/2021024996
LC ebook record available at https://lccn.loc.gov/2021024997

ISBN 978-1-316-51834-2 Hardback
ISBN 978-1-108-99990-8 Paperback

Cambridge University Press has no responsibility for the persistence or accuracy of URLs for external or third-party internet websites referred to in this publication and does not guarantee that any content on such websites is, or will remain, accurate or appropriate.

For Saoirse

Contents

List of Tables		*page* ix
Acknowledgments		x
	Introduction	1
	PART I ANTITRUST TODAY	
1	Competition Law's Role	9
2	Antitrust Fact, Fiction, and the Unknown	33
3	The Missing Link Concentration and Market Power	73
	PART II THE CASE FOR CHANGE	
4	Warning Signs in the Economy Has Competition Declined?	111
5	A Liberal Call to Arms, But Is Deconcentration the Answer?	137
6	Testing the Neo-Brandeisian Vision	174

PART III   ANTITRUST REFORM

7   Taking a Finger Off the Scale
    Revisiting Decision Theory   229

8   Rethinking the Consumer-Welfare Standard   250

9   The Antitrust Evolution   269

    Conclusion
    Key Recommendations   293

Index   308

Table

4.1 Change in market concentration by sector, 1997–2012 *page* 118

Acknowledgments

The views expressed in this book belong to the author alone, and should not be attributed to Latham & Watkins LLP, its clients, lawyers, or staff. The author would like to thank Mark Lemley, Elizabeth Bailey, Mitchell London, Robert Kulick, Sebastian Sohn, Alexandra Clark, Ethan Hoffman, Emily Veillette, and John Gellatly for their thoughtful comments on a prior draft.

Introduction

Antitrust needs an overhaul. So cry neo-Brandeisians, who urge a crackdown on industrial concentration. To the alarm of mainstream antitrust thinkers, the critics have found traction. Hostility to modern competition policy, however, did not arise in a vacuum. This polarized era has seen political upheaval, a populist revival, and diminished faith in capitalism. Implicated in that phenomenon is a renewed focus on antitrust.[1] The left desires a fundamental rethink. Some on the right, dispensing with once-cherished principles, yield to protectionist impulses. Antitrust policy thus finds itself at a rare juncture. A shift in emphasis seems certain; a more radical overhaul is possible.[2]

This point in antitrust history presents an opportunity. A national conversation is upon us – a rare moment for such a wonkish field. Working within a framework largely untouched since 1981, competition law has built on decades of agency experience informed by industrial economics. Today's antitrust thought leaders are rightly proud of the law that they have shaped.[3] Yet, familiarity can impede progress. Some anti-monopolists advance iconoclastic positions. For those warmly accustomed to the status quo, it is easy to reject such claims outright. Yet, reformists have pointed to evidence that, though incomplete and ambiguous, raises troubling questions. Now is a time for introspection.

This book explores US competition policy, both where it is and where it ought to go. Evaluating the latest evidence, it recommends enhancing antitrust scrutiny and offers numerous recommendations accordingly. The book examines policy levers with which to effect suitable changes. The goal is to do so without suppressing procompetitive investments, mergers, agreements, and practices.

In presenting its vision for reform, the book targets the error-cost framework that has long led enforcers to stay their hand in marginal cases. It envisions a recalibration, one that shrinks the incidence of Type II errors – that is, false

---

[1] See, e.g., Daniel A. Crane, *Antitrust's Unconventional Politics*, 104 Va. L. Rev. Online 118 (2018).
[2] See, e.g., Barak Orbach, *The Present New Antitrust Era*, 60 Wm. & Mary L. Rev. 1439 (2019).
[3] See, e.g., FTC Commissioner Noah Joshua Phillips, Prepared Closing Remarkets, 2019 Antitrust Writing Awards Gala Dinner, Mar. 26, 2019, pp. 1–3.

acquittals – and, in turn, fosters enhanced antitrust oversight. Enforcers have overweighted Type I errors – that is, false convictions – in deciding whether to intervene. The result has been suppressed intervention at the margin. Empirical evidence bears out this fact. The number of mergers, restraints, and practices that rest on the liability frontier, and that this point thus implicates, may be limited. But they likely account for most serious antitrust misses. If appropriate reform is afoot, that is where change needs to occur. As the book emphasizes, however, revisiting decision theory does not imply unconstrained antitrust enforcement.

For its part, antitrust's conservative block has oversimplified the law and economics equation. Elevating proof of harmful effects impedes the prosecution of deserving and bad cases alike. Thus, maximizing antitrust's economic content and the robustness of proof required to sustain an antitrust violation may not always be optimal. This observation warrants care because it is easily misunderstood. Enforcers should move further away from structuralism and more closely embrace competitive effects. That is one of the book's principal arguments. Price theory has much to commend it, and represents an important methodology within a larger toolkit. Yet, mathematical identity between antitrust doctrine and economic theory is *necessarily* a deserving goal only in the abstract. Other things being equal, it is desirable when antitrust becomes "purer" as a matter of economics. Yet, it is a mistake conclusively to deem every forward movement along the spectrum a benefit. There may come a point – given practical impediments to suit – beyond which further increments in the requisite proof harms consumers. It is therefore worth exploring whether antitrust's consistent march toward ever-more rigorous economic sophistication has hit an inflection point.

But how to define that point, even assuming that we have passed it? Today's debate implicates coherence, workability, and an analogue to the First Rule of Medicine. The more extreme elements of the reform movement are dubious on each of those grounds. If the curse of history is that we are destined to repeat it, then perhaps looking to the past is in vain. For those inclined to look, however, prior experiences tell much. And the antitrust tale is rich indeed.

Today's approach stands on a robust foundation. The Chicago School overstated efficiency rationales and underestimated the propensity for certain actions to harm competition. Nevertheless, it brought coherence to a policy that had little or none. Indeed, it responded to a stunning lack of lucidity in antitrust law. The tools of price theory – modeling choice through constrained optimization – rationalized analysis, and shifted policy away from the subjective resolution of antitrust questions based on prevailing appetites for trends in concentration. In that respect, we should take stock of everything achieved in the past several decades. Idealism drives well-intentioned calls for reform. The mistake is assuming what is, and asking only what could improve. This is Voltaire's famous line, "Perfect is the enemy of the good."

In that respect, truly radical calls for reform abound. To appreciate how sharply today's neo-Brandeisian movement deviates from the quiet incrementalism of the past several decades, it is worth stepping back. Antitrust's enduring bipartisan support was remarkable, for the field lends itself to division. The law's tenets are bold, implying the antecedent resolution of fundamental questions. Those issues include how best to spur economic activity while cabining private commercial power, the efficacy of state intervention, the roles of wealth creation and distribution, the limits of property rights and contractual freedom, and the virtue of a free market. These are core societal questions. In setting the rules of marketplace behavior, antitrust law judges contestable propositions. One might thus expect competition policy to be more controversial than it has typically been.

Instead, antitrust found itself so definitively resolved that, for a time, it lay in academic doldrums. Arguably neglected by the academy after a period of transformative writing in the 1970s and 1980s, competition law seemed to have had its day. Disagreement centered on judgments at the periphery of the law – particularly dominant-firm liability. Perhaps the most controversial policy disagreement concerned how to distinguish legitimate and improper forms of exclusionary conduct.[4] Few questioned core propositions that define modern antitrust law.

No longer. The field is engulfed in controversy, as political movements from both sides of the spectrum question free-market propositions. A precision instrument honed to protect competitive constraints on the exercise of market power, antitrust stands accused of missing the big picture. The economic meltdown of 2008 formed the tinderbox. Corporate consolidation, the rise of Silicon Valley, an exodus from centrism, populism's resurgence, and a countermovement on the left lit the match. Issues larger than antitrust are at play. Open markets may no longer be a core – let alone definitional – societal value in the west. Some observers apparently view them as fallible constructs founded on dubious foundations. Effects-based antitrust no longer finds favor across the spectrum. Many observers think it due a transformation.

For some on the left, "neoclassical" has become a dirty word – one synonymous with a free-market dogma that has allowed corporations to run wild. Activists see resurgent economic power and an alarming rate of industrial consolidation. A failed competition policy, tracing in particular to the "law and economics" movement, looms large in the imagination. The dominant antitrust methodology, antimonopolists say, focuses on static market effects to the exclusion of larger economic phenomena. The prevailing antitrust mindset, they add, suffers a Chicago School-inspired affliction – a naïve supposition that markets rapidly self-correct and that interventionist policy would chill investment. On such critics' view, the results speak

[4] Cf. U.S. DEP'T OF JUSTICE, COMPETITION AND MONOPOLY: SINGLE-FIRM CONDUCT UNDER SECTION 2 OF THE SHERMAN ACT (2008) (revoked 2009) *with* Statement of Commissioners Harbour, Leibowitz and Rosch on the Issuance of the Section 2 Report by the Department of Justice 1 (Sept. 8, 2008), http://www.ftc.gov/os/2008/09/080908section2stmt.pdf, *and* Statement of Federal Trade Commission Chairman William E. Kovacic, Modern U.S. Competition Law and the Treatment of Dominant Firms: Comments on the Department of Justice and Federal Trade Commission Proceedings Relating to Section 2 of the Sherman Act (Sept. 8, 2008), http://www.ftc.gov/os/2008/09/080908section2stmtkovacic.pdf.

from themselves: the Great Recession flowed from unchecked concentration, while Big Tech now dominates the digital sector. Gathering consumer data and distorting input markets through monopsonistic buying positions, large intermediaries allegedly face too few constraints. These results – supposedly – flow from an anemic antitrust policy, one blind to the big picture and in thrall to an orthodox economic theory good only for advancing laissez faire principles.

Today's anti-monopoly movement has not been shy in diagnosing American competition policy. No longer a centrist anchor, antitrust is in a "regrettable place."[5] Staking out extreme positions, some question whether "we even really have a competition policy at all."[6] Such critics harbor skepticism of any social value from mergers and acquisitions. It has been conventional wisdom that M&A activity can realize scale and scope economies, productivities, reduced input costs, and maintain a market for corporate control that disciplines incumbent management and replaces incompetents. For interventionists, however, "there is in fact no meaningful proof that consolidation generates social benefits."[7] Some progressive politicians echo such views, with Senator Elizabeth Warren warning, for example, that "today, in America, competition is dying. Consolidation and concentration are on the rise in sector after sector. Concentration threatens our markets, threatens our economy, and threatens our democracy."[8] Some believe that recent Supreme Court jurisprudence "devastates antitrust law."[9]

To those warmly disposed to contemporary policy, the debate's direction is troubling. Respected scholars leading the charge champion some radical overhauls. Consider Timothy Wu, a Columbia Law Professor noted for his work on net neutrality and generally considered a free-market skeptic. He equates contemporary antitrust with the rise of totalitarianism, extremist populism, and even fascism. In his view, modern enforcement has made a "mockery" of the antitrust laws, yielding "concentrated economic power in ways that are dangerous to the polity."[10] In March 2020, he became a special assistant to President Biden on technology and competition policy as a member of the National Economic Council. Lina Khan, now Chairwoman of the FTC, is another example. She calls for Title II-style common carrier regulation of digital-platform intermediaries or for a rewriting of antitrust law to prohibit their vertical integration. She has also suggested that the agencies discontinue their use of divestitures in resolving mergers that involve limited horizontal overlaps, obliging them to sue to enjoin every merger with a problematic horizontal overlap, no matter

---

[5] Chris Sagers, *American Antitrust Is Having a Moment: Some Reactions to Commissioner Ohlhausen's Recent Views*, ProMarket, Sept. 16, 2016, https://promarket.org/american-antitrust-moment-reactions-commissioner-ohlhausens-recent-views/.
[6] *Id.*
[7] *Id.*
[8] https://www.warren.senate.gov/files/documents/2016-6-29_Warren_Antitrust_Speech.pdf.
[9] Tim Wu, *The Supreme Court Devastates Antitrust Law*, N.Y. Times, June 26, 2018.
[10] Tim Wu, *Be Afraid of Economic 'Bigness.' Be Very Afraid*, N.Y. Times, Nov. 10, 2018, https://www.nytimes.com/2018/11/10/opinion/sunday/fascism-economy-monopoly.html.

how discrete or severable it may be vis-à-vis the larger transaction.¹¹ The *New York Times* has lauded her scholarly work on what she perceives to be antitrust problems with Amazon's business model, among others.¹²

Such denunciation is not the exclusive province of the far left. Rather, it has been part of a crescendo of policy debate over the past several years. The birthplace of the modern economic approach to antitrust law, the University of Chicago, has even been at the forefront of calls for revisiting competition policy.¹³ It has hosted academic debate not so much on whether today's antitrust laws have gone astray, but how transformative a fix is necessary. Even classically liberal voices, including from *The Economist*, conclude that the United States has a monopoly problem.¹⁴ Giving weight to the movement for reform, the Federal Trade Commission began hearings in September 2018 devoted to questioning the most sacred of cows – including the propriety of antitrust's guiding lodestar since the 1970s, the consumer-welfare standard. Meanwhile, certain of those on the right question international trade agreements, laud tariffs, and have even suggested – however obliquely – that antitrust be wielded as a political tool. Meanwhile, even some economists have suggested that antitrust has failed at its game.¹⁵ In that respect, calls for reform go beyond the far-left and now trace to a growing progressive consensus about the need to strengthen antitrust intervention.

This book takes seriously claims that antitrust, in its pursuit of economic precision, may overlook larger effects. Indeed, after careful exposition, it concludes that we should indeed explore the periphery of today's doctrine and – with care – venture beyond. This does not imply a wholesale expansion of antitrust liability. To the contrary, reform should focus at the margin   that is, on those investigations that hover on the edge of impermissibility and turn on questions of uncertainty. The agencies should revisit how they think about error costs, and no longer uniformly err on the side of nonintervention. The default approach should minimize the raw number of errors. A weighting exercise should follow based on analyzing the candidate universe of outcomes. Meanwhile, a flexible reimagination of doctrinal antitrust analysis would work wonders. Market definition stands out for particular attention. And competition policy would benefit were courts to go beyond simplistic appeal to "consumer welfare" in framing antitrust's normative content. That is the book's central contribution, and the focus of Part III.

---

[11] Lina Khan, *How to reboot the FTC: The agency's antitrust policy isn't up to the challenge of the 21st century. Here's how to fix it*, POLITICO, Apr. 13, 2016, https://www.politico.com/agenda/story/2016/04/ftc-antitrust-economy-monopolies-000090.

[12] David Streitfeld, *Amazon's Antitrust Antagonist Has a Breakthrough Idea*, N.Y. TIMES, Sept. 7, 2018, https://www.nytimes.com/2018/09/07/technology/monopoly-antitrust-lina-khan-amazon.html.

[13] Schumpeter, *The University of Chicago worries about a lack of competition*, THE ECONOMIST, Apr. 12, 2017.

[14] *The problem with profits: Big firms in the United States have never had it so good. Time for more competition*, THE ECONOMIST, Mar. 26, 2016.

[15] See, e.g., Joseph E. Stiglitz, *America Has a Monopoly – and It's Huge*, THE NATION, Oct. 23, 2017.

Competition policy goes hand in hand with the free market. By design, antitrust serves a secondary function. Its role is subordinate and prophylactic. It never seeks to dictate the "right" level of competition – much less to increase it. Its goals are modest. It protects whatever competition exists, but otherwise hands the keys of economic activity over to market participants. Monopoly is perfectly lawful, and has (at times) even been celebrated as the fuel of a generally self-defeating pursuit of victory over one's rivals. Antitrust policy presumes that markets work better than government intervention when they are free of artificial restraints on trade, exclusionary practices, and anticompetitive mergers. Buttressed by suitable regulations – that is, those that project useful information without unjustifiably burdening firms – markets will attract entrants, grow more competitive, and produce better outcomes for consumers and society.

That is a system worth defending. The book champions antitrust's free-market foundation, debunks calls to reinvigorate structuralism, and proposes reforms that will enhance competition as evolving markets raise new challenges. Above all, this debate turns on the evidence. Part I explores antitrust's normative underpinnings, and then evaluates vital questions that inform competition policy. These include the propensity of the market to self-correct, the relationship between seller concentration and market power, and how often mergers create valuable efficiencies. An objective assessment of the empirical literature should guide reform discussions – not impressionistic assessments that characterize many calls for a revolution.

By necessity, this books covers much ground in its quest to identify suitable reforms. For the busy reader interested in bottom-line recommendations, the Conclusion represents the port of call.

PART I

Antitrust Today

1

Competition Law's Role

1.1 INTRODUCTION

Antitrust stands accused of failure. That charge, of course, presupposes a normative metric. One cannot evaluate a policy – much less proclaim its shortcomings – without one. Alas, some reformists obscure their message. In their view, Silicon Valley, drug prices, airline concentration, and other salient issues demonstrate antitrust failure. Whether the problem lies in execution or a misguided lodestar, however, receives little attention. Obfuscation results. Evaluating antitrust incursions requires a goal, for without one analytic rigor is impossible and enforcement thus arbitrary.

What does antitrust seek to accomplish? To that elementary question, there is no universal or widely accepted answer. To the uninitiated, such a state of affairs may seem bizarre, not least because the Sherman Act has existed for 130 years. Although the late twentieth century saw progress toward a common goal, the matter is again subject to contentious debate. To be sure, antitrust policy is neither capricious nor bereft of guiding principles. At a certain level of abstraction, evident themes emerge. Passed in response to widespread collusion and monopolization through trusts in the late nineteenth century, the Sherman Act reflects an obvious procompetitive mandate. Hardcore price-fixing cartels obviously violate the law's most essential principles. So, too, mergers to monopoly do violence to the spirit of the antitrust laws. Unfortunately, delving into less egregious conduct reveals ambiguities and contradictions. Simple normative theories quickly unravel. Peering into the antitrust enterprise reveals complexity, nuance, and – ultimately – ambiguity.

The difficulty lies in competition itself. Markets witness an ostensible paradox. In order to enhance competition, firms often must restrain it. Investment in anticipation of future demand is the essential ingredient of economic growth. Technological innovation, infrastructure development, product-line extensions, and market entry – to name just a few – require upfront expenditures. Investment fuels the dynamic competition that matters over time, but it is vulnerable to appropriation. Anticipated free riding may act as a break. Just as our patent and copyright laws seek to promote expenditures in technological and artistic endeavors, so certain private restraints on competition can drive socially valuable investment over time. This is the genesis of the ancillary-restraint doctrine, which justifies, among other things, productive joint ventures. The premise is that multiple companies can sometimes offer superior products together than they could apart. Indeed, the same principle underlies the firm itself. Every company eliminates competition between its employees and executives.

That is why the Supreme Court has long recognized that antitrust's most important statutory rule – every contract, combination, or conspiracy in restraint of trade is illegal – cannot mean what it says. Only unreasonable restraints violate the antitrust laws. What reasonableness means, of course, brings us back to the underlying question. What is the Sherman Act's purpose, its raison d'être? Only with the answer can one meaningfully address what the antitrust laws *should* prohibit. And, for the reasons just discussed, it is no response to point to competition alone. Maximizing competition in the most simplistic sense of the term would be self-destructive.

The most simplistic view of competition means atomistic markets populated by myriad sellers, homogeneous goods, perfect information, and prices tending toward the marginal cost of production. That is the textbook model of perfect competition. Premised on outlandish assumptions, it is an abstraction never realized in the real world. It has long been a useful benchmark in applying neoclassical price theory. It may also serve as the ultimate vision for neo-Brandeisians who clamor for a world free of industrial concentration and accumulations of economic and political power.

Perfect competition is, however, a decidedly poor aspiration for most markets. It leaves no room for economic profits, meaning that firms cannot recoup fixed-cost investments. The allocative and productive efficiencies associated with perfect competition are obviously desirable, but only from a *static* perspective. Certain mature "bricks and mortar" industries are good candidates for antitrust policy not only informed – but driven – by price-theoretic models. The static efficiencies engendered in price's trending toward marginal cost likely dominate. Two problems, however, remain.

First, the relationship between concentration and market outcomes is not fully understood. From a static perspective, of course, monopoly is bad and perfect competition is good. We are not entirely ignorant about the middle part of the spectrum. In some industries, price outcomes improve with numerous successive entrants, making duopolistic or oligopolistic market structures undesirable. In other settings, however, concentrated industries appear competitive even with just a handful of competitors. Customer sophistication matters. If capable of playing one seller off against another, buyers may not need many options in order to discipline attempted exercises of market power.

Hence, few hard "rules" govern across all markets. Some industries have fixed-to-marginal cost relationships that cause firms' long-run average-cost curves to decline over a large output range. The ultimate example is natural monopoly, where one firm can most efficiently (from the perspective of cost) supply all consumer demand. But numerous less pronounced examples exist. Those markets naturally gravitate toward concentrated industry structures. This means that, even from a static perspective, "maximizing competition" is no straightforward task. Price-cost tradeoffs result, even in the short run.

Second, few industries are so staid that innovation would not yield better products or reduced costs over time. The dynamic element changes everything. Competition can mean maximizing downward competitive pressure on price in the short run or preserving incentives to invest by refusing to encumber property rights through antitrust intervention. It can mean pervasive intervention in the name of industry deconcentration or just the opposite. Dynamic effects, though complex and sometimes impossible accurately to gauge, are of the utmost importance. Antitrust enforcers cannot simply ignore them.

As the complexities come into focus, tradeoffs abound. The Sherman Act – like the Clayton, FTC, and Robinson–Patman Acts – envisions some legal curtailment of private firms' freedom of contract in order to protect competition. The measure of competition thus envisioned, however, is most unclear. Indeed, the statutes mentioned are themselves in tension on the subject, with the Robinson–Patman Act's proscription of certain price discrimination evincing a protectionist goal in tension with the consumer focus typically read into Sherman Act jurisprudence in the modern era. And we have not yet considered the view that promotes deconcentration as a standalone antitrust purpose.

Competition, therefore, cannot in itself define policy. Nor can the past 130 years of Sherman Act jurisprudence provide the requisite clarity. Untethered to a fixed goal, antitrust has meandered over time. Its historical arc is one of wild contradiction. It broke up trusts, blessed others, suspended enforcement, later prohibited mergers conferring scant economic power on the parties, outlawed many vertical restraints, and has since reversed course across the board. History teaches that an objective framework for administering competition policy is critical. Without it, enforcement reduces to ad hoc determinations, subjectivities, and inconsistencies. That was perhaps the most enduring insight of the 1970s Chicago revolution, which brought a focus on neoclassical economics and consumer welfare that has endured to the present day. Neo-Brandeisians, by contrast, look with affection on the Warren Court's inhospitality tradition – the last enforcement period characterized by opposition to consolidation and size as standalone issues.

We cannot resolve today's resurgent antitrust debate without first exploring the law's underlying purpose. Calls to break up today's most successful digital platforms, for example, may reflect an antitrust mandate to limit concentration of economic (or political) power as an end in itself. Or they may reflect a judgment that the accused companies achieved their dominance by unscrupulous methods, and that intervention is necessary in order to restore lost competition. Consider the following hypothetical:

An innovator competes on the merits, racing ahead of its rivals in a network market. Supracompetitive prices ensue, and no credible rival emerges to challenge the monopoly rents. Depending on the relevant goal, the ensuing dominance may be (i) problematic if competition policy opposes monopoly, however obtained; (ii) laudatory if revealed consumer preference dominates other values, the monopolist does not invest in inhibiting other channels of potential competition, and the law wishes to preserve incentives to innovate; (iii) unacceptable if the resulting concentration of wealth and power distorts the democratic process; (iv) ambiguous if consumer demand produced the monopoly, but network-effect-driven path dependence or other obstacles insulate the dominant firm from competitive pressures over time; or (v) even more equivocal if the prescriptive goal blends several considerations. Indeed, any manner of normative permutations is possible depending on the facts.

Even that illustration reveals a critical point. Any debate over antitrust's future lacks meaning without an antecedent resolution of the normative question – to what end? Never has that reality been more clear than today, given increasingly hysterical claims of market failure and the need for an antitrust revolution. Amazon, Apple, Facebook, Google, Microsoft, Uber, and other leading technology firms are the most frequent objects of condemnation. But the criticism brought to bear on them and the economy more generally reflects a painful lack of nuance. Some radical views reflect barely veiled swipes at capitalism. Other commentary, by contrast, has been incremental, evidence-based, and thoughtful.

No antitrust mandate has emerged that is both rigorously defined and widely accepted. The uninitiated might find that claim surprising. Antitrust conferences, for example, often imply a broader consensus than exists. Enforcers laud global "convergence" in substance and procedure. Those claims are at best aspirational, however, because disparities abound. Yes, there is agreement, but generally about uncontroversial propositions. Naked horizontal price-fixing and mergers to monopoly offend a spectrum of normative goals. Venturing beyond the banal, however, reveals glaring divergence. Perhaps in the interests of civility, agencies seldom interrogate the soundness of other countries' antitrust goals. Exceptions are often received coolly. And, even in the United States, the two federal antitrust agencies have repeatedly been at odds. Despite assurances to the contrary, little agreement exists on the *precise* goals of competition law.

That dynamic is regretful because the global antitrust community would benefit from more rigorous debate. Too often, government officials retreat behind empty platitudes, embracing concepts that are uncontroversial because they are too abstract to be meaningful. The line that "antitrust protects competition, not competitors," for example, has become de rigueur. It is hollow. It equally supports honoring a successful monopolist's right not to deal with its rivals (antitrust does not worry about their welfare) as it does unbounded compulsory dealing (one cannot have competition without competitors). The view that consumers are the proper beneficiaries of competition policy enjoys similar widespread support. But it, too, possesses little standalone value. Appealing to consumer interest can justify almost any government intervention in a market.

This chapter – the first of nine that collectively address antitrust reform – thus explores the goals of competition law. Resolving this issue by no means resolves the debate. Even with a defined objective, molding antitrust doctrine to achieve sought ends is difficult. To calibrate the ends-means relationship with precision is likely impossible. Exploring antitrust's normative content, however, is an essential first step.

1.2 ANTITRUST'S "POLITICAL CONTENT"

Antitrust is political. That is a controversial assertion, which often leads competition lawyers to bristle. They rightly value their chosen field's analytic purity. Although unhealthy orthodoxy may have taken root in the past two decades, antitrust today employs a rigorous methodology. Enforcers dispassionately apply industrial organization and econometrics to predict harms under the consumer-welfare standard. To invoke politics is to suggest the whimsy of executive interference or the arbitrary promotion of preferred actors' interests over those of others. That conception is a world apart from contemporary US antitrust practice. No wonder that counsel view charges of political content as impugning their craft.

In many practitioners' view, the scientific apparatus of economics contrasts favorably with the capricious jurisprudence of value-driven fields of law. To impute political judgments to antitrust – as one might to constitutional law – taints the enterprise. This illustrates a phenomenon true of law and economics more generally. Modeling, mathematics, and empiricism conjure up an image of objectivism and precision. But although there is indeed an exacting methodology afoot, it rests on a normative foundation. It is in that sense that antitrust law displays a political character. As a policy, it requires value judgments. Many of those determinations are contestable, and trace to priors and norms on which there is – and has always been – a spectrum of views.

That is why antitrust has an inescapable political dimension. It traces to fundamental choices about how to structure society. Indeed, antitrust laws themselves imply a prior resolution of core value-based questions, most obviously whether to employ a capitalistic market system in the first place. Communism, to draw on an obvious example, displaces private property rights. It is therefore inconsistent with the competitive pressures attendant on voluntary exchange that antitrust laws, at least in their neoclassical conception, protect. Under any standard, however, antitrust is meaningless without competition. Hence, by extinguishing property rights over the means of production, socialism also deprives the country's industrial and production processes of the benefits of competition. There, too, antitrust has no role beyond protecting whatever rivalry may emerge in the alienation of personal property. In short, antitrust presupposes a market system for allocating scarce property rights.

To have antitrust is therefore to accept – to at least some degree – the role of capitalism in spurring economic growth. But it is also to admit the fallibility of markets themselves. If markets quickly dispatched restraints, exclusionary practices, and efforts to charge supracompetitive prices, there would be no need for the Sherman, Clayton, and FTC Acts. Not even the most ardent free-marketeer, however, would embrace such a characterization of the real world. All markets are imperfectly competitive, allowing firms to exercise a measure of market power. Self-correction occurs, but to varying degrees and with dissimilar speed across industries. Antitrust helps markets achieve their promise. At root, competition laws reflect a belief that markets freed of artificial restraints, exclusionary practices, and anti-competitive mergers will produce superior outcomes than those left free of oversight or ones controlled by the state. That much should be – and the author ventures to say is – uncontroversial. Much of the debate centers on what further ends – if any – to which society ought to direct its antitrust laws.

It is worth pausing here to dispatch a caricature often conjured up by those who reject a neoclassical approach to antitrust policy. In particular, critics equate adherents to the "Chicago School" with an ideological bent that uncritically presumes markets to be efficient and government intervention to range from ineffectual to harmful. In surveilling what they consider to be the sad state of antitrust today, such reformists take center aim at the Chicago School's injection of neoclassical price theory into the hard of US competition policy.

Chicago is thus the principal villain of neo-Brandeisians. Their reform movement, however, is merely the latest in a long line of detractors who mischaracterize antitrust's modern constitution. In their terminology, "neoclassical" is a dirty word – one laden with implied laissez faire malice. Critics have long equated the Chicago School's use of price theory with far-fetched suppositions like perfectly efficient capital markets, rapid market self-correction, pervasive merger-generated efficiencies, regulatory capture, and government overview characterized by clumsy and ill-informed intervention decisions.[1] Any association with Chicago implies destructive policy premised on the unsubstantiated dogma that "the market will sort it out." This is one of antitrust's most enduring falsehoods, and it ought to be put to rest.

That strawman approach is ill-informed and, at times, disingenuous. The truth is that evaluating any industry under a neoclassical framework reveals a pervasive failure to achieve perfect competition. In theory, such shortcomings open the door to intervention. The challenge for antitrust is to unleash the potential of flawed markets. Indeed, the industrial-organization field that informs antitrust is, by

---

[1] Even leading members of the antitrust bar have fallen prey to mischaracterizing what the Chicago School represents. A prominent example lies in a subset of essays edited by the late Bob Pitofsky. How the Chicago School Overshot the Mark: The Effect of Conservative Economic Analysis on U.S. Antitrust (Robert Pitofsky ed., 2008).

definition, the economic analysis of imperfectly competitive markets. True laissez faire policies are therefore inconsistent with neoclassical antitrust models.

Of course, prominent advocates of the Chicago School in decades past championed policy that too readily dismissed the plausibility of anticompetitive conduct. It is a mistake, however, to conflate methodologies with priors. The Chicago School's enduring tenet is to construe antitrust as "a branch of applied economics."[2] The field develops in line with the industrial-organization literature from which it draws. As economists refine their understanding and identify new circumstances in which practices harm competition, so antitrust's prohibitory scope will evolve in kind. A more interventionist policy than found favor in the halls of the University of Chicago in the 1970s is perfectly in tune with the School's methodological prescriptions.

In that respect, shortcomings associated with the early Chicago literature are best understood as the product of an incomplete industrial-organization literature. That body of knowledge was itself in flux during the 1960s and 1970s – driven in no small part by Chicago economists' debunking previously established Structure-Conduct-Performance/SCP methodologies. The excesses of the early Chicago School may also reflect an overreaction to the incoherent antitrust jurisprudence of the Warren Court. The Chicago School's principal contribution is as valuable today as it was forty years ago. Antitrust should draw on industrial economics, using the best models available to predict future competitive effects or econometrics to measure the impact of past conduct. Neoclassical economics and game theory remain integral to those efforts. Learning and evolving views on the frequency and significance of exclusionary conduct and market self-correction pay homage to that legacy. By no means do they indict the Chicago tradition.

Hence, on no plausible reading does antitrust reduce to a laissez faire capitalist ideology. Far from it; antitrust exists in opposition to unbridled capitalism. It reflects a basic insight from law and economics. Private contracting inures to the public interest only when bargaining is free of negative externalities. Consumers do not have a seat at the table (let alone a veto) when rivals agree to fix prices, allocate territories, limit output, merge to monopoly, and the like. Hence, firms left to run wild would contract for their mutual benefit at buyers' expense. The law must therefore limit freedom of contract in order to preserve a free market – a paradox that lies at the heart of antitrust. Similar analysis extends to acquisitions and unilateral conduct.

Free markets thus do not work efficiently without some intervention. The difficulty is to find the right blend of private and public control. Effective policy harnesses the power of profit-maximization in a socially valuable direction, leading firms to innovate and compete for success rather than to take it for themselves through mutual agreement. An information problem, of course, afflicts government

---

[2] RICHARD A. POSNER, THE PROBLEMATICS OF MORAL AND LEGAL THEORY 229 (1999).

decision-making. Markets have a systemic advantage because private actors – firms and consumers – reveal their own preferences through voluntary exchange. The state could never hope to efficiently allocate scarce resources to their highest value uses. Yet, a hands-off approach to market oversight allows sellers (and, in some cases, buyers) to appropriate value that would otherwise flow to third parties.

Economic activity is not a zero-sum game. Markets do not simply reallocate wealth, creating recurring sets of winners and losers. Economic growth creates additional value, which can – at least in theory – make everyone better off. Save in the rare case of infinitely inelastic demand, any exercise of market power (on the sell side) will reduce output and raise the market-clearing price. A wealth transfer results in sellers' favor. Similarly, firms that exercise market power on the buy side restrict the quantity of sold inputs, shifting wealth in their favor. An ensuing forfeiture of social value – deadweight loss – ensures that the net harms experienced dominate the benefits conferred. That elementary analysis leads to a basic insight. Firms that either conspire to eliminate competition between them or achieve monopoly power reduce social welfare.

That much is clear and widely understood. It is, however, an incomplete picture. As noted, dynamic considerations can swamp short-term efficiency effects. But there is a more fundamental complication, which goes to the concept of social welfare itself.

The social-welfare criterion is the root of perennial disagreement. Determining which effects are socially valuable, innocuous, or harmful rests on a value judgment. Those determinations are inherently political. Bipartisan – if not unanimous – opposition to naked cartel activity and mergers to monopoly can obscure this point. The reality is contested normative underpinnings.

Wealth maximization and horizontal equity lie in age-old tension. Antitrust cannot meet the Pareto superior criterion, which requires that reallocations make at least someone better off without harming anyone. Third-party effects are pervasive and impossible to remediate. A workable criterion is the Pareto improvement standard, which requires net increases in welfare, but does not demand the compensation of those harmed by a "procompetitive" practice. For example, antitrust does not require a successful innovator and its consumer beneficiaries to compensate rivals bankrupted by the winner's technological achievements. Nevertheless, Pareto improvements can be controversial. For instance, society may take issue with a competition policy that promotes rapid economic growth at the expense of aggravating income inequality. That concern, among others, is a principal motivator of the neo-Brandeisian movement.

Equally storied is the question of which stakeholders' interests should dominate others if the law is not to treat all actors equally. A societal preference for advancing certain actors' welfare has long informed competition policy. A state may value the interests of small businesses over others, yielding protectionist policies that inhibit competition. The Robinson–Patman Act, which prohibits certain forms of price discrimination, exemplifies that goal.³ Given contemporary norms, federal antitrust agencies do not enforce the statute. Those of a different political persuasion may wish for more aggressive enforcement. Here, again, we see a force behind today's antitrust-reform debate. Some commentators recoil at homogeneous national chains, and would rather embrace an eclectic array of smaller-scale (perhaps family-owned) businesses that infuse neighborhoods with character and distinctiveness at an acceptable increment in price.

Of course, such value determinations need not embrace extremes. A citizenry may wish for economic growth founded on efficiency-enhancing competition, and yet choose to limit excess by engendering certain protections in the law. As we shall see below, the result is an internally contradictory policy, but choosing to embrace or reject such a policy remains a value-driven (and hence arguably political) determination.

Political values go beyond whether to pick winners and losers. Even with broad consensus as to antitrust's overarching goals, priors inform – and arguably control – competition policy. Conflicting views on the efficacy of markets inform almost every stage of the antitrust enterprise. The persistence of market power, the relationship between concentration and incentives to innovate, capital market efficiency, entry barriers, and above all the tradeoff between static and dynamic efficiency are all disputed.

Some people may accept in the abstract that markets serve a useful purpose, and yet doubt their workings. They may view profit-maximization incentives with suspicion, and question the equity of a system that reallocates scarce property to "higher value uses" when that value reflects not utility, but willingness and ability to pay. Wealth, in turn, typically reflects initial property allocations of dubious merit. People whose moral compass and intuition point in this direction will prefer antitrust goals that depart sharply from those articulated by free-marketeers. Their natural inclination may be to intervene in order to correct market outcomes that deviate from their preferred result. In their view, antitrust guards against capitalism's excesses.

On that account, competition policy assumes a broad role within a capitalistic economy. It does not merely safeguard competition – for, in some critics' estimation, markets do not work well absent governmental correction. Antitrust becomes something more – a tool with which to engineer superior outcomes. Four phenomena can result.

First comes an effort to *increase* (as opposed merely to preserve) competition. If enforcers look askance at a dominated industry, for example, they may seek to "fix" the market's structure. They may wish to break up large companies or impose compulsory-dealing obligations in order to buttress fledgling rivals. They may do so not as a remedy for exclusion, but simply to improve the market's competitiveness.

---

³ 15 U.S.C. § 13.

Scale economies that naturally drive a degree of concentration may receive little credit. On the merger front, without evidence that the deals will enable the post-closing entity more effectively to compete, horizontal transactions may be categorically disfavored. Such deals, after all, entail some loss of competition. Horizontal restraints may attract even greater scrutiny, and joint venturers may experience pressure to demonstrate that they have structured their otherwise-legitimate collaboration in such a way as to minimize any ancillary restraints.

Second, free-market critics may doubt the extent to which restraining trade enhances competition. Every firm, of course, supplants rivalry between its members in order to coordinate economic activity more efficiently than would be possible through contract. By the same token, maximum competition does not mean minimum concentration. Shoehorning atomistic competition onto high-fixed-cost industries would be enormously destructive, yielding higher costs, prices, and dynamism. It is hard to deny those basic facts, but it is fair to probe the circumstances in which the tradeoff is net positive.

Hence, those who reject neoclassical antitrust often question whether it is truly necessary to inhibit competition in order to secure disproportionate benefits elsewhere. This tends to align with a structural view of competition in which antitrust's purported goal is not to protect pricing pressures, but to foster unconcentrated industry. On that view, firms that restrain competition in order to foster efficiencies or become more effective competitors may receive a cool welcome. The foremost villain may be merger-driven consolidation. Critics of modern antitrust policy take particular issue with the FTC's and DOJ's crediting merger-specific efficiencies in approving acquisitions.[4]

Focusing on a static form of competition – particularly one grounded in structuralism – leaves little room for dynamic effects. This perspective may flow from priors that elevate the power of atomistic competition over claimed benefits flowing from restraints. This line of thought, of course, produces a less accommodating antitrust policy. Vertical restraints often come within the crosshairs. Exclusive selling territories and minimum resale prices, for example, shield certain distribution channels from competition. Economists have long explained that such protection can enhance interbrand competition by limiting free riding and spurring distributors to invest in the relevant product. The manufacturer wishes only to minimize its cost of distribution, of course, and would thus generally restrain competition within its own vertical chain only in anticipation of a demand-enhancing benefit. Absent upstream or downstream collusion, resale price maintenance may be presumptively efficient. With this example as with many others, however, market skeptics may see

---

[4] *See, e.g.*, Chris Sagers, *American Antitrust Is Having a Moment: Some Reactions to Commissioner Ohlhausen's Recent Views*, ProMarket, Sept. 16, 2016, https://promarket.org/american-antitrust-moment-reactions-commissioner-ohlhausens-recent-views/. ("Contrary to what Federal Trade Commissioner Maureen Ohlhausen says, there is in fact no meaningful proof that consolidation generates social benefits.").

imbalance. The fact of restrained competition is plain for all to see, while the offsetting benefits may appear conjectural. A worry that resale price maintenance stabilizes prices and denies consumers a form of valuable intrabrand competition may take root.

Depending on where one stands on distrusting markets and favoring public intervention, it can be easy to discount (or even reject) the proposition that limiting head-to-head competition may enhance a more productive form of rivalry. Further to this effort, one might argue in favor of a rule of reason standard that allows procompetitive restraints on trade only when the ancillary restraint on competition is the *least* restrictive one possible.[5]

Third, antitrust expands beyond its neoclassical conception. It does not simply preserve competitive pressures on firm behavior. Rather, it assumes a regulatory dimension. This view blurs the distinction between (1) the ex ante preservation of market constraints and (2) ex post price and service regulation. A distrust of capitalism drives this view: flawed markets do not warrant deference, and market-clearing prices are not the sacrosanct product of a reliable process. From that perspective, imperfect competition yields market failures that justify intervention.

To be sure, certain industries may require price and quality-of-service regulation – specifically, natural monopolies. But market skeptics may bring a broader array of industries within the regulatory umbrella. Rather than be satisfied with preserving competition, they may scrutinize market outcomes and work to change them if they depart from acceptable ranges. At this juncture, antitrust leaves its neoclassical role of maintaining competitive pressures and enters the regulatory fold.

In recent US history, error concerns have left agencies humble about the scope of their knowledge and their capacity to intervene to desirable effect. Such considerations may ring hollow, however, to those whose natural inclination is to trust the government over markets in identifying and solving failures. And even those who generally support market processes may object to opportunistic conduct – price gouging is a common example – and support employing competition laws accordingly.

Antitrust prohibitions on "unfair" transactions result, leading to legal proscriptions on excessive prices or draconian trading terms. Although such rules do not presently exist in the United States, they are an established part of most competition regimes around the world. Those looking to correct a perceived loss of competition in the economy – or to protect vulnerable consumers against excessive pricing – may favor expanding antitrust's reach beyond preserving market constraints to condemn undesirable effects themselves. In practice, the closest that US antitrust law has come to this position is the FTC's infrequent (and controversial) use of Section 5 to enjoin unfair methods of competition that do not violate the Sherman Act. Notably, in June 2019, the FTC's two Democratic Commissioners issued a statement

---

[5] Under the rule of reason, most circuits require a plaintiff to prove that there was a substantially less restrictive restraint than the challenged restriction (which has a legitimate procompetitive justification).

exploring the possibility of using Section 5 "to challenge excessive, unjustified drug price increases."[6] That remains a minority position, but a change of administration could elevate that view to policy.

Finally, market skeptics may envision a larger policy role for the federal antitrust laws. Specifically, they may view antitrust as guarding against systematic threats flowing from the concentration of economic power, even if those dangers do not flow from lost competition. It is at this point that political values coalesce around antitrust policy. Competition laws may not simply preserve market-based constraints on the exercise of pricing power, but diffuse wealth and guard the democratic process against usurpation at the hands of those who secure outsized influence. The pervasive trusts of the late 1800s – and the various magnates who wielded undeniable power to effect industrial (and to a degree political) policy in the country – loom large on this account. Some commentators now equate that state of affairs with present day Silicon Valley and larger corporate America.

In those reformists' view, big is bad. That diagnosis holds true regardless of scale- or scope-driven efficiencies, lower prices, or even higher innovation. The Supreme Court itself adhered to this view in the 1960s, accepting higher prices as the justifiable cost of disaggregation.[7]

The dangers associated with accumulating economic power may not simply be political. Companies may efficiently grow by competing on the merits or acquiring complementary businesses. Yet, if an intermediary of critical value to the economy results, other questions may arise. The banking crisis of 2008 was held up as a failure of antitrust policy, but not in the sense that acquisitions, restraints, or exclusionary conduct had eliminated competitive constraints. Rather, some critics believe that competition policy should never have allowed any bank to grow so indispensable

---

[6] Statement of Commissioners Rohit Chopra and Rebecca Kelly Slaughter, Federal Trade Commission Report on the Use of Section 5 to Address Off-Patent Pharmaceutical Price Spikes, June 24, 2019, https://www.ftc.gov/system/files/documents/reports/ftc-report-standalone-section-5-address-high-pharmaceutical-drug-biologic-prices/p180101_section_5_report_dissenting_statement_by_chopra_and_slaughter_6-27-19.pdf. More specifically, Commissioners Chopra and Slaughter considered employing the Section 5 proscription on "unfair or deceptive acts or practices" – which drives the Commission's consumer-protection (rather than competition) mission – when "(1) a price increase involves off-patent drugs that lack therapeutic alternatives, and where research, production, and regulatory barriers would prevent near-term entry, (2) the price increase bears no reasonable relationship to manufacturing or production cost increases or changes in supply and demand conditions, and (3) the harm to patients is not outweighed by other benefits[.]" Id. They also recommended exploring circumstances in which unjustified price increases could amount to an unfair method of competition, citing to a controversial statement by former Commissioner Thomas Rosch that eliminating a reputational price constraint could violate Section 7 of the Clayton Act. Id. p. 3 n.9 (citing Concurring Statement of Commissioner J. Thomas Rosch, Federal Trade Commission v. Ovation Pharmaceuticals, Inc., Civil No. 08-6379 (U.S. D. Minn.) (Dec. 16, 2008), https://www.ftc.gov/system/files/documents/public_statements/418091/081216ovationroschstmt.pdf.).

[7] See, e.g., United States v. Brown Shoe Co., 370 U.S. 294, 344 (1962) ("Congress appreciated that occasional higher costs and prices might result from the maintenance of fragmented industries and markets. It resolved these competing considerations in favor of decentralization.").

that its failure would bring catastrophe, with an enormous loss of consumer (and producer) welfare.[8]

These four characteristics represent one vision for antitrust that contrasts with today's neoclassical paradigm. To varying degrees, that perspective is discernible in EU competition law, and is more pronounced still in many other competition-law jurisdictions around the world. One could articulate many other conceptions that flow from priors that look skeptically on market processes. These views flow from beliefs about the state's superior power to effect improvements. Such views need not descend to outright socialism. Rather, they reflect an ideological view along a continuum. In travelling along the spectrum, one might favor distinct revisions to the antitrust apparatus. In that respect – and coupled with the epistemological limitations of industrial organization – divergence as to antitrust's normative direction is inevitable.

1.3 WHAT DOES POLITICAL ANTITRUST LOOK LIKE?

Antitrust may be political – as in value-driven – but that does not make all normative visions equally sound. The book champions the core tenets of modern US antitrust policy, and argues for evidence-based refinement rather than a neo-Brandeisian or populist expansion.

This section facilitates that argument, and illustrates how distinct values produce different competition policies. It does so by giving expression to two interpretations of competition law – what one might call neoclassical antitrust (i.e., the "law and economics" or modern US approach) with one that accommodates nonefficiency factors in evaluating restraints, practices, and mergers (the "political approach").[9] Each contrasting vision is expansive, with its own ambiguities and murky outer limits. Myriad finer divisions are possible. Nevertheless, the distinction between neoclassical and political antitrust is meaningful, and usefully captures the thrust behind two competing visions for competition law's future. In a real way, today's debate concerns which of those frameworks should govern US antitrust policy in the twenty-first century.

1.3.1 Neoclassical Antitrust

The law and economics approach eludes definition. In particular, there are complications about which normative criterion does (or should) govern – a question with which this chapter ends. Further, there are countless difficulties in terms of

---

[8] See, e.g., Jonathan R. Macey & James P. Holdcroft, *Failure Is an Option: An Ersatz-Antitrust Approach to Financial Regulation*, 120 YALE L.J. 1368 (2011).

[9] The scholar who most famously gave expression to the latter perspective is the late Bob Pitofsky, the FTC's fifty-fourth chairman. Robert Pitofsky, *The Political Content of Antitrust*, 127 U. PA. L. REV. 1051 (1979).

quantification and implementation – challenges that feed disagreement even within the neoclassical framework. Still, meaningful clarity accompanies the law's direction. Whether under an aggregate- or consumer-welfare standard, a measure of efficiency sets antitrust's lodestar. Using economics to predict competitive effects, neoclassical antitrust aspires to the scientific method. Antitrust economics defines its assumptions and generates testable hypotheses through objective analysis.

If the chosen framework is defined with precision, then ensuing analysis can be empirically driven. This is not to deny limited information and incommensurability. Those problems arise, and they introduce uncertainty surrounding intervention decisions. Indeed, how best to resolve that challenge is a critical reform topic that Chapter 7 addresses. Nevertheless, uncertainty is neither pervasive nor significant to much of antitrust's *core* function.

Meanwhile, the neoclassical focus on efficiency hones analysis in a unitary direction. This trait bears sizeable benefits. In particular, it renders explicit bases for divergence, and facilitates efforts dedicated to marginal, evidence-based improvement. Although the limits of antitrust economics will never disappear, they will shrink over time.

Economists have advanced empirical methodologies at their disposal. With sufficient transactional data to estimate consumer-demand functions econometrically, they can use merger simulation to predict price effects or to test whether transaction-specific efficiencies will offset price increases. In employing that tool and countless others, economists can reach for an abundance of oligopolistic models founded on rational choice and game theory. Coupled with in-depth factual investigations, that toolkit helps enforcers predict likely competitive effects. As industrial organization evolves, so does the agencies' experience with the industries that they oversee.

Here, a crisply articulated standard aligns enforcers' investigative and analytic efforts. The agencies can source points of ambiguity, identify the informational deficit responsible, and work to minimize uncertainty in a particular matter through targeted investigation. The economic method lends itself to validation, replication, and refinement. It remains, of course, imperfect. Lingering uncertainty feeds divergence even among experts. But far from characterizing the entirety of antitrust, those instances are largely confined to a subset of hard cases, often involving single-firm conduct or transactions in dynamic markets. Meanwhile, ongoing empirical work seeks to reduce the scope of antitrust uncertainty.

In short, an exclusively economic construction bears compelling virtues for antitrust analysis. In that respect, neoclassical antitrust is noteworthy for what it excludes. Specifically, it ignores factors like fairness, employment, wealth distribution, and environment. More controversially today, it also excludes considerations like data privacy as standalone values – meaning that it consider such factors only insofar as they materialize as manifestations of competition. Such omissions are arguably a source of weakness, in that they leave antitrust with blind spots. In other words, competition policy overlooks considerations that may matter a great deal to society. Neoclassical antitrust's narrow focus, however, offers compelling advantages. The problem with reaching further lies in workability, demarcation, usurpation, and transparency.

First, the excluded values are incommensurate with each other and with consumer benefits from competition. They are difficult, if not impossible, to reduce to a viable utilitarian calculus. Any number of examples illustrate the point. Rationalization is a frequent merger goal, as buyers pursue efficiency gains that may reduce prices. If a transaction creates no market power, then modern US antitrust would approve it. Asset rationalization, however, often produces job losses and a wealth transfer to stockholders. How should we weigh those effects? If we took the preservation of jobs seriously, anticipated layoffs become the basis for a prohibition decision. But how can one weigh lost jobs against efficiency gains? It seems impossible to credit the former over the latter in all circumstances, no matter the disparity, but where should one draw the line? There is no grand unified theory of social utility through which regulators can define optimal decision points. A merger-by-merger assessment would produce splintered decisions, little predictability, and decisions that lie on flimsy – likely conjectural – quantifications of tradeoffs.

The problem grows when one adds further criteria to the mix. In a polluting industry, should an antitrust agency impose commitments to invest in superior filters or higher safety if the buyer has a weaker record than the seller? When should such concerns warrant blocking an otherwise-procompetitive transaction? The answer is twofold. First, such factors do not sound in competition, and thus lie beyond the neoclassical purview of the antitrust laws. Second, it is better to address specific noncompetition issues under a separate process, whether it be wealth distribution through the taxation system or environmental protection under a prescriptive or proscriptive code. This approach guards the integrity of antitrust analysis. This not only promotes transparency – everyone knows the rules – but it hastens refinement. Parties can test and litigate intervention decisions uncorrupted by noncompetition values and rendered pursuant to clear principles.

Other noneconomic factors obviously lie outside a legitimate antitrust structure. Ad hoc executive intervention on a case-by-case basis in favor of preferred actors like national champions, family-owned businesses, or companies with close ties to the administration flouts a law-based system, and would render antitrust capricious.

A more weighty consideration is whether to use antitrust to preserve a "competitive" market structure. Neoclassical antitrust focuses on competitive effects, not on concentration. The efficient scale at which firms can most effectively compete varies across industries. "One important finding of the economics literature is of substantial variation across industries in features most relevant to antitrust."[10]

---

[10] Jonathan B. Baker & Timothy F. Bresnahan, *Economic Evidence in Antitrust: Defining Markets and Measuring Market Power*, in HANDBOOK OF ANTITRUST ECONOMICS 23 (Paolo Buccirossi ed. 2008).

Optimal concentration may be a three-firm oligopoly or a market subject to atomistic competition. The neoclassical approach evaluates each market on its own terms, employing the best empirical data and models available to predict the effects of a merger, practice, or agreement.

By contrast, noneconomic factors may yield an anti-concentration mandate. As explored below, one rationale is that concentrated industries distort democracy by putting excessive power in the hands of a few. Atomistic markets, by contrast, ensure freedom of opportunity and a diffusion of wealth and influence. On that account, although scale or scope economics may be independently desirable, they do not justify a merger (or even, perhaps, single-firm expansion) that yields unwarranted size.

The law and economics approach pays little or no heed to those hypotheses, considering them beyond the remit of sound antitrust enforcement. As before, importing noneconomic considerations blurs the normative thrust of competition law, obscures the basis for agency action, erodes objectivity, relies on incommensurate values and hence arbitrary intervention decisions, and risks allowing stakeholders to capture the antitrust process and employ it to their private benefit and against consumer interests, all on the pretense of opposing rising concentration.

An additional, arguably more fundamental, objection also exists. When does an efficient increase in size or concentration endanger liberal democracy? There is no reliable basis for identifying this point. An entire spectrum of possible antitrust intervention policies thus becomes possible, fed not by econometrics or robust models, but by intuition, priors, and values. Such an approach to competition law abandons any pretense of objectivity. To be sure, even an exclusively economic approach falls prey to informational deficits, requiring enforcers and courts to appeal to common sense and instinct in resolving indeterminate issues. But it is easy to exaggerate the frequency and scale of those challenges, and simply wrong to suggest that the neoclassical antitrust enterprise lies on guesswork and subjective policy-making. By contrast, employing antitrust in service of an anti-corporate-power effort aimed at preserving democracy may sound noble. But it would rest on a hollow evidentiary foundation, and introduce unexplored levels of capriciousness into the law.

At this point in exploring neoclassical antitrust, it is worth touching on some critiques. First, there are those who think modern antitrust has failed because it dogmatically adheres to price theory – a deficiency that they tie to the law's Chicago roots. A more thoughtful exposition, however, reveals a different insight. If there is a failure, it is one of execution rather than conception.

Neoclassical price theory plays a central role in modern antitrust, evaluating whether a given restraint will likely restrict output, and thus fail scrutiny. Importantly, the law and economics approach goes beyond price, which simply measures static outcomes. Properly understood, neoclassical antitrust preserves any qualitative metric through which firms strive to capture sales from their rivals. In other words, it protects competitive pressures that constrain firm behavior. In many markets – particularly those involving commodities or goods of limited differentiation – price is the principal criterion by which to attract consumers. Hence, antitrust's focus on price is not in the slightest bit surprising. The law seeks to limit the acquisition of market power, the exercise of which restricts output and hence raises price.

Yet, competition often surpasses price, and it is a profound mistake to think such rivalry beyond the scope of neoclassical antitrust.[11] Quality dominates other factors in some markets, particularly those for technological products that rapidly become obsolete. There, innovation is the principal criterion for advancing consumer welfare, and the deserving focus of antitrust protection. At this point, the normative focus shifts beyond static efficiency to the dynamic efficiencies likely to flow from competition. This is a crucial point in the new economy, as distinct from relatively staid "bricks and mortar" industries that evolve incrementally. Further, "quality" itself may find several different forms depending on consumer demand. It may be advanced functionality or another attribute altogether. It could be data privacy.

That last point warrants further mention because it weighs on today's antitrust-reform debate. In manufacturing industries, firms typically compete for market share on price, but usually face U-shaped, long-run-average-cost curves that inhibit domination or high concentration. Antitrust principles largely developed out of such "bricks and mortar" markets, where price is the locus of competition and increments in productive efficiency plausibly inure to consumers' benefit. Today's technology markets are a different species. Silicon Valley could be another planet. Explosive growth founded on winner-takes-all innovation is the order of the day. For the consumer, Google's Internet search algorithm and Facebook's social network are transformative services of untold value and yet offered for free. With a price of zero and output racing upward, neoclassical's price-theoretic core sees reason only to celebrate. Though not selling for free, Amazon, Apple, Uber, and others offer services and products of unprecedented quality and convenience, while undercutting rivals' prices. Silicon Valley sees consolidation of existing markets and rapid expansion into new ones, all in pursuit of a consumer-pleasing path.

The antitrust-reform crowd has reacted with alarm. They argue that Google's and Facebook's consumer offerings are by no means free, but paid through consumer data. As to Amazon and Uber, they worry that sky-high market capitalizations fueled by expectations of monopoly have facilitated predatory pricing – a phenomenon to which modern antitrust is not merely agnostic, but incredulous. The result, they fear, is that technology firms will dominate the economy feeding on users' data, while antitrust, enthralled by narrow price considerations, sits helplessly on the sidelines. In their view, the noneconomic factors that neoclassical antitrust eschews

---

[11] *See, e.g.*, Brown v. Pro Football, Inc., 518 U.S. 231, 241 (1996) ("[A]ntitrust law forbids all agreements among competitors ... that unreasonably lessen competition among or between them in virtually any respect whatsoever.").

come to the fore here: accumulation of power in a manner destructive of democracy, income inequality, lost consumer freedom, and distorted input markets as technology firms wield monopsony power.

Has focusing on price blinded antitrust to Silicon Valley? That objection is dubious. Nonprice effects matter under the existing model. The question is whether a nonprice dimension is an active channel of competition. Consumers are masters of their destiny under the neoclassical account. If they value qualities other than price, firms will compete on those metrics to entice users. Antitrust protects that process, whether on a neoclassical foundation or otherwise. Hence, for example, there is no reason why a merger between two competitors that discipline one another in offering ever-better privacy guarantees to their prospective customers may not raise antitrust issues under the traditional law and economics framework, even absent price effects.

Importantly, because this vision of antitrust protects channels of competition driven by *consumer preferences*, it will necessarily prove unsatisfactory to some critics. Some reformists dislike the industry structures that emerge in response to consumer demand. This observation brings us full circle to antitrust's political dimension. As the law requires a priori value determinations on contestable points, unanimity is likely to prove elusive.

1.3.2 *Political Antitrust*

Every antitrust policy has value-based underpinnings. But while today's approach is utilitarian, there is another view. Specifically, anti-monopolists argue that competition law should incorporate noneconomic values.

That view radically departs from the status quo, but it is hardly novel. The late Bob Pitofsky, a former Georgetown Law professor and FTC Chairman, famously made the case for venturing beyond law and economics. In a 1979 article, he embraced noneconomic considerations in service of antitrust's mission.[12] Neo-Brandeisians, of course, view his diagnosis as prescient, and find much to like in his prescriptions.

Though plenty controversial in mainstream antitrust circles, *The Political Content of Antitrust* was not as radical as some recent calls for reform.[13] It did not call to burn the house down. Nor did it seek to transform competition law into an amorphous brew of discordant policies. Pitosfky's article was a measured, though provocative, contribution, as one might expect of an experienced regulator and academic.

For want of feasibility and congruity, Pitofsky excluded certain political goals. He disclaimed any "useful role" for interpreting antitrust to protect small business against competition, guaranteeing distributors' continued access to suppliers' products, and redistributing income, which he considered to be a "farfetched" use of the

---

[12] Pitofsky, *supra* note 9.
[13] *Id.* Chapter 5 explores recent calls for reform, many of which are radical when measured against the set of antitrust principles that has governed since the 1970s.

antitrust laws.[14] In his view, it is impossible to preserve competition while protecting small entrepreneurs.[15]

An organizing theory is vital. Without it, offsetting factors are not susceptible to resolution. Conclusions replace analysis, yielding intervention rationales that beg the question. Subjectivity makes various weightings – and hence enforcement decisions – equally valid. If antitrust became a tool for advancing a hodgepodge of conflicting values, it would lose traction in pursuing the public interest. Untethered to a cohesive set of goals, antitrust could not be refined through empirical validation and refinement. It could only serve the ends of those wishing to employ it. Such an inconsonant policy would likely meander over time, imperfectly calibrated to advance any one goal well and likely doing a disservice to the society in whose service it is purportedly employed.

An unbounded incorporation of noneconomic factors would be unworkable. To his credit, Pitofsky recognized as much. He conceded the superiority of taxation, welfare, and subsidization programs in protecting small businesses and promoting income distribution. In doing so, however, he arguably surrendered his larger position.[16]

So, what noneconomic factors did Pitofsky think to be suitable for antitrust? His vision aligns with many progressive reformists today. He observed that "conflicts between political and economic goals do arise – for example, when a merger generating efficiencies contributes significantly to economic concentration in a given market."[17] In his view, if "a single wealthy family" bought the leading newspaper in each major city "the Sherman Act should be sufficiently flexible to take into account that threat to political values."[18] Similarly, if a complementary merger yielded efficiencies with no loss of competition, nevertheless antitrust should object on account of the "concern that the welfare of the country is being placed in the hands of a few economically powerful firms and individuals."[19] Interestingly, he did not perceive the issues that he was addressing as urgent. At the time of writing, he observed that "there are relatively few situations today in which a political dimension must be incorporated" due to a lack of increased concentration among US companies.[20] Neo-Brandeisians, of course, view today's economy altogether differently.

Fusing economic and political factors raises formidable analytic difficulties. It is the antitrust equivalent of mixing oil and water. Pitofsky did not offer any magic solution. Rather, his answer was that precision is an illusion.[21] An economic approach, in his opinion, is equally susceptible to the vagaries of subjective

[14] Id. at 1058–59.
[15] Id. at 1059.
[16] Id. at 1060.
[17] Id. at 1064.
[18] Id.
[19] Id. at 1057.
[20] Id. at 1058.
[21] Id.

judgment, priors, intuition, and experience. From his perspective, incompatible factors already impede antitrust law. On that ground, he rejects concerns about importing political values into antitrust.²² In his view, an economic approach to antitrust "already incorporates large doses of hunch, faith, and intuition[,]" and is thus not "an otherwise reliable enforcement system[.]"²³ Hence, injecting political factors will not introduce "an element of unpredictability[.]"²⁴

That last assertion entails quite a leap. Neoclassical antitrust has not perfected the scientific method, of course. Uncertainty and subjective judgment remain. Yet, we have made real advances in evaluating business conduct. It would be cynical to dismiss today's methodologies as whimsical. The economic approach suffers from noneliminable gaps of knowledge, but that is unremarkable. Introducing discordant values would corrupt the process, foreclosing coherent – if imperfect – evaluations of the kind that occur today.

Adopting noneconomic factors would muddy the antitrust waters. Even the most passionate reformists would surely concede as much. Anti-monopolists, however, may see those costs as justified. In their view, deficiencies associated with law and economics make adopting political factors worth the candle.

Neoclassical antitrust presumes that markets freed of anticompetitive restraints produce desirable outcomes. Suppose that presumption is false. If so, today's antitrust enforcement would allow concentrations of industrial power to grow. Conglomerate mergers would lead the powerful to grow larger and stronger, all without eliminating competition and thus enjoying a free pass under the neoclassical framework. The result, some would claim, "will be an economy so dominated by a few corporate giants that it will be impossible for the state not to play a more intrusive role in economic affairs."²⁵

The key prediction here is not that some industries will grow more consolidated on account of their cost characteristics. It is rather that this phenomenon will become so acute and pervasive that "efficient" growth will produce an unacceptable concentration of economic – and, hence, political – power. Harms to democracy will result not only from the disproportionate influence wielded by the few who control the country's wealth and production, but from inevitable governmental checks in response to that power. Facing an economy dominated by a handful of corporations, the government will have little choice but to regulate them, potentially to an invasive degree. State control over the economic means of production points a country toward a path either of widespread nationalization, displacing markets in favor of central planning and leading to a communist regime, or (so the argument goes) fascism.²⁶

[22] *Id.* at 1065.
[23] *Id.* at 1065–66.
[24] *Id.* at 1066.
[25] *Id.* at 1051.
[26] *Id.* at 1055.

These claims are renascent. Columbia law professor, Tim Wu, writes that our antitrust laws have contributed to an environment ripe for fascism.[27] Others have echoed such a view.[28] Such claims – as directed at contemporary US enforcement – are at best overblown. The US economy is not consolidated to the point of triggering expansive state intervention. It remains globally competitive, innovative, and – though concentrated in part – not so deeply and widely dominated as realistically to create dangers that Wu and others proclaim. In short, the "rising tide of concentration" remains far short of some critical intervention threshold.[29]

To be fair, one could imagine circumstances in which a rampant accumulation of economic power could threaten democracy. If antitrust should indeed incorporate noneconomic factors to limit consolidation, the interesting question is when. When should we intervene in the name of competition policy (or, perhaps more accurately, industrial policy) to arrest efficient mergers – be they horizontal, vertical, or conglomerate – or break up dominant firms that are not excluding competitors? The technical answer requires identifying the all-important dividing line, the point at which incremental conglomeration tips an economy on a path toward totalitarianism. It is impossible to define that threshold, of course, so the question becomes how early in the accretion process to intervene.

If arresting competitively innocuous merger activity or breaking up successful firms absent wrongdoing is costly, then even proponents of the anti-concentration position should agree that some balance is desirable.[30] A flat-out prohibition on mergers and on any firm's holding a dominant position would yield economic harms, while going much further than necessary to protect democratic values. Even working within the political antitrust framework championed by Pitofsky and others, there is a question of balance.

This is another point of acute divergence. Chicago School devotees, of course, would reject noneconomic factors outright. But some accept, variously as dogma or merely as a theoretical possibility, that an unrestrained build-up of corporate power may, at some point, risk destabilizing liberal democracy. Such thinkers must decide where to draw the line. A threshold inquiry here is whether neoclassical antitrust makes the entire question academic. In other words, do markets

---

[27] Wu, Tim Wu, *Be Afraid of Economic 'Bigness.' Be Very Afraid*, N.Y. TIMES, Nov. 10, 2018, https://www.nytimes.com/2018/11/10/opinion/sunday/fascism-economy-monopoly.html; *see also* TIM WU, THE CURSE OF BIGNESS: ANTITRUST IN THE NEW GILDED AGE 14–16, 19–22, 139 (2018).

[28] *See, e.g.*, Ganesh Sitaraman, *Unchecked Power*, THE NEW REPUBLIC, Nov. 29, 2018 (arguing that a rise in authoritarianism flows from "widening inequality and the rising concentration of economic power" and concluding that, in "today's global contest between democracy and nationalist oligarchy, economic power is a critical element and, as a result, antitrust law is an essential tool").

[29] *Accord* Daniel A. Crane, *Rethinking Merger Efficiencies*, 110 MICH. L. REV. 347, 385 (2011).

[30] Neo-Brandeisians, of course, question whether merger-driven consolidation generates efficiencies that benefit consumers. Chapter 3 explores that vital question.

freed of anticompetitive conduct tend toward unacceptable concentrations of economic power? The answer is almost certainly not.[31]

Not being empirically testable, claims of a link between corporate size and harm to democracy flow from subjective judgments. In theory, one might imagine no change at all vis-à-vis today's paradigm (i.e., today's law and economics approach suffices), minor changes at the margin (i.e., deviating from an exclusively economic analysis only in rare, outlier cases involving "mega deals" likely to transform industry structure or diversity of control of media outlets), or a radical, far-reaching departure from the status quo. In practice, reformists who champion noneconomic factors support the last option.

That is why neo-Brandeisians protest large transactions, even if they do not raise colorable antitrust issues under the traditional law and economics framework. *Amazon-Whole Foods*, for example, involved no meaningful overlap. Any rivalry between the parties was limited to a narrow slice of online grocery deliveries, which is a competitive space. Yet, there were widespread calls for the FTC to block the deal.[32]

Other deals not obviously problematic on the neoclassical vision received similar condemnation from the left. Consider *Staples-Essendant*, which – like all vertical mergers in potentially concentrated markets – required economic analysis to identify whether the resulting firm would have the incentive and ability to harm competition. This inquiry, at heart, is a quantitative exercise. It evaluates margins and demand elasticities to determine whether downstream gains from diverted sales from rivals would exceed losses in raising input prices to competitors above profit-maximizing levels. If the answer is yes, then the remaining question is whether efficiencies dominate. If so, then the standard procedure is to approve the transaction with behavioral remedies in place to prevent strategic foreclosure (or input price increases).

The *Staples-Essendant* matter, however, became an unlikely battle ground for a clash of ideas about the future of antitrust. Dissents from the two Democratic Commissioners led to over 1,870 public comments on what would otherwise be an unremarkable consent order.[33] Part of the controversy was the role of private-equity funds in driving acquisitions, given Sycamore Partners' ownership of Staples. Those espousing a neo-Brandeisian view, of course, took exception to the FTC's limited remedy and clearance.[34]

---

[31] As Professor Daniel Crane has observed, the modern law and economics approach to antitrust may have prevented the accumulations of power that infamously led to trouble during the Weimar Republic in Germany. Daniel A. Crane, *Fascism and Monopoly*, 118 MICH. L. REV. 1315 (2020).

[32] *See, e.g.*, Chris Sagers, *Crack Down on Amazon*, SLATE, June 19, 2017, https://slate.com/business/2017/06/yes-there-is-an-antitrust-case-against-amazon.html.

[33] *In re* Sycamore Partners II, L.P., FTC Matter No. 181-0180, https://www.ftc.gov/policy/public-comments/2019/02/initiative-797; *In re* Staples, Inc./Essendant, Inc., FTC Matter No. 181-0180, Statement of Commissioner Rohit Chopra & Statement of Commissioner Rebecca Kelly Slaughter, Jan. 28, 2019, https://www.ftc.gov/enforcement/cases-proceedings/181-0180/sycamore-partners-ii-lp-staples-inc-essendant-inc-matter.

[34] *See, e.g.*, Open Markets Institute, *The FTC's Crisis of Legitimacy: Comment from the Open Markets Institute on the FTC's 3-2 Clearance of the Staples-Essendant Merger*, Feb. 27, 2019, https://open

Other recent blockbuster mergers – like *T-Mobile/Sprint* ($26 billion), *Cigna/Express Scripts* ($67 billion), *AT&T/Time Warner* ($85 billion), *Bayer/Monsanto* ($66 billion), and *Dow Chemical/du Pont* ($130 billion) – raised legitimate questions under the governing neoclassical framework, spurring in-depth government investigations and, in certain cases, litigation challenges or divestiture remedies.[35] Some reformists, however, reacted with dismay to these transactions on grounds exceeding traditional competitive-effects concerns.[36] Similarly, vertical or conglomerate acquisitions involving prominent technology companies attracted fierce opposition, even in the absence of any meaningful loss of head-to-head competition – for example, Microsoft's $27 billion acquisition of LinkedIn in 2016.

In short, neo-Brandeisian thinkers object to large mergers, regardless of whether they are vertical or conglomerate and thus do not eliminate head-to-head competition. They disfavor divestitures, and would rather block horizontal mergers outright.[37]

Chapter 2 explores the extent to which monopolies are impervious or vulnerable to displacement. Direct incursions into a dominated market and an ensuing overthrow of an incumbent do happen. More typically, however, a rival ousts an entrenched monopolist from the side, often by riding a wave of technological advancement.[38] This is particularly true of new-economy industries. In short, long-term competition may emerge not only from within a relevant market, but aside it. Start-ups will naturally focus on contiguous markets, targeting gaps or improving on what exists. Each such neighboring space, which runs adjacent to dominant platforms, yields new offerings susceptible to efficient acquisition. Yet, they may be the embryo from which a network emerges to topple the adjacent giant. This tension bears witness to what critics decry as a "kill zone."

Yet, there are compelling reasons not to block adjacent acquisitions. As large technology companies absorb complementary businesses, their offerings become

---

marketsinstitute.org/public_comments/ftcs-crisis-legitimacy-comment-open-markets-institute-ftcs-3-2-clearance-staples-essendant-merger/.

[35] *See* United States v. AT&T, Inc., 916 F.3d 1029 (D.C. Cir. 2019) (affirming district court decision that the Justice Department had failed to show that the vertical merger would likely have anticompetitive effects); United States v. Bayer AG, No. 1:18-cv-1241, Competitive Impact Statement (D.D.C. May 29, 2018), https://www.justice.gov/atr/case-document/file/973951/download (requiring the divestiture of overlap products); United States v. Dow Chemical Co., No. 1:17-cv-1176, Competitive Impact Statement (D.D.C. June 15, 2017), https://www.justice.gov/atr/case-document/file/973951/download (same).

[36] *See, e.g.,* Zephyr Teachout, *Mega-mergers Like AT&T and Time Warner Crush American Democracy,* THE GUARDIAN, June 13, 2018 ("Gilded age-style monopolies are back. We should take this setback to recommit to a new anti-monopoly movement.").

[37] Lina Khan, *How to Reboot the FTC: The Agency's Antitrust Policy Isn't Up to the Challenge of the 21st Century. Here's How to Fix It,* POLITICO, Apr. 13, 2016, https://www.politico.com/agenda/story/2016/04/ftc-antitrust-economy-monopolies-000090.

[38] *See, e.g.,* Randy Picker, *Platforms and Adjacent Market Competition: A Look at Recent History,* PROMARKET, Apr. 16, 2018, https://promarket.org/platforms-adjacent-market-competition-look-recent-history/.

more compelling to users (and, in many cases, to advertisers). Further, and most importantly, the market for acquisition itself stimulates innovation through start-ups. The prospect of "being bought out" is often the prize that brings new technologies from conception to reality. That process, however, also nips in the bud platforms that may otherwise have achieved scale to threaten the giant next door. The odds that any one such acquired company would have grown in this way are, of course, long.

As this brief account makes clear, the law and economics analysis here is difficult. The necessary information is elusive, the risk of erroneous condemnation is high, and the doctrinal impediments to successfully challenging a particular acquisition are towering. In the author's view, contemporary antitrust is up to the challenge. And its administrators should have the confidence to determine that no good case exists if that is where the evidence leads.

"Political antitrust" could, in theory, approach these difficulties with similar assiduousness. In practice, however, those espousing the adoption of noneconomic principles make short work of the challenge. Their diagnosis is clear, unyielding, and absolute: Silicon Valley giants are hoovering up their competitors, and they must be stopped. This perspective is unsurprising. Identifying the factors that one considers in an analysis is merely a threshold step. The weighting is everything. Neo-Brandeisians put a thumb heavily on the scales toward prohibition based on size and momentum toward concentration. For such thinkers, the consolidation trend in Silicon Valley and the power of the "GAFA" set are reason enough to say, "no more." Merger-driven growth is itself problematic.

In short, those invoking "political antitrust" have far bolder ideas than marginally adjusting the scope of today's framework. Closing this section with the account that opened it, consider Pitofsky's bottom line. Lest there were any ambiguity about how political and economic factors meld, Pitofsky voiced "general support" for the 1960s' antitrust decisions of the Supreme Court.[39] As he readily acknowledged, "it is extremely difficult to defend, strictly on economic grounds, outlawing the kind of five-to-ten percent horizontal mergers" in those cases.[40] Neo-Brandeisians want to return to that era.

Today's antitrust-reform debate – whether to adopt noneconomic values, discard the consumer-welfare standard, embrace structuralism once more, break up leading technology and platform companies, and so on – is about nothing less than the law's soul, its very purpose.

---

[39] Pitofsky, *supra* note 9, at 1069.
[40] *Id.* at 1070 (citing Brown Shoe v. United States, 370 U.S. 294 (1962); United States v. Von's Grocery, 384 U.S. 270 (1966); United States v. Pabst Brewing Co., 384 U.S. 546 (1966)).

2

Antitrust

Fact, Fiction, and the Unknown

We are in the midst of an antitrust dispute not seen in half a century. As reformists clash with traditionalists, debate rages over a sea of conflicting priors. There is a way out. Some facts remain unknowable, of course, which is why error analysis remains fundamental to effective policy.[1] And baseline normative judgments matter, ensuring that unanimity will remain a distant goal.[2] Nevertheless, voluminous evidence illuminates core issues. Cabining (if not resolving) the dispute requires dispassionately reviewing the empirical literature. So, too, it is possible to glean valuable insights from industry dynamics and historical variation in competition policies.

We cannot perfect antitrust, but we can refine it. To do so, we must look to the most essential questions on which competition policy rests. That is the goal of this chapter and the next one. Together, they address four issues: (1) market self-correction, (2) antitrust's role in facilitating competitive market cycling, (3) merger efficiencies, and (4) whether structuralism is a reliable means of resolving antitrust questions. Conclusions flowing from that analysis go a long way to informing suitable reform. They can – and do – reveal various, frequently advanced positions as overstated, hollow, or plain wrong.

We begin with the most fundamental question: How common is timely and effective market-correction? In particular, to what extent do commanding market positions endure or falter in the face of a new competitor's superior product? This issue underlies the entire antitrust enterprise, including agency intervention into dominated markets and the principles governing merger review. It obviously bears on Silicon Valley, where neo-Brandeisians demand structural antitrust remedies like divestiture-drive break-ups or potential price and quality-of-service regulation to which utilities and common-carriers have traditionally been subject.[3]

---

[1] *See* Chapter 7.
[2] *See* Chapter 1.
[3] *See, e.g.*, Asher Schechter, "It's Crucial to Break Up Facebook," ProMarket, Jan. 4, 2019, https://promarket.org/crucial-break-up-facebook/ (interviewing Professor Tim Wu, who asserts, "I think it's crucial to break up Facebook, particularly from WhatsApp and Instagram"); Kaitlyn Tiffany, *A Simple Plan to Dissolve Facebook, Google, and Amazon*, Vox, Nov. 8, 2018, https://www.vox.com/the-goods

This chapter also delves into merger efficiencies. Though complex, this matter is of inestimable importance. The US economy saw $1.8 trillion in aggregate M&A volume in 2019 alone.[4] Over 10,000 mergers and acquisitions have occurred in the United States each year since 2010.[5] Most transactions close without antitrust review. There were 16,919 Hart-Scott-Rodino (HSR) filings between 2010 and 2019.[6] Of those, 502 transactions (less than 3 percent) were subject to in-depth investigation through Second Request.[7] Fewer still were subject to an enforcement action. Illustratively, the agencies brought 38 merger enforcement actions in 2019 – a number that represents less than 2 percent of the 2,089 transactions notified that year.[8]

Antitrust thus poses no impediment to the vast majority of transactions. Only a few dozen mergers each year encounter serious (or fatal) headwinds on competition grounds. Modern review standards are permissive outside of heavy consolidations. The principles employed under Section 7 today presume that M&A activity is a valuable source of social gains. The question whether mergers generally, rarely, or never yield productivities is thus indispensable. Depending on the answer, today's merger-review standards could be built on a faulty construct or properly calibrated. It seems hard to imagine a constructive discussion on antitrust reform without seriously grappling with the literature on that phenomenon.

To preview what follows, rapid erosion of market power appears to be an industry-specific phenomenon, rather than a universal truth. Nevertheless, when subjected to market forces, perpetual dominance remains a mythical creature. What emerges is a market process – seldom perfect, but often dynamic – at odds with the neo-Brandeisian narrative. Those who would dismiss market processes in favor of regulatory intervention by the state rest on dubious evidentiary grounds.[9] Widespread market failure is something breezily asserted and, for some, intuitively resonant. But it has scant factual support.[10]

/2018/11/8/18076440/facebook-monopoly-curse-of-bigness-tim-wu-interview; Lina M. Khan, Note, *Amazon's Antitrust Paradox*, 126 YALE L.J. 710, 800 (2017) ("One approach would apply public utility regulations to all of Amazon's businesses that serve other businesses. Another would require breaking up parts of Amazon and applying nondiscrimination principles separately.").

[4] See, e.g., Greg Roumeliotis & Pamela Barbaglia, *Dealmakers Eye Cross-Border M&A Recovery as Mega Mergers Roll On*, REUTERS, Dec. 31, 2019.

[5] Institute for Mergers, Acquisitions and Alliance, *M&A in the United States*, https://imaa-institute.org/m-and-a-us-united-states/.

[6] Fed. Trade Comm'n & Dep't of Justice Antitrust Division, *Hart-Scott-Rodino Annual Report: Fiscal Year 2019*, p. 1 (2019), https://www.ftc.gov/reports/hart-scott-rodino-annual-report-fiscal-year-2019.

[7] *Id.*, Appendix A.

[8] *Id.* at 1–2.

[9] See, e.g., Lina M. Khan, Note, *Amazon's Antitrust Paradox*, 126 YALE L.J. 710, 798 (2017) ("Given that Amazon increasingly serves as essential infrastructure across the internet economy, applying elements of public utility regulations to its business is worth considering.").

[10] See, e.g., Hon. Douglas Ginsburg, *Judging a Book: Ginsburg Reviews "The Curse of Bigness"*, LAW360, Dec. 3, 2018 (reviewing TIM WU, THE CURSE OF BIGNESS: ANTITRUST IN THE NEW GILDED AGE (2018)) (reviewing a leading neo-Brandeisian book, which advocates an expansion of antitrust to address "bigness," and finding it "thin not just in size but also intellectually; lawyers, economists and historians will find its broad brush maddening").

By the same token, however, the most ardent free-marketeers exaggerate the pace with which monopoly power erodes, and discount the value of sound antitrust intervention against unilateral conduct. In particular, they understate the risk that incumbents can delay procompetitive cycles that oust them based on new products, solutions, and technologies. In doing so, they underestimate the propensity for market failure and the potential benefits of antitrust intervention, even in difficult monopolization cases.[11]

Finally, evidence supporting core propositions of conservative antitrust – in particular, the view that mergers invariably wield significant efficiencies – is light. But the literature does surrender valuable insights at odds with progressive reformists' belief that M&A activity lacks social value. The relevant insights for competition policy are nuanced. In particular, horizontal mergers apt to be caught by a significance expanse in the prohibitory arc of Section 7 are those most likely to yield valuable synergies.

2.1 MARKET SELF-CORRECTION: IS DOMINANCE TRANSIENT?

Few antitrust questions are more contested than whether markets promptly self-correct. None is more important. If monopoly power is fleeting, then antitrust interventions should be limited. Conversely, if an industry once dominated stays so, then competition enforcers must either strictly police exclusionary practices or – if a firm's control of a market remains stubbornly entrenched against consumer demand – consider regulatory intervention.[12] Neoclassical antitrust's premise is that markets, freed of artificial restraints of trade, will produce good outcomes – or, at least, results superior than what the state could achieve directly.

It would be marvelous if the economy lent itself to universal evaluation. The reality, alas, is complex. Industries are too multifaceted and idiosyncratic to surrender universal and usefully broad truths. In fact, the speed with which monopoly power decays varies. That is why the agencies put each relevant market under a microscope to understand its competitive dynamics, including entry barriers and incumbent supply responses to exercises of market power.

Alas, this reality does not inhibit sweeping generalizations about market efficacy.[13] On one view, dominated markets are apt to remain bereft of competition without

---

[11] For an extreme example, see Ryan Young & Clyde Wayne Crews, *The Case Against Antitrust Law*, Competitive Enterprise Institute, Apr. 17, 2019, https://cei.org/content/the-case-against-antitrust-law.

[12] Absent exclusionary conduct, even a monopolist may lawfully (and indefinitely) charge profit-maximizing prices without violating the antitrust laws. Verizon Commc'ns Inc. v. Law Offices of Curtis V. Trinko, LLP, 540 U.S. 398, 407 (2004). The premise behind this rule is twofold: (1) supracompetitive rents will attract entry and (2) intervening to prohibit legitimately obtained monopoly power would suppress incentives to compete. A problem would emerge, of course, if monopoly rents indefinitely proved impervious to entry. Such a market failure may require a solution beyond the antitrust laws. *Cf. id.* (acknowledging that indefinite supracompetitive rents may be problematic – the "opportunity to charge monopoly prices – *at least for a short period* – is what attracts 'business acumen' in the first place") (emphasis added).

[13] As Chapter 3 explores, the problem similarly infects widespread claims of falling competition within the US economy.

antitrust intervention. These days, Silicon Valley features with particular alarm on this account. Others argue that antitrust monopolization actions are a fool's errand because the market will self-correct faster and more effectively than agencies and courts could ever hope to do. Neither view represents sound policy.

2.1.1 The Myth of Perpetual Monopoly

One fallacy warrants immediate repudiation. The claim that a dominant firm controls its own destiny – and is thus impervious to effective competition – is as old as the antitrust laws themselves. It is also wrong. History is replete with failed firms that once led their industries. Yet the myth of entrenched dominance endures. As today's winners loom large and assume an invincible mantle, yesterday's leaders fade into obscurity.

Today's hullabaloo focuses on Amazon, Apple, Facebook, Google, Netflix, Uber, and the like. Twenty years ago, it was Microsoft. And before the software giant, there were AT&T, IBM, and a series of behemoths going back to Standard Oil, US Tobacco, and other monopolists of the Sherman Act's founding era. Antitrust enforcement has followed a recurring historical arc. A firm ascends to dominance, alarms the public, and triggers a public monopolization action. The debate is whether enforcers correctly diagnose anticompetitive conduct and intervene in a manner that hastens the arrival of superior competitors. The historical record is mixed. Looming overhead, however, is whether market forces naturally erode dominance even without agency action and, if so, execute that function quickly.

Calls for antitrust intervention in Silicon Valley are reaching fever pitch. As people fret about digital platforms, it is worth stepping back. The companies may be new and their business models idiosyncratic, but the larger issues are far from unprecedented. History has revealed the perennial monopolist to be a rare species. Absent state sanction, even the most powerful firms eventually topple. Indeed, despite the network effects associated with scale in technology industries, we have seen dramatic failures from seemingly impervious positions. Many such falls have occurred with breathtaking speed, leaving empty proclamations of monopoly in their wake. Anyone interested in antitrust reform should begin by reflecting on what market forces can themselves achieve. Even the largest digital platforms are more vulnerable than they first appear. Some topical examples illustrate the point.

Consider AOL. In 2000, it was the country's largest Internet provider with twenty-six million subscribers and a market capitalization of $125 billion.[14] A veritable Internet giant, AOL had a particularly commanding lead in instant messaging. At the time, commentators worried that "AOL's messaging dominance [was] as clear as Microsoft's PC operating system monopoly."[15] They fretted that not even Microsoft

---

[14] Lily Rothman, *A Brief Guide to the Tumultuous 30-Year History of AOL*, TIME, May 22, 2015, https://time.com/3857628/aol-1985-history/.

[15] Joe Salkowski, *AOL May Also Have Monopoly*, CHICAGO TRIBUNE, June 19, 2000.

could meaningfully contest an IM market, which depended on a user base that AOL controlled.

In 2000, AOL announced an agreement to buy Time Warner for $165 billion – then a record amount.[16] That proposed merger proved to be controversial, raising antitrust calls for prohibition that – in hindsight – look silly.[17] In December 2000, the FTC demanded a remedy to address what it anticipated to be likely anticompetitive effects in markets for broadband Internet access, last-mile access, and interactive-television services.[18] AOL rapidly bled users to free email services like Gmail and Hotmail, and became competitively immaterial in short order. In 2009, Time Warner spun off AOL.

Social-media platforms are demonstrably assailable. Friendster seems like ancient history, though it once had over 115 million users. Google tried to buy it in 2003, and launched its own failed social media effort in 2004 with Orkut. Friendster botched its attempt to scale, suffering major quality-of-service issues, while Orkut ran out of steam. The first social-media platform to gain true scale was Myspace, which has since faded from memory. In 2006, however, it was the most visited website in the United States. It is worth addressing the Myspace example, which raises many parallels to today's debate.

Launched in 2003, Myspace had attained over a million users per month less than a year later. Explosive growth followed with the social-media platform attracting twenty-two million users as of July 2005, when News Corp bought it for $580 million. Its future looked secure. In 2006, Google signed a $900 million, three-year agreement to be the exclusive provider of ad sales for Myspace. Later that year, Rupert Murdoch envisioned a $6 billion market valuation for the company and 200 million users by mid-2007.[19]

People began to fret about Myspace's dominance. *Tech News World* concluded that it was a natural monopoly, and predicted, "Other sites will be condemned to niche markets and subsets while MySpace becomes the only site of significance[.]"[20] *The Guardian* worried about Myspace's monopoly, observing that, if "it were a country, MySpace would be the seventh biggest[.]"[21] The newspaper predicted that it "it may already be too late for competitors to dislodge MySpace, except in

---

[16] Stephen Grocer, *What Happened to AOL Time Warner?*, N.Y. TIMES, June 15, 2018, https://www.nytimes.com/2018/06/15/business/dealbook/aol-time-warner.html.

[17] See, e.g., Alec Klein, *AOL Defends Merger Despite Concerns of Media Monopoly*, Wash. Post, Sept. 8, 2000 (summarizing AOL-competitor testimony from Tribal Voice Inc. that the "'wall that AOL has built around the IM (instant messaging) marketplace today will become virtually impervious to competition[.]'"); Joe Salkowski, *AOL May Also Have Monopoly*, CHICAGO TRIBUNE, June 19, 2000.

[18] Press Release, FTC Approves AOL/Time Warner Merger with Conditions, FTC Matter No. 0010105, Dec. 14, 2000, https://www.ftc.gov/news-events/press-releases/2000/12/ftc-approves-aoltime-warner-merger-conditions.

[19] Nicholas Jackson & Alexis C. Madrigal, *The Rise and Fall of MySpace*, THE ATLANTIC, Jan. 12, 2011, https://www.theatlantic.com/technology/archive/2011/01/the-rise-and-fall-of-myspace/69444/.

[20] John Barrett, *Myspace Is a Natural Monopoly*, TECHNEWSWORLD, Jan. 17, 2007, https://www.technewsworld.com/story/55185.html.

[21] Victor Keegan, *Will MySpace Ever Lose Its Monopoly?*, THE GUARDIAN, Feb. 8, 2007, https://www.theguardian.com/technology/2007/feb/08/business.comment.

niche markets[,]" and that the social network "won't stop its continuing expansion which ... could eventually extend Murdoch's influence in ways that would make his grip on satellite television seem parochial."[22] It proceeded with an avalanche of concerns about winner-take-all characteristics in network markets, in which scale entrenches dominance.

While critics lost sleep over Myspace's monopoly, Facebook was busy supplanting it. As a deluge of users abandoned the platform for its superior rival, Myspace lost competitive significance. A January 2011 *New York Times* article observed that, while Myspace was laying off almost half of its workforce, "Facebook was negotiating a half-billion-dollar investment from Goldman Sachs[.]"[23] The article, which contrasts sharply with the newspaper's recent coverage of Silicon Valley, observed that "the decline of MySpace again shows the fragility of social media where fickle consumers and changing tastes can make sensations out of services like Tribe and Friendster that quickly fade from public imagination."[24]

Competitive fragility is not exclusive to social media platforms. Nokia was the world's largest mobile-phone maker. In 1998, as the industry was shifting from analog to digital, it surpassed Motorola for the top spot. Despite a setback in 2001, it launched its first 3G phone in 2002, allowing users to browse online and download music for the first time. The company sold its billionth phone in 2005. In 2007, it accounted for almost half of global smartphone sales. But 2007 was also the year of its undoing. Apple launched the iPhone – a challenge to which Nokia had no effective response. The following year, its profits fell by 30 percent, while iPhone sales grew by over 300 percent. By 2011, Samsung and Apple had surpassed Nokia, leading its CEO to tell his staff that "we are standing on a burning platform."[25] He continued, "The first iPhone shipped in 2007, and we still don't have a product that is close to their experience. Android came on the scene just over 2 years ago, and this week they took our leadership position in smartphone volumes. Unbelievable." Microsoft bought the company's phone business in 2013 for $7.2 billion.

BlackBerry once looked unstoppable, too, with a famously devoted fan base. Launched in 2003 by Research In Motion, it had fifty million subscribers by 2009. A CNN article the same year noted that RIM had represented over 55 percent of US smartphone sales in the first quarter, observing that the "BlackBerry maker continues to hold dominant market share over Apple and Palm" (the latter another victim to competitive innovation).[26] Within two years, more people had iPhones

---

[22] *Id.*
[23] Tim Arangojan, *Hot Social Networking Site Cools as Facebook Grows*, N.Y. TIMES, Jan. 11, 2011, https://www.nytimes.com/2011/01/12/technology/internet/12myspace.html.
[24] *Id.*
[25] Eric Savitz, *CEO's "Burning Platform" Memo Highlights Nokia's Woes*, FORBES, Feb. 9, 2011, https://www.forbes.com/sites/ericsavitz/2011/02/09/ceos-burning-platform-memo-highlights-nokias-woes/#5455ea388296.
[26] David Goldman, *BlackBerry Is Still Leader of the Pack*, CNN MONEY, June 17, 2009, https://money.cnn.com/2009/06/17/technology/rim_blackberry_preview/.

than BlackBerries. By 2016, BlackBerry had a 0 percent share of the device market. That year, it announced that it would no longer make phones, but would focus on software.

Motorola continues the theme of short-lived cell-phone giants. A pioneer in mobile telephony, it made the world's first mobile-phone call in 1973. In 1994, it accounted for 60 percent of all US cell-phone sales. Although Nokia leapfrogged it just three years later, it remained a leading competitor for some time.[27] In 2005, for example, its slim Razr product was a hit, and there was talk of the company's soon overtaking Samsung. In reality, of course, it quickly ceded market position to its rivals. A 2008 article observed that Motorola's "rapidly declining fortunes in the past few years have sent shock waves through the wireless industry, providing a stark reminder that what is cool one day may be deeply out of favor the next."[28] In 2011, the company split into Motorola Mobility (wireless telephony) and Motorola Solutions (public safety and enterprise). The same year, Google paid $12.5 billion for Motorola Mobility, principally for its 17,000 telecommunications patents. The phones that followed, like the Moto X, struggled commercially. Given the losses and dubious prospects of a turnaround, Google sold Motorola Mobility to Lenovo in 2014 for $2.9 billion.

Today Google is synonymous with internet search, but it was not always so. Leading internet search engines once included WebCrawler, Lycos, AltaVista, Ask Jeeves, Yahoo!, and many others, which are now relics of history. From 1999 to 2002, for example, Yahoo! was the leading US search provider, followed by AltaVista (1999 and 2000), Microsoft (2001), and Google (2002).[29] Such was Yahoo!'s success that, in 1998, *Fortune Magazine* ran an article, *How Yahoo! Won the Search Wars*.[30] The rest, as they say, is history. Despite being far from the first mover, and launching from a point of little scale vis-à-vis its competitors, Google offered a superior product and eclipsed its rivals.

Kodak was an icon: one of the world's most successful companies. It was a famous pioneer in film and camera, and known for its marketing – so much so that a "Kodak moment" was a generational term of art. At one point, it had 90 percent of the US film market and almost as strong a position in cameras. Unsurprisingly, the company was no stranger to antitrust. Concerns about its dominance in film and photofinishing produced consent decrees in 1921 and 1954, which endured until newly

---

[27] Ted C. Fishman, *What Happened to Motorola*, CHI. MAGAZINE, Aug. 25, 2014, https://www.chicagomag.com/Chicago-Magazine/September-2014/What-Happened-to-Motorola/.
[28] Sinead Carew, *Motorola's Decline Seen as Cautionary Tale*, REUTERS, Feb. 14, 2008, https://www.reuters.com/article/us-mobile-fair-motorola/motorolas-decline-seen-as-cautionary-tale-idUSN1444261220080214.
[29] *See* Manish Agarwal & David K. Round, *The Emergence of Global Search Engines: Trends in History and Competition*, 7 COMPETITION POL'Y INT'L 115, 127 (2011).
[30] Randall E. Stross, *How Yahoo! Won the Search Wars*, FORTUNE, Mar. 2, 1998, https://archive.fortune.com/magazines/fortune/fortune_archive/1998/03/02/238576/index.htm ("Once upon a time, Yahoo! was an Internet search site with mediocre technology. Now it has a market cap of $2.8 billion. Some people say it's the next America Online.").

competitive conditions led to their termination in 1994.[31] It faced numerous antitrust claims filed by competitors, some successful and others not.[32] In 1992, the Supreme Court famously (infamously in some quarters) held that Kodak, despite facing competition in the equipment market, had to face trial for monopolizing a derivative aftermarket for replacement parts and services.[33] The company was ultimately found liable.[34]

The film giant's downfall, however, was not a function of antitrust intervention. Kodak sowed the seeds of its own destruction by inventing the digital camera in 1975. Many years later, as the digital revolution was underway, Kodak decided to focus on its core film business. In 2012, having missed the shift to online photo sharing, it declared bankruptcy and exited legacy businesses, while Instagram was sold for $1 billion.

Microsoft, long a byword for monopolist within the public imagination, missed the industry shift to mobile. Outflanked by Google and Apple, the operating systems of which cover the vast majority of today's smartphones, Microsoft finds itself a peripheral player in mobile. This holds true even though it remains dominant in its core market for PC operating system software, and has successfully reinvented itself as a cloud-based software firm. Notably, its Internet Explorer product – the focus of the Justice Department's groundbreaking monopolization case – today has a trivial share of the market. Today, Google's Chrome and Apple's Safari hold sway. Who knows what the future holds?

There are countless other examples. General Electric was a famous American innovator. Founded in 1892, it became a manufacturing behemoth, reaching peak market capitalization of $594 billion in August 2000. By September 2019, after years of struggles, it was worth less than 14 percent of that amount. Blockbuster, a household name in video rental, missed the shift to streaming and went bankrupt in 2010 because it could not compete with Netflix. Borders, one of the largest booksellers in the United States, fell prey to Amazon's recognition of consumer preference for digital purchasing and e-readers. It went bust in 2011.

Uber tapped into acute consumer demand for convenient, on-demand transportation services, disrupting the most stable (and competitively shielded) of industries almost overnight. In the late 1990s, Walmart appeared unstoppable. Some critics from the left called to break up the retail giant on antitrust grounds.[35] Then Amazon

---

[31] United States v. Eastman Kodak Co., 853 F. Supp. 1454 (W.D.N.Y. 1994), aff'd, 63 F.3d 95 (2d Cir. 1995).

[32] For example, a jury in 1978 found Kodak liable for monopolizing the amateur-photographic business in 1978. See, e.g., U.S. Jury Finds a Kodak Monopoly in Amateur-Photography Business, N.Y. TIMES, Jan. 22, 1978. The same decade, the Second Circuit rejected an effort by Kodak's competitors to require the dominant firm to disclose its innovation in advance in order to facilitate their competition. Berkey Photo, Inc. v. Eastman Kodak Co., 603 F.2d 263, 268 (2d Cir. 1979), cert. denied, 444 U.S. 1093 (1980).

[33] Eastman Kodak Co. v. Image Tech. Servs. Inc., 504 U.S. 451 (1992).

[34] Image Tech. Servs. Inc. v. Eastman Kodak Co., 125 F.3d 1195 (9th Cir. 1997).

[35] See, e.g., Barry C. Lynn, Breaking the Chain: The Antitrust Case Against Wal-Mart, HARPER'S MAGAZINE, 2006.

arrived on the scene, capturing voluminous sales from its bricks and mortar competitor.³⁶ In 2015, its market capitalization surpassed that of Walmart. By May 2019, it had tripled in size and overtaken Walmart to become the world's largest retailer.³⁷ Meanwhile, Sears – facing insuperable competition from those companies – went bankrupt. In doing so, it ended an iconic era in which it was surely the Amazon of its day.

The examples keep adding up, but the point is the same. Dominant firms – and even today's digital-tech giants – are more vulnerable than they might appear. Markets in the new economy tend to cycle as consumers gravitate to the latest great thing. Network effects notwithstanding, even firmly established platforms and technology giants must innovate in order to survive. The past is littered with examples of companies that failed to do so. This is the Schumpeterian wave of creative destruction that nicely describes the new economy.³⁸

Of course, it is easy to discount past examples and see today's issues as unique. *Obviously*, the thinking goes, AOL, Myspace, AltaVista, Nokia, BlackBerry, Nokia, Yahoo!, Kodak, Sears, and the like were never going to dominate the future – their very names invoke obsolescence. But the reality of their time was altogether different. It is difficult to predict future paths of innovation, which excel in leaving yesterday's technological trailblazers stranded. To be sure, there is no guarantee that the cyclical rise and fall of past technology companies will mirror those of the present and future. But it does present a forceful case for measured assessment and a skeptical reaction to claims of entrenched monopoly.

2.1.1.1 Public Monopolization Cases Have an Ignominious History, But Antitrust Can Safeguard Access to Consumers and Suppliers

As discussed, competition punishes even the most successful companies that fail to anticipate shifts in consumer demand. The history of toppled giants invites a simple inference: markets self-correct, leaving little need for antitrust enforcement beyond prohibiting cartels and mergers to monopoly or extreme market concentration. Furthering that account is a blemished track record of antitrust intervention against unilateral conduct. Technology far outpaces the courtroom. Hence, some public monopolization actions may have scant utility in addressing specific harms associated with exclusionary conduct. Past debacles cement the point.

That intuition goes too far, though it properly warns against unbounded antitrust enforcement. As explained below, the agencies must ensure that markets remain

---

[36] The lines between the online versus bricks and mortar store business models have since eroded with Amazon's acquiring Whole Foods and Walmart's buying Jet.com.
[37] *See, e.g.*, Lauren Debter, *Amazon Surpasses Walmart As the World's Largest Retailer*, FORBES, May 15, 2019, https://www.forbes.com/sites/laurendebter/2019/05/15/worlds-largest-retailers-2019-amazon-walmart-alibaba/#7063b9f64171.
[38] *See generally* Richard A. Posner, *Antitrust in the New Economy*, 68 ANTITRUST L.J. 925 (2001).

exposed to competition and do not become fortified through exclusionary conduct. Before exploring that point further, though, it is worth reflecting on the dangers of misadventure. Enforcers have in the past embarked on unwarranted interventions, harming markets and distorting incentives instead of benefitting consumers. Nowhere is that risk more acute than in Section 2 cases, which require strong justification, but also serve an important function when properly executed.

INFAMOUS FAILURES AND THE LIMITS OF ANTITRUST. The IBM monopolization case stands out as a particular disaster – "the antitrust division's Vietnam."[39] The government sued in 1969, accusing the computer giant of monopolizing computer markets through predatory innovation, below-cost pricing, bundling, and related marketing practices. The litigation, which came to epitomize the fruitless public-monopolization case, ground on for thirteen years until the DOJ finally dismissed its complaint in 1982.[40] The government's case morphed as innovation obviated the original theory of competitive harm. After 700 days of trial, 17,000 exhibits, and $17 million in litigation costs on the DOJ's side alone, and up to $100 million annual costs in total, one is left to ponder the point of it all.[41]

The FTC, for its part, experienced a similar debacle flowing from its deconcentration push in the 1970s. In particular, the Commission dismissed its administrative litigation against Exxon for shared monopoly in 1981, eight years after issuing a complaint, observing that "completion of discovery is at least several years away."[42]

Administrative limitations matter, too. Unlike most jurisdictions, US antitrust enforcers cannot determine liability and impose remedies.[43] Rather, they must go to court. The antitrust bar cherishes this system, which employs superior due-process safeguards, separates powers, and yields more accurate decision-making. Litigation, however, drives a temporal wedge between an agency's identification of a competition problem and a remedy. Even in meritorious cases, the gulf can be several years. To be sure, productive intervention may be feasible in staid industries. Further, consents through which an accused firm commits to remedial action may be timely and effective. Remediating foreclosure in effervescent markets through litigation, however, can be difficult and even impossible. Technology-driven industries seldom allow for retrospective correction. Rapid innovation, displacement, and competitive cycling elide the traditional antitrust apparatus. As *IBM* perhaps best exemplified, well-intentioned

---

[39] *U.S. vs. I.B.M.*, N.Y. TIMES, Feb. 15, 1981 (quoting Professor Robert H. Bork), https://www.nytimes.com/1981/02/15/business/us-vsibm.html.
[40] *In re Int'l Bus. Machs. Corp.*, 687 F.2d 591, 593 (2d Cir. 1982).
[41] *See* William E. Kovacic, *The Antitrust Law and Economics of Essential Facilities in Public Utility Regulation*, in ECONOMIC INNOVATIONS IN PUBLIC UTILITY REGULATION 1 (Michael A. Crew ed.) (1992).
[42] William E. Kovacic, *Failed Expectations: The Troubled Past and Uncertain Future of the Sherman Act as a Tool for Deconcentration*, 74 IOWA L. REV. 1105, 1109 n.20 (1989) (citing Exxon Corp., 98 F.T.C. 453, 460 (1981)).
[43] Even the FTC, which has an idiosyncratic administrative litigation process known as "Part 3," can only enforce its cease and desist orders through the judicial process.

enforcers can find themselves chasing a moving target, and all for naught. A case that may once have appeared worthy can unravel. Indeed, if markets evolve so quickly that challenged practices become defunct while litigation is pending, are unilateral-behavior cases worth the candle?

It follows, one might argue, that enforcers should bow to markets. And that conclusion gains traction even before one considers the vital issue of error costs, which – as traditionally, but wrongly, conceived – favors nonintervention at the margin. Those concerns properly reach their zenith, however, in unilateral-conduct matters. Defining exclusionary conduct is hard – distinguishing it from hard competition on the merits even more so. Save in the occasional clear case, offsetting considerations abound. It is easy inadvertently to punish merit-based competition.

That line of thought has seduced many conservative thinkers. Certainly, it found favor in the early Chicago School's writings.[44] The Supreme Court has generally ratcheted up the difficulty of successfully prosecuting monopolization cases.[45] And laissez faire became a (short-lived) policy in 2008, when the Bush II administration published a single-firm-conduct report that adopted a substantial disproportionality test to which the Federal Trade Commission refused to adhere.[46]

The most extreme noninterventionist policies in the monopolization space flow from contestability theory. Under certain assumptions, including the absence of entry barriers, a monopoly may yield perfectly competitive outcomes.[47] In reality, of course, potential competition never perfectly disciplines an incumbent monopolist.[48]

Ultimately, monopoly's transience does not justify an antitrust-light or -free policy. A more thoughtful path is to eschew absolutist positions in favor of an

---

[44] See, e.g., ROBERT BORK, THE ANTITRUST PARADOX (1978).
[45] See Pac. Bell Tel. Co. v. linkLine Commc'ns, Inc., 555 U.S. 438, 454 (2009); Weyerhaeuser Co. v. Ross-Simmons Hardwood Lumber Co., 549 U.S. 312 (2007); Verizon Commc'ns Inc. v. Law Offices of Curtis V. Trinko, LLP, 540 U.S. 398 (2004); Brooke Grp. Ltd. v. Brown & Williamson Tobacco Corp., 509 U.S. 209 (1993); Matsushita Elec. Indus. Co. v. Zenith Radio Corp., 475 U.S. 574 (1986); see also Ohio v. Am Express, 138 S. Ct. 2274 (2018) (in a Section 1 decision, requiring proof of harm across two-sided platform market for simultaneous transactions, potentially making future monopolization actions in network markets more difficult). But see N.C. State Bd. Dental Exam'rs v. Fed. Trade Comm'n, 574 U.S. 494 (2015); Fed. Trade Comm'n v. Phoebe Putney Health Sys., 568 U.S. 216 (2013); Eastman Kodak Co. v. Image Tech. Servs., Inc., 504 U.S. 451 (1992); Aspen Skiing Co. v. Aspen Highlands Skiing Corp., 472 U.S. 585 (1985).
[46] Cf. U.S. DEP'T OF JUSTICE, COMPETITION AND MONOPOLY: SINGLE-FIRM CONDUCT UNDER SECTION 2 OF THE SHERMAN ACT (2008), withdrawn (2009) with Press Release, FTC Commissioners React to Department of Justice Report, Competition and Monopoly: Single-Firm Conduct Under Section 2 of the Sherman Act, Sept. 8, 2008, https://www.ftc.gov/news-events/press-releases/2008/09/ftc-commissioners-react-department-justice-report-competition-and.
[47] WILLIAM J. BAUMOL, JOHN C. PANZAR, & ROBERT D. WILLIG, CONTESTABLE MARKETS AND THE THEORY OF INDUSTRY STRUCTURE (1982).
[48] See, e.g., Richard J. Gilbert, The Role of Potential Competition in Industrial Organization, 3 J. ECON. PERSP. 107 (1989); Steven A. Morrison & Clifford Winston, Empirical Implications and Tests of the Contestability Hypothesis, 30 J.L. & ECON. 53 (1987).

intervention calculus that humbly evaluates the art of the possible before employing the antitrust machine.[49]

ANTITRUST REFORM AND EXCLUSIONARY CONDUCT. Economists have modeled scenarios in which dominant incumbents may rationally exclude competitors.[50] The vehicle of foreclosure may take various forms – exclusive dealing, below-cost pricing, bundled discounts, volume rebates, product tying, taxing rivals' sales, vertical integration (whether by merger or contract), and so on.[51] Industrial organization has evolved since the early days of the Chicago School, when price theorists predicted that exclusionary conduct would be irrational. Game-theoretic models identify circumstances, albeit within strict parameters, in which such behavior may indeed be profitable.

Exclusion is thus possible. By extension, the absence of oversight of dominant-firm conduct would invite harmful Type II errors. Those costs may not be fleeting. Dominant positions erode, as we saw above, but not with consistent expedition across markets. Antitrust enforcers analyze entry barriers for good reason – some exercises of significant market power linger. Markets have forceful self-curative properties, but they do not work perfectly. Some industries feature heavy upfront investment in infrastructure needed to compete, meaning that structural changes to the market may affect outcomes for sustained periods. In other sectors, the principal competitive assets may be mobile, thus rendering any meaningful exercise of market power short-lived.

At least in theory, antitrust enforcers can facilitate entry and expansion by condemning exclusionary conduct. The extent to which possibility theorems of rational foreclosure should inform antitrust-liability standards, of course, is contested.[52]

[49] See, e.g., Maureen K. Ohlhausen, *Regulatory Humility in Practice*, Apr. 1, 2015, https://www.ftc.gov/system/files/documents/public_statements/635811/150401aeihumilitypractice.pdf.

[50] See, e.g., Michael Funk & Christian Jaag, *The More Economic Approach to Predatory Pricing*, 14 J. COMPETITION L. & ECON. 292 (2018); Luis M. B. Cabral & Michael J. Riordan, *Learning Curve, Predation, Antitrust and Welfare*, 45 J. INDUS. ECON. 155 (1997); Michael D. Whinston, *Tying, Foreclosure, and Exclusion*, 80 AM. ECON. REV. 837 (1990); Oliver Hart & Jean Tirole, *Vertical Integration and Market Foreclosure*, 1990 BROOKINGS PAPERS: MICROECONOMICS 205, 213, *passim* (1990); Janusz A. Ordover, Garth Saloner, & Steven C. Salop, *Equilibrium Vertical Foreclosure*, 80 AM. ECON. REV. 127 (1990); Michael Salinger, *Vertical Mergers and Market Foreclosure*, 103 Q.J. ECON. 345 (1988); Paul R. Milgrom & John Roberts, *Informational Asymmetries, Strategic Behavior and Industrial Organization*, 77 AM. ECON. REV. 184 (1987); Philippe Aghion & Patrick Bolton, *Contracts as Barriers to Entry*, 77 AM. ECON. REV. 388 (1987); David M. Kreps & Robert B. Wilson, *Reputation and Imperfect Information*, 27 J. ECON. THEORY 253 (1982); Paul R. Milgrom & John Roberts, *Predation, Reputation and Entry Deterrence*, 27 J. ECON. THEORY 280 (1982).

[51] See, e.g., sources cited *supra* note 50. To be clear, these are possibility theorems rather than general predictions. For example, there is good reason to look skeptically on claims of predatory pricing. See, e.g., John S. McGee, *Predatory Pricing Revisited*, 23 J.L. & ECON. 289 (1980). Further, many of these practices are widespread even in competitive markets, demonstrating efficiency justifications that counsel against any general rule against such conduct, even when employed by a dominant firm. It is imperative not to extrapolate a general prohibitory rule from the game-theoretic literature on exclusion. Any such prohibition would be overbroad.

[52] Cf., e.g., Patrick Bolton, Joseph F. Brodley, & Michael H. Riordan, *Predatory Pricing: Strategic Theory and Legal Policy*, 88 GEO. L.J. 2239 (2000) (calling for a broader liability standard for predatory pricing) *with* Kenneth G. Elzinga & David E. Mills, *Predatory Pricing and Strategic Theory*, 89 GEO.

Game-theoretic models of unilateral exclusion are not, however, general cases. Yet, they have given cover to unjustifiably broad prohibitions adopted by many overseas competition enforcers. Under the rubric of "Post-Chicago" thinking, some jurisdictions condemn unilateral conduct without undertaking a cost-benefit calculus or tying practices to consumer harm. In fact, the economics literature does not lend itself to any general proscription on below-cost pricing, exclusive dealing, tying arrangements, or other such practices. Many such practices, even when employed by a dominant firm, increase competitive pressure in both the short and long run. Thankfully, US doctrine employs a more nuanced liability standard under Section 2.

Can we trust the agencies and judiciary, however, to conduct this analysis with precision? We might recognize the academic possibility of exclusion, but query the workability of a conduct standard likely to be applied in practice. At this point, the history of misguided enforcement invites pause. Further, the reality of international competition law is at times alarming. Some overseas "abuse of dominance" cases, including by the European Commission, evince a lack of rigor. In the worst instances, declared abuses have been wholly conclusory. This shortcoming is partially one of design. The concept of an "abuse" is rooted in fairness – a "vagrant" concept.[53] EU competition law has interpreted it to forbid conduct that neither plausibly affects consumers nor bolsters the undertaking's dominant position against displacement or erosion.[54]

Armed with the right guiding principles and leadership, however, the FTC and Justice Department are up to the task. US jurisprudence precludes unilateral-conduct liability of the kind that characterizes many other jurisdictions. The hallmark of a meritorious US case is exclusion, not exploitation. The courts will not allow monopolization cases to proceed absent evidence of harm to the competitive process itself.[55] The vital issue of case selection, of course, raises challenges. Meritorious interventions against dominant firms may be the exception, even in the United States, but they are important.[56]

The need for robust oversight of dominant-firm conduct reflects an essential point. Despite the challenges and past failures, US public monopolization actions have also seen demonstrable success. Those benefits are worth preserving. It is not simply that the FTC and Justice Department have intervened to end harmful conduct. Rather,

---

L.J. 2475, 2476 (2001) ("chid[ing] the courts for failing to heed modern theories of predation and for continuing to rely on 'earlier theory that is no longer generally accepted'").

[53] Phillip Areeda & Herbert Hovenkamp, Antitrust Law: An Analysis of Antitrust Principles and Their Application, ¶ 111d (2019).

[54] By its express terms, for example, Article 102 TFEU prohibits the imposition of "unfair ... selling prices" – an act that *increases* competition by enticing incumbent expansion, repositioning, and entry.

[55] United States v. Microsoft Corp., 253 F.3d 34, 58 (D.C. Cir. 2001) (per curiam) (en banc).

[56] See, e.g., Christine A. Varney, Vigorous Antitrust Enforcement in This Challenging Era, May 11, 2009, http://graphics8.nytimes.com/images/2009/05/12/business/VarneySpeech.pdf (espousing more aggressive interventionist efforts for Section 2 violations).

incentive effects matter most. Appreciating the costs of a meritorious governmental action – from which painful treble-damages class actions are sure to follow – even monopolists will realize that, if they are to overcome their rivals, they may only do so by competing on the merits.

We must take care, of course, not to overexpand the scope of Section 2 liability. Antitrust policy wants all firms, dominant ones included, to compete mercilessly. By necessity, monopolization standards will always be fuzzy and hence bear the potential to over-deter the risk averse. As noted, prohibitory rules would be far too broad, while a permissive (i.e., no liability) rule would yield unacceptable costs. A fact-specific inquiry grounded in economic analysis – that is, a variant of the rule of reason – is the right path. That framework will never yield perfect legal certainty. When optimally calibrated, however, it can allow firms to estimate the risks of conduct likely to exclude their rivals. Duly apprised, monopolists will take heed of governing Section 2 principles. This benefit, however, can only materialize if the agencies visibly act against problematic exclusion when it arises.

The goal of Section 2 policy should be to discipline incumbents, forcing them to innovate and evolve on threat of looming extinction, and to do so by deterring exclusionary conduct.

Pause on this critical point. New-economy markets cycle, often suddenly and unpredictably. Dominant technology firms cannot sustain their positions indefinitely without innovating. Perpetual monopoly profits seem outlandish for digital platforms unless driven by impressive continuous improvements. That is a far cry, however, from positing that every superior technology comes to market – expeditiously or at all. Nor does it suggest that digital networks are vulnerable to displacement in the short term. Well-positioned incumbents can delay their day of reckoning by controlling at least some innovation pipelines and by restricting rivals' access to consumers and distributors. Strategic acquisitions could, at least in theory, reduce the risk of displacement. Indeed, in network industries, even the most promising technologies require sufficient volume to tip the market. Hence, deprived of scale, some fledgling rivals may struggle to get off the ground even with compelling new features or superior offerings.

Antitrust may play a valuable role here, ensuring that dominant firms do not invest in excluding competition, whether from within or abreast their core markets. The stakes are high. If an incumbent successfully postpones (or kills off) a superior technological standard, then consumers may suffer harms exceeding those inflicted by supranormal pricing. Innovation drives economic growth, and, in the new economy, leapfrog competition may be a vital determinant of consumer welfare. Antitrust *can* help to protect that process.

The emphasis reflects the challenge of employing antitrust effectively here. In the digital space, for example, acquiring users may simultaneously enhance network value and impede entry. An incumbent's investment in technological advancement benefits consumers, but closes the door to alternative standards. Adjacent acquisitions may enhance a platform's offerings – itself a good thing – and yet potentially whittle away the universe of incipient threats.[57] Tradeoffs flourish here, requiring caution. There is, perhaps, no other area of antitrust law more rife with the opportunity for miscalculation. Teasing out the impetus, let alone the likely future effect, of various business practices is devilishly tricky.

MONOPOLIZATION ACTIONS, DONE RIGHT. Monopolization cases require compelling facts. Unilateral actions do not endanger competition like horizontal agreements do. Nor, crucially, is a precision rule available to tackle exclusionary conduct by a dominant firm. Effects are far too context-dependent for such a solution. As a result, a good Section 2 case requires careful proof that a practice is likely to harm competition without net offsetting efficiency benefits.

Error analysis matters here. Not only is exclusionary conduct hard to identify, but a misdiagnosis can broadly restrict a firm's ability to compete. By contrast, if a contract unreasonably restrains trade, then the agencies can enjoin it cleanly through judicial action or by consent. The firm involved can otherwise proceed with its business. Indeed, it may lawfully circumvent the prohibition through an agreement that is less restrictive of competition or by pursuing an in-house solution. In these Section 1 cases, the antitrust attack is usually targeted, even surgical.

When the antitrust crosshairs fall on a dominant firm's standalone actions, however, the calculus shifts. The typical accusation is that the monopolist's overall course of conduct – that is, its means of competing in the market – unlawfully excludes rivals.[58] Hence, the ensuing antitrust incursion is broad. Next best alternatives available to the dominant firm may be significantly less attractive. Even instances of input or customer foreclosure often carry efficiency justifications. And because "exclusion" is most effective when the challenged practices benefit consumers, policing single-firm conduct is rife with opportunity for error. If the agencies and courts wrongly intervene, then they condemn a firm for competing on the merits, benefiting its rivals at consumers' expense. It is at this juncture that antitrust risks inverting its pro-consumer mandate. Coupled with powerful evidence that monopolies erode, markets cycle, and public Section 2 cases often stall or become defunct, it is scant wonder that conservative thinkers look skeptically on monopolization actions.

These concerns are real, but public monopolization actions have an important role to play. As explored above, dominant firms have at their disposal means to inhibit new entry or expansion. They may curtail or delay disruptive technologies.

---

[57] See Randy Picker, *Platforms and Adjacent Market Competition: A Look at Recent History*, PROMARKET, Apr. 16, 2018, https://promarket.org/platforms-adjacent-market-competition-look-recent-history/.

[58] See, e.g., City of Mishawaka v. Am. Elec. Power Co., 616 F.2d 976, 986 (7th Cir. 1980) ("The utility would have us consider each separate aspect of its conduct separately and in a vacuum. If we did, we might agree with the utility that no one aspect standing alone is illegal. It is the mix of the various ingredients of utility behavior in a monopoly broth that produces the unsavory flavor.").

Effective strategies can deny consumers the benefits of price, quality, and innovation competition. After all, such firms have incentives rationally to exclude competition in at least some circumstances. Thus, antitrust enforcers could not, in good conscience, abandon the field of unilateral conduct. Doing so would grant monopolists carte blanche to foreclose rivals.

This is all well and good in theory, but if real-life enforcement efforts flounder, what is the point? Despite the inglorious history recounted above, there are several examples of meritorious – indeed, crucially important – public-monopolization cases. The next several pages touch on a selection of meritorious Section 2 cases, concluding with the famous *Microsoft* litigation.[59]

Lorain Journal *Lorain Journal* is the classic example.[60] The city of Lorain, Ohio, had just one major newspaper – the Journal – in the 1930s and 40s. The only other paper was a restricted, Sunday-only circulation. Advertisers wishing to reach the 52,000 people living in Lorain had to use the Journal. In 1948, however, a radio station received FCC approval to begin broadcasting in the area, and began competing for advertising. The Journal responded by boycotting any firm that advertised with WEOL, its radio competitor. The publisher monitored WEOL programming to identify Lorain advertisers, and then terminated their contracts until they agreed no longer to advertise by radio. The campaign worked – several local firms stopped advertising with WEOL.

Those facts present a straightforward Section 2 violation, and the Supreme Court agreed.[61] The exclusionary effect was not a byproduct of competition. The Journal did not lure advertisers away, for example, by offering them lower prices or other attractive terms. Exclusive dealing can expand output by providing incentives to invest in high-quality product distribution, but there were no such benefits at issue in *Lorain Journal*. Indeed, there was no credible efficiency justification of any kind. Rather, the newspaper's actions marked a transparent effort to preserve a dominant position against an emerging rival. The agencies can – and should – quickly arrest such conduct when it occurs.

Notably, Section 2 cases become difficult when the vehicle of exclusion blurs with competition on the merits. The most controversial monopolization cases thus tend to revolve around predatory innovation, below-cost pricing, bundled discounts, volume rebates, and refusals to deal. The dangers of going after exclusionary innovation are axiomatic. So, too, price reductions benefit consumers, and induce competitors themselves to cut price in order to chase volume. Prohibiting such conduct threatens to invert antitrust policy, shielding relatively inefficient firms from Darwinian competition. We want to be awfully sure before condemning a firm for offering consumers terms that were too generous. Separately, imposing

---

[59] United States v. Microsoft Corp., 253 F.3d 34 (D.C. Cir. 2001) (per curiam) (en banc).
[60] Lorain Journal Co. v. United States, 342 U.S. 143 (1951).
[61] *Id.* at 154.

liability for refusing to cooperate undermines property rights – and the incentives to invest attendant upon them – by allowing rivals to free-ride on their successful competitor's infrastructure. Again, we want to be quite certain that imposing a duty to deal will not diminish long-term incentives. By contrast, actions that impede rivals' ability to compete without obvious offsetting efficiency justifications are easier to prohibit.[62]

By contrast, actions like those in *Lorain Journal* reflect an affirmative investment in exclusion itself. In the author's experience, evidence of intent is often soft and unreliable. But, as *Lorain Journal* demonstrates, that is not always the case. When the circumstances make clear that a monopolist acted to exclude a competitor without benefiting consumers, then the case for liability is strong.

AT&T Among the most celebrated Section 2 cases is *AT&T*, which produced what Judge Posner later called the most effective antitrust remedy in history.[63] The settlement marked a transformative moment in the history of the US telecommunications industry. The structural break-up of AT&T on account of its long-running monopoly makes it an appealing analogy for today's progressive reformists. In particular, neo-Brandeisians want to bring similar remedies to bear on today's Silicon Valley giants.

AT&T, however, is singularly inapposite for today's divestiture debate. Some historical context must this clear.

Alexander Graham Bell invented the telephone, of course, and secured pioneer patents that yielded a lawful monopoly for AT&T until 1894. Although thousands of local telephone companies quickly emerged after the core patents expired, they were unable to build an effective long-distance telecommunications network. AT&T grew through acquisitions in the early twentieth century, but soon encountered antitrust headwinds. In a shrewd move that staved off monopolization actions of the kind that had just befallen Standard Oil and American Tobacco,[64] AT&T's Vice President, Nathan Kingsbury, wrote to the Justice Department in 1913. He proposed opening AT&T's network to independents, not acquiring them, and selling Western Union. The "Kingsbury Commitment" resulted in AT&T's enjoying a lawful monopoly – protected from competition by the federal government itself.

The rationale behind AT&T's state-sanctioned position was natural monopoly. Competition offered the unappetizing prospect of incompatible phone systems and inefficient duplication of network infrastructure. Hence, AT&T operated as a natural monopolist for almost seven decades. This reality did not change until technological innovation made effective competition in long-distance workable for

---

[62] *See, e.g.*, McWane, Inc. v. Fed. Trade Comm'n, 783 F.3d 814 (11th Cir. 2015); United States v. Dentsply Int'l, Inc., 399 F.3d 181 (3d Cir. 2005).

[63] United States v. Am. Tel. & Tel. Co., 552 F. Supp. 131 (D.D.C. 1982). *See* RICHARD A. POSNER, ANTITRUST LAW 111 (2d ed. 2001).

[64] Standard Oil Co. v. United States, 221 U.S. 1 (1911); United States v. Am. Tobacco Co., 221 U.S. 106 (1911).

the first time. Specifically, the FCC allowed MCI Communications to enter the space in 1969 using microwave technologies to bypass AT&T's copper-wire network. Other applications for long-distance service quickly proliferated. As MCI sought to enter on terms that it believed the FCC had authorized, it warred with AT&T over interconnection terms.[65]

It was within that context that the Justice Department sued AT&T in 1974 for monopolization. The government's case focused on the telephone giant's efforts to stymie entry in the long-distance market. More specifically, it emphasized AT&T's alleged practice of using profits from its regulated short-distance monopolies to cross-subsidize price cuts in the face of attempted competition in long distance, and refusing to interconnect with competitive networks. Eight years later, the parties announced a settlement in which AT&T agreed to divest its seven local exchange-service carriers – the Regional Bell Operating Companies (RBOCs) – but would retain its long-distance business and keep Western Electric. The RBOCs continued to operate as state-regulated local monopolies, but AT&T became exposed to full competition in the long-distance market. The break-up became effective in 1984, and produced dramatic price reductions in long-distance service.

This case warrants two observations. First, the principal worry in bringing a Section 2 case is that liability will deter future investment. That risk is much reduced where a monopolist achieved its position under the auspices of government protection, rather than through competition on the merits. Second, the Justice Department did not premise its monopolization action on a status offense. In other words, the government did not seek a breakup simply because AT&T was a monopolist and competition would thrive under an industry restructuring. Rather, the government identified *exclusionary* actions undertaken by the telecommunications giant. Those two facts contrast sharply with much of the debate surrounding leading Silicon Valley companies.

Microsoft *Microsoft* looms over today's antitrust debate.[66] Calls for action against Silicon Valley abound. Yet, they seldom display nuanced regard for the constituent elements of a monopolization case. *Microsoft* speaks to the issues that any Section 2 action in the technology space would have to overcome. The case probed the nuances of exclusion in technological network industries. It also illustrates the difficulty of bringing remedies effectively to bear on dominant platforms that foreclose competition. If there were a viable unilateral-conduct case against technology companies with the largest market capitalizations today – it is not clear that there is – then it would surely turn on issues at the frontier of antitrust liability. And, without a doubt, they would raise achingly difficult remedial problems. *Microsoft* is a benchmark by which to judge the soundness of any such proposed intervention in Silicon Valley.

---

[65] MCI Comm'cns Corp. v. AT&T Co., 708 F.2d 1081 (7th Cir. 1983).
[66] United States v. Microsoft Corp., 253 F.3d 34 (D.C. Cir. 2001) (per curiam) (en banc).

This discussion first requires a compendium. After agreeing to build the MS-DOS operating system in 1980 for IBM's PC, Microsoft displaced the previously leading OS provider, Digital Research. Enjoying a commanding lead through its IBM contract – an opportunity that Digital Research famously turned down – Microsoft accelerated its rival's demise in the 1980s through vertical restraints with OEMs.[67] In particular, Microsoft imposed licensing terms that charged OEMs a "per processor" royalty fee that effectively taxed its competitors' sales. Any such manufacturer had to pay Microsoft for building a computer that did not use a Microsoft operating system. Other things being equal, those provisions made rival operating systems more expensive relative to Microsoft's offerings.

The FTC opened an investigation in 1990, but deadlocked 2–2, which led the Justice Department to take over the matter. The DOJ sued in 1994 for unlawful maintenance of a monopoly based, in particular, on per-processor licenses. Microsoft and the government settled the case through a consent decree that the DC Circuit, in reversing the lower court, ultimately blessed in 1995.[68] Under the decree, Microsoft endeavored not to tie sales of its operating system to any of its other products. Under the agreement, however, the firm could lawfully develop integrated products.[69]

The ultimate monopolization case – the one that bears particular relevance to today's climate – grew out of Microsoft's reaction to a perceived threat to its operating system. On the back of millions of IBM computers, Microsoft had created a seemingly impervious ecosystem. Already dominant, the company launched Windows 3.1 in 1992 to acclaim, followed by the revolutionary – and even more successful – Windows 95. Software developers had written myriad programs to run on Windows, enhancing consumer demand and ensuring that any rival operating system would have to achieve large scale in order to supplant Microsoft.[70] This was the "applications barrier to entry" that shielded Microsoft's operating-system monopoly from competition.

Microsoft realized, with some alarm, its lack of control over users' Internet access. Middleware potentially allowed software developers to write code that would work regardless of the underlying operating system. By exposing application programming interfaces (APIs), Sun Microsystems' Java could allow programmers to bypass Microsoft's Windows monopoly. In conjunction with Java, the leading Internet

---

[67] United States v. Microsoft Corp., 56 F.3d 1448, 1451–52 (D.C. Cir. 1995).
[68] Id.
[69] United States v. Microsoft Corp., No. 94-CV-1564, 1995 WL 505998, at *3, § IV.E(i) (D.D.C. Aug. 21, 1995).
[70] This is a typical feature in platform markets. Network effects lead consumer demand for a system to rise with the number of users. If sufficiently powerful, this phenomenon may tip markets toward monopoly in a "winner takes all" contest. Whether dominated network markets resist entry is contested. In theory, network effects may inhibit entry, but may also facilitate rapid displacement of an incumbent. As we saw above, technology markets cycle and often do so dramatically. The D.C. Circuit recognized the theoretical indeterminacy of these offsetting factors. *Microsoft*, 253 F.3d at 50.

browser, Netscape Navigator, could operate as middleware performing this function. In theory, the market could shift, leaving Microsoft stranded with a defunct product.

The software firm recognized the threat. In his infamous "Internet Tidal Wave" memo, Bill Gates stressed on the company's employees a need to "assign the Internet the highest level of importance."[71] He then honed in on a specific competitive threat:

> SUN's Java project involves turning an Internet client into a programmable framework. SUN is very involved in evolving the Internet to stay away from Microsoft.... A new competitor "born" on the Internet is Netscape. Their browser is dominant, with 70% usage share, allowing them to determine which network extensions will catch on. They are pursuing a multi-platform strategy where they move the key API into the client to commoditize the underlying operating system.... One scary possibility being discussed by Internet fans is whether they should get together and create something far less expensive than a PC which is powerful enough for Web browsing.... I want every product plan to try and go overboard on Internet features.... [T]he Platform group [is going] to define an integrated strategy that makes it clear that Windows machines are the best choice for the Internet. This will protect and grow our Windows asset.[72]

The *Microsoft* litigation centered on what happened next. The company launched an all-out effort to supplant Netscape's Navigator browser by investing in Internet Explorer and taking various actions to exclude its competitor. Despite the obvious exclusionary goal, several of those actions were procompetitive, at least vis-à-vis a potential browsing market. Microsoft poured some $100 million per year into developing Internet Explorer, which it then gave away for free. This zero-price competition forced Netscape to make Navigator freely available, too – an undeniable short-term boon to consumers. At the same time, Microsoft developed its own Java Virtual Machine (JVM), designing it to be incompatible with Sun Microsystems' offering, and then worked to move the market toward its proprietary solution. Developing a new product is, of course, procompetitive.

In theory, certain of these actions might violate the antitrust laws. Below-cost pricing may amount to unlawful monopolization if it creates a dangerous probability of recoupment.[73] That looked unlikely in the browser market because Microsoft's goal was to protect its operating-system monopoly. By the same token, predatory innovation – such as designing a product to be incompatible with competitors' goods – can theoretically harm consumers. The law is rightly wary, however, of condemning technological progress. Every incremental product improvement

---

[71] Mem. fr. Bill Gates on the Internet Tidal Wave, May 26, 1995, http://www.justice.gov/atr/cases/exhibits/20.pdf.
[72] *Id.*
[73] Brooke Grp. Ltd. v. Brown & Williamson Tobacco Corp., 509 U.S. 209, 224 (1993).

reflects an effort to capture share from a competitor. Notably, Microsoft's JVM permitted applications to run more quickly on Windows than did Sun's JVM.

The DC Circuit properly reversed liability findings on those two forms of conduct.[74] And, in an important ruling, it held that antitrust's modified per se rule against product tying does not apply to platform software products.[75] Integrating complementary functionality in software carries overwhelming benefits, making a prohibitory rule unworkable.

Nevertheless, a powerful case lay at *Microsoft*'s core. Trying to exclude a rival may represent legitimate – indeed, wholly desirable – competition on the merits. That is so if the *means* and *consequences* of exclusion likely benefits consumers.[76] As noted, some of Microsoft's actions in response to Netscape made consumers better off, at least in the short run. Yet, the core behavior lent itself to no such innocuous reading. The software company invested in restricting its competitor's access to consumers in a manner that harmed users, intermediaries, and Netscape alike.

As a threshold matter, antitrust law *must* prohibit monopolists from excluding nascent threats, even ones not yet developed into viable substitutes. As discussed, new-economy markets cycle as innovation – often from adjacent platforms – suddenly leads a critical mass of users to shift toward an alternative offering. Thus, in network markets, Section 2's principal role may be to protect the apparatus by which such displacement can occur. The goal is to identify exclusionary conduct that will ultimately harm consumers.

Microsoft easily met that standard. In designing Windows, Microsoft commingled code to ensure that any effort to delete Internet Explorer would cripple the operating system. It also excluded Internet Explorer from Add/Remove Programs, and overrode the user's choice of a default browser in certain circumstances. Those actions visited no benefits on consumers, and carried obvious exclusionary effects. Indeed, the anticompetitive animus behind those product-design decisions was so clear and the benefits so elusive that Microsoft had little to say in response. Charged with discharging the simplest of burdens – merely articulating a nonpretextual procompetitive justification – Microsoft could offer *nothing* in defense of those actions.[77]

Certain restrictions on OEMs were similarly difficult to explain. Microsoft prohibited them from removing Internet Explorer icons, altering the initial boot sequence to load a rival browser, or adding icons for competing products. These steps did not plausibly facilitate efficiencies for Microsoft or benefit consumers – justifications of the kind that one might expect for vertical restraints. Instead, the firm generally fell back on an absolutist copyright defense that, with the exception of

---

[74] *Microsoft*, 253 F.3d at 68, 75.
[75] *Id.* at 84.
[76] As the Supreme Court has observed, "Even an act of pure malice by one business competitor against another does not, without more, state a claim under the federal antitrust laws[.]" Brooke Grp. Ltd. v. Brown & Williamson Tobacco Corp., 509 U.S. 209, 225 (1993).
[77] *Id.* at 66–67.

OEMs' loading new interfaces in place of Windows, the DC Circuit rejected.[78] Indeed, in the court's view, Microsoft's "primary copyright argument borders upon the frivolous."[79]

Microsoft also agreed with Internet Access Providers (IAPs) like AOL (itself then dominant) to exclude Netscape, thus further depriving it of effective means of reaching consumers. When asked to justify its exclusive-dealing restraints with IAPs, the company merely argued that it wanted to focus developers focused upon its APIs, which, as the DC Circuit observed, "is to say, it wants to preserve its power in the operating system market."[80]

The litigation was, of course, controversial. Monopolization cases always are. Yet the DC Circuit's limited affirmance was fundamentally sound. Three traits conspire to make the case a tempting template for Section 2 intervention for some in the new economy.

First, the case proceeded expeditiously. Three years separated the complaint from the DC Circuit's en banc decision – a period that included four months of mediation. Second, the merits were clear. Indeed, in the author's estimation, it was not a particularly difficult case. Finally, as corrected by the DC Circuit, the ultimate remedy was measured. It also bore fruit in two respects – internet browsing and mobile OS. Microsoft Explorer has since faded into obscurity as Google's Chrome races ahead, followed by Apple's Safari and Mozilla's Firefox. Critically, the *Microsoft* remedy may have helped Google and Apple ultimately to prevail in mobile OS – a space that, but for the DOJ's monopolization, Microsoft ultimately may have reserved for itself by controlling Internet access.

If there were a flaw, though, it is that the fix was not more forceful as to the monopoly at the center of the case. Although it opened mobile internet browsing and operating software up to competitors, the relief ultimately imposed did little to expose Microsoft's desktop OS monopoly to competition. While structural relief of the kind sought by the Division would have been excessive, perhaps the court could have done more. Nevertheless, the case serves as a welcome example of an effective public monopolization action. And it continues to reinforce the principle that a dominant firm cannot entrench its position by denying, without efficiency justification, its competitors the means by which to reach distributors and ultimately consumers.[81]

2.2 EFFICIENCIES IN MERGER REVIEW

Intervention implies that antitrust can resolve a competitive problem more effectively than the market can. As discussed, market self-correction is more potent than

---

[78] *Id.* at 63.
[79] *Id.*
[80] *Id.* at 71.
[81] *See, e.g.,* McWane, Inc. v. Fed. Trade Comm'n, 783 F.3d 814 (11th Cir. 2015); United States v. Dentsply Int'l, Inc., 399 F.3d 181 (3d Cir. 2005).

progressive reformists often suppose. Claims of perpetual monopoly ring hollow in the face of evidence. But the preceding pages also argued for antitrust, even in the hard case of unilateral misconduct. Markets are capable, but imperfect. Dominant firms have incentives to exclude competition in at least some circumstances, and – occasional debacles notwithstanding – there are clear instances in which the agencies have intervened for the better. The most ardent free-marketeers are therefore wrong to require the most demanding imaginable proof before bringing such cases.

Those observations lay down an important marker for the reform discussion that lies ahead. Being rare, difficult, and controversial, Section 2 cases grab the headlines. There is a persuasive argument, however, that merger review should command more attention in the reform debate. Each of the past ten years, well over 10,000 mergers and acquisitions change the US commercial landscape. By contrast, even under the most aggressive administration, good monopolization cases will be infrequent.

Just as the case for Section 2 intervention turns on markets' propensity to self-correct, so the decision whether to block mergers turns on the presence of efficiencies. There is no question that antitrust policy since the early 1980s has taken a light touch to merger review relative to preceding decades, which saw a strong line against horizontal acquisitions and many vertical ones, too. The remainder of this chapter explores the question of merger synergies. Conservative antitrust thinkers tend to see efficiencies everywhere, while their more liberal colleagues see just the opposite. In fact, there is a more nuanced story to tell here, and the evidence matters greatly for today's reform debate.

2.2.1 Do Synergies Lead Agencies to Bless Anticompetitive Deals?

Efficiencies play a controversial role in merger review. A frequent critique holds them responsible for the industrial malaise that some observe today. On that view, the federal antitrust agencies are enthralled by an empty dogma. They naïvely suppose that deal-driven consolidation realizes marginal-cost reductions, which flow in turn to consumers through lower prices. Yet, rising concentration follows, demonstrating a failure of antitrust policy. Critics imply that the agencies have improperly cleared anticompetitive mergers simply because they promise to yield cost savings.[82]

That image, however, defies reality. True, the agencies credit efficiencies on occasion in blessing some consolidating transactions.[83] But that is very much the exception. In practice, staff are skeptical of claimed efficiencies, which counsel often

---

[82] See, e.g., Jonathan B. Baker & Carl Shapiro, *Reinvigorating Horizontal Merger Enforcement*, in HOW THE CHICAGO SCHOOL OVERSHOT THE MARK: THE EFFECT OF CONSERVATIVE ECONOMIC ANALYSIS ON U.S. ANTITRUST (Robert Pitofsky ed., 2008) at 256; Chris Sagers, *#LOLNothingMatters*, 63 ANTITRUST BULLETIN 7, 25 (2018). For a more extreme view, see Lina Khan & Sandeep Vaheesan, *Market Power and Inequality: The Antitrust Counterrevolution and Its Discontents*, 11 HARV. L. & POL'Y REV. 271–72, 275–76 (2017).

[83] See, e.g., Amanda P. Reeves & Maurice E. Stucke, *Behavioral Antitrust*, 86 IND. L.J. 1527, 1561 (2011) (citing relevant closing statements).

raise, but seldom substantiate. In part, this is because the Horizontal Merger Guidelines impose demanding eligibility criteria.[84]

The requirement of merger-specificity, in particular, disqualifies many efficiencies. Further, the verification condition has teeth. The agencies place the burden on companies, which must devote significant resources to documenting and rigorously verifying anticipated savings. Anyone who has spent time at the agencies, or working across from them, knows that the focus lies squarely on competitive effects. Duly aware of this fact, counsel seldom prioritize efficiency arguments – apart from trying to convince staff that the impetus for a particular deal flows from something other than eliminating a competitor. Other than in retail deals and others in which variable cost savings are apt to put downward pressure on price, antitrust deal lawyers know that they are in trouble if their clearance argument has descended to efficiencies alone.

In reality, the agencies reject the great majority of efficiency justifications for transactions that trigger a Second Request.[85] Such defenses typically flounder on verifiability and merger-specificity.[86] No court has ever upheld an anticompetitive merger on the ground of efficiencies. And the Guidelines expressly prohibit efficiency-enhancing mergers that nevertheless yield or facilitate the exercise of newfound market power.[87] All in all, efficiencies play a limited role in merger-clearance decisions.

Of course, they do play *some* role. Staff evaluate claimed efficiencies, particularly as part of in-depth investigations that go beyond the initial waiting period. It would be odd if they did not. A sophisticated economic analysis of a proposed merger often calculates incentives to raise price. For example, economists often use diversion ratios and margin data to estimate gross upward pricing-pressure indices – GUPPIs – in markets for differentiated goods. That statistic, however, may be incomplete without considering post-transaction marginal-cost savings, which may press price downward. When sufficiently rich data exist, combining them yields a single, more meaningful statistic, namely upward pricing pressure or UPP.[88] Using substantiated variable-cost savings (a proxy for marginal-cost reductions) is hardly grounds for

---

[84] U.S. Dep't of Justice & Fed. Trade Comm'n, Horizontal Merger Guidelines § 10 (2010).
[85] *See* Malcolm B. Coate & Andrew J. Heimert , Fed. Trade Comm'n, Merger Efficiencies at the Federal Trade Commission 1997–2007 35, 36 (2009), https://www.ftc.gov/sites/default/files/documents/reports/merger-efficiencies-federal-trade-commission-1997%E2%80%932007/0902mergereffi ciencies.pdf (the Bureau of Competition staff accepted just 8 percent of advanced efficiency claims in 186 mergers for which the staff completed a Second Request investigation between 1997 and 2007 – the Bureau of Economics staff, by contrast, accepted 27 percent of such claims).
[86] *Id.* at 19.
[87] Horizontal Merger Guidelines, *supra* note 84, at § 10.
[88] *See* Joseph Farrell & Carl Shapiro, *Upward Pricing Pressure and Critical Loss Analysis: Response*, 13 CPI Antitrust J. (Feb. 2010), https://faculty.haas.berkeley.edu/shapiro/uppcritical.pdf; Richard Schmalensee, *Should New Merger Guidelines Give UPP Market Definition?*, 12 CPI Antitrust J. (Dec. 2009), https://www.competitionpolicyinternational.com/should-new-merger-guidelines-giveupp-market-definition/.

criticizing the merger-review process. It informs a more accurate evaluation of competitive effects.

Putting all of this together, are critics barking up the wrong tree with efficiencies? Yes, to the extent that they blame the agencies' supposed propensity to credit unproven cost savings in clearing otherwise-problematic mergers. That simply does not happen. Nor do courts bless challenged mergers on account of synergies.[89] But a larger consideration warrants close attention – namely, the frequency and significance of merger-generated productivities inform the optimal antitrust standard. In other words, regardless of whether the agencies recognize efficiencies in a given transaction, the net social benefit of M&A activity illuminates how strict or lax antitrust merger review standards ought to be.

2.2.2 *Optimal Antitrust Rules Turn on the Frequency and Significance of Merger-Driven Efficiencies*

Merger-driven efficiencies inform the choice of rule.

Suppose that horizontal acquisitions realized no cost savings, failed to enhance buyers' competitiveness in the market, never accelerated innovation, and otherwise had no beneficial effect on consumers. Imagine further that a minority of those deals is anticompetitive, enhancing the post-transaction entities' market power. The agencies, however, struggle to distinguish the relatively innocuous from harmful transactions at the margin. In that hypothetical world, we would prohibit mergers between competitors (or require divestitures of the overlapping segments of larger merging businesses).

This is, in part, an application of error-cost analysis. Prohibiting all mergers between competitors on these assumptions would involve a Type I error cost of zero, and would prevent every anticompetitive horizontal acquisition. Further, by definition, mergers between head-to-head rivals eliminate competition. Absent marginal-cost savings, such acquisitions give the buyer some incentive to raise price. This holds true for mergers between firms that engage in Cournot competition involving homogeneous products.[90] And it is true for horizontal mergers involving differentiated products due to recapturing positive margins on diverted sales to the seller. Without entry, incumbent expansion, efficiencies, or sophisticated buyers that can discipline attempted exercises of market power (which are more likely in bidding markets or others with large, infrequent sales), even horizontal mergers between firms with small market shares may yield price increases.[91]

---

[89] *See, e.g.*, St. Alphonsus Med. Ctr.–Nampa Inc. v. St. Luke's Health Sys., Ltd., 778 F.3d 775, 790 (9th Cir. 2015) ("We remain skeptical about the efficiencies defense in general and about its scope in particular.").

[90] *See* Joseph Farrell & Carl Shapiro, *Horizontal Mergers: An Equilibrium Analysis*, 80 AM. ECON. REV. 107, 112, 122 (1990).

[91] In practice, the agencies tend to ignore GUPPIs of 5 percent or less. One might argue that that rule of thumb presumes marginal-cost savings of the same amount or low entry barriers.

Now, flip the hypothetical. If mergers routinely generate powerful efficiencies, then we need a permissive regime that intervenes only to block those deals that will facilitate exercises of market power that swamp any downward-pressure on price. The real world rests between those extremes. How close it lies to either end of the spectrum, however, is both contested and vital. Antitrust reform cannot overlook this fundamental question.

To gauge the issue's significance, consider that companies reported 2,089 transactions under the Hart–Scott–Rodino Act in 2019.[92] Only sixty (3 percent) of those deals received a Second Request – an in-depth investigation by the FTC and DOJ. The government challenged, or required a remedy in, merely thirty-eight (less than 2 percent) of those acquisitions. The federal antitrust agencies sued to block outright only five transactions – less than a quarter of one-percent of notifiable transactions. And, of course, there was a larger universe of non-notifiable transactions that sailed by without any look at all. Clearly, antitrust is a roadblock only to a tiny subset of mergers and acquisitions.

This phenomenon is desirable only if mergers create efficiencies. If they do not, then we should radically enhance antitrust scrutiny of horizontal combinations, in particular. It is true that most transactions individually create no material risk to competition in a given market. But subtle effects associated with a certain deal may go unnoticed, and when any such effects are magnified many times over every year, then we may start to see worrisome consequences in the economy over time. That is the thrust of today's debate about rising concentration in the US economy. It is a concern that we should take seriously. Together, the prevalence and magnitude of efficiencies and markets' tendency to self-correct inform optimal merger review policy.

2.2.3 *The Strong Theory – and Mixed Evidence – of Merger Efficiencies*

Do merger-specific efficiencies exist, and how often do they materialize? Those calling for less permissive merger review tend to answer with a variant of "rarely, if ever." Professor Sagers, for example, claims that "there is in fact no meaningful proof that consolidation generates social benefits."[93] In the Open Markets Institute's view, "horizontal mergers ... generally fail to produce efficiencies."[94] The Institute's Diana Moss further observes that "many claimed merger efficiencies never materialize."[95]

---

[92] FISCAL YEAR 2019, *supra* note 6.
[93] Chris Sagers, *American Antitrust Is Having a Moment: Some Reactions to Commissioner Ohlhausen's Recent Views*, PROMARKET, Sept. 16, 2016, https://promarket.org/american-antitrust-moment-reactions-commissioner-ohlhausens-recent-views/.
[94] Open Markets Institute, *The Failure and Potential Redemption of Federal Merger Policy*, FTC Comment, p. 2 (Aug. 20, 2018), https://www.ftc.gov/system/files/documents/public_comments/2018/08/ftc-2018-0053-d-0021-154978.pdf.
[95] Testimony of Diana Moss, President, Am. Antitrust Institute Before the U.S. Senate Committee on the Judiciary, Subcommittee on Antitrust, Competition and Consumer Rights, p. 6., Dec. 13, 2017, https://www.judiciary.senate.gov/imo/media/doc/12-13-17%20Moss%20Testimony.pdf.

If such critics are right, particularly in their more categorical claims that acquisitions produce few or no social gains, then our merger-review process suffers a gaping flaw. The Guidelines' express premise – that is, that "a primary benefit of mergers to the economy is their potential to generate significant efficiencies" – would be false.[96] The antitrust agencies would uncritically permit horizontal acquisitions, permitting accretions of market power with few offsetting gains.

As explained below, however, merger-generated efficiencies do exist and are not merely fleeting phenomena. It is true, nevertheless, that companies often overstate synergies and many acquisitions fail to achieve their full promised cost-savings, cross-sell opportunities, and related benefits. But that is a far cry from disclaiming merger efficiencies across the board or thinking a radically expanded antitrust threshold for merger clearance cost-free.

As a threshold observation, there are compelling *theoretical* reasons to think that efficiencies exist. Theory without fact has little ultimate value, of course, but it is a useful starting point.

First, most acquisitions do not reduce competition. It follows that few transactions seek to "take out a rival." Some rationales may be neutral from a competitive-effects standpoint – for example, empire-building to satisfy managerial egos, tax benefits, or income diversification through conglomerate mergers. Yet, procompetitive goals drive many transactions, including portfolio enhancement through complementary acquisitions, technology transfer, scale-driven input procurement savings, asset rationalization, anticipated superior management, and, of course, scale economies. Owners and management may be wrong, driven astray by various cognitive biases and imperfect information, but they often act in the belief that merger-driven efficiencies are attainable. So, too, a healthy market for corporate control may displace inferior management and discipline incumbents.[97] Hence, transactions *can* realize a host of potential efficiencies. Those benefits are plausible, and dealmakers often present them as express goals. The key question, of course, is how often mergers *in fact* successfully generate such efficiencies.

The evidence of actual cost savings, however, is surprisingly meagre. Empirical work suggests that (i) mergers can yield synergies that benefit consumers, (ii) some transactions generate powerful efficiencies, but (iii) many acquisitions fail to achieve material productivities – at least in the short term. In that last respect, the evidence shows that horizontal mergers can yield long-run efficiencies that dominate market-power increases, ultimately benefiting consumers, though many such productivities take time to materialize. Notably, horizontal mergers are relatively likely to yield

---

[96] HORIZONTAL MERGER GUIDELINES, *supra* note 84, at § 10.

[97] See, e.g., FTC Commissioner Noah Joshua Phillips, Competing for Companies: How M&A Drives Competition and Consumer Welfare, Opening Keynote, May 31, 2019, https://www.ftc.gov/system/files/documents/public_statements/1524321/phillips_-_competing_for_companies_5-31-19_0.pdf. As a matter of law and economics, markets cause property rights to flow to higher-value uses, unless the transaction facilitates supracompetitive pricing by eliminating price constraints, which is, of course, what antitrust guards against.

efficiencies by eliminating duplicative assets and infrastructure in favor of an optimized allotment. Nevertheless, many transactions fail to achieve efficiencies, while some mergers yield dissynergies. The picture, in short, is nuanced.

These observations raise important questions. In particular, why do so many mergers fail to produce significant efficiencies? Part of the problem lies in rosy ex ante projections.[98] Buyers tend to overestimate potential synergies, underestimate the difficulty of ones that are technically available, underrate cultural impediments to integration, undervalue the expertise of the target's management, and discount dissynergies like customer losses. Inflated net-present-value may result, leading optimistic buyers into deals the benefits of which, if any, may flow disproportionately (or entirely) to the seller's stockholders. A McKinsey study of 160 mergers found, for example, that buyers were most likely to miss targets for revenue synergies like cross-selling, for which almost 70 percent of the transactions failed to achieve expected benefits.[99] That is significant because "revenue synergies form the basis of the strategic rationales for entire classes of deals[.]"[100]

This section explores the empirical literature on merger efficiencies.

2.2.3.1 1980s Studies

The antitrust laws of the 1960s proscribed horizontal and vertical acquisitions. When a US merger wave arrived, then, it focused on conglomerate deal. The M&A activity that followed gave rise to valuable empirical work in the 1980s.

In 1983, Fisher and Lande – then an economist and attorney, respectively, at the FTC – published an influential article on merger efficiencies.[101] Thinking available econometric work to be insufficient, they embarked on case studies. They found that "many mergers create significant efficiencies, while many others result in unexpectedly higher overall costs."[102] Although "mergers often result in efficiencies," identifying which ones will do so ex ante is exceptionally difficult.[103] In that respect, they found that "the record of predictions for individual cases has been shockingly poor[.]"[104]

---

[98] Scott A. Christofferson et al., *Where Mergers Go Wrong*, McKinsey Quarterly, May 2004, https://www.mckinsey.com/business-functions/strategy-and-corporate-finance/our-insights/where-mergers-go-wrong (observing that "the average acquirer materially overestimates the synergies a merger will yield").

[99] *Id.*

[100] *Id.*

[101] Alan A. Fisher & Robert H. Lande, *Efficiency Considerations in Merger Enforcement*, 71 Cal. L. Rev. 1580 (1983).

[102] *Id.* at 1605, 1619–24, *passim*. Nevertheless, Fisher and Lande cautioned that studies' focus on conglomerate mergers (in light of the strict policy against horizontal and vertical mergers after the Celler–Kefauver Amendment of 1950), are "likely to understate the efficiency potential of mergers in general." *Id.* at 1606.

[103] *Id.* at 1693–94.

[104] *Id.* at 1693.

In 1985, the Council of Economic Advisers to the President reported to Congress on the economic effects of merger activity.[105] Lauding a competitive market for corporate control, it identified "powerful evidence that takeovers as a group are beneficial."[106] It referred principally to event studies, which measure increases in stock prices in the weeks following announced transactions. In the Council's view, "takeovers tend to be beneficial, ... mergers and acquisitions increase national wealth, ... and takeovers generate net benefits to the economy."[107] Those views nicely encapsulate the intuition shared by many conservative-minded thinkers who address antitrust merger policy.

The 1985 Council's reading of the frequency and significance of merger efficiencies, however, was too rosy. Ravenscraft and Scherer, the authors of the leading relevant empirical study of the 1980s, found the Council's interpretation of the evidence to be "quite wrong" on account of its preoccupation on the short-term reaction of common stock investors.[108] Ravenscraft and Scherer studied nearly 6,000 transactions from the 1960s involving firms for which the FTC had collected performance data, broken down by line of business, between 1974 and 1977.[109] Using and augmenting that data, Ravenscraft and Scherer found that "the merger wave of the 1960s ... led to efficiency losses substantially exceeding identifiable gains."[110]

It is important not to extrapolate too much, however, from the Ravenscraft and Scherer study. Despite its thoroughness, the mergers that it studied were overwhelmingly nonhorizontal. The conglomerate merger wave of the 1960s is likely not representative of contemporary M&A activity.[111]

Importantly, synergies are more likely both to arise and to be significant in horizontal deals than in conglomerate mergers, particularly with respect to fixed-cost savings. Horizontal transactions involve overlapping assets, the most efficient of which the post-merger can keep in lieu of the rest. Further, any of the problems that robbed transactions of value as identified by Ravenscraft and Scherer – including the absence of knowledge about the markets in which the acquired businesses operate – do not apply to deals that bring two firms in the same market together. Indeed, the "horizontal acquisitions in [their] main statistical sample had higher post-merger profitability than the pure conglomerate acquisitions" – a phenomenon that a delta in market power could not readily explain.[112] In Ravenscraft and Scherer's view, even

---

[105] ECONOMIC REPORT OF THE PRESIDENT (1985).
[106] Id. at 187, 191.
[107] Id. at 191, 196, 198.
[108] DAVID J. RAVENSCRAFT & F.M. SCHERER, MERGERS, SELL-OFFS, AND ECONOMIC INEFFICIENCY 216 (1987).
[109] Id. at 17–18.
[110] Id. at 217.
[111] Indeed, Ravenscraft and Scherer warned that their analyzes "provide little direct guidance" to the efficiency effects of large horizontal merger. Id. at 219.
[112] Id. at 224.

if the evidence of an average effect remained unclear, "both in principle and from our sell-off case studies, horizontal mergers *can* confer efficiencies."[113]

A 1985 study by an FTC economist, Mueller, sought to measure transaction-generated efficiencies by measuring changes in post-merger firms' market share.[114] An exercise of market power would shrink the firm's share, while an increase in the company's efficiency or product quality would increase it. Drawing on FTC surveys of the 1,000 largest companies in each year between 1950 and 1972, he found evidence that "acquired firms experienced a loss in efficiency and/or product quality following the mergers."[115] He continued, "The results presented here strongly imply that mergers do not improve operating efficiency or product quality, and may even worsen them."[116] Mueller noted, however, that the "deterioration in performance is more pronounced for conglomerate acquisitions than for horizontal[.]"[117]

Nevertheless, the 1980s did produce some impressive evidence of merger-generated efficiencies. In 1988, Tremblay and Tremblay studied the dramatic evolution in the US brewing industry after World War II.[118] Between 1950 and 1984, the four-firm concentration ratio rose from 20.2 percent to 74.9 percent, as the number of independent beer producers fell from 369 to 34.[119] Mergers had little to do with this trend until the late 1970s, when the Chicago School began to make its influence felt at a policy level, relaxing the strict rules against horizontal combinations that had held sway since 1950. Evaluating 170 horizontal acquisitions, the economists concluded that "mergers are an efficient means of transferring assets from failing to successful firms" and that, in "retrospect, the evidence that mergers in brewing have been due primarily to efficiency rather than market power reasons suggests that the antitrust constraint may have been too restrictive."[120] In particular, the authors observed, "scale economies have been rising faster than market demand since the late 1950s, making exit by merger or bankruptcy inevitable for a majority of brewers."[121] Hence, they viewed the Justice Department's 1984 acceptance of an efficiency defense as "justified in light of the evidence from this study that efficiency forces can be a powerful cause of horizontal mergers."[122]

---

[113] *Id.* at 225 (emphasis in original). They continued to observe that the evidence "provides no reason to believe that *on average* the efficiency gains have been appreciable." *Id.* (emphasis in original).
[114] Dennis C. Mueller, *Mergers and Market Share*, 67 Rev. Econ. & Statistics 259 (1985), https://www.ftc.gov/system/files/documents/reports/mergers-market-share/wp092.pdf.
[115] *Id.*
[116] *Id.*
[117] *Id.*
[118] Victor J. Tremblay & Carol Horton Tremblay, *The Determinants of Horizontal Acquisitions: Evidence from the U.S. Brewing Industry*, 37 J. Indus. Econ. 21 (1988).
[119] *Id.* at 22–23.
[120] *Id.* at 33–34.
[121] *Id.* at 34.
[122] *Id.*

In 1987, Lichtenberg and Siegel analyzed data on over 18,000 US manufacturing plants, comparing the ~21 percent of facilities subject to an ownership change between 1972 and 1981 to those plants that remained under constant ownership.[123] The authors sought to understand, in particular, whether shareholder gains that typically accrue from acquisitions bring private or social benefits.[124] They found that inefficient plants were more likely to be sold.[125] They also found that changes in ownership eventually yielded efficiency gains.

Specifically, sold "plants exhibit both lower initial levels of productivity and a deterioration in relative performance through the year in which these acquisitions occur. But after changing owners, their improvement in performance reduces and eventually (after seven years) almost eliminates the productivity gap that existed between them and the control group before takeover."[126] They deemed Ravenscraft and Scherer's work to be largely consistent because they, too, found that sell-offs in the 1970s increased efficiency. The difference, of course, is that Ravenscraft and Scherer tied the need for those divestitures to inefficient acquisitions during the 1960s. Recognizing the need for more work, Lichtenberg and Siegel nevertheless concluded that their "evidence is consistent with the view that ownership change or asset redeployment is an important mechanism for correcting lapses from inefficient producer behavior."[127] Finally, they opined that horizontal mergers are more likely to generate productivity gains given buyers' existing experience in the relevant business.[128]

2.2.3.2 The 1990s

The 1980s saw another merger wave, albeit of a different character than its 1960s predecessor. A radical shift in antitrust policy, associated with the Chicago School, found full effect beginning in 1981, when the Reagan Administration appointed leadership at the agencies and soon after judges versed in the law and economics approach. Horizontal acquisitions increased relative to the conglomerate transactions of the 1960s. This phenomenon presented new opportunities for empirical research in the 1990s.

These studies, which focused on the banking industry, revealed sparse evidence that deal-driven consolidation produced efficiencies.

---

[123] Frank R. Lichtenberg & Donald Siegel, *Productivity and Changes in Ownership of Manufacturing Plants*, in BROOKING PAPERS ON ECONOMIC ACTIVITY: SPECIAL ISSUES ON MICROECONOMICS 643, 645 (1987). Note that a modern literature review has observed that the Lichtenberg-Siegel study did not control for endogeneity or selection bias in estimating productivity, which could bias productivity estimates. *See, e.g.*, Michael D. Whinston, *Antitrust Policy Toward Horizontal Mergers, in* HANDBOOK OF INDUS. ORG. 2435 (2007).
[124] *Id.* at 645.
[125] *Id.* at 665.
[126] *Id.* at 666.
[127] *Id.* at 667.
[128] *Id.* at 668.

In 1992, Berger and Humphrey sought to build on the 1980s literature, which had found little evidence that banking mergers yielded cost savings.[129] Observing methodological problems with those studies, they sought to blaze new ground by reviewing fifty-seven US banking megamergers, which they defined to mean transactions in which both the buyer and target had over $1 billion in assets.[130] Observing claims by consultants and the trade press that acquisitions would yield savings as high as 30 percent of a target's operating costs, the authors found little evidence to support those claims.[131] Although acquiring banks were more efficient than acquired ones, the ensuing mean X-efficiency (i.e., management-driven, as distinct from scale-driven) cost savings varied from 1.9 percent to 4.7 percent across the three data sets.[132] None, however, was statistically significant.[133] Within the data, the most successful megamerger saw an X-efficiency improvement of 80 percent, while the least successful one saw a decline of between 50 percent and 70 percent.[134] The authors concluded that, although "there do appear to be some very successful individual mergers[,]" "there were no significant cost efficiency benefits from the [banking] megamergers of the 1980[]s on average."[135]

Several studies followed in the 1990s. They similarly found that banking mergers from the prior decade had failed, on average, to produce significant efficiencies.[136] A 1993 study, for example, examined data governing ~ 2,000 banks from 1984 to 1988.[137] Focusing on 160 acquiring banks and measuring productivity trends two years before and after each merger, the authors found that "acquiring banks achieve no gains in efficiency."[138] The economists inferred that "mergers are evidently

---

[129] Allen N. Berger & David B. Humphrey, *Megamergers in Banking and the Use of Cost Efficiency as an Antitrust Defense*, 37 ANTITRUST BULL. 541 (1992).
[130] *Id.* at 541.
[131] The researchers explained the discrepancy between consultants' predictions and empirical evidence on several grounds, including that consultants typically analyze the potential for savings, neglect bank operations likely to experience scale diseconomies, and focus on few most successful mergers, rather than the larger universe of bank acquisitions. *Id.* at 563.
[132] *Id.* at 577.
[133] *Id.*
[134] *Id.* at 578.
[135] *Id.* at 579.
[136] *See, e.g.*, Stavros Peristiani, *Do Mergers Improve the X-Efficiency and Scale Efficiency of U.S. Banks? Evidence from the 1980s*, Fed. Res. Bank of New York Research Paper No. 9623, p. 23 (Aug. 1996) (finding that "in-market mergers yield no significant improvements in postmerger performance"); Stephen A. Rhoades, *Efficiency Effects of Horizontal (in-market) Bank Mergers*, 17 J. BANKING & FINANCE 411, 419–22, *passim* (1993) (studying 898 bank mergers between 1981 and 1986 – horizontal ones "thought to have the greatest potential to result in efficiency gains" – but finding that "horizontal bank mergers during 1981–1986 did not generally result in efficiency gains"); Babu G. Baradqaj et al., *Bidder Returns in Interstate and Intrastate Bank Acquisitions*, 5 J. FIN. SERVS. RES. 261 (1992) (studying 108 bank acquisitions between 1981 and 1987, and finding negative returns for bidders in tension with the shareholder wealth maximization model).
[137] Dennis J. Fixler & Kimberly D. Zieschang, *An Index Number Approach to Measuring Bank Efficiency: An Application to Mergers*, 17 J. BANKING & FINANCE 437 (1993).
[138] *Id.* at 440–41.

neither better nor worse than internal growth in achieving an expansion of operations[,]"[139] and they agreed with prior "findings that suggest that there are no economies of scale to exploit."[140] They did find, however, that acquiring banks tend to be more productive than average institutions, and maintain their productivity advantage after merging.[141]

Those findings contributed to a general shortcoming of evidence of merger efficiencies.[142] What was true of the banking industry, however, was not universally accurate.

Using data on 28,294 manufacturing plants, McGuckin and Nguyen examined productivity changes for plants that sold between 1977 and 1987 relative to those that stayed under consistent ownership during the same period.[143] To measure productivity, they used relative labor productivity – that is, the ratio of plant labor productivity to average four-digit industry labor productivity (dollar output divided by number of employees). Granting that their conclusions lay "in sharp contrast to much of the existing literature," they found that transferred plants experienced significant productivity improvements.[144] The effect was not uniform. Large plants that were not acquired experienced higher productivity growth than acquired ones. Otherwise, plants that changed hands did better than those that did not. The authors inferred that "gains from synergies ... are the most important motive for ownership changes during the 1977–1982 period."[145] They explained their iconoclastic findings by reference to prior studies' likely aggregation biases and measurement errors.[146]

Like other studies of the period, the McGuckin-Nguyen study potentially suffers from endogeneity problems in terms of how it measures productivity. To measure total factor productivity, economists regress output on production inputs. If higher rates of productivity correlate with input usage, however, then regressions may be biased.[147] Nevertheless, it remains a valuable study and more recent work, which capitalizes on advances in econometrics, provide related support.

---

[139] *Id.* at 446.
[140] *Id.* at 449.
[141] *Id.*
[142] *See, e.g.,* John F. Stewart & Sang-Kwon Kim, *Price Changes and Mergers in U.S. Manufacturing 1985–86, in* EMPIRICAL STUDIES IN INDUSTRIAL ORGANIZATION: ESSAYS IN HONOR OF LEONARD W. WEISS 79, 83 (1992) (granting that "researchers have not found overwhelming support for the hypothesis that 'efficiencies' have been realized through mergers" and observing that "the available evidence is not strongly supportive of the hypothesis that mergers result in cost saving efficiencies").
[143] Robert H. McGuckin & Sang V. Nguyen, *On Productivity and Plant Ownership Change: New Evidence from the Longitudinal Research Database,* 26 RAND J. ECON. 257 (1995).
[144] *Id.* at 259.
[145] *Id.*
[146] *Id.*
[147] The author thanks Dr. Robert Kulick of NERA for discussing this issue.

Finally, empirical evidence gathered in various 1990s studies reveal that hospital mergers can produce significant efficiencies.[148] A 1998 study evaluated the effects of 122 mergers – using data on 3,500 US hospitals from 1986 to 1994, which represented some two-thirds of the country's general hospitals.[149] Consistent with prior studies, the researchers found that merging hospitals experienced 5 percent cost savings, on average.[150] Those institutions saw 5 percent price reductions, too, implying that they passed merger-generated cost savings onto consumers.[151] Certain prior studies had observed slightly lower efficiencies. The authors observed, however, that those earlier studies had measured results within only a year or two of the merger. The evidence suggested that "it may take a few years for merger savings to be achieved due to the organizational turmoil during a merger."[152] The authors observed, though, that mergers yielded much lower price reductions in highly concentrated markets relative to competitive ones.[153] More recent studies also bear out this phenomenon, albeit with qualifications.[154]

2.2.3.3 Recent Studies: 2000 to Present

The 2000s saw useful research into not just the fact, but the *timing*, of merger-generated synergies.[155] Horizontal transactions can harm consumers without offsetting cost savings. Given data limitations, merger retrospectives typically study short-term price effects. By the same token, many studies of merger efficiencies evaluate cost savings using short-run data following the transaction.

That reality could mask a vital detail. Mergers are messy affairs, requiring buyers to navigate logistical, managerial, and sales-related challenges. When synergies arise, they do not take full form overnight. Horizontal mergers may simultaneously create market

---

[148] *See, e.g.*, Ugar Tony Sinay, *Pre- and Post-Merger Investigation of Hospital Mergers*, 24 E. ECON. J. 83, 94, 96 n.9 (1998) (studying 131 pre-merger hospitals and 63 post-merger hospitals between 1987 and 1990, and finding that merger activity "reduced the cost of production by achieving scale and scope economies, allowing hospitals to become more efficient").

[149] Robert A. Connor et al., *The Effects of Market Concentration and Hospital Mergers on Hospital Costs and Prices*, 5 INT'L J. ECON. BUS. 159, 177–78 (1998).

[150] *Id.* at 174.

[151] *Id.*

[152] *Id.*

[153] *Id.* at 176.

[154] *See, e.g.*, Stuart Craig et al., *Mergers and Marginal Costs: New Evidence on Hospital Buyer Power*, Nat'l Bureau of Econ. Research, Working Paper No. 24926 (2018) (studying six years' supply-purchase data from a sample of hospital mergers, finding that target hospitals secured 1.5 percent cost savings on average (less than merging parties typically project), and identifying only mixed evidence of cost savings for acquirers).

[155] For a literature review effective at the turn of the century, see Paul A. Pautler, Bureau of Economics, FTC, *Evidence on Mergers and Acquisitions*, Sept. 25, 2001, https://www.ftc.gov/sites/default/files/documents/reports/evidence-mergers-and-acquisitions/wp243_0.pdf. Six years later, an in-depth literature review concluded that "the evidence on the efficiency effects of horizontal mergers provides little guidance at this point." Michael D. Whinston, *Antitrust Policy Toward Horizontal Mergers, in* Vol. 3 HANDBOOK OF INDUS. ORG. 2435 (2007).

power, thus yielding short-run price increases, and also produce offsetting cost savings over a longer time frame. This dynamic may plausibly govern many horizontal transactions. Two important pieces of research from the 2000s explore this possibility.[156]

First, in 2003, Focarelli and Panetta observed that the preceding literature had tied consolidation to price increases.[157] Because those prior studies "may well have missed effects that take longer to become manifest[,]" the authors examined long-run pricing effects in Italian markets for bank deposits.[158] They considered those markets to be attractive on account of their local competition – thus isolating merger-specific local effects from larger industry dynamics – concentration, entry barriers, and product homogeneity.[159] Consistent with prior work, they found that consolidation increased market power, as revealed through deposit rate reductions (equivalent to price increases). Over time, however, those trends not only reversed, but led to rates exceeding the pre-merger levels. Those findings, the researchers explained, "lend empirical support to the hypothesis that in the long run mergers improve efficiency."[160] Importantly, they concluded, "in the long run the efficiency gains from mergers prevail over the market power effects, so that consumers benefit."[161]

Second, in 2015, Ashenfelter, Hosken, and Weinberg set out to explain the surprising lack of "direct empirical evidence that efficiencies can offset the incentive to raise prices."[162] They embarked on a detailed study of the joint venture between Miller and Coors, the brewing industry's then second and third largest firms. That transaction was particularly suitable because the Justice Department had approved it without conditions, notwithstanding the highly concentrated industry, because of its expected shipping and distribution variable-cost savings.[163] Further, as the industry involves numerous separate geographic markets at the metropolitan level, and because anticipated cost savings differed across those geographies, the data lent itself to useful analysis. Using retail scanner data for forty-eight regional markets, the authors found that rising concentration led lager prices to increase both for the joint venturers, as well as for other suppliers. Crucially, however, the "effect of the increase in concentration on pricing was nearly exactly offset by efficiencies created

---

[156] See also Ugar Tony Sinay, *Pre- and Post-Merger Investigation of Hospital Mergers*, 24 E. ECON. J. 83, 94 (1998) (finding that merged hospitals achieved efficiencies "two years after the merger[,]" but observing that "[o]ne year after the merger is not sufficient time to achieve efficiencies as indicated by relatively high marginal costs"); Robert A. Connor et al., *The Effects of Market Concentration and Hospital Mergers on Hospital Costs and Prices*, 5 INT'L J. ECON. BUS. 159, 174 (1998).

[157] Dario Focarelli & Fabio Panetta, *Are Mergers Beneficial to Consumers? Evidence from the Market for Bank Deposits*, 93 AM. ECON. REV. 1152 (2003).

[158] Id. at 1152–53.

[159] Id. at 1152.

[160] Id. at 1154.

[161] Id. at 1170.

[162] Orley C. Ashenfelter et al., *Efficiencies Brewed: Pricing and Consolidation in the US Beer Industry*, 46 RAND J. ECON. 328, 328–29 (2015).

[163] Id. at 329.

by the merger in the average market."¹⁶⁴ The effects were not simultaneous. Rather, it took two years after the merger for pricing to fully incorporate the ultimate cost reductions.¹⁶⁵

A 2003 study looked at thirty-one horizontal mergers in the paper and paperboard industry in the 1980s, estimating merger-generated cost savings by contrasting investment decisions made by firms before and after the merger wave.¹⁶⁶ It found that, "all else equal, marginal cost falls subsequent to an acquisition due to an increase in the capacity and an increase in the number of plants."¹⁶⁷ Results, however, varied widely. "About one-fourth of mergers exceed the expectations and achieve additional cost savings, while three-fourths are below the expected effect."¹⁶⁸ Most acquiring firms, however, experienced an increased cost advantage after the acquisition.¹⁶⁹ Going further, the author estimated that the 1980s merger wave yielded a net total welfare gain per year of $891.2 million, of which $602.8 million and $288.4 million represented consumer and producer surplus, respectively.¹⁷⁰

In 2001, Professors Maksimovic and Phillips looked beyond stock market data to measure actual productivity changes in individual plants that were sold relative to other plants in the industry.¹⁷¹ The efficiency implications of these transactions – including partial-asset sales – are crucial. Indeed, almost 4 percent of large US manufacturing plants undergo ownership changes every year.¹⁷²

Using US Census data on manufacturing facilities at the plant level between 1974 and 1992, Professors Maksimovic and Phillips found that "most transactions in the market for assets result in productivity gains."¹⁷³ This finding supported their hypothesis that the market facilitates an efficient redistribution of assets to firms with a superior ability to exploit them. Further, productivity gains dominated the enhanced managerial costs to the buyer of running a larger organization. More generally, less productive firms were more likely to sell, while "the probability that a firm is a buyer of additional assets increases with its efficiency and size."¹⁷⁴ This

---

¹⁶⁴ *Id.* at 330.
¹⁶⁵ *Id.*
¹⁶⁶ Martin Pesendorfer, *Horizontal Mergers in the Paper Industry*, 34 RAND J. ECON. 495 (2003). Although the study is notable, some economists have questioned the reliability of its results. *See, e.g.*, Michael D. Whinston, *Antitrust Policy Toward Horizontal Mergers*, in HANDBOOK OF INDUS. ORG. 2435 (2007).
¹⁶⁷ Pesendorfer, *supra* note 166, at 508.
¹⁶⁸ *Id.*
¹⁶⁹ *Id.* at 509.
¹⁷⁰ *Id.* at 511.
¹⁷¹ Vojislav Maksimovic & Gordon Phillips, *The Market for Corporate Assets: Who Engages in Mergers and Asset Sales and Are There Efficiency Gains?*, 56 J. FINANCE 2019, 2020 n.6 (2001).
¹⁷² *Id.* at 2019.
¹⁷³ *Id.* at 2021, 2060; *see also* Antoinette Schoar, *Effects of Corporate Diversification on Productivity*, 57 J. FIN. 2379, 2401–02 (2002) (observing that "diversified firms are more productive than stand-alone firms" – a finding that "is not the result of conglomerates' buying into high productivity plants" – but rather because "it seems that diversified firms actually add value to the plants they acquire").
¹⁷⁴ Maksimovic & Phillips, *supra* note 171, at 2058.

phenomenon could explain why buyers pay a premium over stock market value. Efficiency gains were not universal, of course – a minority of acquisitions yielded productivity losses.[175] More notably, Professors Maksimovic and Phillips identified "one category of transactions, full-firm acquisitions by buyers with lower productivity than that of the assets they purchase, for which overall firm productivity declines."[176]

A subsequent paper by Maksimovic, Phillips, and Prabhala in 2011 revealed that, following transactions, firms sold 27 percent or closed 19 percent of acquired plants.[177] The authors found that retained plants saw productivity gains, while sold ones did not. This observation was consistent with the hypothesis that acquisitions can enhance firm-level efficiency by shuttering relatively high-cost manufacturing facilities. These outcomes, however, "are not consistent with the notion that pure empire building by managers explains the disposition of assets and the operating decisions following mergers. The outcomes are more consistent with the neoclassical comparative view of firm growth[.]" Hence, "even if the initial decision to acquire a target involves overpayment, empire building or simple hubris, our results indicate that economic rationality asserts itself soon afterwards. Acquirers find it advantageous to enter into post-merger restructuring and deals with other firms that result, on average, in an improved allocation of resources following mergers."

It is worth noting, however, that transactions could increase productivity by removing inefficient productive assets from the market, while also reducing competition.

In 2007, Kwoka and Pollitt studied a merger wave that occurred in the US electricity industry between 1994 to 2003.[178] The prior literature suggested that a market for corporate control facilitates efficient allocations of underperforming assets, but also that some transactions reflect the pursuit of market power or can otherwise yield social costs.[179] Kwoka and Pollitt observed that stock-market event studies generally corroborate the efficient-merger hypothesis, while operating-effects studies "tend to show that gains from merger[s] are the exception rather than the rule."[180] Examining a database of seventy-three electric utilities, however, they found "a rather remarkable inversion of the efficient-merger hypothesis, it is poor-performing companies that apparently search out and acquire better performers and that selling firms' efficiency declines rather than improves after merger."[181] They floated explanations that range from managerial motives to defensive acquisitions to

---

[175] *Id.* at 2022.
[176] *Id.* at 2060.
[177] Vojislav Maksimovic et al., *Post-Merger Restructuring and the Boundaries of the Firm*, 102 J. FIN'L ECON. 317 (2011).
[178] John Kwoka & Michael Pollitt, *Industry Restructuring, Mergers, and Efficiency: Evidence from Electric Power* (2007), http://www.eprg.group.cam.ac.uk/wp-content/uploads/2008/11/eprg07081.pdf.
[179] *Id.* at 1.
[180] *Id.*
[181] *Id.* at 3.

stave off takeovers, but did not test them. In their view, however, their evidence poured cold water on expectations that post-regulation asset reallocation would enhance efficiency – at least in the US electricity sector.[182]

In a sophisticated 2016 study, Blonigen and Pierce endeavored to separate out efficiency from market-power effects from M&A transactions.[183] This effort mattered because prior studies of transactional effects had failed to disentangle the two, potentially yielding unreliable conclusions. For example, a considerable literature from the 1980s and 1990s on stock-market events generally showed that mergers enhance firm profitability, while gains predominantly flow to the acquired firm's shareholders. Those profit increases, however, could reflect achieved market power, enhanced productivity, a blend of the two, or other factors altogether.[184] Recognizing those problems, some more recent efforts – like the Ashenfelter and Focarelli studies explored above – take the form of case studies. That work, though illuminative, has limited value because it cannot be generalized on account of its suffering from selection bias and being focused on particular industries.

Focusing on acquired plants relative to comparison groups, Blonigen and Pierce found that "M&As significantly increase markups on average, but have no statistically significant average effect on productivity."[185] More specifically, they saw "little evidence for plant- or firm-level productivity effects from M&A activity on average, nor for other efficiency gains often cited as possible from M&A activity, including reallocation of activity across plants or scale efficiencies in non-productive units of the firm."[186] Unsurprisingly, the markup effect was most pronounced for horizontal transactions. Interestingly, though, the economists found "some evidence that M&As have positive impacts on plant-level productivity for M&As that are not horizontal."[187]

Finally, an emerging literature is beginning to grapple with one of the most important questions to antitrust merger review – whether horizontal transactions create sufficient productivities as to outweigh the effects of an increase in market power. One recent study of mergers in the ready-mix concrete industry, for example, finds that horizontal mergers do achieve productivity gains, but that market-power effects dominate.[188]

Studying retail grocery mergers, FTC economists found in 2012 that acquisitions in unconcentrated or moderately concentrated markets "are often associated with

---

[182] Id. at 25–26.
[183] Bruce A. Blonigen & Justin R. Pierce, *Evidence for the Effects of Mergers on Market Power and Efficiency*, Nat'l Bureau of Econ. Research, Working Paper No. 22750 (2016), https://www.nber.org/papers/w22750.pdf.
[184] Id. at 5.
[185] Id. at 3.
[186] Id. at 24.
[187] Id. at 3.
[188] Robert Kulick, *Ready-to-Mix: Horizontal Mergers, Prices, and Productivity* (Nov. 2018) (working paper) (on file with author).

reductions in consumer prices."[189] This observation supports the Horizontal Mergers Guidelines' use of market concentration as a screening mechanism because their results imply that "competitively benign mergers can confer significant efficiencies that are passed on to consumer[s] in the form of lower prices."[190]

2.2.4 What Does This Evidence Mean for Antitrust Policy?

Neo-Brandeisians suggest that M&A activity has little or no social value. That view lacks empirical support. The question for larger antitrust policy is not whether some transactions fail to achieve their predicted efficiencies – clearly many do. And, for that reason, the agencies ought to be skeptical of claimed productivities without robust substantiation by the parties.[191]

But the real question for competition policy is whether merger activity as a whole improves economic welfare, thus justifying an antitrust merger review program that permits transactions with the potential to yield productivities, whilst screening out and remediating the subset of mergers that endanger competition. On that more important question, the empirical literature supports today's modern antitrust approach, as encapsulated in the 2010 Horizontal Merger Guidelines.[192]

Some reformists envision a far stricter merger review process than we have today. Such critics need not look hard for evidence that mergers fail to yield productivity gains. The conglomerate merger wave of the 1960s, for example, realized few net efficiency gains. Evidence that consolidation in the financial services sector generated net productivity improvements is likewise thin. Studies finding that divestitures in the 1970s and 1980s achieved such benefits may be meaningful, but could simply reflect the undoing of dissynergies associated with inefficient conglomerate transactions of the prior era.

In construing the literature, however, it is vital to observe the kind of transactions being assessed for productivity gains. Most evidence that merger activity produced no productivity gains flowed from conglomerate mergers. Such mergers, of course, are the least likely to produce efficiencies, and also the least interesting from an

---

[189] Daniel Hosken et al., *Do Retail Mergers Affect Competition? Evidence from Grocery Retailing* 30 Fed. Trade Comm'n Bureau of Econ., Working Paper No. 313 (2012), https://www.ftc.gov/sites/default/files/documents/reports/do-retail-mergers-affect-competition%C2%A0-evidence-grocery-retailing/wp313.pdf.
[190] *Id.*
[191] Jonathan B. Baker & Carl Shapiro, *Reinvigorating Horizontal Merger Enforcement*, in HOW THE CHICAGO SCHOOL OVERSHOT THE MARK: THE EFFECT OF CONSERVATIVE ECONOMIC ANALYSIS ON U.S. ANTITRUST 256 (Robert Pitofsky ed., 2008) ("Evidence from the finance, managerial, and economics literatures ... certainly does not support the view that merger-specific efficiencies are common or that claims of efficiencies made by merging parties should generally be credited.").
[192] Indeed, the agencies seek to "avoid[] unnecessary interference with mergers that are either competitively beneficial or neutral." HORIZONTAL MERGER GUIDELINES, *supra* note 84, at § 1.

antitrust perspective.[193] The crucial question for antitrust involves horizontal transactions, which can reduce competition, but also allow for productivity gains in removing underperforming duplicative assets and are more likely to see control bestowed on knowledgeable management. Even well into the 2000s, however, the evidence was unclear. Since then, however, more sophisticated econometric work suggests that horizontal mergers do indeed enhance productivity efficiency, even if market-power effects can dominate them.[194]

These observations reduce to a simple proposition: the agencies should continue to review each merger on its own facts. In light of the preceding evidence, it would be clearly wrong to presume that any one deal will yield its vaunted benefits. It would be equally wrong, though, to reject M&A activity as a net driver of social value.

---

[193] Frederic M. Scherer, *A New Retrospective on Mergers*, 28 REV. INDUS. ORG. 327, 330 (2006) ("One might expect opportunities for cost savings and benefits from complementarity to be much stronger for horizontal and vertical mergers than for conglomerates, and so the record of widespread failure we documented may simply have become irrelevant.").

[194] *See supra* notes 156–165; *see also* Joel M. David, *The Aggregate Implications of Mergers and Acquisitions* 2 (July 9, 2014), https://wpcarey.asu.edu/sites/default/files/uploads/department-economics/david-paper.pdf; Gennaro Bernile & Evgeny Lyandres, *The Effects of Horizontal Merger Operating Efficiencies on Rivals, Customers, and Suppliers*, 23 REV. FIN. 117 (2019) (finding that "the pass-through of efficiency gains along merging firms' supply chains is as important as the effects of post-merger changes in market power").

3

The Missing Link

Concentration and Market Power

3.1 INTRODUCTION

Antitrust is rich in nuance. An interdisciplinary field, its methods are at once empirical and theoretic. It absorbs the idiosyncratic features of countless markets. Its enforcement, if not its mission, concerns the regulation of business strategy. That focus puts squarely at issue the nature of the firm, how companies make decisions, the role and societal value of contracts, the implications of consolidation, and the machinery of competition itself. This endeavor requires an understanding of how markets work. Few undertakings are more complex. And yet, despite the impassioned howls of its most devoted followers, competition law remains technocratic only at the surface. Underneath lurk foundational, divisive, and ever-evolving societal values.[1] Few think competition policy simple. Fewer still see its administration as uncontroversial, as today's debate makes all too clear.

One surveying this field might think it immune to simplification. Few would expect antitrust to reduce to a single question. And yet it does. The relationship between concentration and market power is antitrust. No question in the field has been the object of greater scrutiny. None has proven so impervious to final resolution.

Industrial organization is the study of imperfectly competitive markets. Its very existence is to examine market structure and performance.[2] The field traces back to Adam Smith in the late 1700s, emerged through the breakthrough work of Edward Chamberlin and Edward Mason in the 1930s, achieved full-throated expression via the Structure-Conduct-Performance paradigm of the 1940s through early 1970s, and attained its modern form in the decades since.[3] Research continues apace, as industrial economists probe the outer bounds of knowledge. Their methodologies have grown more sophisticated, resulting in studies of extraordinary precision.

---

[1] *See* Chapter 1.
[2] *See, e.g.*, Dennis W. Carlton & Jeffrey M. Perloff, Modern Industrial Organization (4th ed. 2005).
[3] Pioneers of Industrial Organization: How the Economics of Competition and Monopoly Took Shape (Henry W. de Jong & William G. Shepherd eds., 2007).

Industrial economists strive to understand the very question on which the relationship between concentration and market power turns – under which conditions do markets fail to deliver efficient outcomes? Perhaps more specifically, given the ubiquity of market power, which changes lead to worse outcomes? From the earliest days, industrial economists have posited an intuitive hypothesis. Competition is a function of market structure. Faced with fewer sellers, companies experience less biting competitive pressures and fewer impediments to coordinating with one another. Small firms struggle to constrain their larger rivals. When the latter cut output, the former would have to disproportionately increase production relative to their prior levels in order to make up the shortfall. Doing so is costly, and hence market shares matter. Entry barriers matter, too. If new sellers must invest heavily in capital infrastructure, advertising, intellectual property, and the like, then they may not enter even in pursuit of supranormal rents.

If this reasoning is correct, then markets with certain structures ought to perform better than others. Firms in unconcentrated industries will lack market power, price closer to margin cost, and reap modest profits. Consolidated markets will feature elevated pricing and profits, especially if industry conditions inhibit entry. Scant wonder that economists have systematically examined whether real-life markets bear out this hypothesis.

The answer is truly dispositive. Should higher concentration necessarily cause market power to increase, and if that relationship held true across industries, then antitrust policy becomes straightforward. Enforcers need not examine the constituent elements of competition in a market, learn the nuances of the industry, measure the proximity of competition between the parties, gauge customer preferences, anticipate buyer and seller responses to the transaction, substantiate merger-specific efficiencies, or otherwise predict future effects. They need merely preserve a competitive market structure. Concentration ratios – be they n-1, C_4, C_8, or the Herfindahl-Hirschman Index – answer the antitrust question.

Hence, the million-dollar question: Is there a causal, universal relationship between concentration and market power? The answer is contested. Associational trends consistently emerge, but remain dogged by serious econometric challenges that inhibit reliable causal inferences. Progressive reformists, however, see powerful confirmatory evidence for their worldview in the literature. Decades of research throughout the SCP era found a weak association between concentration and profits that held true across industries, supporting the market-power hypothesis. That literature observed a stronger relationship between market shares and profits. More recent intra-industry studies tie price to concentration, further confirming a link that structuralists consider obvious. As they digest the literature, such critics also see ample evidence in tension with the pro-consolidation efficiency hypothesis that links concentration and profits.

At first blush, the literature appears to confirm the progressive diagnosis at every turn. Anti-monopoly campaigners advance a simple message: markets become less competitive as they consolidate, and US industries have grown more concentrated over the past several decades.[4] In their view, tying intervention decisions to competitive effects is folly because doing so requires predicting the future – an impossible exercise. It would be much better, they argue, to embrace the policies of old. They look with fondness on the enforcement priorities of the 1950s and 1960s, as perhaps best encapsulated by the virulently anti-consolidation mindset of the Justice Department's 1968 guidelines.[5] That structuralist approach may have been crude, but they argue that it worked.

This charge warrants close attention. As a threshold matter, the DOJ and FTC should be open to – and not defensive about – the possibility of systematic underenforcement. No one should doubt their resolve in protecting competition. Optimizing antitrust policy, however, is devilishly tricky. And while the agencies are by no means hamstrung, they face a more challenging merger policing framework than their overseas counterparts. Unlike the administrative systems that tend to dominate elsewhere, in which competition agencies wield quasi-regulatory powers with limited judicial process, US enforcers bear the burden of proof in front of an impartial (and sometimes skeptical) judiciary. Thus, it is hardly outlandish to question whether the intervention calculus has drifted too far toward noninterventionism.

Competition policy must reflect the best available evidence. Retrospectives, critical self-reflection, and a penchant for asking hard questions should be goals to live by within the agencies. Hence, in addressing the reformists' critique, one must scrutinize today's methodologies. Doing so requires looking to empirical studies and the larger industrial-organization literature.

More specifically, determining the basis for – and proper extent of – reform involves several steps. We must critically analyze the evidence that US industries have grown less competitive.[6] We need to understand whether horizontal mergers, in particular, carry social value absent negative competitive effects.[7] How the agencies make decisions, weigh the propensity for error, and think about market efficacy illuminates the plausibility of insufficient enforcement.[8] Above all, though, the extent to which rising concentration leads to increased market power matters. To the extent that such a causal relationship exists and consistently holds across industries and various deltas, then it may effectively end the debate.

For that reason, this chapter may be the book's most important one. Ultimately, the evidence does not support claims that an increase in concentration, even within a relevant market, necessarily *causes* market power to increase. A change in market

---

[4] See Chapter 5.
[5] U.S. Dep't of Justice, 1968 Merger Guidelines, https://www.justice.gov/archives/atr/1968-merger-guidelines.
[6] See Chapter 4.
[7] See Chapter 2.
[8] See Chapter 7.

concentration, no more than a change in industry structure, is not itself the mechanism by which price, output, and quality effects take form. The causal chain of unilateral effects is now well understood. Such effects depend, in the first instance, on diversion ratios and margins. Their ultimate disposition reflects various dynamic factors, including customer and supplier responses, as well as the proximity of the next most preferred seller to the acquired firm. Concentration in a well-defined antitrust market is relevant. But it is relevant only because it serves as an imperfect proxy for causal factors like diversion ratios and consumer preferences.

The agencies should therefore rely on more reliable, direct evidence of competitive effects when it is available. As for interpreting the competitive significance of rising concentration in a relevant market, qualified inferences about potential price effects are warranted, though with caution. To the extent that a causal relationship exists between concentration and price, it is bidirectional. Superior competition on the merits will lead an innovator to capture share and consolidate a market, which is nevertheless performing optimally. Market structure is endogenous. Hence, drawing steadfast conclusions from observed correlations between it and market outcomes is a fool's errand.

3.2 MARKET STRUCTURE'S FLOW AND EBB IN ANTITRUST POLICY

Economists have long explored structuralism's role in antitrust policy.[9] The following pages explore relevant insights, tentative conclusions, and swings in policy over time. They culminate in the latest learning.

3.2.1 *The Early Twentieth Century: Economists Struggle to Reconcile Market Structure with Classicist Theories, and Fear Competition*

Marginalism represented an important moment in the development of economics. In the last thirty years of the nineteenth century, it led economists to move beyond the descriptive manner in which the classicists had approached competition and monopoly. Mathematical principles of optimization unlocked insights that had previously eluded the profession. In the 1870s, Léon Walras developed the first recognized theory of general equilibrium, and in doing so presented a rigorous conception of perfect competition.[10] Alfred Marshall, the Nobel Laureate typically associated with the rise of neoclassicism, subsequently developed an alternative, quantity-based theory of general equilibrium. His leading 1890 text on microeconomics addressed the concept of perfect competition, though he ultimately

---

[9] For an excellent treatment of the pre-Chicago School period, see Herbert Hovenkamp, *United States Competition Policy in Crisis: 1890–1955*, 94 MINN. L. REV. 311 (2009).
[10] LÉON WALRAS, ELEMENTS D'ECONOMIE POLITIQUE PURE: OU THEORIE DE LA RICHESSE SOCIALE (1874); LÉON WALRAS, ELEMENTS OF PURE ECONOMICS OR THE THEORY OF SOCIAL WEALTH (Routledge 2010).

expressed skepticism that the impeccable knowledge necessary for its attainment would be realized.[11]

Hence, in the early twentieth century, economists were familiar with static models of perfect competition and monopoly. Those two frameworks provided a useful normative baseline, but had little descriptive power. Real markets tended to be oligopolistic, characterized by some market power, and subject to competition of a sub-perfect kind. None was truly atomistic, homogeneous, free of switching and entry costs, and possessed of perfect information in the stylized vision of perfect competition. Few were monopolistic in the sense of featuring no competition whatsoever.

Economists thus labored without a theory to describe the markets that they were responsible for understanding. Lacking generally applicable models and testable hypotheses, they turned to case studies. The ensuing work was laborious, and the general implications of notable insights dubitable. Such anecdotal observations, of course, have limited utility. But an enduring consensus among economists focused on fixed costs. The model of perfect competition did not allow for the recovery of capital infrastructure investments. Observing heavy fixed costs across a variety of industrial sectors, economists worried that entry would yield insolvency – hence, the frequent invocation of ruinous competition and a prevalent belief in natural monopoly. The government was thus quick to displace market competition in favor of public regulation of utilities and common carriers. This line of thinking led to skepticism within the economics profession about the merits of aggressive antitrust intervention in favor of regulatory solutions.

Of course, the period just discussed bore witness to the Sherman Act of 1890 and its aftermath. After a slow start, the government moved against the largest trusts of the day. In 1906 and 1907, the Justice Department sued John D. Rockefeller's Standard Oil and the American Tobacco trust, respectively, for monopolization. In 1911, the Supreme Court found for the government in both cases.[12] The result was a break-up of Standard Oil, though American Tobacco escaped with less serious consequences. The same year, the Taft administration sued J. P. Morgan's US Steel.

In 1920, however, the Supreme Court handed the government a crushing defeat.[13] The decision remains significant to today's reform debate. The Court remarked upon the absence of exclusionary practices, the company's share of less than half of market sales, and that US Steel had grown to achieve scale efficiencies. It remains the seminal opinion on the incompatibility of faultless monopoly with liability under the Sherman Act.[14] Seven years later, the Court reinforced the view that no

---

[11] ALFRED MARSHALL, PRINCIPLES OF ECONOMICS (1st ed. 1890); (8th ed. 1920).
[12] Standard Oil Co. v. United States, 221 U.S. 1 (1911); United States v. Am. Tobacco Co., 221 U.S. 106 (1911).
[13] United States v. U.S. Steel Corp., 251 U.S. 417 (1920).
[14] Id. at 451 ("[T]he law does not make mere size an offence, or the existence of unexerted power an offence.").

size offense exists in US antitrust law in rejecting the government's case against International Harvester.[15]

Through deft maneuvering, AT&T had managed to stave off similar litigation. It did so by tapping into intuition shared by economists and politicians that competition was harmful under natural monopoly. Following the 1913 Kingsbury commitment to preserve some interconnection with independents, Congress rolled back antitrust limits on the company in 1921.[16]

Of course, today we understand the conditions for natural monopoly to be more limited than previously supposed. A long-run average cost curve that continues to decline when it intersects with the demand curve defines the existence of natural monopoly. In practice, only pockets of traditionally regulated industries satisfy that condition. That realization led to a regulatory rollback many decades later. No less importantly, however, the tendency of price in network industries to collapse to marginal cost is less acute than was commonly supposed in the first thirty years of the twentieth century. Oligopolistic markets seldom witness perfectly competitive pricing. As much as economists of the early 1900s lacked models with which to frame more realistic means of competition, two vital theories of oligopolistic competition did exist.

In 1838, Cournot developed a quantity-based model of duopolistic competition.[17] The mathematical nature of its exposition contrasted sharply with conventions among economists of the time. Perhaps for that reason, his work received scant attention for several decades. In an 1883 review of Cournot's work, Bertrand presented an alternative view in which duopolists compete based on price, rather than quantity, and end up at the competitive price point.[18] Both were static models in which firms compete with homogeneous goods. Yet, they produce radically different predictions. The Cournot outcome falls between monopoly and competition. By contrast, Bertrand competition yields perfectly competitive results. Both models represented a Nash equilibrium through a one-shot game, and were thus far ahead of their time.

Indeed, today's industrial economists routinely employ derivative versions of these models. In the first half of the twentieth century, however, Cournot's and Bertrand's work received limited attention. Firms seldom choose to compete based on quantity, let alone set quantity levels on the expectation that their rival's output would remain fixed. Such issues put in question the realism of the Cournot model. Meanwhile,

---

[15] United States v. Int'l Harvester Co., 274 U.S. 693, 708 (1927) ("The law ... does not make the mere size of a corporation, however impressive, or the existence of unexerted power on its part, an offense, when unaccompanied by unlawful conduct in the exercise of its power.").
[16] Willis-Graham Act, Pub. L. No. 15, ch. 20, § 1.
[17] ANTOINE AUGUSTIN COURNOT, RECHERCHES SUR LES PRINCIPES MATHÉMATIQUES DE LA THÉORIE DES RICHESSES (1838).
[18] Joseph Louis François Bertrand, *Review of Recherches sur les Principes Mathématiques de la Théorie des Richesses*, J. DES SAVANTS 499 (1883) (reviewing ANTOINE AUGUSTIN COURNOT, RECHERCHES SUR LES PRINCIPES MATHÉMATIQUES DE LA THÉORIE DES RICHESSES (1838)).

Edgeworth's 1925 critique identified serious equilibrium problems with Bertrand competition absent constant marginal cost.[19] Economists instead focused on neoclassical theories of monopoly and perfect competition, and labored to understand observed industries that displayed supracompetitive pricing, idle capacity, and fungible products.

3.2.2 1933: *The Imperfect Competition Revolution*

In 1933, two economists simultaneously happened on a solution that had previously eluded the academy. That year, Edward Chamberlin and Joan Robinson published the *Theory of Monopolistic Competition* and the *Economics of Imperfect Competition*, respectively.[20] Their work demonstrated that, even with free entry and competition, firms could face downward-sloping demand curves and thus exercise market power. The key was product heterogeneity. By investing in differentiated goods and advertising in order to engender unique consumer tastes for their goods, firms could eliminate the requisite fungibility of perfect competition.

Their insights proved to be influential. Some questioned the models.[21] Other industrial economists, however, found in them both descriptive value and normative implications. Firms in the real world advertised heavily, striving at every turn to distinguish their products from others. So, too, companies earned positive economic rents short of full-blown monopoly profits. Although this prediction undermined concerns that had motivated the natural-monopoly mindset at the turn of the century, it also pointed to pervasive market failure and a need for antitrust intervention.

Among other things, the theories tied product differentiation to inefficient outcomes that harmed consumers. Chamberlin's and Robinson's theories implied that advertising represented an investment in avoiding head-to-head competition. A further inference of monopolistic competition was that industries develop socially costly excess capacity. The ensuing shift in thinking among economists coincided with, and may have helped to drive, the Roosevelt Administration's dramatic expansion in antitrust enforcement after an era of near-nonenforcement.[22]

In many respects, Chamberlin's work laid the intellectual foundation for the SCP paradigm to follow. Suspicions about marketing, product differentiation, and excess capacity filled the SCP era, as economists viewed them as indicia of suboptimal market performance. Such thinking would later lead the FTC astray, as it sought to

---

[19] FRANCIS YSIDRO EDGEWORTH, PAPERS RELATING TO POLITICAL ECONOMY (1925).
[20] EDWARD HASTINGS CHAMBERLIN, THE THEORY OF MONOPOLISTIC COMPETITION (1933); JOAN ROBINSON, THE ECONOMICS OF IMPERFECT COMPETITION (1933).
[21] *See, e.g.*, Nicholas Kaldor, *Professor Chamberlin on Monopolistic and Imperfect Competition*, 52 Q.J. ECON. 513 (1938).
[22] *See, e.g.*, Herbert J. Hovenkamp, *The Neal Report and the Crisis in Antitrust*, 5 COMPETITION POL'Y INT'L 217 (2009).

deconcentrate industries characterized by large advertising investment in brand differentiation, most notably the cereal industry.[23]

Chamberlin influenced the path of industrial organization for another reason. Beyond creating a legacy at Harvard that others would soon follow, Chamberlin inspired research in the field that would ultimately become experimental economics – an area that has interesting implications for antitrust policy today.[24]

3.2.3 1939–1940s: *The SCP Paradigm Takes Root, Antitrust Reemerges, and Workable Competition Sees (Fleeting) Influence*

Edward Mason, the famous Harvard economist, sowed the roots of the SCP paradigm in the late 1930s. Gaining tenure in 1932, he focused his research on the economics of business. Market structure, firm pricing decisions, corporate governance, antitrust, and regulation attracted his attention.[25] His interests, in turn, attracted others. In the mid-1930s, he began teaching Industrial Organization and Control.[26] One of his Ph. D. students, Joe Bain, would go on to give full expression to the SCP hypothesis – an approach that dominated antitrust law and economics for several decades to come. As Bain later recognized, "Professor E. S. Mason of Harvard ... in large part created and developed the modern Industrial Organization field and ... introduced me to it in the 1930s."[27]

In an influential article in 1939, Mason explored how firms make pricing decisions, the difficulty of teasing out the determinants of those choices, and the problematics of conceptualizing competition through price alone.[28] The descriptive analysis, as was then typical, contrasts sharply with today's formal mathematical expositions. Mason's writings, however, presented an unmistakably structural vision.

In laying out the path ahead for industrial economics, Mason highlighted an argument that "runs from differences in market structure to differences in price responses to the consequences of these differences for the functioning of the economy."[29] Both on that question and others, Mason saw urgent need for statistical analysis. Indeed, two years previously – while exploring a dichotomy between the treatment of monopoly by economics and law – he had previously made the case for studying "industrial markets and business practices" in an effort to identify harmful market controls.[30]

---

[23] See Chapter 5 § 3.1.
[24] See, e.g., Don Bellante, *Edward Chamberlin: Monopolistic Competition and Pareto Optimality*, 2 J. Bus. & Econ. Res. 17, 18–19 (2004).
[25] See, e.g., Raymond Vernon & John T. Dunlop, *Edward Sagendorph Mason (22 February 1899–29 February 1992)*, 138 Proceedings Am. Phil. Soc'y 342 (1994).
[26] Id. at 343.
[27] Id. (quoting Joe Staten Bain, Industrial Organization (1968)).
[28] Edward S. Mason, *Price and Production Policies of Large-Scale Enterprise*, 29 Am. Econ. Rev. 61 (1939).
[29] Id. at 73–74.
[30] Edward S. Mason, *Monopoly in Law and Economics*, 47 Yale L.J. 34, 49 (1937).

Mason's work exhibited a nuance, however, that many SCP studies to follow overlooked. Specifically, he was attuned to the dangers of inter-industry regressions. He warned that "the attempt to correlate measures of price behavior with other data such as industrial concentration ... on an economy-wide basis is apt to include irrelevant and exclude relevant determinants of price policy."[31] Instead, he predicted, "empirical work will achieve better results by a more intensive examination of specific market situations."[32] Observing that "very little has been done to formulate tests of undesirable price behavior applicable to public action[,]" he threw down the gauntlet. Mason's doctoral student, Joe Bain, would seize the mantle. A little over a decade later, Bain wrote the seminal article on the SCP paradigm.[33]

The intervening period – the 1940s – saw antitrust emerge with force. Under Roosevelt, Thurman Arnold took over the Justice Department in 1938, and radically changed its direction. The 1930s, pursuant to the New Deal, had seen the federal government pursue industrial planning. Blessing industry-wide cartel agreements passed in the form of codes under the auspices of the National Industrial Recovery Act, the era marked a low point for free markets and competition. The Supreme Court lent its own support to the anticompetitive policies of the time, infamously blessing a cartel in its 1934 decision in *Appalachian Coals*.[34]

Arnold set things right. He transformed the Division, which grew several-fold during his five-year watch, and launched a flurry of antitrust cases.[35] He indicted a host of firms in the car industry for agreeing to exclude independent financiers. He sued the movie industry for anticompetitive licensing practices and vertical integration into theater ownership. The case ultimately led the Supreme Court to rule in the government's favor in 1948, and forced film studios to divest their cinema chains.[36] The ensuing consent decree endured all the way until late 2019, when the Division moved to terminate them.

The Justice Department's antitrust activism far exceeded those examples. Arnold brought criminal charges in the dairy industry. He led a series of interventions against perceived abuses of patent rights. Arnold himself successfully argued the *Univis* and *Ethyl Gasoline* cases before the Supreme Court, which prohibited various restraints outside the scope of the patent grant.[37] In the oil sector, he oversaw the prosecution of a host of companies and their executives for conspiring to stabilize prices by coordinating the purchase of distress gasoline in the spot market. That

---

[31] Mason, *supra* note 28, at 65–66.
[32] Edward S. Mason, *Price and Production Policies of Large-Scale Enterprise*, 29 AM. ECON. REV. 66 (1939).
[33] Joe S. Bain, *Relation of Profit Rate to Concentration: American Manufacturing, 1936–1940*, 65 Q.J. ECON. 293 (1951).
[34] Appalachian Coals, Inc. v. United States, 288 U.S. 344 (1933).
[35] For a terrific account, see Spencer Weber Waller, *The Antitrust Legacy of Thurman Arnold*, 78 ST. JOHN'S L. REV. 569 (2004).
[36] United States v. Paramount Pictures, Inc., 334 U.S. 131 (1948).
[37] United States v. Univis Lens Co., 316 U.S. 241 (1942); Ethyl Gasoline Corp. v. United States, 309 U.S. 436 (1940).

effort ultimately saw the Supreme Court hold that horizontal price-fixing is per se unlawful.[38] Perhaps the most famous case on his watch, however, was the monopolization case against Alcoa. The government eventually won in 1945 in a still-celebrated decision by Judge Learned Hand.[39]

Meanwhile, an evolution took place within the economics literature. John Clark's 1940 article on workable competition, in particular, prompted the academy to think of industrial organization outside of the abstract neoclassical theories of monopoly and perfect competition.[40] Clark made a pragmatic argument. His writings depicted perfect competition as an apparition not worth chasing. In its place, he insisted, one should strive for a competitive process that is both attainable and desirable. To that point, the neoclassical literature had implied that deviations from the competitive paradigm were ubiquitous. Further, the 1933 conceptions of imperfect competition suggested that markets would not gravitate toward competitive outcomes, but would instead rest in an equilibrium characterized by supracompetitive pricing.[41] The combination propelled a market-failure narrative that did little to dissuade the predilection toward regulation. With Clark's prescription of working toward effective competition, antitrust enforcers need not attain perfection, but rather should foster a market structure in which results exceeded those likely to be associated with regulation.

At the close of the decade, Mason observed that the question for economists was to identify "the conditions of market structure, the limitations on the market position or scope of action of firms, deemed necessary to the maintenance of effective competition."[42] His student, Bain, was on the cusp of developing a structuralist hypothesis that would ignite a surge of econometric work for decades to come.

3.2.4 1950: *The Celler–Kefauver Anti-Merger Act*

Despite the Antitrust Division's activism during Arnold's tenure, merger control was not, and had never been, a focus of antitrust enforcement. The aftermath of World War II brought with it widespread concern, however, about industrial consolidation of the kind that had accompanied the rise of fascist governments elsewhere. Economists observed that concentration had been steadily rising in the US economy[43] – a trend attributed to the failure of the Clayton Act of 1914 to halt anticompetitive mergers. In part, that shortcoming reflected a loophole in the statute itself, which failed to catch asset, as distinct from stock, acquisitions. The result was an environment in the 1940s that grew increasingly hostile to M&A activity.

---

[38] United States v. Socony-Vacuum Oil Co., 310 U.S. 150 (1940).
[39] United States v. Alum. Co. of Am., 148 F.2d 416 (2d Cir. 1945).
[40] John M. Clark, *Toward a Concept of Workable Competition*, 30 AM. ECON. REV. 241 (1940).
[41] Hovenkamp, *supra* note 9, at 339, 346.
[42] Edward S. Mason, *The Current Status of the Monopoly Problem in the United States*, 62 HARV. L. REV. 1265, 1267 (1949).
[43] Hovenkamp, *supra* note 9, at 352.

The Justice Department brought its first prospective M&A challenge in 1947, suing to enjoin US Steel's acquisition of Consolidated Steel. Finding the market shares at issue to be too modest to sustain the complaint's theory of competitive harm, the Supreme Court rejected the government's case in 1948.[44] This failure reinforced public conviction that existing antitrust laws were not up to the task. An FTC report of the same year magnified the urgency. Noting a "sharply upward" trend in merger activity following World War II, the Commission observed how firms "plainly circumvented" the antitrust laws through asset acquisitions or by acquiring stock and then using that stock to acquire the underlying assets if challenged.[45] It characterized Section 7 as a "virtual nullity."[46]

Congress responded by passing the Celler–Kefauver Act, which strengthened Section 7 of the Clayton Act.[47] The amendment closed the asset loophole, and clarified the statute's application to nonhorizontal transactions. The Supreme Court first addressed the 1950 Act twelve years later.[48] Remarking on the bountiful legislative record, it observed that the "dominant theme pervading congressional consideration of the 1950 amendments was a fear of what was considered to be a rising concentration in the American economy."[49] That was why, it noted, Congress provided "authority for arresting mergers at a time when the trend to a lessening of competition in a line of commerce was still in its incipiency."[50]

3.2.5 1950s–1970s: A Profusion of Empirical Work Validates SCP Theories, and Leads to Structuralist Antitrust Policies

Post-war distaste for consolidation dovetailed with economic consensus on structuralism. For a quarter of a century, prevailing evidence and theory had convinced economists of a simple proposition – safeguarding competition required preserving unconcentrated market structures. The ensuing alignment between political values and economic science created the most hostile environment to M&A activity in the history of the country.

Meanwhile, the generation's most influential economist, Joe Bain, was about to make his mark. Grappling with the concept of effective competition introduced by John Clark a decade before, Bain framed the problem for industrial organization as identifying the set of conditions under which markets would fail to achieve such

---

[44] United States v. Columbia Steel Co., 334 U.S. 495 (1948).
[45] ANNUAL REPORT OF THE FED. TRADE COMM'N FOR THE FISCAL YEAR ENDED JUNE 30, 1948, 18, https://www.ftc.gov/sites/default/files/documents/reports_annual/annual-report-1948/ar1948_0.pdf.
[46] Id. at 16.
[47] United States v. Phila. Nat'l Bank, 374 U.S. 321, 340–42 (1963); see also United States v. Cont'l Can Co., 378 U.S. 443, 453 (1964).
[48] Brown Shoe Co. v. United States, 370 U.S. 294 (1962).
[49] Id. at 315.
[50] Id. at 317; see also Cont'l Can, 378 U.S. at 462.

workable competitiveness.⁵¹ Such indicia of failure, he explained, may include unusual rates of return, excess capacity, firms at scale "outside the optimal range," excessive pricing, and "persistent lag in adoption of cost-reducing technical changes or persistent suppression of product changes which would advantage buyers."⁵² In presenting this argument, he championed "the potential association of price results to market structure" as the key explanatory variable.⁵³

The following year – shortly after the Celler–Kefauver Act – Bain articulated the SCP vision in a pivotal article.⁵⁴ He hypothesized a causal relationship between concentration and profit. More specifically, he posited that seller and buyer concentration, entry barriers, and product differentiation affected profits, selling costs, and scale and capacity efficiencies.⁵⁵ Importantly, he evinced that relationship empirically. Observing 340 US manufacturing industries, but finding sufficient data for only 42 of them between 1936 and 1940, he found that profits correlated with seller concentration when the C8 ratio exceeded 70 percent.⁵⁶

Although a "conclusive indication" of a continuous association between concentration and rate of return did not emerge from the data, Bain viewed his study as a launching pad for further empirical work. The goal that he had laid out the year before – investigating the structural conditions under which workable competition will break down – was underway. In his view, "we have a very provisional and tentative hypothesis for further testing. Should it be further verified, we may be on the road to an answer to the question of what is a ... 'workable' number and size distribution of sellers[.]"⁵⁷

Bain developed his structuralist hypothesis over the ensuing five years. In 1954, he published a new study, this time focusing on industry data between 1947 and 1951.⁵⁸ There, he argued that profit was not simply a function of concentration, but of structure. Structural impediments to entry were key. Bain insisted that "basic environmental circumstances" determine entry, and thus "affect the probability that monopoly will emerge and remain."⁵⁹

His efforts culminated in a 1956 book, which gave the SCP paradigm its definitive expression.⁶⁰ There, he argued that scale economies, related cost and technology advantages enjoyed by incumbents, and product differentiation impede entry. His

---

[51] Joe S. Bain, *Workable Competition in Oligopoly: Theoretical Considerations and Some Empirical Evidence*, 40 AM. ECON. REV. 35 (1950).
[52] *Id.* at 37.
[53] *Id.* at 38.
[54] Bain, *supra* note 33.
[55] *Id.* at 293.
[56] *Id.* at 313–14.
[57] *Id.* at 324.
[58] Joe S. Bain, *Conditions of Entry and the Emergence of Monopoly, in* MONOPOLY AND COMPETITION AND THEIR REGULATION (Edward H. Chamberlin ed., 1954).
[59] *Id.* at 215.
[60] JOE S. BAIN, BARRIERS TO NEW COMPETITION: THEIR CHARACTER AND CONSEQUENCES IN MANUFACTURING INDUSTRIES (1956).

view was intuitive. To compete effectively in a market subject to falling long-run average-cost curves, an entrant must enter at scale or suffer a cost disadvantage. The capital required to ramp up production or overcome consumer preferences for well-established brands through advertising may deter entry that would otherwise be profitable given mark-ups. As a result, Bain intuited, market leaders rationally price at supracompetitive levels in the presence of entry barriers. This conclusion mattered, of course, because – on Bain's conception of entry barriers – few markets lacked them.

Bain rounded out the decade with an authoritative text on industrial organization, which became de rigueur for the upcoming generation of economists.[61] Similarly influential was Kaysen and Turner's book on antitrust policy in 1959.[62] Together, Bain's, Kaysen's, and Turner's work in the 1950s captured the imagination of the industrial economics and antitrust communities. Although there was a lag between Bain's empirical and theoretical work and the myriad econometric studies that would follow, the SCP wave arrived in the 1960s. Work exploring the relationship between structure, conduct, and performance flourished.

The hypothesis was straightforward. Competition is a function of the number and symmetry of sellers, as well as impediments to entry. Atomistic industries are not conducive of coordinated pricing, and so no firm can exercise market power. Concentrated markets, by contrast, allow incumbents to monitor each other's pricing. Brand differentiation allows firms to earn supranormal margins. Structural impediments to entry prevent supply-side responses that would neutralize exercises of market power. The result is that, as such markets grow more consolidated, their economic performance for society will suffer. The relationship is simple: Structure → conduct → performance.[63]

One study after another in the 1960s bore out Bain's structure-profit hypothesis.[64] Those studies typically involved cross-sectional, least-squares regressions of a concentration ratio on price-cost margins. A positive correlation generally emerged. Indeed, the 1960s produced little evidence to the contrary.[65] The consistency of

---

[61] JOE S. BAIN, INDUSTRIAL ORGANIZATION (1959).
[62] CARL KAYSEN & DONALD F. TURNER, ANTITRUST POLICY: AN ECONOMIC AND LEGAL ANALYSIS (1959).
[63] For good reviews on the econometric evidence underlying the SCP hypothesis, see STEPHEN MARTIN, ADVANCED INDUSTRIAL ECONOMICS 5–9, 117–41 (2d ed. 2002); Richard Schmalensee, *Inter-Industry Studies of Structure and Performance*, in 2 HANDBOOK OF INDUS. ORG. (1989).
[64] See, e.g., Leonard W. Weiss, *Quantitative Studies of Industrial Organization*, in FRONTIERS OF QUANTITATIVE ECONOMICS 362 (1971); H. Michael Mann, *Seller Concentration Barriers to Entry and Rates of Return in Thirty Industries, 1950–1960*, 48 REV. ECON. & STATISTICS 296 (1966); Leonard W. Weiss, *Average Concentration Ratios and Industrial Performance*, 11 J. INDUS. ECON. 237 (1963); Victor R. Fuchs, *Integration, Concentration, and Profits in Manufacturing Industries*, 75 Q.J. ECON. 278 (1961); Kazuo Sato, *Price-Cost Structure and Behavior of Profit Margins*, 1 YALE ECON. ESSAYS 360 (1961). But see HAROLD M. LEVINSON, POSTWAR MOVEMENTS OF PRICES AND WAGES IN MANUFACTURING INDUSTRIES 22 (Study Paper No. 21, 1960) ("No consistently strong relationship was found between price changes and concentration ratios.").
[65] A lonely exception lay in work by George Stigler, who in 1963 found no support for the hypothesis that structure determines profitability. GEORGE STIGLER, CAPITAL AND RATES OF RETURN IN MANUFACTURING INDUSTRIES (1963). A few years later, he did observe some evidence linking concentration to

results across time, datasets, and industries reinforced consensus – the SCP paradigm enjoyed strong evidentiary support.[66] Nevertheless, the observed correlation between concentration and profitability remained weak.[67]

To a degree, the SCP paradigm absolves firms of responsibility of their conduct. Coordination, supracompetitive pricing, building excess capacity, vertical integration, and product diversification in order to evade head-to-head competition are a rational response to market conditions. Indeed, by definition, oligopolistic interdependence makes each firm's profit-maximization calculus a function of other sellers' expected reactions. For structuralists, the fix is simplicity itself. Policymakers should deconcentrate industries and, to the extent possible, dissolve entry barriers. Doing so would foster competition, and yield more efficient market outcomes. By contrast, it would be ineffective to bring conduct cases. Incumbents merely make rational decisions. Antitrust should instead focus on the root cause.

Thus arose an environment perfectly calibrated to inhibit horizontal and vertical mergers. Public hostility to consolidation pervaded the 1940s to 1960s. Those political values fused with an industrial economics literature that lent empirical and theoretical support to an anti-concentration antitrust agenda. The Warren Court received the government's anti-merger efforts with open arms. It adopted a structural presumption of 30 percent, which remains to this day.[68] The Court blocked mergers that implicated trivial market shares based on little more than a discernible trend toward concentration – even if the industry remained near-atomistic at the time of decision.

Even in "an industry as fragmented as shoe retailing," the Court in *Brown Shoe* prohibited a merger that would have given the buyer control of 7.2 percent of the country's stores.[69] It did one better in *Pabst Brewing*, preventing a merger to just 4.49 percent of national beer sales.[70] In *Von's Grocery*, the Court held illegal a merger with a combined market share of 7.5 percent.[71] Scanning the precedent, an exasperated Justice Stewart remarked that the "sole consistency that I can find is that in litigation under s 7, the Government always wins."[72]

In the face of these policies, horizontal and vertical transactions largely ceased. A boom in conglomerate mergers thus took their place.

---

profitability, though with caveats. George Stigler, A Theory of Oligopoly, 72 J. POL. ECON. 44, 56–59 (1964). Stigler would later become one of the most ardent critics of the SCP hypothesis.

[66] See, e.g., Leonard W. Weiss, The Concentration-Profits Relationship and Antitrust, in INDUSTRIAL CONCENTRATION: THE NEW LEARNING (1974).
[67] See, e.g., id.; NORMAN R. COLLINS & LEE E. PRESTON, CONCENTRATION AND PRICE-COST MARGINS IN MANUFACTURING INDUSTRIES (1968); Stigler, supra note 65.
[68] United States v. Phila. Nat'l Bank, 374 U.S. 321 (1963).
[69] Brown Shoe Co. v. United States, 370 U.S. 294, 345 (1962).
[70] United States v. Pabst Brewing Co., 384 U.S. 546 (1966).
[71] United States v. Von's Grocery Co., 384 U.S. 270, 272 (1966).
[72] Id. at 301.

3.2.6 1970s–1980s: *The Chicago School Revolution and Subsequent Embrace of Game Theory*

Accepted by economists and policymakers alike throughout the 1960s, the SCP paradigm began showing cracks at the turn of the decade.

In 1969, Yale Brozen pointed out numerous flaws.[73] In particular, SCP researchers had improperly inferred that observed profit margins represented exercised market power – a criticism that Eugene Singer would also articulate a year later.[74] The critics had identified serious errors. Accounting profits differ from economic rents, industries characterized by risky investment are likely to become concentrated, and cross-sectional work takes a potentially misleading static picture of a dynamic market that may be in disequilibrium.[75] Indeed, in 1971, Brozen found empirical support for the proposition that "rates of return observed by Bain in his concentrated industries were not at equilibrium levels and were not an appropriate test of his hypothesis."[76]

This opening critique of the SCP hypothesis was powerful. As it impugned conventional wisdom, proponents of the status quo unsurprisingly mounted a hearty defense.[77] But the kill shot followed in 1973. The celebrated UCLA economist, Harold Demsetz, penned a devastating critique of the SCP literature.[78] His essential point remains indisputable – market structure is endogenous, which prevents one from ascribing causality to observed correlations. Demsetz showed that competition in technology and quality naturally leads to heightened concentration and price-cost margins. Consumers reward firms that bring superior offerings to the market, and those firms' shares will rise at less capable rivals' expense. Hence, structure need not determine competitive behavior. The opposite may be true. He then demonstrated that much of the evidence marshalled in the preceding two decades in support of the SCP hypothesis more plausibly pointed to this efficiency/competitive hypothesis.

Demsetz's takedown reverberates through the present day. Few serious economists would now infer a one-way causal link from observed associations between market structure and profit.[79] A host of critiques followed in Demsetz's wake,

---

[73] Yale Brozen, *Significance of Profit Data for Antitrust Policy*, 14 ANTITRUST BULL. 119 (1969).

[74] Eugene M. Singer, *Industrial Organization: Price Models and Public Policy*, 60 AM. ECON. REV. 90 (1970).

[75] Brozen, *supra* note 73; *see also* Yale Brozen, *Bain's Concentration and Rates of Return Revisited*, 14 J.L. & ECON. 351 (1971); John T. Wenders, *Profits and Antitrust Policy: The Question of Disequilibrium*, 16 ANTITRUST BULL. 249 (1971).

[76] Yale Brozen, *The Antitrust Task Force Deconcentration Recommendation*, 13 J.L. & ECON. 279, 288 (1970).

[77] *See, e.g.*, Paul W. MacAvoy et al., *High and Stable Concentration Levels, Profitability, and Public Policy: A Response*, 14 J.L. & ECON. 493 (1971).

[78] Harold Demsetz, *Industry Structure, Market Rivalry, and Public Policy*, 16 J.L. & ECON. 1 (1973); *see also* Harold Demsetz, *Two Systems of Belief About Monopoly*, in INDUSTRIAL CONCENTRATION: THE NEW LEARNING (1974).

[79] The fact of bidirectional causal influences has now been clear for decades. *See, e.g.*, Alan A. Fisher & Robert H. Lande, *Efficiency Considerations in Merger Enforcement*, 71 CAL. L. REV. 1580, 1609 (1983)

including impactful ones by Peltzman and McGee.[80] Meanwhile, Carter showed that concentration correlated with leading firms' margins, but not with those of firms behind the top four.[81] In other words, the most successful firms had greater profit margins than those further behind, an observation that strengthened the efficiency hypothesis.

It became clear that SCP models had been misspecified. Worse, there was no good way to fix the problem. Cross-sectional, inter-industry studies pose insurmountable problems. To be sure, the Chicago critique did not immediately quash any defense or advancement of the SCP paradigm. As late as 1979, some associated with the tradition continued to propound structuralism as having a strong evidentiary basis and justifying no-fault deconcentration efforts of the likes proposed by the Neal Report.[82] In reality, though, the SCP movement's swan song had long since passed. As Stigler observed, "[B]y 1980 there remained scarcely a trace of the two Harvard traditions of Chamberlin and Mason in the current work of economists."[83]

Ultimately, it became clear that line-of-business data did not even support the core SCP hypothesis.[84] Cross-sectional regressions after the 1960s revealed that concentration in US manufacturing did not correlate positively with profits.[85] Indeed, more sophisticated studies after the core SCP period of the 1960s through 1970s even found a negative association between concentration and price-cost margins, thus flipping the SCP paradigm on its head. Cross-sectional evidence that structure affects profits was tied to large market shares, not to HHI or Cn concentration ratios.[86] This insight has important consequences.[87]

The sea change in industrial economics wrought an equivalent shift in policy. Yet, the two events did not occur simultaneously.

(observing that "the evidence tentatively suggests that both market-power and efficiency effects contribute to the overall relationship between concentration and profitability").

[80] Sam Peltzman, *The Gains and Losses from Industrial Concentration*, 20 J.L. & ECON. 229 (1977); Sam Peltzman, *The Causes and Consequences of Rising Industrial Concentration: A Reply*, 22 J.L. & ECON. 209 (1979). John McGee, *Efficiency and Economies of Size*, in INDUSTRIAL ORGANIZATION: THE NEW LEARNING (1974).

[81] John R. Carter, *Collusion, Efficiency, and Antitrust*, 21 J.L. & ECON. 435 (1978).

[82] Leonard W. Weiss, *The Structure-Conduct-Performance Paradigm and Antitrust*, 127 U. PA. L. REV. 1104 (1979).

[83] GEORGE J. STIGLER, MEMOIRS OF AN UNREGULATED ECONOMIST 166 (2003).

[84] See, e.g., Schmalensee, *supra* note 63, at 976.

[85] See, e.g., F.M. SCHERER & DAVID ROSS, INDUSTRIAL MARKET STRUCTURE AND ECONOMIC PERFORMANCE (1990).

[86] See, e.g., Paul A. Pautler, Bureau of Economics, FTC, *Evidence on Mergers and Acquisitions*, Sept. 25, 2001, https://www.ftc.gov/sites/default/files/documents/reports/evidence-mergers-and-acquisitions/wp243_0.pdf, at 54.

[87] The observation that a positive correlation does not consistently exist between concentration and price, but does between *market share* and price, may be significant. It supports the hypothesis that a cost advantage or asymmetric innovation explains higher prices – if the top firms' share of a market explains higher prices better than market-wide metrics of concentration, then it suggests that the spoils are going to the victor.

Though it traces to the early 1970s, the modern era began in earnest in 1981. That was when Bill Baxter, a Stanford law professor, became head of the Antitrust Division. He decreed that the Justice Department would only bring cases that were grounded in rigorous economics. His tenure marked the last truly radical shift to date in US competition enforcement at the agency level. Baxter threw out the *I.B.M.* case, which the government had filed in 1969 and had long since been a debacle. He settled the *AT&T* case through divestitures that reshaped the telecommunications industry. He revoked the economically unsound "Nine No-Nos" of patent licensing. And he issued transformative merger guidelines in 1982. Economists like Stigler, Demsetz, and Peltzman may have laid the foundation in industrial organization for the law and economics revolution. Scholars like Bork, Posner, and Director gave it legal expression. But it was Baxter, above all others, who made it policy.[88]

The decades since Baxter's 1981–83 reign at the DOJ have witnessed acerbic debate about the merits of intervention in particular cases, including as to the sufficiency of underlying economic evidence. Nevertheless, a bipartisan consensus has since prevailed, namely that antitrust should be employed in service of economic principles alone. It is only in the past few years, with the rise of the antimonopoly movement, that thinkers beyond the fringe are beginning to question core tenets of the law and economics approach to competition law.

In the meantime, though, antitrust economics itself evolved. The Chicago School of the 1970s drew heavily on neoclassical price theory. Its models solved for price and quantity outcomes using mathematical techniques of constrained optimization. Scholars working in the Chicago tradition employed models suggesting that vertical integration, bundling, tie-ins, exclusive contracts, below-cost pricing, price discrimination, monopoly leverage, and the like are variously efficient or irrational means of exclusion. The pendulum swung far from the Warren Court's inhospitable tradition, which some of the Chicago School's most influential writers had Bork ridiculed.[89] Although he, Posner, and others laid the intellectual foundation for antitrust that continues to this day, some of their initial prescriptions too casually disregarded the potential for anticompetitive conduct and hence the value of antitrust intervention.[90]

---

[88] *See, e.g.*, Richard A. Posner, *Introduction to Baxter Symposium*, 51 STAN. L. REV. 1007 (1999); Richard Schmalensee, *Bill Baxter in the Antitrust Arena: An Economist's Appreciation*, 51 STAN. L. REV. 1317 (1999).

[89] ROBERT BORK, THE ANTITRUST PARADOX 66 (1978).

[90] *See, e.g.*, HOW THE CHICAGO SCHOOL OVERSHOT THE MARK: THE EFFECT OF CONSERVATIVE ECONOMIC ANALYSIS ON U.S. ANTITRUST (Robert Pitofsky ed., 2008). Although some parts of the book inaccurately caricature the Chicago School, which is better understood as adhering to the prevailing industrial-organization insights of the time and teaching that antitrust policy ought to adhere to robust economics principles, there is no doubt that certain proponents of the Chicago School overstated the innocuous nature of various restraints and unilateral practices.

The 1980s brought with them a new revolution, this time in the direction of game theory. A literature focused on problems associated with imperfect information followed. Two 1982 articles, in particular, demonstrated that dominant firms could use asymmetric information to build reputations for an aggressive response to competitors, and thus inhibit entry.[91] A literature modeling Nash-equilibria blossomed. Much of it focused on how incumbents might credibly signal potential rivals that their costs are lower than what they really are, and thus deter competition. The ensuing literature showed that, under certain assumptions, various means of exclusion could be rational, even though they remain costly in the short run. No one encapsulated that work better than Jean Tirole, whose game-theoretic models arguably defined the brand and whose 1988 textbook became the quintessential graduate resource on industrial organization.[92] This brings us to the modern evidence.

3.3 THE PRICE-CONCENTRATION RELATIONSHIP: MODERN EVIDENCE

3.3.1 *New Empirical Industrial Organization (NEIO)*

Pause to reflect on the association between concentration and profits. As we have seen, industrial economists grappled with the competitive implications of structuralism for decades. Neoclassical abstractions in the early twentieth century fed worries about ruinous competition – concerns that dissipated in the 1930s with models of imperfect competition. Within industrial organization, case studies gave way to broader empiricism.

Chamberlin, Mason, and Bain moved the academy toward the SCP paradigm and the first efforts systematically to trace the relationship between industry concentration and price-cost margins. Initial empirical efforts in the 1950s gave way to a horde of SCP studies in the 1960s and into the 1970s. Work in that tradition ceased, however, due to withering criticism. The SCP inter-industry studies experienced intractable problems including endogeneity, reverse causality, simultaneity bias, misspecification, and measurement problems. Industrial organization then swung back toward theory, as Chicago economists reached to neoclassical economics. The 1980s saw industrial economics become yet more theoretical with an abundance of game-theoretic models. Empirical work that formally tested antitrust's most important relationship – market structure and performance – had fallen out of fashion.

An empirical renaissance, however, was about to get underway. The post-Chicago focus on game theory frustrated policymakers and academics alike. Models yielded wildly different outcomes, and hence insights, depending on assumptions. Antitrust

---

[91] David Kreps & Robert Wilson, *Reputation and Imperfect Information*, 27 J. ECON. THEORY 253 (1982); Paul Migrom & John Roberts, *Predation, Reputation and Entry Deterrence*, 27 J. ECON. THEORY 280 (1982).
[92] JEAN TIROLE, THE THEORY OF INDUSTRIAL ORGANIZATION (1988).

economics had become the thing of possibility theorems. Although advances in theory suggested a need for antitrust intervention in some settings, they did not provide useful guidance as to when those scenarios would actually arise.

Dissatisfaction with the endless possibilities associated with game theory led to renewed interest in empiricism. Econometrics itself grew more sophisticated. In light of the SCP critique, economists recognized that inter-industry studies were never going to produce reliable results. They turned instead to formulating and testing hypotheses using *intra*-industry data. This effort has become known as the New Empirical Industrial Organization (NEIO), and has proven itself to be of immense value to competition policy. Comparative statics between pre- and post-event equilibria have obvious applications to antitrust enforcement. Economists have proven adept at using market data to estimate supply and demand functions, thus allowing merger simulations and other counterfactuals constructions needed to quantify competitive effects.

NEIO goes beyond merger analysis. Econometricians have explored structural parameters at the single-industry level in order to tease out relationships of interest to antitrust. Recognizing that industries differ across virtually all metrics, they focus instead on a common product market in which numerous regional or local geographic markets exist. Ideally, this approach permits comparisons of like with like – that is, all parameters remain constant except for price and concentration. For that reason, economists try to focus on markets with homogeneous products or product mixes and for which price dominates other forms of competition. As relevant geographic markets invariably differ in HHIs, Cn, and the like, econometricians can regress concentration against price and – if necessary – control for observable differences. Markets for retail, gasoline stations, cement, airlines, railroads, cars, and livestock are popular objects of study for that reason.

The modern literature is superior than the SCP studies of old for another reason. It avoids a measurement problem that plagued efforts to regress *profit* on concentration. NEIO economists recognize that profit levels are a dubious proxy for market power, and that accounting-derived markups can deviate seriously from economic rents. NEIO economists thus focus on price rather than profit. Hence, they explore the intra-industry relationship between the former dependent variable and concentration.

3.3.2 Intra-industry Studies Find an Association between Concentration and Price, But Endogeneity Remains and Little Evidence Supports a Direct Causal Relationship

Beginning in the 1980s and accelerating from there, NEIO economists have systematically explored the relationship between concentration and price. Their intra-industry studies have found reasonably consistent results – a positive (albeit modest) association holds in a variety of settings.

Timothy Bresnahan coined the NEIO term in 1989, in a book chapter on industrial organization.[93] In 1990, Weiss published a book collecting numerous studies that found a positive relationship between concentration and price in markets for Portland cement, advertising, retail, railroads, livestock purchasing, and banking.[94] Econometricians have observed a positive correlation between price and concentration through countless intra-industry studies in the years since then. Examples include banking,[95] cement,[96] movie theaters,[97] airfares,[98] gasoline,[99] office-supply superstores,[100] beer,[101] natural gas,[102] hospitals,[103] and even motels on motorways.[104]

Observed correlations, however, are not always strong. Further, some evidence contradicts the price-concentration hypothesis. In 1992, Dunne and Roberts found no relationship between the number of bread producers on price or output.[105] In 1990, an FTC economist found studies observing a positive association between

---

[93] Timothy F. Bresnahan, *Empirical Studies of Industries with Market Power*, in HANDBOOK OF INDUS. ORG. (1989).

[94] LEONARD WEISS, CONCENTRATION AND PRICE (1990).

[95] *See, e.g.,* Anthony W. Cyrnak & Timothy H. Hannan, *Is the Cluster Still Valid in Defining Banking Markets? Evidence from a New Data Source*, 44 ANTITRUST BULL. 313 (1999); Timothy Hannan, *The Functional Relationship Between Prices and Market Concentration: Evidence from the Market for Consumer Deposits*, 107 Q.J. ECON. 657 (1992); David Neumark & Steven Sharpe, *Market Structure and the Nature of Price Rigidity: Evidence from the Market for Consumer Deposits*, 107 Q.J. ECON. 657 (1992).

[96] *See, e.g.,* David I. Rosenbaum, *Efficiency v. Collusion: Evidence Cast in Cement*, 9 REV. INDUS. ORG. 379 (1994).

[97] *See, e.g.,* Peter Davis, *Spatial Competition in Retail Markets: Movie Theatres*, 37 RAND J. ECON. 964 (2006); Peter Davis, *The Effect of Local Competition on Admission Prices in the U.S. Motion Picture Exhibition Market*, 48 J.L. & ECON. 677 (2005).

[98] *See, e.g.,* José Azar et al., *Anticompetitive Effects of Common Ownership*, 73 J. FIN. 1513 (2017); E. Han Kim & Vijay Singal, *Mergers and Market Power: Evidence from the Airline Industry*, 83 AM. ECON. REV. 549 (1996); William N. Evans & Ioannis N. Kessides, *Living by the Golden Rule: Multimarket Contact in the US Airline Industry*, 109 Q.J. ECON. 341 (1993); Steven A. Morisson & Clifford Winston, *The Dynamics of Airline Pricing and Competition*, 80 AM. ECON. REV. 389 (1990).

[99] *See, e.g.,* Paul R. Zimmerman, *The Competitive Impact of Hypermarket Retailers on Gasoline Prices*, 55 J.L. & ECON. 27 (2012).

[100] *See, e.g.,* Mark D. Manuszak & Charles C. Moul, *Prices and Endogenous Market Structure in Office Supply Superstores*, 56 J. INDUS. ECON. 94 (2008).

[101] *See, e.g.,* Orley C. Ashenfelter et al., *Efficiencies Brewed: Pricing and Consolidation in the US Beer Industry*, 46 RAND J. ECON. 328 (2015).

[102] *See, e.g.,* John R. Morris, *The Relationship Between Industrial Sales Prices and Concentration of Natural Gas Pipelines*, Fed. Trade Comm'n, Bureau of Economics, Working Paper No. 168 (1988), https://www.ftc.gov/sites/default/files/documents/reports/relationship-between-industrial-sales-prices-and-concentration-interstate-natural-gas-pipelines/wp168.pdf.

[103] *See, e.g.,* Emmett B. Keeler et al., *The Changing Effects of Competition on Non-profit and For-profit Hospital Pricing Behavior*, 18 J. HEALTH ECON. (1999).

[104] *See, e.g.,* Michael J. Mazzeo, *Competitive Outcomes in Product-Differentiated Oligopoly*, 84 REV. ECON. & STATISTICS 716 (2002).

[105] Timothy Dunne & Mark J. Roberts, *Costs, Demand and Imperfect Competition As Determinants of Plant-Level Output Prices*, in EMPIRICAL STUDIES IN INDUSTRIAL ORGANIZATION: ESSAYS IN HONOR OF LEONARD W. WEISS 13 (1992).

price and concentration in grocery retailing to be unreliable.[106] Indeed, the one study that he identified as coming closest to having controlled for inter-market differences in costs and intra-market differences in provided services found no association between market share and price.[107]

In 1990, using manufacturing data from 1972 to 1982, Salinger found an association between an increase in concentration and lower prices.[108] In 1984, Lynk found that consolidation in the beer industry correlated with reduced prices.[109] Ravenscraft found in 1983 that regressing profit on market share and concentration revealed a *negative* coefficient on concentration.[110] By contrast, the coefficient on market share was significant and positive. More generally, some NEIO studies that find positive relationships between price and concentration have been called into question.[111] And some merger retrospectives find a link between consolidation and price decreases.[112]

Intra-industries thus do not uniformly link concentration to price. Nevertheless, the prevalence of the observed relationship is impressive, transcending all manner of products and settings. It provides useful background context to antitrust policymakers. As discussed below in this section, it yields qualified support for the use of structural considerations in enforcing competition laws. NEIO studies, however, do *not* reliably indicate a linear causal relationship between price and concentration. Most importantly, they reveal little or nothing that answers the antitrust question of interest – whether (and when) a marginal delta in concentration in a given market will result in anticompetitive effects. A merger policy that prohibited increments in HHIs, Cns, or market shares would be vastly overbroad. In other words, structural antitrust remains blunt, overbroad, and error-prone. Further, those errors matter because situations exist in which consolidation may be associated with output increases, either in the short or long run.

Consider the statistical infirmities that afflict price-concentration studies. First, structure remains endogenous.[113] The danger of false causality thus looms overhead.

---

[106] Keith B. Anderson, *A Review of Structure-Performance Studies in Grocery Retailing: A Review*, in COMPETITIVE STRATEGY ANALYSIS IN THE FOOD SYSTEM 203 (1993).

[107] Id. at 205 (citing Phillip R. Kaufman & Charles R. Handy, *Supermarket Prices and Price Differences: City, Firm, and Store-Level Determinants*, USDA Econ. Research Serv. (1989)).

[108] Michael Salinger, *The Concentration-Margins Relationship Reconsidered*, in 21 BROOKINGS PAPERS ON ECONOMIC ACTIVITY: 1990 MICROECONOMICS 287, 309–10 (1990).

[109] William J. Lynk, *Interpreting Rising Concentration: The Case of Beer*, 57 J. BUS. 43 (1984).

[110] See, e.g., David J. Ravenscraft, *Structure-Profit Relationships at the Line of Business and Industry Level*, 65 REV. ECON. & STATISTICS 22 (1983).

[111] See, e.g., Craig M. Newmark, *A New Bottle for the Profits-Concentration Wine: A Look at Prices and Concentration in Grocery Retailing*, Bureau of Economics, Fed. Trade Comm'n (1989).

[112] See, e.g., Pauline Affeldt & Rainer Nitsche, *A Price Concentration Study on the European Mobile Telecom Markets*, (European Sch. Mgmt. Tech., Working Paper, 2014), https://www.e-ca.com/wp-content/uploads/esmt_working_paper_nitsche-affeldt.pdf. See generally *Market Concentration Can Benefit Consumers, but Needs Scrutiny*, THE ECONOMIST (Aug. 31, 2017).

[113] See, e.g., Vishal Singh & Ting Zhu, *Pricing and Market Concentration in Oligopoly Markets*, 27 MARKETING SCI. 1020 (2008).

Superior competition on the merits rewards the winner with market share, thus concentrating the market. Innovation may yield temporary market power with that share, evincing a price-concentration relationship that is entirely consistent with a healthy competitive market process. Further, if risk variables affect price, then ignoring them may bias the results of a price-concentration study.[114] While price may be a function of concentration and vice versa, it is also possible that another variable drives both of them. In short, econometricians lack good observations of exogenous variation in market concentration.

Second, regressing price on concentration overlooks nonprice-based competition.[115] Hence, price-concentration studies are vulnerable to omitted-variable bias. More specifically, almost no market sees competition occur solely through the price channel. In the presence of quality-based competition, regressing price on concentration without adequately controlling for other dimensions of competition (a difficult task) will produce biased results. Adjusting prices to account for quality, however, is a fraught exercise.

Third, it is difficult or impossible to account for all cost differences between various intra-industry markets. For example, Kimmel showed that a positive correlation might exist between price and concentration across different geographic markets for the same product even if the markets are competitive.[116] The measurement would simply capture differences in costs, between for example large and small markets.

Most importantly, however, almost no theoretical causal relationship exists between a change in concentration and price. Absent evidence or theory pointing to a causal relationship, it is a fundamental error to infer one from correlation alone.[117] Endogeneity prevents robust proof of a causal relationship. Economic theory offers just one example: quantity-based competition between symmetric firms with constant marginal costs and selling fungible products. That classic case of Cournot-Nash competition, however, is seldom – if ever – encountered in the real world. Hence, something other than concentration affects price. That something is the determinants of upward-pricing pressure – margins, diversions, and efficiencies. Concentration relates to unilateral effects only insofar as it correlates with one of those variables. It does not relate to margins. At most, it can be an imperfect proxy for diversion ratios. This basic fact has led some leading economists to acknowledge the

[114] See, e.g., Elijah Brewer III & William E. Jackson III, The "Risk-Adjusted" Price-Concentration Relationship in Banking, Fed. Reserve Bank Atlanta, Working Paper No. 2004-35 (2004), https://core.ac.uk/download/pdf/6924589.pdf.
[115] Craig M. Newmark, Price-Concentration Studies: There You Go Again (2004), https://www.justice.gov/atr/price-concentration-studies-there-you-go-again.
[116] Sheldon Kimmel, A Fundamental Bias in Studying Effects of Concentration on Price (U.S. Dep't of Justice, Economic Analysis Group, Antitrust Div., Working Paper 91-9, 1991).
[117] See, e.g., Letter from Timothy J. Muris, Chairman, Fed. Trade Comm'n to James E. Wells, Dir., Nat. Res. & Env't, U.S. Gen. Accounting Office (Aug. 25, 2003), https://www.ftc.gov/sites/default/files/attachments/press-releases/statement-federal-trade-commission-chairman-timothy-j.muris-gao-study-1990s-oil-mergers-concentration-released-today/040527petrolactionsftcresponse.pdf.

inherent limits of price-concentration studies. As one such economist observed, most of these studies "lack an economic foundation."[118]

Putting the serious empirical issues aside, it is also important to acknowledge what price-concentration studies do *not* show. The literature finds an association between concentration and price. It does not imply, however, that a positive increment in HHIs or Cns will itself lead to a price increase. For that reason, structural merger review is inherently imprecise. The observed relationship is not continuous.[119] The "critical" ratio beyond which further deltas in concentration yield higher prices is unknown. If it exists, then it is almost certainly transient, varying between industries. The price-concentration association is no more ubiquitous than it is linear. Indeed, as stated above, the two metrics sometimes display a negative relationship.[120] The fact that concentration and price (or profit) may be inversely correlated should obviously give any structuralist pause.[121]

3.4 HOW TO THINK ABOUT STRUCTURALISM IN ADMINISTERING ANTITRUST: SIX PRINCIPLES

To many reformists, the connection is obvious. *Of course* rising concentration equates to diminished competition. Fewer sellers mean fewer opportunities for buyers to play vendors off against each other and an environment more conducive to coordination. Large shares allow firms to move markets. The empirical literature confirms this audience's intuition at every turn. Decades of SCP research showed a positive relationship between structure and profitability across industries. And decades of intra-industry studies reveal a similar association between concentration and price. How much more do you need, they might ask, to accept the obvious?

On closer inspection, however, the picture becomes far more complex. The evidence simply does not bear out the hypothesis that increments in market concentration *cause* price increases. The relationship is bidirectional, oblique, and variable. Endogeneity issues are stubborn, good instruments are in rare supply, a causal mechanism by which deltas in concentration themselves lead to price effects seldom exists, and the correlation may be weak or even negative. There is a great deal of

---

[118] Daniel P. O'Brien, *Price-Concentration Analysis: Ending the Myth, and Moving Forward* (Working Paper, 2017).

[119] *See, e.g.*, Timothy F. Bresnahan & Peter C. Reiss, *Entry and Competition in Concentrated Markets*, 99 J. POL. ECON. 977, 978 (1991) (observing that, in "markets with five or fewer incumbents, almost all variation in competitive conduct occurs with the entry of the second or third firms[,]" but finding that, "[s]urprisingly, once the market has between three and five firms, the next entrant has little effect on competitive conduct.").

[120] *See, e.g.*, Sam Peltzman, *The Gains and Losses from Industrial Concentration*, 20 J.L. & ECON. 229 (1977). *See also supra* notes 108–112.

[121] For example, Salinger studied data from 1972 to 1982 and found that "increases in concentration are associated with cost and price decreases." Salinger, *supra* note 108, at 291. He suggested that "the process by which markets become concentrated is part of a dynamically competitive process that is beneficial to the economy." *Id.*

variation across markets. Even when done properly, intra-industry studies that find a connection between concentration and price do not permit researchers to extrapolate such a relationship beyond the observed markets. Efforts to get at a broader, cross-industry relationship floundered on the rocks of econometric impossibility. Inter-industry, cross-sectional studies that regress price (or, worse, margins) on market structure are inherently unreliable.

These statistical difficulties pose obvious challenges for antitrust policy. Industrial organization has focused on a single question, which has yet defied resolution. As a result, the evidence may prove bewildering and its general lessons unclear. This section tackles the issue head-on. Based on the preceding literature review, it articulates six principles that should guide the agencies as they think about structuralism in pursuing their mandate.

First, concentration must be tied to a properly defined relevant market. That means an area of effective competition within which firms vie for mutually exclusive opportunities in selling products that are functional substitutes. The resulting market may be narrow – surprisingly so for businesspeople.[122]

Second, concentration is relevant. It illuminates the competitive landscape, and can help predict effects. Yes, unconquerable statistical challenges afflict the empirical study of market power and industry structure. And we should avoid drawing unjustifiable causal inferences from observed correlations. Nevertheless, studies across a broad range of industries find a positive connection between price and concentration. Such a relationship also enjoys one source of theoretical support. Cournot competition between symmetric firms selling homogenous goods predicts worsening effects based on rising HHIs.

Importantly, concentration ratios provide useful context if the market is properly defined. 1-n statistics are the first port of call. Extremes presage an almost inevitable outcome. C4 or C8 ratios provide a richer competitive picture by illuminating the relative dispersion of share at the top of the market. HHIs weight each seller according to its share, and thus shed light on the structural composition of the whole market. That is why they are the agencies' preferred means of weighing structural concerns.

Each of these ratios provides increasingly helpful insights. Markets that are already concentrated, for example, bear greater vulnerability to unilateral and coordinated effects. Moreover, further consolidation in such markets is less likely to produce significant scale economies than in unconcentrated ones. In other words, although price and concentration may be inversely correlated in the presence of large fixed costs, when merging firms already account for the lion's share of sales in a market, it becomes more likely that they have exhausted efficiencies associated with

---

[122] Although the government's predilection for alleging razor-thin markets, excluding differentiated products that are nevertheless reasonable substitutes, is regrettable – see Chapter 9 – the relevant market must be bounded so as to capture material competitive constraints. Otherwise, concentration indices will be misleading at best and economically meaningless at worst.

larger output. (Of course, scale economies are far from the only sources of firm productivity, and mergers can yield efficiencies from many sources.) Combining these insights yields a simple conclusion: the agencies have good reason to investigate possible harm to competition when rivals propose to merge in concentrated markets.

Third, while concentration is a useful metric, it remains a deeply flawed proxy for competitive effects. A causal relationship between changes in market structure and price is undetermined. The only exception is the unrealistic Cournot setting outlined above. Industrial economists know what factors cause unilateral effects. They are not HHI deltas, Cn statistics, or n-1 changes. Structuralism cannot replace a granular assessment of the mechanics of competition in a relevant market.

Of course, studies find a correlation between price and concentration, and that connection persists across an eclectic array of markets. Yet, it remains unclear what precisely those studies are capturing. To be sure, some results reflect a loss of competition. Others, however, may flow from exactly the opposite phenomenon. Quality-based competition will lead superior innovators to capture share, and thus consolidate their markets, and yet the ensuing structure is indicative of exactly the kind of competition that society needs. Similarly, the competitive structure of a market subject to high ratios of fixed to marginal costs will inevitably be concentrated.

Structural ratios are associated with price effects not because they cause them, but because they correlate with factors that do. That correlation, however, is never generalized. It requires substantiation through a case-specific inquiry. Market shares may be a proxy for consumer preference – an important causal driver of competitive effects – but they also may not be. It is impossible to tell without first studying the market. Worse, price correlates with concentration because market structure is itself a function of competition. Industrial economists widely agree on that proposition, and it is fatal to any casual effort to conflate rising concentration and increased market power. Practices, agreements, and mergers may simultaneously consolidate a market and make it more competitive. And there are, of course, myriad scenarios in which consolidating mergers will not harm competition. The economics literature makes that possibility clear.

Ultimately, concentration ratios are information-deprived. They reduce each seller to a number, ascribing no weight to its real-life significance, consumer preferences, proximity of competition, merger-generated efficiencies, or to the many dynamic considerations that comprise the competitive space at issue in an investigation. To administer antitrust in obeisance to such statistics is to blind it to the factors that actually matter. That reality brings us to the next point.

Fourth, enforcers have superior tools at their disposal than structural factors. The great achievement of modern antitrust has been to move beyond crude policies of the kind that characterized the SCP era. The agencies now focus on competitive effects, and principally weigh concentration metrics only to the extent that they illuminate the actual determinants of price.

A post-merger firm's incentive to raise price does not depend on market concentration. Rather, it is a function of two factors: diversion ratios and margins. By calculating the percentage of lost sales that went to the target and the markup on those diverted sales, economists can calculate pricing-pressure indices. The insight thus garnered is itself incomplete. Actual effects turn on much more than GUPPIs. Merger-generated efficiencies may exert net downward pressure on price. Static indices ignore dynamic phenomena, which are crucial. Sellers and customers do not stand still. A critical factor is the gulf between the target and the next best placed competitor. Customer indifference can obviate effects. Indeed, sophisticated buyers may effectively discipline sellers even in a tightly packed oligopoly. That is one reason why experimental economics often finds that four sellers and four buyers are enough to bring about competitive outcomes.[123]

In short, no responsible antitrust enforcer should make intervention decisions based on structural factors when reliable indicia of competitive effects are available.

Fifth, there are circumstances in which structuralism provides sufficient basis for government action. This setting is not limited to the extreme case of merger to monopoly. An enforcer should turn to the most reliable evidence available. In a perfect world, that would involve robust bidding data from the merging parties and other sellers in the market, good margin data, fruitful natural experiments like entry and exit events, customers that are forthcoming in interviews, penetrating insight into potential entrants' plans, and so forth. In reality, data can be fragmented or unavailable, instruments sparse, interviewees reluctant, and the future track of a market decidedly unclear.

Absent such information, the agencies must do what they can, turning to ordinary-course documents to glean insights into proximity of competition and falling back on concentration ratios as the best-available proxies for the determinants of competition. Enforcers deprived of win/loss data may not know customers' ordinal preferences for sellers, for instance, but may see stable market shares over time as a workable proxy. In such settings, the choice is to do nothing or act to protect competition using what evidence is available. As explored above, with the predicate fact of the relevant market established, concentration has a legitimate role to play.[124]

---

[123] *See, e.g.*, Martin Dufwenberg & Uri Gneezy, *Price Competition and Market Concentration: An Experimental Study*, 18 J. INDUS. ORG. 7 (2000).

[124] Another setting in which the agencies may legitimately rely on structural factors alone is where the parties to a merger wish to offer up a divestiture in order to fix a horizontal overlap in a concentrated product market in order to close their deal without having first to comply with a Second Request and then give the government time to complete its investigation. It would seem odd to put merging parties to the time and expense required to sustain an effects-based analysis in that setting. *Cf., e.g.*, In re Holcim/LaFarge, Statement of the Federal Trade Commission, May 4, 2015, *with id.*, Statement of Commissioner Wright, Dissenting in Part and Concurring in Part.

Finally, theory must cede to facts. Suppose that empirical work *established* that incremental changes in concentration in a particular market are consistently associated with price effects. In that setting, it is academically interesting – but practically irrelevant – to understand the causal chain at issue. Little work meets this condition. Even within an industry, a generalized relationship between price and concentration reveals little about whether a marginal change in structure at the prevailing concentration level will produce anticompetitive effects. And, as industrial economists retreated from cross-industry studies, they largely abandoned any pretense toward positing generalized relationships.

Nevertheless, some work establishing the requisite connection does exist. Economists have now convincingly demonstrated, for example, that generic drug markets see declining prices with additional entry until eight sellers compete.[125] That insight is profoundly important from an enforcement perspective, though caution is still warranted. In particular, the fact that prices drop with numerous sequential entrants does not itself demonstrate that a 6–5 merger, for example, will be associated with unilateral effects. As ever, the enforcer's job remains a difficult one.

3.5 HAS THE MOVE AWAY FROM STRUCTURALISM LED TO HARMFUL CONSOLIDATION?

It is common in the antitrust bar to celebrate the pivot to the modern approach. Law and economics gave competition law its attractive intellectual constitution. Today, antitrust entails rigorous analysis pursuant to an objective framework applied to hard data. The law itself has grown sophisticated, as has the agencies' methodological toolkit. Ultimately, modern antitrust is about finding the right answer. Lawyers and economists unite in an effort to predict how a restraint, practice, or transaction will affect market outcomes. Seldom easy, that undertaking offers abundant intellectual reward. It contrasts favorably with the blunt structuralism of the prior era. Few, if any, practitioners or enforcers pine for a time when analysis began and ended with concentration ratios and the structural direction of an industry.

Nevertheless, it would be naïve to suppose that the move from structure to effects lacked cost. In fact, antitrust's shift to modernity four decades ago did carry a price. This section explains why this is so. It begins by contextualizing that downside with the weighty benefits associated with antitrust's shift to the modern era. This discussion sets up Chapter 4, which evaluates whether the US economy has suffered diminished competition over the past several decades – the period associated with the law and economics approach.

---

[125] *See, e.g.*, David Reiffen & Michael R. Ward, *Generic Drug Industry Dynamics*, 87 REV. ECON. & STAT. 37 (2005).

3.5.1 Chasing Precision: How Antitrust Escaped Nescience

Structuralism once reigned in the United States. Many reformists clamor for its return.[126] It is worth pausing, however, to consider the extraordinary advantages associated with today's focus on competitive effects. In terms of applied competition policy, the SCP era suffered from two critical deficiencies.

First, enforcement was confused. The agencies floundered about without rhyme or reason. Consolidation roused their passions, of course, and no one doubted the FTC's and DOJ's structural focus. Some of their headline merger challenges, however, can only be described as arbitrary. Blocking mergers in fragmented markets that would have given the parties 7.5 percent and 4.49 percent shares of sales has an attenuated link to protecting competition.[127] Even transactions involving no horizontal overlap or vertical issues succumbed. The government blocked purely complementary acquisitions, treating efficiencies as sources of competitive harm.[128] Yet, while intervening against some trivial combinations, the agencies blessed others. Their moves to block mergers, though frequent and aggressive, spoke of no readily discernible plan. Meanwhile, the government embarked on harebrained schemes like the FTC's effort to deconcentrate the cereal industry and the DOJ's monopolization case against IBM.

Such erraticism reflected the lack of a coherent objective. The intervention calculus was incongruous. An act of consolidation may obscure that issue or highlight it. Take the easy case. Two firms merge in a concentrated market, eliminating a unique competitive constraint that the target had imposed on the buyer. Prices rise, harming consumers. No efficiencies arise. The merger accelerates a trend of growing concentration, contributing to an amassing of economic power that undermines democracy. The post-merger firm exercises heightened buyer power in labor markets, harming workers and exacerbating income inequality. An anti-concentration mandate of the sort that reigned in the 1950s and 1960s would nip it in the bud. So would an effects analysis, even though it (wisely) asks nothing about such abstractions as the relationship between market structure and democracy.

Now consider a transaction in a six-firm oligopoly characterized by large investment and high margins. The third and fourth largest firms propose to merge, creating the new largest seller, with 35 percent of the market. The pre-closing market shares are 30 percent, 25 percent, 23 percent, 12 percent, 6 percent, and 4 percent, respectively. The 6–5 transaction significantly increases concentration. The HHI rises to 2,802 with a delta of 552. The post-merger firm, however, achieves powerful scale economies. Unilateral effects are unlikely because consumers do not prefer the merging parties over other suppliers. In fact, the deal will put downward pressure on

---

[126] *See* Chapter 4.
[127] United States v. Von's Grocery Co., 384 U.S. 270, 272 (1966); United States v. Pabst Brewing Co., 384 U.S. 546, 550 (1966).
[128] *See, e.g.,* Fed. Trade Comm'n v. Procter & Gamble Co., 386 U.S. 568 (1967).

the buyer's pricing due to marginal-cost savings. The parties' customers support the deal.

This transaction, though hypothetical, is representative of some deals. For structuralists, it poses a dilemma. To be sure, they would look askance at the HHIs. Yet, as an enforcer, it is hard to blind oneself to consumer benefit. Should the agencies employ structuralism as a strong presumption, and thus approve the occasional consolidating merger on the right facts? Or should it serve as an ironclad rule, lending itself to no exceptions? The answer would be obvious if the antitrust mandate were clear. In practice, the SCP-era agencies considered the preservation of existing industry structure to be a discrete and important goal.

Ascribing independent value to market structure, however, fatally compromises the analysis. It introduces a need to weigh incommensurate factors. Return to the 6–5 hypothetical. On the modern question – whether the deal would create newfound market power – the answer is clear. Structure matters, but only as a proxy for effects. For structuralists, however, market concentration becomes an end in itself. Now the answer is unclear. The transaction is unpalatable because it raises HHIs. Yet it is attractive because it benefits consumers and increases efficiency. There is no principled way to resolve the tradeoff. An absolutist may stay true to beliefs, say consequences be damned, and block the merger anyway. A more thoughtful enforcer might be wary given the concentration figures, but also consider other factors. The ensuing sanction decision, however, turns on a subjective value determination. Precisely that quality drove the haphazard nature of SCP-era enforcement.

Neoclassical antitrust solved that problem. The Chicago School identified a single defined objective, namely the pursuit of economic efficiency. A utilitarian calculus thus became possible, and price theory allowed economists to model welfare effects that not only informed, but determined, the intervention decision.

Second, structuralism is crude by design. Markets are complex. Many constituent elements combine to form the competitive pressures that firms experience in selling to consumers, improving their products, investing in R&D, and so forth. Industrial economists have made great strides in understanding how transactions affect this process. Diversion ratios, margins, merger-generated efficiencies, buyer sophistication, customer preferences, and dynamic responses determine whether a transaction will allow the post-merger firm sustainably to exercise newfound market power. An antitrust philosophy that reduces intervention decisions to structure alone purposively blinds itself to these all-important nuances.

The law and economics revolution marked a shift not just of analysis, but of vision. Policymakers were no longer content to universalize simplistic rules of thumb. They embarked in pursuit of greater accuracy, plumbing the depths of each relevant market, understanding its unique characteristics, and reaching the most informed possible view on the likely effects of the transaction at issue. The modern era has brought with it sophisticated econometric techniques. With the right data, the agencies' economists can estimate post-closing pressure to raise price, estimate demand, and engage in merger simulation.

In evaluating claims that the pendulum has swung too far, allowing markets to grow more concentrated through anticompetitive transactions, it is worth recalling the weighty benefits associated with the law and economics approach. The question is whether the evidence justifies reinvigorated structural policies, no change at all, or an incremental adjustment within the effects-based framework.

3.5.2 *Throwing Out the Good with the Bad: Did the Move to Effects Succumb to the Law of Unintended Consequences?*

Every antitrust intervention risks misadventure. An effects case requires showing inferior market outcomes relative to the but-for world. As the counterfactual is never observable, this approach involves a modeling exercise. It might be an implicit calculus. Naked horizontal restraints typically carry harmful effects, and neither the agencies nor courts waste effort quantifying the harm before prohibiting them. More complex investigations, however, may require data-intensive econometrics in order to estimate model parameters that allow a projection of price and output. The overarching effort – from the simplest restraint to the most complex monopolization case – involves the art of prediction.

That quality defines the modern approach to antitrust. Effects-based analysis gets into the mechanics of competition in order to understand the future (or, in retrospective matters, a hypothetical past). Paradoxically, this pursuit of precision carries with it an inescapable element of risk. Every enforcement decision, however assiduous the investigation or talented the staff, rests on incomplete knowledge. The absence of perfect information guarantees mistakes.

The shift in enforcement in 1981 set antitrust away from structuralism and toward effects. As the agencies strive to identify the subset of consolidating mergers that will not harm competition, they inadvertently bless some transactions that do. That is the price of discarding a rule in favor of a standard. Errors arise in both directions, and any movement along the spectrum introduces fewer of one kind of mistake and more of another. The tradeoff is inevitable. An adjustment is worthwhile if the frequency and significance of the costs eliminated outweigh the new ones created. Contemporary merger review relieves the harm of overbroad prohibition. Enforcers never knowingly allow a harmful transaction, of course. They endeavor to get it right.

The point for today's reform debate is that the agencies cannot always get it right. They can make the "correct" decision – correct in that it reflects the best determination possible based upon the universe of knowable evidence – and yet get it horribly wrong. Available win/loss data may understate the proximity of competition between the parties. Buyers may be less sophisticated than anticipated, and thus accept price increases rather than discipline the post-merger firm by moving supply around. But for the acquisition, the parties may have become closer competitors. Subsequent events may not bear out the reviewing agency's expectations of imminent entry, and so on.

This point matters because of a growing chorus that the US economy has suffered a systematic loss of competition over the past four decades.[129] That period, of course, corresponds with the law and economics revolution and promotion of competitive effects over structuralism. Critics blame the agencies and courts for having succumbed to Chicago School ideology, approving consolidating mergers based on pseudoscientific methodologies that find clever ways to justify the indefensible.[130] Reformists may see it as backward to weigh purity of theory and administration over long-term results. They might concede that structuralism forces the courts and agencies to grapple with incommensurate values. And their approach would see the government prohibit some transactions that would have proven harmless. For structuralists, however, the benefit of their policies lies in holding the line, ensuring that one transaction after the next does not lead to harmful consolidation over years and decades – the very phenomena that they purport to observe today.

That raises the question – has the effects approach let harmful deals slip through the net? That is an hypothesis worth taking seriously. For all their many flaws, the structural antitrust policies of the 1950s and 1960s offered a benefit. By prohibiting consolidating mergers of nearly any stripe, the agencies prevented accretions of market power.

To be sure, that grand interdiction caught up a great many innocuous and procompetitive transactions. The normative question turns, in part, on the social value of allowing those deals to close. Although some reformists attach little or no value to such transactions, the weight of evidence supports that merger and acquisition activity is a source of social value.[131] Further, productivities are most likely in horizontal combinations, which involve duplicative assets and thus allow optimization of a kind less frequently available in conglomerate or even in vertical transactions. The remainder of the normative calculus reflects the social costs inflicted by anticompetitive mergers permitted to close.

We know that there were, and will always be, mistakes. But how many, and how serious have they been? Alas, this is an exceptionally difficult question to answer. Rigorous evidence of a strong cross-industry causal relationship between deltas in concentration and price effects would help to answer it. Of course, no such reliable evidence exists. Antitrust economists have retreated from efforts to measure general relationships across industries toward narrower intra-industry studies. The resulting methodology is more defensible, and the observed associations are more reliable. Alas, they are also less generalizable. This raises a challenge for diagnosing the state of competition by looking at concentration trends across the economy.

---

[129] See Chapter 4.
[130] See Chapter 5.
[131] See Chapter 2.

Still, in order to gauge whether the post-1980 agencies have presided over industries in which competition is in decline, one could study HHI movements in relevant markets. That approach, however, would be extraordinarily burdensome. There is no freestanding list of antitrust markets, the boundaries of which regularly fluctuate and require detailed economic analysis to define. Suppose that the agencies were nevertheless given the resources and time necessary to engage in this exercise over many thousands of markets across the country. What might the results show? With our current knowledge about concentration and price, one could draw tentative inferences about the state of competition as a broad matter, knowing that correlations in some markets would mask some false associations. But not even this effort is possible. Only national-industry-level data are available. Such statistics yield few reliable insights about the state of competition.[132]

These limitations mean that industry-level evidence is merely directionally helpful. In order to determine whether the government has approved harmful transactions, the only rigorous evidence available takes the form of transaction-specific reviews. To a degree, this is industrial economics gone full circle because case studies were a hallmark of the pre-SCP literature. It is precarious to extrapolate principles of broad application from individual retrospectives. Nevertheless, merger retrospectives are valuable for a purpose going beyond the discrete question whether the Justice Department or Commission got it wrong in a particular transaction. They can shed light on a critical issue. If the agencies have systematically erred, they have likely done so at the margin, tending to terminate investigations in close cases when they should have sued. Retrospectives focused on such cases may reveal valuable evidence whether the agencies could profitably ratchet up their level of scrutiny in critical investigations.

Almost inevitably, the agencies will permit some anticompetitive mergers. That is the unavoidable cost of trying to reach the correct result in each investigation. Retrospective studies bear out this expectation. This evidence is not an indictment, of course, because some erroneous determinations are inevitable at the margin. The question is whether the cited studies, construed in light of the industry-level consolidation and rising profits explored in Chapter 4, suggest that antitrust enforcers ought to employ tougher standards in close merger reviews.

3.5.3 *The Agencies Have Cleared Harmful Transactions*

Merger retrospectives have a strong history both from within and outside the agencies. The FTC launched its modern hospital-merger program after a Section 6(b) industry study that focused on consummated mergers. The effort identified actual anticompetitive effects, and led the Commission to bring an after-the-fact

---

[132] *See* Chapter 4; *see also* Carl Shapiro, *Antitrust in a Time of Populism*, 61 INT'L J. INDUS. ORG. 714 (2018) ("The real question is whether those modest increases in concentration have been accompanied by a decline in competition, leading to higher prices or other consumer harms. One cannot answer that question just by looking at measures of concentration, no matter how good the data.").

challenge to Evanston's acquisition of Highland Park Hospital in the suburbs of Chicago.[133] That particular undertaking was easy in the sense that it was not the agencies, but the courts, that had impeded antitrust enforcement in the healthcare-provider space. Indeed, the government lost seven back-to-back hospital merger cases in the 1990s and early 2000s.

The exercise grows uncomfortable when the agencies revisit mergers that they themselves cleared. The FTC has undertaken valuable studies of the efficacy of its merger remedies, most recently in 2017.[134] That effort did not entail econometrics, and thus did not shed light on the existence or absence of price effects, but instead reflected a qualitative inquiry. Outside of remedies, however, the Commission and Antitrust Division have not systematically evaluated and published which, if any, of their past approvals in marginal investigations were mistaken. A partial exception lies in the FTC's Bureau of Economics, which has long facilitated research by its economists.[135] That shortcoming is, in part, a function of resources.[136] Some observers posit that it may also reflect an institutional resistance to exposing uncomfortable truths. Either way, this is something that the agencies ought to tackle with urgency and that Congress ought to facilitate with funding.

Hence, economists outside of the agencies have undertaken the bulk of published retrospective analysis of approved transactions. Lacking the compulsory process available to the FTC, they tend to focus on industries for which there is good publicly available pricing data. Airlines, banking, oil, and hospitals are the key examples. Contrary to what one might expect, it is not always easy to determine whether a merger created newfound market power.[137] Economists need to construct the but-for world – that is, control for all changes in the market not tied to the merger – and compare outcomes there to those observed in the post-closing data. The ensuing results are often debatable, and it is not always clear whether a certain transaction led to price increases or not.

It is clear, however, that some horizontal transactions produce anticompetitive effects.[138] The question is whether the federal antitrust agencies have successfully

---

[133] *In re* Evanston Nw. Healthcare Corp., FTC Dkt. No. 9315, Opinion of the Commission, Aug. 6, 2007.
[134] THE FTC'S MERGER REMEDIES 2006–2012, A REPORT OF THE BUREAUS OF COMPETITION AND ECONOMICS (Jan. 2017), https://www.ftc.gov/system/files/documents/reports/ftcs-merger-remedies-2006-2012-report-bureaus-competition-economics/p143100_ftc_merger_remedies_2006-2012.pdf.
[135] For helpful merger retrospectives undertaken by FTC economists, *see, e.g.*, Joseph Farrell et al., *Economics at the FTC: Retrospective Merger Analysis with a Focus on Hospitals* (2009), https://www.ftc.gov/sites/default/files/documents/reports/economics-ftc-retrospective-merger-analysis-focus-hospitals/farrelletal_rio2009.pdf.
[136] *See, e.g.*, Rebecca Kelly Slaughter, *Merger Retrospective Lessons from Mr. Rogers*, Remarks at Hearings on Competition and Consumer Protection in the 21st Century: Merger Retrospectives, Apr. 12, 2019.
[137] *See* Gregory J. Werden, *Inconvenient Truths on Merger Retrospective Studies*, 3 J. ANTITRUST ENFORCEMENT 287, 288 (2015) (critiquing econometric work showing merger-specific price increases).
[138] *See, e.g.*, Bruce A. Blonigen & Justin R. Pierce, *Evidence for the Effects of Mergers on Market Power and Efficiency*, Nat'l Bureau of Econ. Research, Working Paper No. 22750 (2016), https://www.nber.org/papers/w22750.pdf.

blocked all such mergers, while allowing others to proceed. What emerges from the literature on retrospectives, however, is that the agencies have indeed allowed some harmful transactions.

Noting that most merger retrospectives have focused on marginal clearance decisions – often controversial ones – a 2008 literature review by Hunter observed "perhaps the expected result" that a majority of studies found prices increases, while a "significant minority of studies have found no price effects."[139] In 2010, Ashenfelter and Hosken identified five retail transactions between 1997 and 1999 that they determined to have been the most problematic of approved mergers from the perspective of the agencies.[140] Using retail scanner data, they conducted econometric analysis to determine their impact on pricing. They found that four of the five mergers had anticompetitive effects, with price increases varying between 3 and 7 percent. In 2013, an FTC economist and two academics studied a 2006 transaction that combined two of the country's largest appliance manufacturers.[141] The merger likely hovered on the edge of permissibility. The economists found that the transaction led prices for dishwashers and clothes dryers to increase, with no price effects for refrigerators or clothes washers.

More generally, retrospective merger reviews have found price effects in the airline industry.[142] The same is true for banking,[143] health care,[144] and

[139] Graeme Hunter et al., *Merger Retrospective Studies: A Review*, 23 ANTITRUST 34, 34 (2008).
[140] Orley Ashenfelter & Daniel Hosken, *The Effect of Mergers on Consumer Prices: Evidence from Five Mergers on the Enforcement Margin*, 53 J.L. & ECON. 417 (2010).
[141] Orley C. Ashenfelter et al., *The Price Effects of a Large Merger of Manufacturers: A Case Study of Maytag-Whirlpool*, 5 AM. ECON. J.: ECON. POL'Y 239 (2013).
[142] John Kwoka & Evgenia Shumilkina, *The Price Effect of Eliminating Potential Competition: Evidence from an Airline Merger*, 58 J. INDUS. ECON. 767, 769 (2010); Craig T. Peters, *Evaluating the Performance of Merger Simulation: Evidence from the U.S. Airline Industry*, 49 J.L. & ECON. 627, 647 (2006); E. Han Kim & Vijay Singal, *Mergers and Market Power: Evidence from the Airline Industry*, 83 AM. ECON. REV. 549, 550 (1993); Gregory Werden et al., *The Effects of Mergers on Economic Performance; Two Case Studies from the Airline Industry*, 12 MANAGERIAL & DECISION ECON. 341 (1991); Severin Borenstein, *Airline Mergers, Airport Dominance, and Market Power*, 80 AM. ECON. REV. 400 (1990). *But see* Dennis W. Carlton et al., *Are Legacy Airline Mergers Pro- or Anti-Competitive? Evidence from Recent U.S. Airline Mergers* (working paper, Oct. 25, 2016), https://papers.ssrn.com/sol3/papers.cfm?abstract_id=2851954 (finding improved post-merger performance)).
[143] Dario Focarelli & Fabio Panetta, *Are Mergers Beneficial to Consumers? Evidence from the Market for Bank Deposits*, 93 AM. ECON. REV. 1152 (2003); Paola Sapienza, *The Effects of Banking Mergers on Loan Contracts*, 57 J. FIN. 329 (2002); Robin A. Prager and Timothy H. Hannan, *Do Substantial Horizontal Mergers Generate Significant Price Effects? Evidence from the Banking Industry*, 46 J. INDUS. ECON. 433, 450 (1998).
[144] Jose R. Guardado et al., *The Price Effects of a Large Merger of Health Insurers: A Case Study of UnitedHealth-Sierra*, 16 HEALTH MGMT. POL'Y & INNOVATION 1, 2 (2013); Deborah Haas-Wilson & Christopher Garmon, *Hospital Mergers and Competitive Effects: Two Retrospective Analysis*, 18 J. ECON. BUS. 17, 30 (2011); Leemore Dafny, *Estimation and Identification of Merger Effects: An Application to Hospital Mergers*, 52 J.L. & ECON. 523, 544 (2009); Steven Tenn, *The Price Effects of Hospital Mergers: A Case Study of the Sutter-Summit Transaction*, 18 INT'L J. ECON. BUS. 65, 79 (2011); Ranjani A. Krishnan & Hema Krishnan, *Effects of Hospital Mergers and Acquisitions on Prices*, 56 J. BUS. RES. 647, 655 (2003); Michael Vita & Seth Sacher, *The Competitive Effects of Not-For-Profit Hospital Mergers: A Case Study*, 49 J. INDUS. ECON. 63 (2001).

petroleum.[145] Further, an influential meta-analysis of prior retrospectives by Kwoka in 2014 found harmful price effects, notwithstanding the imposition of divestitures and other remedies by the FTC and DOJ.[146]

The finding in any one study may, or may not, be correct. As noted, even with good data, merger retrospectives pose significant challenges. Kwoka's work itself was the object of a scathing critique by two leading FTC economists in 2018.[147] In short, one ought not to accept dire claims of antitrust failure uncritically. Nevertheless, the merger retrospectives conducted to date tell us something important as we grapple with antitrust reform. The number of studies, breadth of industries touched, and consistency of results point to a reality. The move from structuralism to competitive effects brought with it merger policies that have, if only in marginal cases, allowed some harmful consolidations to pass.[148]

This observation does *not* prove, however, that antitrust merger review is miscalibrated. The fact of error is inevitable. Its significance depends on the cost of those mistakes relative to those associated with other candidate policies. The answer, as ever, lies at the margin. If tightening the screws meant blocking a disproportionate number of price-reducing or innovation-enhancing transactions, for example, then the agencies would be right not to clamp down further in close cases. That is a difficult question. We can be more confident about judging the merits of large swings in policy. It would clearly be harmful to revert to the SCP era, for example, which inhibited efficient combinations and surely denied consumers lower pricing.[149] Individual mergers sometimes fail to achieve their sought productivities, but overall M&A activity carries social value.[150] Importantly, efficiencies are most likely in horizontal transactions in markets that are not highly concentrated – the very ones implicated by a proposal to make antitrust merger review more strict.

Proper reform is evidence-based and incremental. Evidence that the agencies have let anticompetitive mergers go has limitations. Largely taking the form of case

---

[145] Justine Hastings & Richard Gilbert, *Market Power, Vertical Integration and the Wholesale Price of Gasoline*, 53 J. INDUS. ECON. 469 (2005); Justine Hastings, *Vertical Relationships and Competition in Retail Gasoline Markets: Empirical Evidence from Contract Changes in Southern California*, 94 AM. ECON. REV. 317 (2004); Christopher Taylor & Daniel Hosken, *The Economic Effects of the Marathon-Ashland Joint Venture: The Importance of Industry Supply Shocks and Vertical Market Structure*, 55 J. INDUS. ECON. 419 (2007).

[146] JOHN KWOKA, MERGERS, MERGER CONTROL, AND REMEDIES: A RETROSPECTIVE ANALYSIS OF U.S. POLICY (2014); *see also* John Kwoka, Jr., *Does Merger Control Work? A Retrospective on U.S. Enforcement Actions and Merger Outcomes*, 78 ANTITRUST L.J. 619 (2012).

[147] *See* Michael Vita & F. David Osinski, *John Kwoka's Mergers, Merger Control, and Remedies: A Critical Review*, 82 ANTITRUST L.J. 361 (2018); *cf.* John E. Kwoka, Jr., Mergers, Merger Control, and Remedies: A Response to the FTC Critique (Apr. 6, 2017).

[148] *See, e.g.*, Orley Ashenfelter et al., *Did Robert Bork Understate the Competitive Impact of Mergers? Evidence from Consummated Mergers*, 57 J.L. & ECON. 67 (2014).

[149] *See, e.g.*, Ashenfelter, *supra* note 148, at 96 ("Given the aggressiveness of horizontal merger policy when Bork was writing *The Antitrust Paradox*, it is quite probable that the price effect of the marginal merger was then negative.").

[150] *See* Chapter 2.

studies, individual retrospectives do not readily surrender insights of universal application. This was the very limitation that brought industrial organization toward inter-industry, cross-sectional work in the first place, where economists ultimately hit a wall. Still, evidence of harmful price effects matters. In a real way, it points to Type II errors that a modest increment in scrutiny could prevent. Given the economic sophistication of modern merger review, it is likely that mistakes cluster around the margin. That is where gains are to be had. The agencies can work to limit losses associated with heightened scrutiny at the enforcement frontier by delving into the proffered benefits associated with a significant consolidation and requiring convincing substantiation by the parties of claimed efficiencies.

By contrast, evidence of an economy-wide loss of competitive pressure is far more ambiguous. That is the object of the next chapter. Given the lack of evidence that existing antitrust laws are too hostile at the margin, however, the broader perspective is one that supports a strengthening of enforcement. Perhaps the most important vehicle for realizing that change lies in revisiting how the courts and agencies think about error. That is the weighty topic addressed in Chapter 7.

PART II

The Case for Change

4

Warning Signs in the Economy

Has Competition Declined?

4.1 INTRODUCTION

Antitrust is resurgent. Some progressives want to give agencies bold new powers to block mergers. Investigating technology companies has become bipartisan sport. Meanwhile, op-eds, social-media posts, and articles paint ever-more-extreme visions of a corporate takeover of America. Their prescriptions range from overhauling the antitrust laws to regulating large digital platforms. Antitrust enforcers do not fare well in this account. They stand variously accused of being asleep at the wheel or enslaved to laissez faire dogma.

The question whether competition has declined is truly foundational. Yet, too often, the conversation has been frenzied, hyperbolic, and unsubstantiated. Yes, the FTC has held hearings. And some leading commentators have weighed in on the state of competition in the US economy and the associated role of antitrust. The larger maelstrom, however, threatens to drown out such thoughtful contributions. It is important to consider whether the din obscures valid concerns.

Hence, what to make of the fact that one commentator after another heralds the death of US competition? Is it empty populistic rhetoric or something worth taking seriously? Does a kernel of truth underlie claims of an American monopoly problem? Has a failure to pursue antitrust with vigor actually led to a dearth of competition? This chapter addresses those questions.

4.2 EVIDENCE OF DECLINING COMPETITION

One fact is clear – concentration in many US industries has increased. Today, fewer firms account for more sales across the economy than in the past. The effect in certain sectors has been pronounced. What is less clear is the effect on *competition*. For those who wish to see antitrust curb accumulations of economic power, of course, concentration trends at the industry level end the analysis. But if we are concerned about preserving competitive pressure in relevant product (or service) markets, then the picture is far more opaque.[1]

Nevertheless, progressive reformists are reacting to a real phenomenon and asking antitrust-policy questions that need to be taken seriously.

4.2.1 Rising Consolidation in Specific US Industries

Even a casual observation of US industries reveals consolidation. This phenomenon explains why claims of rising corporate power resonate.[2] The pages that follow address concentration, including the role of mergers, in the airline, beer, mobile telephony, video programming and distribution, healthcare insurance, vision, home compliances, food, and credit-card industries. They conclude with some brief observations about Silicon Valley. The recurring theme is one of compression, as firms grow larger within their industries, arguably leaving consumers with fewer choices.

Of the US legacy airlines, only three remain. This result followed a wave of M&A-driven consolidation. Delta purchased Northwest in 2008, United bought Continental in 2010, and American merged with US Airways in 2013. The companies won antitrust approval in each of those transactions, albeit with conditions in the last two.[3] Today, along with low-cost carrier Southwest, the legacy three of American, United, and Delta account for almost three-quarters of US industry sales.[4] Profits are up (pre-Covid), and on some accounts service is down.[5]

The beer industry has seen dramatic consolidation. Anheuser-Busch InBev (ABI), which may brew as many as one-quarter of all beers consumed worldwide, grew through acquisitions of Interbrew in 2003, Anheuser-Busch in 2008, and SABMiller

---

[1] Two factors obscure analysis. First, industries are not antitrust markets. Concentration may rise in the former and drop in the latter, vice versa, or change in one but not in the other. Second, as per Chapter 3, economists dispute the degree to which structural changes even in a relevant market affect competition.

[2] As we shall see, however, the neoclassical antitrust question is far more nuanced – and much reviled by the neo-Brandeisian movement for that reason. For economists studying relevant antitrust markets, *industry*- (as opposed to market-) level changes in concentration reveal little, or no, reliable information about competition.

[3] Press Release, Justice Department Requires US Airways and American Airlines to Divest Facilities at Seven Key Airports to Enhance System-wide Competition and Settle Merger Challenge, Nov. 12, 2013, https://www.justice.gov/opa/pr/justice-department-requires-us-airways-and-american-airlines-divest-facilities-seven-key; Press Release, United Airlines and Continental Airlines Transfer Assets to Southwest Airlines in Response to Department of Justice's Antitrust Concerns, Aug. 27, 2010, https://www.justice.gov/opa/pr/united-airlines-and-continental-airlines-transfer-assets-southwest-airlines-response; Statement of the Department of Justice's Antitrust Division on Its Decision to Close Its Investigation of the Merger of Delta Air Lines Inc. and Northwest Airlines Corporation, Oct. 29, 2008, https://www.justice.gov/archive/opa/pr/2008/October/08-at-963.html.

[4] *See, e.g., Europe's Airline Industry Is Consolidating,* THE ECONOMIST, Apr. 27, 2019 (largest five US carriers account for roughly 70 percent of sales).

[5] *See, e.g., A Lack of Competition Explains the Flaws in American Aviation,* THE ECONOMIST, Apr. 22, 2017.

in 2016.[6] In challenging ABI's SABMiller acquisition and requiring divestiture of the target's entire US business (including MillerCoors), the DOJ observed that the two companies accounted for 72 percent of US beer sales.[7] Today, ABI and MillerCoors still account for a majority of beer sold in the United States, while Constellation Brands, Heineken, Pabst Brewing, Carlsberg, and Diageo play a smaller role. On the other hand, the industry has witnessed a surge in craft brewing as myriad small firms enter.

Mobile telephony has witnessed a similar trend. T-Mobile and Sprint recently overcame a determined antitrust effort by several states to block the transaction by closing in April 2020.[8] The result was a three-firm oligopoly. Verizon, AT&T, and T-Mobile/Sprint now compete in the industry, though a DOJ remedy seeks to create a fourth competitor in Dish.[9]

Consolidation in mobile telephony, however, long preceded that $26 billion merger. In 2014, AT&T purchased Leap Wireless for $1.2 billion. That acquisition followed T-Mobile's $1.5 billion acquisition of rival wireless carrier, MetroPCS, in 2013 and Sprint's purchase of US Cellular's spectrum and Midwest customers for $480 million in 2012. The DOJ was not a passive observer, however, during this period. In 2011, it blocked AT&T's $49 billion attempted acquisition of T-Mobile, which later emerged as a disruptive competitive force in the industry.[10]

The video-content programming and distribution industry is undergoing momentous change. Over-the-top streaming has changed how people consume content, as subscription video-on-demand services like Netflix, Disney+, and Hulu disrupt traditional cable and satellite companies (known as multichannel video programming distributors). A wave of mega mergers has resulted. In 2018, AT&T successfully overcame a DOJ antitrust challenge to acquire Time Warner for $85 billion.[11] The same year, Disney overcame a rival bid from Comcast to buy 21st Century Fox for $71.3 billion. In response, Comcast acquired Sky for $39 billion later the same year. Those transactions followed 2009's $30 billion merger between Comcast and NBC Universal.

Healthcare insurance is another example, where five national insurers serve the industry: Anthem, UnitedHealth, Cigna, Aetna, and Humana. This space saw the Justice Department intervene twice in 2016 to block megamergers. In 2017, the DC Circuit upheld a permanent injunction enjoining Anthem's $54 billion acquisition of Cigna, a deal that would have fused the country's second- and third-largest

---

[6] See, e.g., Brewers at AB InBev Need to Rethink Its Strategy, THE ECONOMIST, May 11, 2019.
[7] United States v. Anheuser-Busch InBEV SA/NV, No. 1:16-cv-1483, Compl., ¶¶ 3–4 (D.D.C. July 20, 2016).
[8] New York v. Deutsche Telecom, 439 F. Supp. 3d 179 (S.D.N.Y. 2020).
[9] Press Release, Justice Department Welcomes Decision in New York v. Deutsche Telecom, the T-Mobile/Sprint Merger, Feb. 11, 2020, https://www.justice.gov/opa/pr/justice-department-welcomes-decision-new-york-v-deutsche-telecom-t-mobilesprint-merger.
[10] United States v. AT&T Inc., No. 1:11-cv-1560, Compl. (D.D.C. Aug. 31, 2011).
[11] United States v. AT&T Inc., 916 F.3d 1029 (D.C. Cir. 2019).

national health insurers.[12] The Division also prevailed in blocking Aetna's effort to buy Humana for $37 billion, focusing in particular on the combination's likely effect in private Medicare health-insurance plans in hundreds of relevant markets across the United States.[13] The industry responded by vertically integrating further. In 2019, Aetna and CVS earned judicial approval to close their $69 billion merger after an unusually searching Tunney Act review by a federal judge.[14] And, in late 2018, Cigna closed its $67 billion merger with Express Scripts, having similarly won antitrust approval.[15]

The vision industry has also consolidated. Essilor and Luxottica were the world's largest lens and frame manufacturers, respectively. Essilor made almost half of all prescription lenses, while Luxottica manufactured roughly a quarter of all glass frames, being particularly prominent in luxury frames. Their $49 billion announced merger in 2017 was a lightning rod of controversy, spurring calls for antitrust intervention.[16] In announcing their *Better Deal: Cracking Down on Corporate Monopolies* in 2017, congressional Democrats specifically identified the merger as being emblematic of the problem of rising concentration.[17] In 2018, however, the FTC cleared the deal without conditions after conducting an exhaustive, year-long investigation.[18] The transaction was largely complementary, and did not raise concerns of vertical foreclosure. The example is one of how many, however, that highlights the distinction between preserving competitive market pressures (today's approach) and fostering unconcentrated industry structures (the neo-Brandeisian view).

The home-compliance industry features a half-dozen large suppliers. Whirlpool, Haier, Electrolux, Samsung, LG, Bosch, and Siemens compete throughout various segments. The degree of US concentration led the Justice Department to challenge a merger between the second- and third-largest players a few years ago. Specifically, in 2015, it blocked Electrolux's $3.3 billion purchase of GE's appliance unit.[19] In doing so, the Division observed that the two parties and Whirlpool sell more than 90 percent of major cooking appliances sold in the contract channel.[20] The

---

[12] United States v. Anthem, Inc., 855 F.3d 345 (D.C. Cir. 2017).
[13] United States v. Aetna Inc., 240 F. Supp. 3d. 1 (D.D.C. 2017).
[14] United States v. CVS Health Corp., Civ. No. 18–2340, Dkt. 7 (D.D.C. Sept. 4, 2019).
[15] Dep't of Justice, Statement of the Department of Justice Antitrust Division on the Closing of Its Investigation of the Cigna-Express Scripts Merger, Sept. 17, 2018.
[16] *See, e.g.*, David Balto, *Get Ready to Pay When One Company Dominates the Eyeglass Market*, THE HILL, Nov. 28, 2017; Sarah Gordon, *EssilorLuxottica Merger Blindsides Customers*, FIN'L TIMES, Jan. 24, 2017; *see also* Sam Knight, *The Spectacular Power of Big Lens*, THE GUARDIAN, May 10, 2018.
[17] A Better Deal: Cracking Down on Corporate Monopolies p. 4, https://www.democrats.senate.gov/imo/media/doc/2017/07/A-Better-Deal-on-Competition-and-Costs-1.pdf.
[18] Statement of the Fed. Trade Comm'n concerning the Proposed Acquisition of Luxottica Group S.p.A. by Essilor International (Compagnie Generale d'Optique) S.A., FTC File No. 171–0060, Mar. 1, 2018.
[19] United States v. AB Electrolux, No. 1:15-cv-1039, Compl. (D.D.C. July 1, 2015).
[20] *Id.* ¶ 2.

next year, Haier bought GE's appliance unit instead. Today, Whirlpool, Haier, and Samsung account for most washer and dryer sales.

Mergers have increased consolidation in home compliances, and antitrust has not always stood in the way. A notable example occurred in 2006, when the Department of Justice allowed Whirlpool to buy Maytag for $1.7 billion.[21] The government's decision to approve the merger provoked much criticism, not least because it gave Whirlpool a ~ 70 percent share of US washer and dryers sales.[22]

A few companies have ascended to the top of the food industry. Agrochemicals and seeds are vital agricultural inputs, and has grown consolidated. As recently as 2015, there was a "Big Seven" of BASF, Bayer, Dow Chemical, DuPont, Monsanto, Syngenta, and ChemChina, which sold various pesticides and seed treatments. Over the following three years, mergers created the Big Four.

In 2017, ChemChina bought Syngenta for $43 billion. The FTC approved the transaction, subject to divestitures meant to protect competition in three US pesticide markets.[23] Despite the size of the transaction, the parties did not compete in seed markets, making the horizontal analysis relatively straightforward under today's governing framework.

In 2018, Bayer completed its $66 billion acquisition of Monsanto. The firms were leading suppliers of seeds and chemicals to farmers, leading the DOJ to require the largest divestiture in its history in order to bless the deal.[24] In finding likely harm to competition in seventeen product markets across various herbicides, seed treatments, genetically modified seeds, and vegetable seeds, the Division alleged that the two companies had market shares ranging from 43 percent to 100 percent.[25]

2018 also saw the $130 billion Dow Chemical/DuPont merger, which supplanted BASF as the world's largest chemical company (before splitting into three separate firms later that year). In a 2017 complaint that preceded a divestiture remedy, the DOJ alleged that those firms were "two of only a handful of chemical companies that manufacture certain types of crop protection chemicals."[26] Indeed, Dow Chemical and DuPont controlled nearly three-quarters of chewing-pest insecticides, over 40 percent of broadleaf herbicides for winter wheat crops, and were the only two US producers of acid copolymers and ionomers.[27]

---

[21] Department of Justice Antitrust Division Statement on the Closing of its Investigation of Whirlpool's Acquisition of Maytag, Mar. 29, 2006, https://www.justice.gov/archive/atr/public/press_releases/2006/215326.htm.

[22] *See, e.g.*, Jonathan B. Baker & Carl Shapiro, *Reinvigorating Horizontal Merger Enforcement, in* How the Chicago School Overshot the Mark 248–50 (Robert Pitofsky ed., 2008).

[23] Fed. Trade Comm'n, Press Release, FTC Requires China National Chemical Corporation and Syngenta AG to Divest U.S. Assets as a Condition of Merger, Apr. 4, 2017.

[24] U.S. Dep't of Justice, Press Release, Justice Department Secures Largest Negotiated Merger Divestiture Ever to Preserve Competition Threatened by Bayer's Acquisition of Monsanto, May 29, 2018.

[25] United States v. Bayer AG, No. 1:18-cv-1241, Compl. (D.D.C. May 29, 2018).

[26] United States v. Dow Chem. Co., No. 1:17-cv-1176, (D.D.C. June 15, 2017).

[27] *Id.* ¶¶ 5, 33, 37, 57, 60.

The food industry has also consolidated further downstream. Meat-packing – that is, the slaughtering of animals and ensuing processing and packaging of meat – has become more concentrated over time. Today, JBS SA, Tyson, Cargill, and Smithfield account for a majority of US meat processing. Studies indicate that the four-firm concentration ratio in livestock slaughter doubled or more between 1980 and 2015.[28] This trend has been underway for some time. For example, a 2000 US Department of Agriculture study found that "four firms handle nearly 80 percent of all steer and heifer slaughter; just two decades ago, concentration was less than half as high."[29] Food distribution at the national level has grown more concentrated, too. The FTC blocked Sysco's $8.2 billion attempted acquisition of US Foods in 2015, for example, alleging that the two parties had a 75 percent market share of broadline foodservice distribution, with the largest remaining competitor's having only 11 percent of the market.[30] Foodservice distribution at the local and regional level, however, is more far more fragmented.

These are by no means the only concentrated industries. Visa, MasterCard, and American Express, for example, process over 90 percent of all credit-card transactions. Large digital platforms attract much attention.

Today, Google accounts for over 90 percent of US internet search, with Microsoft's Bing accounting for a few percent. Hence, companies wishing to advertise online to capitalize on user searches are immediately attracted to Google's AdWords and Microsoft Advertising (formerly Bing Ads). Mobile operating-systems are synonymous with Apple's iOS and Google's Android. Facebook has the most users of any social-networking site. Google has more data than other companies, arguably making it uniquely attractive to prospective advertisers. Amazon, of course, has a leading position in online retail sales.

None of this means that a given firm has monopoly power or that consolidation has produced less competitive outcomes in the form of unilateral or coordinated effects or otherwise. Indeed, as discussed in Chapter 3, the relationship between market concentration and performance is complex. But the anecdotal observations discussed in this section have a salience that explains why claims of an economy-wide consolidation trend resonate with many people, especially on the left. We now turn to formal studies.

---

[28] See, e.g., James MacDonald, *Consolidation and Competition in Agribusiness*, p. 3, Feb. 23, 2018, https://www.usda.gov/oce/forum/2018/speeches/James_MacDonald.pdf; see also Tina L. Saitone & Richard J. Sexton, *Concentration and Consolidation in the U.S. Food Supply Chain: The Latest Evidence and Implications for Consumers, Farmers, and Policymakers*, FED. RESERVE BANK OF KANSAS CITY ECON. REV. 25, 33 (2017) (observing a sum of market shares of the four largest firms in the industry in 2012 of 85 for steer and heifer slaughter, 56 in cow and bull slaughter, 64 in hog slaughter, and 62 in sheep and lamb slaughter).

[29] James M. MacDonald et al., *Consolidation in U.S. Meatpacking*, U.S. Dep't of Agriculture, Agricultural Econ. Report No. 785 (2000), https://www.ers.usda.gov/webdocs/publications/41108/18011_aer785_1_.pdf?v=41061.

[30] In re Sysco Corp., FTC Dkt. No. 9364, Compl., Feb. 19, 2015.

4.2.2 Cross-Industry Evidence of Growing Concentration Emerges

Statistical analysis of US industrial concentration tells a comparable story. Trends of rising consolidation emerge.

A 2019 study by Grullon et al. concluded that over 75 percent of US industries have become more concentrated over the past two decades.[31] Using public-firm data, the authors measured changes in HHI in industries defined by three-digit NAICS codes (i.e., by subsector) between 1997 and 2014. Aggregating their calculated HHIs across industries to calculate a value-weighted HHI, the researchers observed that concentration, after reaching a low point in 1997, rose steadily – and by almost 70 percent – through 2014.[32]

Grullon et al. next explored whether those averages hid intense and localized concentration increases or instead reflected widespread concentration changes. The authors calculated the percentage by which HHI had changed between 1997 and 2014 in each three-digit NAICS industry for public firms.[33] They discovered that the median and mean increases in HHI were 41 percent and 90 percent, respectively, and that HHIs had risen in 80 percent of industries.[34] They illustrated their findings in the following table, which shows the distribution of HHI changes:

The Grullon study, though illuminative, inaccurately characterized its findings as "point[ing] to an increase in product market concentration."[35] Their data show no such thing, but merely reflect changes in concentration at the three-digit NAICS industrial code level. As discussed below, that is a critical difference.

In 2016, the Council of Economic Advisers observed that competition may be declining in the US economy.[36] The Council used an odd concentration measure – one capturing the top fifty firms' share of revenue in an industry, rather than the top four or eight ratio that economists usually employ.[37] Using its chosen index, the Council noted that numerous industries had grown more concentrated between 1997 and 2002, as per its Table 4.1 below. Such "increasing industry concentration" was, in the Council's view, "broadly suggestive of a decline in competition."[38]

---

[31] Gustavo Grullon et al., *Are U.S. Industries Becoming More Concentrated*, 23 REV. FIN. 697 (2019).
[32] See Gustavo Grullon et al., *Are U.S. Industries Becoming More Concentrated?*, draft at 6–7, 43 http://dx.doi.org/10.2139/ssrn.2612047.
[33] The authors found that their results were robust even when they considered private firms' share of sales. *Id.* at 9.
[34] *Id.*
[35] *Id.* at 11; see also *id.* at 5, 7–8, 29.
[36] Council of Economic Advisers Issue Brief, *Benefits of Competition and Indicators of Market Power*, Apr. 2016, at 4, https://obamawhitehouse.archives.gov/sites/default/files/page/files/20160414_cea_competition_issue_brief.pdf.
[37] The difference is important. There are many relevant antitrust markets that are both competitive and yet have far less than fifty competitors.
[38] *Id.* at 4.

TABLE 4.1 *Change in market concentration by sector, 1997–2012*

Industry	Revenue Earned by 50 Largest Firms, 2012 (Billions $)	Revenue Share Earned by 50 Largest Firms, 2012	Percentage Point Change in Revenue Share Earned by 50 Largest Firms, 1997–2012
Transportation and Warehousing	307.9	42.1	11.4
Retail Trade	1,555.8	36.9	11.2
Finance and Insurance	1,762.7	48.5	9.9
Wholesale Trade	2,183.1	27.6	7.3
Real Estate Rental and Leasing	121.6	24.9	5.4
Utilities	367.7	69.1	4.6
Educational Services	12.1	22.7	3.1
Professional, Scientific and Technical Services	278.2	18.8	2.6
Administrative/ Support	159.2	23.7	1.6
Accommodation and Food Services	149.8	21.2	0.1
Other Services, Non-Public Admin	46.7	10.9	−1.9
Arts, Entertainment and Recreation	39.5	19.6	−2.2
Health Care and Assistance	350.2	17.2	−1.6

Note: Concentration ratio data is displayed for all North American Industry Classification System (NAICS) sectors for which data is available from 1997 to 2012.
Source: Economic Census (1997 and 2012), Census Bureau.

Also in 2016, *The Economist* concluded that two-thirds of America's 893 industry sectors became more concentrated between 1997 and 2012.[39] In doing so, it observed that the top four firms' weighted average share of each sector rose from 26 percent to 32 percent in that period.[40]

Using employment, payroll, and profit data, a 2017 study out of NYU found that there has "been a moderate but continued increase in aggregate concentration since the mid 1990s" – though it remained lower than levels seen in the early 1980s.[41] This

[39] *The problem with profits: Big Firms in the United States Have Never Had It So Good. Time for More Competition*, THE ECONOMIST, Mar. 26, 2016.
[40] *Too Much of a Good Thing: Profits Are Too High. America Needs a Giant Dose of Competition*, THE ECONOMIST, Mar. 26, 2016.
[41] Lawrence J. White & Jasper Yang, *What Has Been Happening to Aggregate Concentration in the U.S. Economy in the 21st Century?*, Mar. 30, 2017 draft, https://papers.ssrn.com/sol3/papers.cfm?abstract_id=2953984.

observation was inconsistent with the magnitude of the concentration rise that "political and media references to large corporations might indicate."[42] A number of the study's charts are worth reproducing.

First, a time series drawn from the Census Bureau's "Census of Manufactures" revealed how much value the largest 50, 100, 150, and 200 manufacturers added to the economy.[43] After a relatively flat period between the 1970s and 1990s, aggregate concentration has grown – albeit at a modest rate. The authors warned, however, that the manufacturing sector has become less significant to the larger US economy.[44] Indeed, it represented merely 13.8 percent of private-sector GDP in 2015, as compared to 32.6 percent in 1953.[45]

Using Census Bureau data on employment and payroll from 1988 through 2014, the authors found that more firms employed over 10,000 people at the turn of the century than they had in 1988.[46] Growth in that metric between 2000 and 2014, however, was uneven and ultimately modest.

The NYU authors also reported data showing the percentages of the workforce hired by the largest 100, 500, and 1,000 companies in the United States from 1988 to 2014.[47] This metric of concentration fell from 1988 until 1995, but has since risen steadily – albeit modestly and with a dip in the 2000s – since then.

4.2.3 Interpreting Evidence of Rising Concentration

To summarize, some high-profile industries have become visibly more concentrated. This makes the phenomenon noticeable at the voter level, helping to fuel a political reawakening in antitrust. Formal studies generally indicate that concentration is rising across many – though not all – US industries. Nevertheless, the trend is more modest than many alarmist claims would suggest.

The anti-monopoly movement, of course, sees things differently. Neo-Brandeisians diagnose a serious loss of competition. And they use that conclusion to justify overhauling antitrust law, breaking up tech companies, replacing effects-based analysis with structuralism, prohibiting more mergers, and even introducing price and quality-of-service regulation. Unfortunately, many competitive assessments of the US economy lack rigor. Even sophisticated voices, like those of the Council of Economic Advisers and *The Economist*, have fallen prey to appealing, but unreliable, inferences.

Many progressive reformists take the preceding evidence as proof positive that market power is rising in the United States. In Barry Lynn's view, for example, the

---

[42] Id. at 17–18.
[43] Id. at 10–11.
[44] Id. at 11.
[45] Id.
[46] Id. at 11–12.
[47] Id. at 14.

"idea that America has a monopoly problem is now beyond dispute."[48] The Open Markets Institute with which he affiliates similarly concludes that America has a "concentration crisis" that represents "[g]rowing monopoly power[.]"[49] And that "monopoly problem" flows from the fact that "[n]early every marketplace in America is vastly more consolidated than a generation ago."[50] A 2018 Roosevelt Institute report holds that "available economic data all point to declining competition, increasing concentration, higher prices, and widening wealth and income inequality" – all of which are indicia of "failures of the current antitrust regime[.]"[51]

The examples continue, including from leading progressive thinkers. Paul Krugman finds "direct evidence" of "a decline in competition" from the fact that, "in many industries the combined market share of the top four firms ... has gone up over time."[52] Joseph Stiglitz thinks it "obvious" that the US "economy is marked in industry after industry by large concentrations of market power[.]"[53] And Professor Sagers observes that "[m]arkets are now so concentrated and ripe for abuse ... that our antitrust laws seem increasingly hopeless."[54]

These claims are overblown, and simply do not flow from the industry-level concentration figures on which they rely. It is vital to interpret data correctly. Otherwise, critics risk falsely diagnosing a problem. On the neo-Brandeisian world view, of course, consolidation at the level of national industry may be inherently problematic. But that is not the case from the perspective of competitive effects (i.e., market outcomes). Antitrust economists worry about competitive pressure, and consider changes in industry structure only to the extent that it illuminates likely effects.

The study of concentration and market power is nothing new. Today's antitrust economists have a wealth of knowledge and a deep literature on which to draw. It is no accident that the Justice Department and the Federal Trade Commission define "relevant markets" under a rigorous process before ascribing market shares and measuring changes in concentration. The agencies identify as a market only that "group of products and a geographic area that is no bigger than necessary to satisfy" the hypothetical-monopolist test.[55] That group is the smallest collection of products

---

[48] Barry C. Lynn, *America's Monopolies Are Holding Back the Economy*, THE ATLANTIC https://www.theatlantic.com/business/archive/2017/02/antimonopoly-big-business/514358/.
[49] Open Markets Institute, *America's Concentration Crisis*, https://concentrationcrisis.openmarketsinstitute.org/.
[50] Open Markets Institute, *Monopoly by the Numbers*, https://openmarketsinstitute.org/explainer/monopoly-by-the-numbers/.
[51] MARSHALL STEINBAUM & MAURICE E. STUCKE, THE EFFECTIVE COMPETITION STANDARD: A NEW STANDARD FOR ANTITRUST 55 (2018), https://rooseveltinstitute.org/wp-content/uploads/2018/09/The-Effective-Competition-Standard-FINAL.pdf.
[52] Paul Krugman, *Monopoly Capitalism Is Killing US Economy*, The IRISH TIMES, Apr. 19, 2016.
[53] Joseph E. Stiglitz, *America Has a Monopoly Problem – and It's Huge*, THE NATION, Oct. 23, 2017.
[54] Chris Sagers, *Everyone Wants to Get Tough on Antitrust Policy, but Not Really*, N.Y. TIMES DEALBOOK, Apr. 29, 2016.
[55] U.S. Dep't of Justice & Fed. Trade Comm'n, Horizontal Merger Guidelines § 1 (2010).

(or services) over which a single owner could raise price 5–10 percent over the competitive level without suffering a critical loss of sales.[56]

Such a market is often narrow, and typically far narrower than the larger national industry of which it is part.[57] Consider "retail trade" – the industry in which the Council of Economic Advisers found the second largest rate of increase in concentration between 1997 and 2012. With respect to supermarkets alone, the FTC investigated mergers in 153 *distinct relevant markets* between 1996 and 2007.[58] The "retail trade" industry is massively broad. Computing statistics based on concentration changes reveals nothing about the locus of competition. Even large deltas may have nothing to do with competition. For example, if a previously local company goes national and enters relevant markets around the country, it will simultaneously raise industrial concentration and *increase* competition.[59]

The agencies define markets rigorously in order to avoid false inferences. As explained above, there is a positive correlation between price and concentration in relevant antitrust markets, though that relationship does not always hold, is not linear, and can vary between markets.[60] There is no reliable causal relationship, however, between concentration in an area of the economy that is not a relevant market (e.g., a national industry) and competitive outcomes.

Economists know this, not least because their predecessors famously got it wrong. During the Structure-Conduct-Performance era of the 1950s and 1960s, industrial economists regressed profit against structure across industries and found weakly positive correlations.[61] Today, we understand that those studies suffered from a fatal endogeneity problem.[62] Firms that grow to achieve scale economies (or that successfully innovate), and thus become more effective competitors, will

---

[56] In the merger context, the agencies employ the hypothetical-monopolist test at prevailing market prices in order to identify binding competitive constraints at existing prices. In monopolization cases, by contrast, they define markets by asking which substitutes would make an attempted SSNIP unprofitable at competitive (i.e., non-prevailing) prices. Failing to do so in a dominant-firm case exaggerates the scope of the relevant market, and is known as the Cellophane Fallacy in light of the Supreme Court's historical failure to catch this nuance. United States v. E.I. DuPont de Nemours & Co., 251 U.S. 377 (1956).

[57] Sometimes, the agencies define the relevant market too narrowly. But that is a separate issue. *See* Chapter 9.

[58] See Daniel Hosken et al., *Do Retail Mergers Affect Competition? Evidence from Grocery Retailing* p. 2 (2012), https://www.ftc.gov/sites/default/files/documents/reports/do-retail-mergers-affect-competition%C2%A0-evidence-grocery-retailing/wp313.pdf.

[59] Indeed, even modestly misstating a relevant market can seriously distort the analysis of competitive effects. For example, expanding a relevant market to include distant substitutes overstates the degree of competition to which incumbents are actually subject. Hence, concentration at the national-industry level may be meaningless to antitrust analysis.

[60] *See* Chapter 3.

[61] A seminal work in the SCP literature was Joe S. Bain, *Relation of Profit Rate to Industry Concentration: American Manufacturing, 1936–1940*, 65 Q.J. ECON. 293 (1951).

[62] For two leading critiques, see Sam Peltzman, *The Gains and Losses from Industrial Concentration*, 20 J.L. & ECON. 229 (1977) and Harold Demsetz, *Industry Structure, Market Rivalry, and Public Policy*, 16 J.L. & ECON. 1 (1973).

simultaneously experience higher profits and lead concentration to rise.[63] But higher concentration may increase profits by facilitating coordinated or unilateral price effects. Both hypotheses are equally valid a priori. Hence, observing a correlation between profit and concentration tells you nothing about the direction of the causal relationship, if one exists at all. That problem is magnified if one uses cross-sectional data across industries, which are most unlikely to display the same economic relationship between structure and performance. Many SCP studies were indeed cross-sectional.

Traditional SCP studies had a laundry list of other deficiencies, too. First, the firm accounting profits available to researchers are heavily biased proxies for the economic profits relevant to a competition analysis. (The latter are profits relative to the opportunity cost of capital.) Second, companies typically report profit across aggregated products, obscuring potentially asymmetric competitive conditions. Product-level data are more reliable, but are not always available. Third, being static, cross-sectional studies may capture false results if the industry being studied is in disequilibrium. This issue is particularly serious if the industry is producing supranormal returns at a particular moment in time. Absent long-run barriers to entry, new competition will erode those profits. Fourth, SCP studies often unrealistically presume a linear relationship between concentration and performance.[64]

Ultimately, concentration is exogenous. It does not simply determine competition, but reflects it. Any effort simply to regress structure against performance will therefore suffer from simultaneity bias. As a leading treatise on industrial organization observes, the "barrage of criticism has caused most research in this area to cease."[65] As a result, econometricians working in the "new industrial organization" no longer pursue cross-sectional studies, but instead look for suitable instruments that allow them to study the relationship between concentration and price (not profit) either at an industry level or – more accurately – between separate geographic markets in the same relevant product market. As explained below, and subject to considerable variation among markets, those studies often find a relationship between concentration and market power.[66]

These principles are well understood. Yet, many claims today about lost competition overlook them. This is disappointing. Indeed, the FTC and Justice Department have felt obliged to remind observers of the limited utility of industrial-concentration statistics.[67] Some reformists, however, harbor strong intuitions about the concentration of economic power. For them, given what they see in industries from airlines to Silicon Valley, formal economy-wide measures of

---

[63] Id.
[64] Dennis W. Carlton & Jeffrey M. Perloff, Modern Industrial Organization 266 (4th ed. 2005).
[65] Id. at 268.
[66] See Chapter 4.
[67] Market Concentration – Note by the United States, OECD, June 7, 2018, https://www.ftc.gov/system/files/attachments/us-submissions-oecd-2010-present-other-international-competition-fora/market_concentration_united_states.pdf.

concentration simply confirm the obvious. They then leap to unsupported conclusions about diminishing competition. An unfortunate example comes from Professor Wu, who – despite recognizing "a technical difference between 'bigness' and 'industry concentration' – the former refers just [to] the size of firms, while the latter refers to the number of firms competing in each properly defined market" – goes on to asserts that, "in practice, the two tend to overlap[.]"[68] This is not merely wrong, but dangerously misleading.

For example, there is evidence that entry into relevant markets may simultaneously increase both competition and national concentration.[69] Hence, one can easily reach the wrong conclusion by observing rising consolidation at the industry level and inferring a loss of concentration in relevant markets. Indeed, where data have been available at the level of relevant antitrust markets, there is little evidence that competition has in fact declined.[70]

To their credit, other observers acknowledge that it is precarious to infer rising market power from national concentration metrics. White and Yang of NYU observe, for example, that "aggregate concentration has little or no relevance for antitrust[.]"[71] In grappling with these issues, the IMF in 2019 observed that "[b]road market concentration is generally not a good gauge of market power; it is hard to measure and can be misleading."[72] The Council of Economic Advisers under Obama, for its part, granted that it was merely observing "national statistics across broad aggregates of industries" and acknowledged that "an increase in revenue concentration at the national level is neither a necessary nor sufficient condition to indicate an increase in market power."[73] In 2020, the Council under the Trump Administration saw that point as fatal and repudiated the 2016 report, observing that "concentration may result from market features that are benign or even benefit consumers."[74] Alas, politicization threatens to obscure what should be robust, objective statistical analysis.

---

[68] TIM WU, THE CURSE OF BIGNESS: ANTITRUST IN THE NEW GILDED AGE 14–16, 19–22, 139 (2018).
[69] Rossi-Hansberg et al., *Diverging Trends in National and Local Concentration*, Working Paper (2019), https://www.princeton.edu/~erossi/DTNLC.pdf.
[70] Gregory J. Werden & Luke M. Froeb, *Don't Panic: A Guide to Claims of Increasing Concentration*, 33 ANTITRUST 74 (2018), https://papers.ssrn.com/sol3/papers.cfm?abstract_id=3156912 (observing that HHIs had dropped in relevant markets for airlines and banking, but had risen in wireless telecommunications, notwithstanding the government's blocking a number of mergers). *But see* Adil Abdela & Marshall Steinbaum, *The United States Has a Market Concentration Problem*, ROOSEVELT INSTITUTE ISSUE BRIEF (Sept. 2018), https://rooseveltinstitute.org/wp-content/uploads/2018/09/The-United-States-has-a-market-concentration-problem-brief-final.pdf.
[71] White & Yang, *supra* note 41, at 3.
[72] INT'L MONETARY FUND, WORLD ECONOMIC OUTLOOK 55 (2019).
[73] CEA, *supra* note 36, at 4. Nevertheless, it cited other studies that had found evidence of rising concentration along narrower lines that may more closely track relevant markets as defined by economists – specifically, hospitals, wireless providers, and railroads.
[74] Economic Report of the President, Together with the Annual Report of the Council of Economic Advisers 199–226 (Feb. 2020).

Rounding out the universe of measured observers is the OECD, which in a 2018 report evaluated much of the preceding evidence of rising concentration in the US economy.[75] In that international body's view, it "does appear ... that concentration in US markets is more likely to be increasing than decreasing, though the increase is not a dramatic one." The OECD observed that, even on *The Economist*'s assessment of rising concentration at the four-firm level, the results were consistent with intense competition in the "typical" market.[76] The OECD concluded that, "even where there is evidence to suggest an increase in concentration, in the absence of evidence on the movements of other indicators it is extremely difficult to draw any conclusion on whether there has been a change in competitive intensity or not."[77]

4.2.4 *The More Worrisome Evidence of Market Power Goes Beyond Concentration Measures*

Industry-concentration measures are not a reliable barometer for the state of competition. But they are not the only available data point. In particular, firm profits and markups have been at historical highs across many industries (pre-Covid).[78] What should we make of this?

Large returns on invested capital may indicate healthy, competitive markets in which successful companies enjoy rents born of risky investments in technology, infrastructure, and other forms of quality. Further, it is dangerous to infer the existence of market power from profits. Among other points, a static measure of profit may overlook entry, thus signaling market power that does not exist. And, of course, accounting profits are not economic rents. Overlooking the opportunity cost of capital, the former may seem large and yet be competitive.

That is the innocuous reading. Unusually high ROIs, however, can also reflect profits flowing from sustained exercises of market power. Interpreted in light of rising industrial concentration and a falling labor share of GDP, one might naturally infer that supracompetitive rents born of lax antitrust enforcement are responsible.[79]

It is somewhat more concerning, however, that profits are not merely high, but resilient. As noted, there are two broad possibilities. Large public-company profits may, in fact, reflect competitive rates of return on risky investment in technology, infrastructure, or growth. Or those profits may reflect supranormal rents. If that is the

---

[75] OECD, *Market Concentration*, Apr. 20, 2018, https://one.oecd.org/document/DAF/COMP/WD(2018)46/en/pdf.
[76] *Id.* at ¶ 33 (citing Carl Shapiro, *Antitrust in a Time of Populism*, INT'L J. INDUS. ORG. (2017)).
[77] *Id.* at ¶ 36.
[78] *See, e.g.*, Jan De Loecker et al., *The Rise of Market Power and the Macroeconomic Implications*, NBER, Working Paper No. 23687 (2017), https://www.nber.org/papers/w23687 (observing aggregate markups held steady between 1955 and 1980, after which they rose "from 21% above cost to 61% over cost in 2016" – with the distribution falling disproportionately on a small minority of firms).
[79] *See, e.g.*, Gauti B. Eggertsson et al., *Kaldor and Piketty's Facts: The Rise of Monopoly Power in the United States*, NBER Working Paper 24287 (2018).

case, then the durability of elevated profits would be worrying. It would indicate that markets are not self-correcting as rapidly as they should.[80] Supracompetitive profits attract entry, which should lead firms to compete away elevated rents. If that is not happening, it points to long-term barriers to entry. That would be of great concern to competition policy. As discussed below, there is no doubt that many such barriers exist across various markets. Alas, many are the function of state action, and thus lie beyond the purview of federal antitrust agencies. But they ought to be a priority for anyone interested in pursuing a pro-competition mandate.[81]

4.3 PROCOMPETITIVE FACTORS MAY EXPLAIN RISING CONCENTRATION, PROFIT MARGINS, AND FIRM-TO-LABOR GDP SHARE TRENDS

This discussion makes for grim reading. Identifying the explanatory variables behind such macroeconomic phenomena, however, is notoriously difficult. Causal factors may not be obvious. It would be tragic to blame a loss of competition if movements in industrial concentration, profit margins, and the labor share of wealth reflected something else. Such a misdiagnosis would be especially perverse if those effects flowed from competition on the merits. Hence, we must carefully evaluate whether innovation, efficiency, or other procompetitive developments drive these trends. Unless we can confidently exclude that possibility, we need to tread carefully in reforming our antitrust laws.

4.3.1 *The FTC and DOJ: Unlikely Villains in the Monopoly Story*

Some reformists comfortably embrace the loss-of-competition hypothesis. Nevertheless, their contention is, in many respects, counterintuitive. For a sustained loss of competition to have occurred, the DOJ and FTC must have committed systematic – and not merely isolated – errors. That is an hypothesis worth taking seriously. There can be no "sacred cows" when it comes to optimizing economic policy. A priori, however, it is a surprising proposition.

Many reformists do not share that skepticism. They blithely accept that the federal antitrust agencies underenforce the law – typically invoking their supposed adherence to Chicago School ideology.[82] In reading some of the more cutting accounts, a newcomer would be forgiven for thinking the Antitrust Division and Federal Trade

---

[80] Special Report: *Across the West Powerful Firms Are Becoming Even More Powerful*, THE ECONOMIST, Nov. 15, 2018, https://www.economist.com/special-report/2018/11/15/across-the-west-powerful-firms-are-becoming-even-more-powerful.
[81] The Conclusion provides recommendations on this point.
[82] *See, e.g.*, JONATHAN TEPPER, THE MYTH OF CAPITALISM: MONOPOLIES AND THE DEATH OF COMPETITION 155 (2019) ("We would not have highly concentrated industries if it were not for Robert Bork and the Chicago School"); WU, *supra* note 68, at [83–92]; Lina M. Khan, *Amazon's Antitrust Paradox*, 126 YALE L.J. 710, 798 (2017), at 719–22. For an excellent account of how an obsession with the Chicago School

Commission obsessed with price effects, dismissive of nonprice competitive harms, quick to see efficiencies in every merger, and disciples of market self-correction. In their worst moments, some critics have even impugned staff's integrity, most often by pointing to a revolving-door and inviting cynical inferences about the agencies' propensity to take hard positions.[83]

The critique is plainly wrong. It portrays an image of agency life that exists only in critics' minds. Is it possible that the two agencies' enforcement falls short of the social optimum? Of course. Judged by the standard of perfection, even the most capable and industrious of enforcers will come up short. Antitrust is simply too complicated – and the facts needed to inform optimal intervention decisions too elusive – for it to be any other way. But, larger evidence aside, is it likely that the Antitrust Division and the Commission have systematically allowed competition to degrade throughout much of the economy over the past two decades? Hardly. If the Federal Trade Commission and Antitrust Division get it wrong, it is not for want of expertise or effort.

The agencies are populated not by blind dogmatists, but by experts deeply experienced in the workings of the industries that they oversee, in empirical methods, and in economics. They are, by far, the world's most experienced antitrust agencies. Industrial economists – whose profession is to understand how imperfectly competitive markets work – are more integrated and play a more central role in enforcement decisions in the US agencies than they are in any other country.[84] Notably, the FTC's economists formally devote time not only to enforcement, but to research that advances the state of the art in industrial organization. The agencies routinely embark on empirical projects and retrospectives. No recluses, they hold public hearings to invite input from leading thinkers beyond their ranks. They constantly speak at conferences and with their international peers, debating best practices and contemporary issues.

Bestowed of impressive credentials, agency staff forego lucrative private-sector opportunities in pursuit of the public interest. It beggars belief that hundreds of talented antitrust lawyers and economists pursue such careers with a gusto driven not by a compulsion to do their best for consumers, but to further a noninterventionist agenda focused on facilitating the growth of corporate power.

Robust debate is a hallmark of agency work. To be sure, staff hold a spectrum of views about market self-correction, merger efficiencies, the assuredness of position required to sustain a challenge recommendation, and many other issues besides.

has done a disservice to antitrust policy, see William E. Kovacic, *The Chicago Obsession in the Interpretation of US Antitrust History*, 87 U. CHI. L. REV. 459 (2020).

[83] See, e.g., Andrea Beaty, *How Biden Can Prove He's Serious About Busting Corporate Monopolies*, WASH. MONTHLY, June 19, 2020; Jonathan Tepper, *Why Regulators Went Soft on Monopolies*, THE AM. CONSERVATIVE, Jan. 9, 2019; Public Citizen, *The FTC's Big Tech Revolving Door Problem*, May 23, 2019, https://www.citizen.org/article/ftc-big-tech-revolving-door-problem-report/.

[84] That fact matters because the economics literature does not always point in directions that neo-Brandeisians welcome.

Some are more interventionist in philosophy, others the opposite. This is not merely unsurprising, it is vital. Important gaps in knowledge persist. Although narrowed by fact-intensive investigations, the mission often calls on the DOJ and FTC to act (or not) in the absence of critical information, particularly with respect to the market's future evolution and the but-for world – neither of which can be observed.

In this setting, debate is critical. It guards against group think and an uncritical embrace of empirically uncertain propositions. Priors are constantly tested. The agencies are structured in a way to formalize these safeguards, ensuing that decision-makers enjoy an eclectic array of voices beyond the parties. To take but one example, before the Commission decides whether to act, it receives formal written recommendations separately from the reviewing antitrust shop (e.g., Mergers IV), the Bureau of Competition leadership, the staff economist, and the Director of the Bureau of Economics. The Commissioners receive separate recommendations from their attorney advisors. In difficult cases, dissenting voices often emerge. This leads to hard questions, robust debate, and close scrutiny of the record. The Commission's independent bipartisan constitution furthers this dynamic.

This is not a setting conducive to embracing absolutist free-market principles at the altar of the Chicago School. The idiosyncratic structure of US antitrust enforcement, in which two agencies divvy up industries and responsibilities, further protects against uncritical excess or dogmatism. Indeed, the agencies came closest to embracing unadulterated Chicago School principles at the close of the Bush II Administration, when they held joint hearings on Section 2 enforcement. But the Federal Trade Commission refused to sign onto the ensuing report, which adopted a philosophy that would have limited monopolization actions to narrow circumstances in which harm from inaction would have been disproportionate to the gains from intervention.[85] The report ultimately survived for one year, before being withdrawn.

Ultimately, Chicago is a frail hypothesis for systemic underenforcement at the FTC and DOJ. The most extreme laissez faire assumptions of Chicago's foundational era are an extinct species at the agencies today.[86] Staff believe in effective antitrust enforcement, and strive to advance procompetitive policies. The Chicagoan assumptions most often pilloried – rapid market self-correction, near-ubiquitous efficiencies from mergers, and the irrationality of unilateral exclusion by the dominant firm – simply do not fill the Commission's and Division's halls. This is not merely an anecdotal observation from the author's time managing the FTC's Bureau of Competition, but is obvious from the agencies' guiding principles. To

[85] Press Release, FTC Commissioners React to Department of Justice Report, Competition and Monopoly: Single-Firm Conduct Under Section 2 of the Sherman Act, Sept. 8, 2008, https://www.ftc.gov/news-events/press-releases/2008/09/ftc-commissioners-react-department-justice-report-competition-and.

[86] Chicago endures today consistent with its founding principles – a devotion to economic analysis grounded both in developing the most accurate models to predict effects and in testing them empirically. The field of industrial organization has developed mightily since the 1970s, and so should the prescriptions of even the most devoted Chicagoan.

take a prominent example, the Horizontal Merger Guidelines look skeptically on merger efficiencies, define markets narrowly, expressly incorporate nonprice effects in the enforcement calculus, and reject the Stiglerian definition of entry barriers.[87] In short, they contradict almost everything that neo-Brandeisians accuse the agencies of doing.

The fact of the matter is that neo-Brandeisians dislike the state of the art in industrial organization. Theirs is not a principled critique flowing from the economics literature. It is, rather, a wholesale repudiation of decades of learning.[88] By contrast, precision characterizes antitrust review today. Soft factors like imputed market shares, HHIs, and party documents play an important role, but they are not in themselves dispositive. Parties can convince staff to close investigations when the evidence shows that the transaction, practice, or agreement at issue will not likely have anticompetitive effects. The field's quasi-scientific nature makes antitrust an intellectually rich and enjoyable area in which to practice. More importantly, it yields more accurate determinations than a structuralist approach. Some progressive reformists, by contrast, would happily sacrifice that precision in favor of broad prohibitions.

Two agency characteristics, in particular, rankle neo-Brandeisians – the "revolving door" between the public and private bars, and the agencies' burden of proof in litigating mergers. In fact, these are vital sources of strength for US antitrust enforcement.

First, unlike many of their overseas counterparts, the DOJ and FTC regularly hire from the private bar. This process allows them to draw on a deeper pool of talent. Those who join the government from law firms bring with them distinct and valuable perspectives, which complement those of long-term staff. The talent cycle leads to richer analysis within the agencies, fosters transparency, and disrupts mutual distrust. These benefits extend to the very top positions.[89] Neo-Brandeisians have launched a scathing attack on this system, arguing that leading antitrust lawyers who take senior positions at the agencies abandon the public interest in favor of currying favor with corporations that will be their future clients.[90] That argument is wrong. No one is subject to be more rigorous treatment, or held to higher standards, than the alumni who return to the agencies on behalf of private clients.

---

[87] HORIZONTAL MERGER GUIDELINES, *supra* note 55, at *passim*.

[88] Critics also object that the consumer-welfare standard distorts intervention decisions. Chapter 8 scrutinizes that claim, and finds it wanting. Progressive reformists' invocation of the lodestar is empty posturing. They mischaracterize the standard, its role within the agencies, and the significance of its reform. Theirs is a means of backward induction – envision a preferred industry structure and then reverse into the framework that support it. This process leads them to a place of textual alignment with the author, albeit with radically different meanings. Specifically, the author supports clarifying that antitrust's goal is not literally to enhance, maximize, or simply preserve consumer welfare, but rather to protect the competitive process. Neo-Brandeisians say the same thing. But what they see as harm to competition is often anything but.

[89] To take just one recent example, this process allows the agencies to get people like Debbie Feinstein, who, as one the country's top antitrust lawyers, left her position as chair of Arnold & Porter's antitrust group to direct the FTC's Bureau of Competition from 2013 to 2017.

[90] *See supra* note 83.

Second, on the burden-of-proof point, having to prove one's case before an independent decision-maker has marvelous benefits for competition policy. It disciplines staff, guarding against runaway enthusiasm that leads to the adoption of overly aggressive or inventive theories of harm. One need merely look at overseas competition agencies, which typically enforce the law unilaterally and without biting judicial review. Such agencies tend to adopt rules that ease their administration of the law, rather than rules that maximize the precision of their decisions. A good example is the European Commission, which has long made liberal use of the "by object" label to condemn restrictions that, in fact, have nuanced effects. To be sure, the courts sometimes get it wrong. Antitrust proves to be too complicated for some generalist judges. But the occasional unjustified loss – which may be overturned on appeal[91] – is a worthy price for the long-term qualitative benefits and due-process protections engendered in a litigation approach.

In short, the agencies are not bound to the Chicago School, though there are committed to the economic method. They house a great deal of learning, both in industrial organization and in the administration of antitrust law. It is, of course, possible that the FTC's and DOJ's refined methodologies have led to underenforcement. Indeed, in reviewing the evidence, the author concludes that the agencies should bring more cases at the margin. But the proposition that any such shortcoming encompasses wholesale failures to protect competition is deeply counterintuitive. Again, it is a possibility worth considering. But it surely behooves us to take another hypothesis seriously – namely that the agencies know what they are doing, and that observed deficiencies in competition trace back not to antitrust, but to the myriad impediments to trade that government itself constructs.

Of course, anecdotal experience with industries invites an inference of lost competition. Formal measures of industry-level concentration increases and apparently inflated firm profits cement the implication. But it is vital not to rush to embrace a diagnosis. That is particular true where, as here, it would be truly surprising if the DOJ and FTC had allowed systematic losses of competition to take root in the economy. Could there be an innocuous – or even procompetitive – explanation for troubling observations in concentration and returns on invested capital? Crucially, the answer is yes.

4.3.2 Competition on the Merits May Explain Changes in Industrial Concentration, Profit Margins, and the Labor Share of GDP

Factors unrelated to lost competition may cause industry concentration to rise, firm profits to increase, and the labor share of GDP to fall.

---

[91] See, e.g., FTC v. Penn State Hershey Med. Ctr., 838 F.3d 327 (3d Cir. 2016); FTC v. Advocate Health Care Network, 841 F.3d 460 (7th Cir. 2016).

Innovation is one explanation. Quality-based competition, including in the form of R&D, is likely the greatest long-term contributor to consumer welfare. Dynamic efficiencies, of course, do not inure to the benefit of all firms equally. Rather, they flow to those that can employ them. Trade secrecy and patent protection allow innovators to deny their competitors use of their technologies, at least for a time, while first-mover advantage bestows further benefits. Market shares grow, as will margins facilitated by product differentiation. Further, if innovation yields productive-efficiency gains, investor returns on equity will rise relative to the labor share of surplus.

The effect may be especially dramatic in industries that display "winner takes all" (or most) characteristics. Importantly, we would not expect the effects of technological progress to hold steady over time. Innovation is lumpy, and changes in technology can radically affect consumer preferences. More generally, if firms increasingly focus on areas in which they are efficient relative to their competitors, they will enter an increasing number of geographic markets within the same industry. As a result, competition and profits will increase, even as national industries become more concentrated. In short, if a minority of firms is becoming more productive relative to competitors, then we would see these symptoms.

The question, of course, is whether these are mere possibility theorems or instead enjoy evidentiary support. In fact, impressive emerging work suggests that innovation and productivity credibly explain the industrial trends explored at the outset of this chapter. In 2019, for example, the IMF examined whether corporate market power had increased. Although markups over marginal costs have risen by almost 8 percent since 2000, those increases have "been concentrated among a small fraction of dynamic – more productive and innovative – firms[.]"[92] Hence, "rising corporate market power seems, so far, more reflective of 'winner-takes-most' by more productive and innovative firms than of weaker pro-competition policies[.]"[93]

A group, including David Autor of MIT, has produced important research. Consistent with the trends observed above, their paper notes that concentration has risen at the four-digit industry level "across the vast bulk of the US private sector[.]"[94] The economists attribute that result to leading firms' increasing specialization on core competencies and growth. Their hypothesis is that "superstar firms" – that is, uniquely productive ones – have emerged, along with a "winner takes most" trend within their industries.[95]

Autor and his coauthors hypothesize that globalization and changing technology have led the most productive firms to grow, thus increasing markups and reducing

---

[92] Int'l Monetary Fund Research Dep't, *The Rise of Corporate Market Power and Its Macroeconomic Effects*, in WORLD ECONOMIC OUTLOOK, Ch. 2., Apr. 2019.
[93] *Id.*
[94] Daniel Autor *et al.*, *The Fall of the Labor Share and the Rise of Superstar Firms*, 135 Q.J. ECON. 645 (2020), public version *available at* https://scholar.harvard.edu/lkatz/publications/fall-labor-share-and-rise-superstar-firms.
[95] *Id. passim.*

the labor share of GDP. Using micro-panel US Census data from 1982 to 2012 for 676 industries across six sectors, they find powerful support for their hypothesis. In particular, they observe that "the industries that are becoming more concentrated are those with faster growth of productivity and innovation."[96] Superstar effects, they note, may reflect network effects – as may explain "the dominance of companies such as Google, Facebook, Apple, Amazon, AirBNB, and Uber in their respective industries" – or the emergence of technology that requires large fixed costs or confers disproportionate benefits with scale.[97] With respect to the latter possibility, the authors give the example of Walmart, which "has made substantial technology investments to enable it to monitor supply chain logistics and manage inventory to an extent that, arguably, would be infeasible for smaller competitors."[98]

There is, of course, a third explanation for their observed "superstar firm" effect. This is the proposition that weakened antitrust enforcement has allowed firms to benefit from reduced competition.[99] Autor *et al.* consider that possibility – one seen by neo-Brandeisians, of course, as self-evidently true – and discount it for two reasons. First, they observe similar trends across the United States and the European Union, notwithstanding the latter jurisdiction's more demanding competition laws. Second, they note that "the concentrating sectors appear to be growing more productive and innovative [.]"[100] Hence, a loss of competition "is unlikely to be the primary explanation[.]"[101]

In 2019, economists from Princeton and the University of Chicago similarly observe rising concentration at the national-industry level between 1977 and 2013, but only within the services, wholesale, and retail sectors.[102] The manufacturing sector, by contrast, has seen concentration fall. Hsieh and Rossi-Hansberg posit that new ICT technologies are driving this trend, not a loss of competition. They argue that technologies now allow firms to achieve scale in services over numerous locations, rather than a centralized one – a change akin to the famous manufacturing-scale efficiencies realized a century ago. Surveying the services, wholesale, and retail sectors, the economists find that "rising concentration in these sectors is entirely driven by an increase in the number of local markets served by the top firms."[103] In other words, innovative firms are entering geographic markets that would otherwise have not been profitable to contest, thus enhancing competition. Why does this increase concentration? The answer is because, with "a large enough fixed cost, only the most efficient firms find it profitable to adopt the new technology,

---

[96] *Id.* at 3.
[97] *Id.* at 3–4.
[98] *Id.* at 4.
[99] Many critics, of course, hold this view notwithstanding the work explored in this section. *See, e.g.*, David Wessel, *Is Lack of Competition Strangling the U.S. Economy?*, Harv. Bus. Rev. 106 (Mar.–Apr. 2018), https://hbr.org/2018/03/is-lack-of-competition-strangling-the-u-s-economy.
[100] Autor *et al.*, *supra* note 94, at 4.
[101] *Id.*
[102] Chang-Tai Hsieh & Esteban Rossi-Hansberg, *The Industrial Revolution in Services*, July 5, 2019, https://faculty.chicagobooth.edu/chang-tai.hsieh/research/services.pdf.
[103] *Id.* at 4.

which leads to more concentration in the industry."[104] In conclusion, the authors find, "top firms are now more specialized, are larger in the chosen industries, and these are precisely the industries that have experienced concentration growth."[105]

Hsieh and Rossi-Hansberg's findings build on prior observations by Professor James Bessen, who, in 2017, concluded that successful "IT systems appear to play a major role in the recent increases in industry concentration and in profit margins, more so than a general decline in competition."[106]

This work should give any thoughtful reformist pause. The analysis by Autor, Dorn, Katz, Patterson, and Reenen is especially important. Theirs is a rigorous study, and it suggests that *increasing competition* may be responsible for the concentration, profit, and labor share of GDP phenomena to which many observers are now reacting with alarm. If they are right, then a substantial expansion of antitrust prohibitions may work considerable mischief to the economy.

4.4 WHERE DOES THIS LEAVE US?

All told, the preceding evidence does not reveal the systematic loss of competition that some reformists claim to be obvious. Interpreting the evidence to date is more difficult than neo-Brandeisians admit. The challenge is to construe ambiguous data – that is, information reasonably consistent with dueling hypotheses – and use it to inform responsible competition policy. In the author's view, the better reading supports heightened antitrust scrutiny and intervention in close cases associated with a significant loss of competition.[107] It does not, however, lend credence to more radical calls for reform that would put antitrust beyond its neoclassical foundation.

What does the evidence show? Though not uniformly, US *industries* have become more concentrated. Merger-driven consolidation has surely contributed to that trend. A merger wave has been underway since the early 2010s, and 2017 marked an all-time high of 15,558 US transactions.[108] The following year, global M&A activity reached $3.7 trillion – exceptionally high, though still short of the $5 trillion record set in 2015.[109] At the same time, the US new-firm creation rate has

---

[104] *Id.* at 5.
[105] *Id.* at 18.
[106] James Bessen, *Information Technology and Industry Concentration*, No. 17-41 Boston University School of Law, Law & Economics Paper Series (2017), https://scholarship.law.bu.edu/faculty_scholarship/267.
[107] To be clear, that does *not* lend support to extreme proposals like making dominance a status offense or reversing evidentiary burdens in merger review. As Part III explores in detail, the proper reaction is a shift in emphasis, particularly in marginal cases. For purposes of this chapter, however, it behooves us to explain why the preceding evidence supports a stronger antitrust-enforcement mandate.
[108] Institute for Mergers, Acquisitions and Alliances, *United States – M&A Statistics*, https://imaa-institute.org/m-and-a-us-united-states/.
[109] Andrew Brownstein *et al.*, *Mergers and Acquisitions – 2019*, HARV. L. SCH. FORUM ON CORP. GOVERNANCE & FIN'L REG., Jan. 15, 2019, https://corpgov.law.harvard.edu/.

diminished.[110] But, just as M&A has contributed to concentration, so, too, have organic growth rates, the degree of market entry, and innovation. At least in the digital space, technology races and a winner-takes-most (or -all) phenomenon explains the rise of "superstar firms" that are now household names.

In themselves, however, these facts say little of significance to competition policy. Industries are not relevant markets. A national industry may grow more concentrated with – or without – a parallel trend in an antitrust market. Indeed, mergers can simultaneously increase competition in relevant markets and increase industry consolidation. Consider a low-cost supplier that enters new geographic markets by acquiring a less-efficient firm in each locale.

Nevertheless, consolidation in relevant product markets can produce the same effect at the industry level. Such a scenario would generally lead competition to decrease. The economics literature shows that, in oligopolies fairly characterized by Cournot quantity competition, HHIs track closely with competitive outcomes. Has this occurred? There is evidence to support that hypothesis, but not to the exclusion of dueling – procompetitive – ones. Yes, profit margins for US companies have risen. A loss of competition could explain those trends, in whole or part.

Again, though, this phenomenon supports an innocuous reading. If firms have heavily pursued R&D, for example, their healthy margins may reflect normal returns on risky investments. As discussed, recent studies suggest that the emergence of ICT and related technologies may allow unusually productive firms to achieve previously unattainable scale economies, increasing competition by leading efficient firms to compete within their area of advantage, while exiting from others. That phenomenon would certainly yield higher industry concentration. Similarly, if companies expanded to realize scale economies, their margins and profits would rise. Further, automation and globalization have reduced many firms' per-unit costs, thus inflating those profit figures. Certainly, digital platforms have proven extraordinarily profitable, but to date the returns from their innovation-driven scale largely reflect competition on the merits. These hypothesis are plausible, and have some evidentiary support. We should be cautious before ignoring them.

Perhaps the most worrisome fact, however, is that US corporate profits have not merely been elevated, but have proven to be resilient. The industrial-organization literature teaches that industry structure does not cause sustained supranormal rents – long-term barriers to entry do so.[111] Static profit margins can mask disequilibrium. If margins remain stubbornly elevated across industries *and* over time, however, they may reflect a systemic issue. Compounding the problem is that firm-level investment appears to have declined, not risen in a manner that might explain inflated margins. And, while there is no doubting the superstar-firm phenomenon in

---

[110] CEA, *supra* note 36; Ian Hathaway & Robert E. Litan, *Declining Business Dynamism in the United States: A Look at States and Metros*, BROOKINGS, May 2014, https://www.brookings.edu/wp-content/uploads/2016/06/declining_business_dynamism_hathaway_litan.pdf.

[111] CARLTON & PERLOFF, *supra* note 64, at 267.

Silicon Valley, those giants' experience is not that of the larger economy. Certainly, long-term trends in automation and globalization bear considerable explanatory power, but they may not in themselves explain the full picture here.

Ultimately, the evidence shares a common theme. It largely points in the same direction. Few studies suggest that US markets have generally become more competitive or – more relevantly – that the FTC, DOJ, and other antitrust enforcers have overstepped their bounds, and inadvertently put the brakes on incentives to invest. By contrast, those who argue that competition across the US economy remains unchanged have to explain many data points. Though individually explicable, the individual pieces of evidence collectively prove worrisome. To be clear, we can neither confidently state that market power has both risen in the US economy nor that it has done so in a manner problematic for antitrust policy. But we are not reduced to agnosticism and inaction. Two bottom-line takeaways emerge.

First, the most natural reading of the evidence is that consolidation has contributed to rising firm profits. (As noted, those profits may or may not be a function of reduced competition.) Second, although competitive pressures have not obviously eased in relevant markets, error-cost analysis suggests that we have reached a new threshold. Specifically, at the margin, the agencies should worry less about over-enforcement and more about the ill effects of not challenging a borderline practice, merger, or agreement that may harm competition.

This a natural incremental reform. Antitrust is a fluid policy. Enforcers should continuously revisit the tradeoffs that inform their intervention decisions. Given the larger macroeconomic context in which antitrust features today, agencies ought not to shy away from enforcement actions that target conduct or transactions that, on balance, appear likely to introduce competitive dangers without offsetting procompetitive effects. If a concern for avoiding Type I errors stayed enforcers' hands in the past, they should feel liberated now.

Why not mount a more vigorous response? If the evidence points toward merger-driven consolidation and rising market power across numerous industries, notwithstanding expert antitrust review at the federal antitrust agencies, does it not imply a need for bolder action? On this account, merely tweaking enforcement at the margin in close cases will not provide the needed medicine. Such urgency, of course, drives neo-Brandeisian calls for larger reform.

Here is the answer – we could be wrong.[112] Diagnosing the state of competition at the level of the US economy is extraordinarily difficult. The observations discussed above, though worrisome, is consistent with forces that are socially valuable or not a function

---

[112] *Accord* Chad Syverson, *Macroeconomics and Market Power: Facts, Potential Explanations and Open Questions*, BROOKINGS, p. 2, Jan. 2019, https://www.brookings.edu/wp-content/uploads/2019/01/ES_20190116_Syverson-Macro-Micro-Market-Power.pdf ("I do not think there is yet a rich enough collage of evidence to justify presuming aggregate market power has risen substantially.... In the meantime, there is a case for caution before calling for policy changes (antitrust or otherwise) that assume as fact a size-able, across-the-board increase in market power.").

of antitrust. The digital network economy may very well reflect a Schumpeterian process of dynamic competition driven by technological innovation and leapfrog displacement. To date, Silicon Valley has unquestionably been a net engine of extraordinary value creation for consumers. Companies in other industries may generally be becoming more efficient, simultaneously competing more effectively and enjoying higher profit margins as a result, even while squeezing the labor share of wealth generated. If firms are competing on the merits and winning, then the macroeconomic signals that follow merely reflect healthy capitalistic processes.

The question here is not whether competition has diminished in some relevant antitrust markets – of course it has, just as it has strengthened in some others. The issue is twofold. First, has there been a systematic trend of lost competition across industries? Possibly. But that it is not clear, and the prospect of misdiagnosis ought to be terribly unsettling if used to effect a transformative change in antitrust. Second, to the extent that competition has indeed diminished, does it reflect a failure of antitrust policy? There is no question that competition across the US economy is suboptimal, largely on account of governmental barriers to entry. State impediments to competition abound – from occupational-licensing requirements to certificate-of-need laws – and they warrant careful scrutiny. But, given federalism principles, they are seldom within the scope of competition laws. As for antitrust itself? There is evidence that, unsurprisingly, some *marginal* enforcement decisions that erred in favor of nonintervention got it wrong.[113]

Humility should accompany any process as difficult and consequential as antitrust reform. That is not a call to inaction, but rather for a careful weighing of the offsetting consequences of moving the needle in various directions. It seems most unlikely that ratcheting up antitrust scrutiny of horizontal mergers, in particular, will yield serious net social harms if effected in incremental fashion directed at significant losses of competition. The calculus is altogether different in contemplating a reversion to structuralism. The neo-Brandeisian vision for antitrust would occasion transformative effects, not all of which can readily be predicted.

4.5 CONCLUSION

We should fortify antitrust enforcement at the margin. Contrary to some claims, however, today's fundamentals are sound. The federal agencies are repositories of massive institutional knowledge, born of industry experience, empirical studies, and the close attention of dedicated Ph.D. economists devoted to antitrust policy. The 2010 merger guidelines, like the agencies' larger toolkit, are analytically rigorous.

The agencies should continuously refine their intervention decisions in light of the best available evidence. That holds true regardless of whether we are in the midst of an iconoclastic debate about reshaping competition policy.

[113] See Chapter 3, § 3.5.3.

That does not mean, however, that today's enforcement calculus is optimally calibrated. The evidence discussed above is consistent with inaction in close cases that warranted antitrust intervention. Indeed, it appears that some marginal decisions that tipped in favor of clearance have yielded price increases.[114] No recent studies of which the author is aware suggest that our merger-review standards are too lax. Further, transactional synergies – though real, attainable, and worth crediting in appropriate cases – are by no means pervasive.

What emerges is an incomplete picture, but one suggesting that the federal antitrust agencies should block more borderline transactions. The error analysis conducted in Chapter 7 supports that recommendation. The solution does not lie in prohibiting 4–3 or 3–2 transactions, imposing dogmatic market-share thresholds, flipping burden presumptions for "megadeals," or adopting other inflexible concentration rules. Such tenets characterize imprecise analysis of the kind that some non-antitrust agencies presently employ in assessing the "competitive" dimensions of mergers.[115] The FTC and DOJ have done better, and should continue to do so. The call is rather to weigh more heavily demonstrable losses of head-to-head competition, and – above all – to bring *and lose* more cases.

Litigation is important. It clarifies the scope of the law, limits the troublesome practice of soft-law creation through untested consents, and leads doctrine to evolve in light of the best available economics. No less important is losing. The agencies should probably fail more often than they do, such being the symptom of a healthy enforcement mandate. This is not to suggest bringing unmeritorious cases or ones that have little or no chance of success on the merits. But it is to emphasize the importance of challenging every deal that, left to work its course, will ultimately harm consumers based on the reviewing agency's best judgment.

---

[114] See id.
[115] See, e.g., Comment of the U.S. Dep't of Justice & Fed. Trade Comm'n, Modifications for Commission Requirements for Review of Transactions Under Section 203 of the Federal Power Act and Market-Based Rate Applications Under Section 205 of the Federal Power Act, FERC Dkt. No. RM16-21-000, Nov. 28, 2016, https://www.ftc.gov/system/files/documents/advocacy_documents/comment-federal-trade-commission-us-department-justice-federal-energy-regulatory-commission-ferc/v170000_ferc_market_power_comment_28_nov_2016.pdf.

5

A Liberal Call to Arms, But Is Deconcentration the Answer?

5.1 INTRODUCTION: BRANDEIS REVISITED

Louis Brandeis, the distinguished Supreme Court jurist, championed the antimonopoly movement of the early 1900s. Deeply hostile to consolidation, he made an impassioned case for breaking up trusts. He identified a litany of sins associated with monopolistic largesse – problems ranging from the inefficiencies inherent in sprawling enterprise to coddled monopolists' dampened incentive to innovate. Justice Brandeis did not pose the issue simply in economic terms. Rather, he framed antitrust intervention as being essential to preservation of democracy itself. His writings on competition policy were profoundly influential. Indeed, he bore partial responsibility for the Federal Trade Commission's formation in 1914.

Justice Brandeis's views are back in vogue. Incremental consolidation since the mid-1980s, though subtle from one year (or even one administration) to the next, has wrought a degree of concentration unseen in decades. This reality is not the thing of arcane studies, but of common experience. From airlines to telecommunications, consumers perceive that suppliers are few and powerful. Wealth inequality has accelerated to unprecedented extremes – a phenomenon that invites an explanation born of rising market power. Silicon Valley has magnified these issues in the public imagination. Many people fear the clout and scale of leading digital networks. Progressives have identified monopoly power as an urgent issue. Even conservatives echo some of their concerns, especially with regard to technology platforms.

There is more to the story of rising concentration, of course, than meets the eye.[1] Nevertheless, for many on the left, the problem is clear. In their view, conservative antitrust policies tied to the Chicago School have hobbled antitrust, leaving enforcement a shadow of its former self. Price theoretic analysis has blinded the FTC and DOJ to issues of larger significance to competition policy. This myopia has allowing zero-price platforms to grow exponentially free of scrutiny. And it has permitted firms to grow through vertical and conglomerate free and clear of the antitrust laws. Meanwhile an aversion to Type I errors and a naïve belief in the power of market self-

---

[1] *See* Chapter 3.

correction have led them to bless horizontal transactions that should never have been allowed. The result has been an arms race – consolidation begets consolidation as rivals seek to outmaneuver one another. For those who diagnose the problem thus, a solution is sorely needed. A natural source of inspiration lies in Justice Brandeis.

His views, of course, developed in light of the industrial reality of his time. This was the Gilded Age – a paradoxical time when the United States saw unprecedented economic growth and innovation, and yet near-ubiquitous monopolization and severe income inequality. A handful of magnates wielded considerable political clout.

At the turn of the century, trusts controlled swathes of the US economy. By acquiring independent refineries, John D. Rockefeller's Standard Oil had monopolized American oil production. A 1901 merger with Andrew Carnegie's steel company created US Steel, which accounted for almost three-quarters of US production. A five-firm combination in 1890 gave birth to American Tobacco, which then launched a flurry of acquisitions. The company came to dominate all aspects of the tobacco industry. Meanwhile, the American Sugar Refining Company controlled the sugar business at the turn of the century. Its acquisition of the E. C. Knight Co. and other rivals in 1892 provided the trust with 98 percent of the American sugar-refining industry. The federal government sought in vain to enjoin those acquisitions. An 1895 Supreme Court decision hobbled antitrust-enforcement efforts for years to come by holding that the Justice Department lacked jurisdiction to move against a manufacturing monopoly located in one state.[2]

The railroad industry was arguably the most significant growth industry during the Gilded Age. Despite their transformative effect on the economy, railroad companies soon became accused of monopolistic practices, as illustrated by the Granger movement led by farmers upset by grain-transport rates following the Civil War. Legendary for their ruthlessness, dueling railroad tycoons coordinated on carriage rates, and convinced the government of the merits of natural monopoly because competing infrastructure was wasteful. Founded in 1877, the Interstate Commerce Commission sought to impose "reasonable and just" rates on the railroads, but to little effect. Meanwhile, price coordination remained par for the course. In a 1901 effort that spawned a famous antitrust case, for example, rival railroad builders James Hill and Edward Harrimon agreed with J. P. Morgan to combine their railroad stocks in a holding corporation, the Northern Securities Company, in order to dominate the Northwest.[3]

Such were the conditions of the Sherman Act's passing in 1890, and the government's first major incursions into industry on antitrust grounds – in particular against the Northern Securities Company, US Steel, and American Tobacco.[4] They were

---

[2] United States v. E. C. Knight Co., 156 U.S. 1 (1895).
[3] N. Secs. Co. v. United States, 193 U.S. 197, 325–39, 354–60 (1904) (holding that the Northern Securities combination violated Section 1 of the Sherman Act, and requiring its breakup).
[4] Id. at 197; United States v. Am. Tobacco Co., 221 U.S. 106 (1911); United States v. U.S. Steel Corp., 251 U.S. 417 (1911).

also the setting in which Justice Brandeis formed his views about the role of antitrust laws in society.

Brandeis opposed laissez faire capitalism. In his view, "unless there be regulation of competition, its excesses will lead to the destruction of competition, and monopoly will take its place." A recognized "champion of small business" and "The People's Lawyer," Brandeis feared the accumulation of economic power.[5] He worried that "size may, at least, become noxious by reasons of the means through which it was attained or the uses to which it is put."[6] In his estimation, "We can have democracy in this country, or we can have great wealth concentrated in the hands of a few, but we can't have both."[7] He argued that monopoly is "neither inevitable nor desirable."[8] Dominant firms are "less innovative" because their "secure positions freed them from the necessity which has always been the mother of invention."[9] In his later years on the Court, he would write "of the insidious menace inherent in large aggregations of capital" and warn of "such concentration of economic power that so-called private corporations are sometimes able to dominate the State."[10]

Today's US economy, of course, is a world apart from the Gilded Age. At risk of stating the obvious, we have a mature antitrust regime that criminalizes arrangements of the kind that blossomed in the nineteenth and early twentieth century. Mergers to monopoly are not tolerated, and the government typically sues to enjoin 3-2 and 4-3 transactions or impose remedies. In approving mergers with significant horizontal overlaps, the agencies routinely require divestitures in order to preserve existing competitive constraints. Ours is not some Dickensian laissez faire system that leaves capitalists free to accumulate market power. That reality has not stopped frequent invocations, however, of a second Gilded Age and an associated need to reinvigorate the Sherman Act consistent with its founding vision.[11] Louis Brandeis's famous reference to "the curse of bigness" has become reformists' rallying cry.[12] In fact, neo-Brandeisians wish to expand the antitrust mandate beyond protecting competitive market pressures to enact an anti-size vision.

On that point, Brandeis did not simply object to firms' securing market power in order to raise price. Nor did he limit his opposition to excessive shares of what economists would see as relevant antitrust markets today. His was a broader objection – one that would reach expansion across markets through conglomerate

---

[5] See Barak Orbach, *The Antitrust Curse of Business*, 85 S. CAL. L. REV. 605, 624–26 (2012) (collecting sources).
[6] Louis D. Brandeis, *A Curse of Bigness*, HARPER'S WKLY, at 18, Jan. 10, 1914.
[7] JOSEPH R. CONLIN, THE MORROW BOOK OF QUOTATIONS IN AMERICAN HISTORY 48 (1984).
[8] U.S. Congress Subcommittee of the Committee on the Judiciary U.S. Senate, Sixty-fourth Congress, First Session, on the Nomination of Louis D. Brandeis to be an Associate Justice of the Supreme Court of the United States, Jan. 1, 1916, Tr. at 106.
[9] MELVIN I. UROFSKY & DAVID W. LEVY, THE FAMILY LETTERS OF LOUIS D. BRANDEIS (2002).
[10] Louis K. Liggett Co. v. Lee, 288 U.S. 517, 549, 565 (1933).
[11] See, e.g., TIM WU, THE CURSE OF BIGNESS: ANTITRUST IN THE NEW GILDED AGE (2018).
[12] Louis D. Brandeis, *A Curse of Bigness*, HARPER'S WKLY, Jan. 10, 1914.

mergers, for example. Size was a problem in itself, not only for the violence that it visits upon democracy, but for its larger social ills, including wealth inequality.[13]

Notably, Brandeis appears to have harbored doubts about competition itself. He ventured the opinion, for example, that "the worst form of illegitimate competition has been found to be price cutting."[14] He saw monopoly as "the natural outcome of" that process, thus evincing an hostility to price competition on the merits.[15] In his estimation, "unbridled competition" was not something to foster, but to suppress.[16] That theme resonates with many of today's progressive reformists, who worry that antitrust enforcers have been wrong to allow – and have even applauded – uncurbed price-cutting by platforms. Like the Justice from whom they draw inspiration, neo-Brandeisians believe that dominant firms can distort markets even without excluding equally or more efficient competitors. That view implies that antitrust must do more than protect existing competitive constraints on the exercise of market power – a degree of direct intervention is necessary to curb excesses. That is a point of acute divergence between neoclassical antitrust thinkers and those calling for substantial reform.

5.2 NEO-BRANDEISIANS CALL FOR AN ANTITRUST REVOLUTION

The anti-monopoly movement captures not a single viewpoint, but a collection of thinkers united by core beliefs. In their estimation, the modern "law and economics" approach misses something important. They reject Chicago School assumptions about productivities and market self-correction, and disagree that efficiency should guide analysis. In particular, they view the consumer-welfare standard as pernicious. Focusing on downstream price effects, they think, obscures upstream distortions in supply markets. Asset rationalization in the form of layoffs, as well as reduced input prices, should weigh against mergers, not be "efficiencies" that justify them.

Neo-Brandeisians appear to sympathize with workers and small businesses over consumers. They look with suspicion on low pricing – especially by dominant firms – seeing it as a path to consolidation and rising corporate power. Skepticism about markets permeates the movement. Above all, they see "bigness" as a problem in itself, and not one that can be rescued by appealing to competition on the merits, innovation, consumer preference, or lower pricing. Theirs is a view irreconcilable with the paradigm governing US antitrust law today.

---

[13] See, e.g., Louis D. Brandeis, *The Opportunity in the Law*, 39 AM. L. REV. 555, 562 (1905) ("The people are beginning to doubt whether in the long run democracy and absolutism can co-exist in the same community; beginning to doubt whether there is a justification for the great inequalities in the distribution of wealth, for the rapid creation of fortunes, more mysterious than the deeds of Aladdin's lamp.").
[14] U.S. Congress Tr., *supra* note 8, at 107.
[15] *Id.*
[16] New State Ice Co. v. Liebmann, 285 U.S. 262, 307 (1932) (Brandeis, J., dissenting) (taking a deeply skeptical position about the virtues of "unbridled competition").

5.2.1 Parting Company with Some Progressive Antitrust Reformists, Neo-Brandeisians Dominate the Conversation

Who are the neo-Brandeisians or "anti-monopolists"? As always, labels are imprecise, but this book uses the term to mean antitrust reformists who reject competitive-effects analysis in favor of a redistributive structuralism defined at the industry level.

Neo-Brandeisians wish to use the antitrust laws to deconcentrate industries, even if doing so increases consumer prices. This effort goes beyond policing concentration levels in economically defined relevant markets. Rather, conglomerate and vertical growth can also yield unacceptable economic, and thus political, power. In that neo-Brandeisian vision, atomistic markets will yield a more equitable division of surplus to suppliers, small firms, and workers. Of course, cost and demand characteristics dictate an industry's optimal structure. Reconstituting markets to reflect neo-Brandeisian preferences – as opposed to those revealed by buyers and sellers through market transactions – will therefore entail losses in efficiency, pricing pressure, and potentially in investment incentives. For those calling for an antitrust revolution, however, those costs are worth the long-run benefits associated with unconcentrated industries.

The movement's ranks include some progressive old guard from the academy – established faculty who cast a skeptical eye on free-market ideology and call for reinvigorated antitrust enforcement. Energetic writers and prominent thinkers among this group include Professor Tim Wu of Columbia Law School (presently a member of President Biden's National Economic Council) and Chris Sagers of the Cleveland-Marshall College of Law. If one organization is synonymous with the neo-Brandeisian movement, it is the Open Markets Institute. The think tank, led by Barry Lynn, aggressively makes the case for an antitrust revolution. Some economists, such as the Roosevelt Institute's Marshall Steinbaum, have also joined the neo-Brandeisians' ranks.

An impassioned group of young thinkers, however, has given the neo-Brandeisian movement its defining urgency. The standout is Lina Khan. As a third-year law student, she penned a student note arguing that the antitrust laws are ill-equipped to deal with the digital economy.[17] Her principal target was Amazon, which grew explosively on the back of low pricing, massive investment, and strategic acquisitions – all while negotiating low input costs from suppliers and competing with businesses that use its platform. Those characteristics, of course, encapsulate everything that neo-Brandeisians object to in the modern economy. Over ninety-six pages, Khan methodically made the case against Amazon, arguing that the Chicago School's focus on price theory had blinded enforcers to dangers lurking in plain sight. Exquisitely timed, the paper hit the presses just as claims of a monopoly problem were hitting fever pitch. Her work went viral, and led to rave reviews from the left.[18]

---

[17] Lina M. Khan, Note, *Amazon's Antitrust Paradox*, 126 YALE L.J. 710, 798 (2017).
[18] *See, e.g.*, David Streitfeld, *Amazon's Antitrust Antagonist Has a Breakthrough Idea*, N.Y. TIMES, Sept. 7, 2018, https://www.nytimes.com/2018/09/07/technology/monopoly-antitrust-lina-khan-amazon.html.

Khan has since become something of a superstar within the progressive antitrust camp. After graduating from Yale, she spent a stint at the FTC advising Commissioner Rohit Chopra, who has staked out a notably left-wing position. From there, she served as majority counsel to the US House Judiciary Committee's Subcommittee on Antitrust, Commercial, and Administrative Law. In 2021, and at the age of only 32, she became Chairwoman of the FTC. With articulation and thoughtfulness, she continues to write in support of neo-Brandeisian positions.

To be sure, Khan has assumed a high-profile position within the neo-Brandeisian movement. It is important not to overlook, however, the great many young people who have seized onto neo-Brandeisian positions.[19] The movement enjoys a groundswell of support, as brimming op-eds and social-media posts make clear. Progressive think tanks burst with enthusiasm for antitrust reform. Notably, leading Democratic presidential campaigns in 2020 shared that vision, meaning that staffers were (and remain) quietly working away on these issues behind the scenes.

Progressive antitrust thinkers inclined toward incremental reform are contributing to important policy conversations in Washington, DC, but they are not in the political limelight. By contrast, neo-Brandeisians dominate the progressive conversation on antitrust policy. Liz Warren, in particular, has lent her full-throated support for neo-Brandeisian reforms.[20] In her view, "Today, in America, competition is dying ... Consolidation and concentration are on the rise in sector after sector. Concentration threatens our markets, threatens our economy, and threatens our democracy."[21] In March 2019, she rolled out proposals that capture the neo-Brandeisian vision. She expressly envisioned "breaking up Amazon, Facebook, and Google," and called for legislation that would designate large tech networks as "platform utilities" that could not compete with participants on their provided platforms.[22] She further called for the unwinding of several "anticompetitive mergers," including Amazon's acquisition of Whole Foods and Zappos, Facebook's

---

[19] Young activists' and scholars' rousing exhortation for antitrust reform is, of course, inspirational. For those favorably inclined toward the virtues of free-market competition, however, a parallel robust defense of the status quo by young thinkers would be equally welcome.

[20] Sheelah Kolhatkar, *How Elizabeth Warren Came Up with a Plan to Break Up Big Tech*, NEW YORKER, Aug. 20, 2019, https://www.newyorker.com/business/currency/how-elizabeth-warren-came-up-with-a-plan-to-break-up-big-tech.

[21] Press Release, Senator Elizabeth Warren Delivers Remarks on Reigniting Competition in the American Economy, June 29, 2016, https://www.warren.senate.gov/newsroom/press-releases/senator-elizabeth-warren-delivers-remarks-on-reigniting-competition-in-the-american-economy. Even Pete Buttigieg, who ran a centrist campaign, echoed neo-Brandeisian thinking about antitrust's perceived inability to tackle zero-priced technology services. Makena Kelly, *Pete Buttigieg Wants the FTC to Fight Big Tech Monopolies*, THE VERGE, Apr. 23, 2019, https://www.theverge.com/2019/4/23/18512428/pete-buttigieg-facebook-google-amazon-apple-antitrust-ftc-break-up.

[22] Elizabeth Warren, *Here's How We Can Break Up Big Tech*, Mar. 8, 2019, https://medium.com/@teamwarren/heres-how-we-can-break-up-big-tech-9ad9e0da324c.

purchase of WhatsApp and Instagram, and Google's buying Waze, Nest, and DoubleClick.[23]

Importantly, neo-Brandeisians part company with left-leaning antitrust scholars who have long advocated for more intervention within the confines of modern antitrust's analytic framework. More principled thinkers on the left see the antitrust laws as imperfectly calibrated, but do not advocate a wholesale rethinking of our competition policies. For example, Fiona Scott Morton and Jonathan Baker worry that market power has increased in the United States, thus justifying enhanced antitrust intervention.[24] But their proposals for reform fall far short of neo-Brandeisian aspirations.[25] Some other leading economists, like Carl Shapiro, are no fans of Chicago School thinking, but caution against a reactionary shift in antitrust laws absent convincing evidence.[26] Such views display a level of nuance that brings them outside the "big is bad" mindset that seems to motivate neo-Brandeisians. The same applies to some members of the American Antitrust Institute, a think tank that has long worked to move the intervention calculus to the left. It is hard to accuse its adherents, including its president Diana Ross, of laissez faire sympathies. But it is not clear that they adhere to the extremes of the neo-Brandeisian vision.

5.2.2 Neo-Brandeisian Antitrust: Previewing the Critique

Certain deficiencies underlie the neo-Brandeisian ideology.[27] Those shortcomings take the form of evidentiary gaps, which proponents fill with anti-market priors and anecdotal impressions about the prevalence, genesis, and repercussions of industrial concentration. This does not make progressive reformists simple in their exposition. Far from it – their group includes deeply sophisticated thinkers. But it is to observe that ideological underpinnings matter here. Four overarching characteristics stand out.

---

[23] *Id.*
[24] Jonathan B. Baker et al., *Unlocking Antitrust Enforcement*, 127 YALE L.J. 1916 (2018); Fiona Scott Morton, *Antitrust Alone Is Not Enough to Combat the Problems Associated with Digital Platforms*, PROMARKET, May 17, 2019, https://promarket.org/antitrust-alone-is-not-enough-to-combat-the-problems-associated-with-digital-platforms/; see also JONATHAN B. BAKER, THE ANTITRUST PARADIGM: RESTORING A COMPETITIVE ECONOMY (2019); STIGLER COMMITTEE ON DIGITAL PLATFORMS, FINAL REPORT (2019), https://research.chicagobooth.edu/stigler/media/news/committee-on-digital-platforms-final-report.
[25] *See, e.g.*, Sandeep Vaheesan, *The Twilight of the Technocrats' Monopoly on Antitrust*?, 127 YALE L.J. FORUM 980 (2018).
[26] Carl Shapiro, *Antitrust in a Time of Populism*, 61 INT'L J. INDUS. ORG. 714 (2018).
[27] Beyond the author's critique, *see, e.g.*, Herbert J. Hovenkamp, *Whatever Did Happen to the Antitrust Movement*?, 94 NOTRE DAME L. REV. 583 (2019); Joshua D. Wright et al., *Requiem for a Paradox: The Dubious Rise and Inevitable Fall of Hipster Antitrust*, 51 ARIZONA ST. L.J. 293 (2019); Herbert Hovenkamp, *Progressive Antitrust*, 2018 U. ILL. L. REV. 71; Hon. Douglas Ginsburg, *Judging a Book: Ginsburg Reviews "The Curse of Bigness"*, LAW360, Dec. 3, 2018; Alan Reynolds, *The Return of Antitrust*?, REGULATION 24 (2018); Barak Orbach, *Antitrust Populism*, 14 N.Y.U. J. L. & BUS. 1 (2017).

First, the neo-Brandeisian critique remains unsubstantiated. Its proponents express displeasure with today's industry structures. Their claims of an economy-wide lessening of competition, however, lack factual support. Theirs is not an evidence-based reform movement. It is, rather, value-driven. And, in this respect, neo-Brandeisian scholarship is neither profound nor surprising. Its members advance classic left-wing ideology in promoting the interests of workers over consumers, protecting small firms from efficient ones, and trusting government regulation over market processes. Those values permeate its antitrust critique. They arguably define it.

Second, despite insisting that America has been monopolized, neo-Brandeisians are hostile to competition. They equate that concept with an abundance of small sellers (structure), rather than with maximum market-exerted compulsion to reduce price, improve quality, and invest in innovation (competitive pressure). They dislike Darwinian market processes, viewing low pricing with antipathy. That is why they champion the "competitive process" over a consumer-welfare standard. Yet, competition is not a process that they actually seek to protect. Far from it – their goal is to deprive the marketplace of rivalrous pressures created by some of the most effective competitors, especially but not limited to digital platforms.

Third, its proposals for reform are vague. The movement's scholars provides little specificity about how competition policy would work under the neo-Brandeisian vision. The closest that they have come is through the Utah Statement, which the next chapter addresses.

More generally, though, anti-monopolists offer no framework within which to weigh incommensurate factors. If exclusionary conduct is no longer a requisite of violating Section 2, then monopolization becomes a status offense. Is there any way for a successful firm not to run afoul of that law? Will there be any room for effects-based analysis? On the merger front, could transacting firms defend themselves, notwithstanding an increase in concentration, by showing that their combining will make them a more effective competitor or otherwise benefit consumers? Or would such benefits be acceptable as long as the emerging firm is not "too good" and likely to accelerate away from its competitors post-merger? If structure guides the way, what is the critical concentration ratio beyond which further increments in HHI, Cn, and the like become intolerable? How is that ratio established, and can the parties to a transaction mount an evidentiary showing to dispute it? Or would it simply be a fixed rule that applies without regard to the facts at hand?

Further, neo-Brandeisian scholars insist that size matters because it bestows disproportionate political influence on capitalists. But how big is too big? Does it matter whether a firm grows into a towering conglomerate without ever dominating a single relevant product market? Will efficiencies ever count in a merger review? Presumably, on the neo-Brandeisian account, horizontal acquisitions are largely or entirely out. Would vertical mergers ever be acceptable? If so, what principles would guide the clearance decision? These are just a sampling of questions to which neo-Brandeisian scholars have, to date, provided few answers.

Fourth, neo-Brandeisian scholarship evinces little interest in critical reflection. At no juncture does its leaders even acknowledge, for instance, that "law and economics" has, in at least some respect, rationalized antitrust enforcement or provided a methodology more coherent than what preceded the Chicago School. Seldom mindful of the limitations of their own positions, they instead mount a frenzied attack on antitrust norms.

Surety of position fills the neo-Brandeisian movement. Reformists venture few misgivings about the accuracy of their diagnosis. Their staunch assessment, however, lies on ambiguous evidence that is easy to misinterpret.[28] They may very well be mistaken about the existence, pervasiveness, or significance of market power in the US economy. Worse, they may be wrong about the origin of any problem. Myriad factors combine to determine economy-level outcomes, making it difficult to trace problems to underlying causes.

Neo-Brandeisians' certitude extends beyond industry analysis to the cause of the "problem." In particular, they are quick to ascribe dogmatic positions to those who enforce modern antitrust policy. On critics' telling, the Federal Trade Commission and Justice Department are enslaved to a free-market ideology that uncritically presumes that monopoly power is fleeting, entry barriers are trivial, merger-specific efficiencies are ubiquitous, and that fear of getting it wrong impedes challenges in tough cases. This caricature cannot be squared with reality.

Neo-Brandeisians should pause to consider that the federal antitrust agencies are repositories of vast industrial expertise. Antitrust lawyers and Ph.D. economists at the agencies have devoted their careers to evaluating how competition works in the markets that they police. The industrial-organization literature does not stand still, but continues to be refined in light of ongoing empirical and theoretical work. The charge that enforcers shut their eyes in service of the Chicago School is pure fantasy. The antitrust agencies sometimes err, of course, but they work assiduously to discharge their responsibilities for the benefit of consumers. Yet, neo-Brandeisians would throw away a methodology honed with decades of experience in favor of an industrial policy that would break up dominant firms without evidence of exclusion, prohibit mergers without regard to likely competitive effects, and replace economics with structural analysis.

In that respect, neo-Brandeisians venture no misgivings about potential unintended consequences of their preferred antitrust policies. The next section discusses the most influential neo-Brandeisian literature to date. In digesting their writings, the reader should bear in mind the problems identified above. It is truly remarkable how little the movement's scholars have to say about the doctrine and enforcement principles with which they would replace today's antitrust regime.

---

[28] *See* Chapter 3.

5.2.3 *The Neo-Brandeisian Critique*

A tsunami of op-eds and articles has proclaimed the death of competition, and advanced progressive reforms.[29] In the interests of space, however, this section focuses on substantive exposition of the neo-Brandeisian position. In particular, it considers Tim Wu's critique of the status quo and calls for reform. It addresses Lina Khan's influential writings about refashioning antitrust laws for the digital age. It evaluates Chris Sagers' views on reform. And it considers some recent thought leadership from the FTC's most progressive commissioner during the Trump Administration, Rohit Chopra. This discussion facilitates the critique that follows in Chapter 6.

5.2.3.1 Tim Wu

Professor Tim Wu of Columbia Law School – best known for his work on net neutrality – is the leading intellectual proponent of neo-Brandeisian reforms. Distrustful of markets, Wu expects that buyers' revealed preferences lead to unpalatable industry structures.[30] Opposed to the prominence of price theory in modern antitrust analysis, he has condemned recent Supreme Court decisions that he views as reflecting "laissez-faire economic policies[.]"[31] What concerns him most, however, is the cumulative effect of Chicago School policies. Everywhere he looks, Wu sees monopoly and oligopoly.[32]

Alarmed by "the threat to democracy posed by monopoly and excessive corporate concentration," Wu argues that "we are conducting a dangerous economic and political experiment" by having weakened the antitrust laws.[33] Modern antitrust merger review is responsible for this state of affairs, he insists, so much so that "over the last two decades we have allowed successive waves of mergers that make

---

[29] See, e.g., JONATHAN TEPPER, THE MYTH OF CAPITALISM: MONOPOLIES AND THE DEATH OF COMPETITION (Wiley 2019); Jonathan Tepper, *American Corporations Are Winning Their War on Capitalism*, BLOOMBERG, Nov. 26, 2018, https://www.bloomberg.com/opinion/articles/2018-11-26/tech-monopolies-strangle-economic-growth; Tim Wu, *The Oligopoly Problem*, NEW YORKER, Apr. 15, 2013, https://www.newyorker.com/tech/annals-of-technology/the-oligopoly-problem; Jordan Weissmann, *The Return of the Monopoly: An Infographic*, Apr. 2013, https://www.theatlantic.com/magazine/archive/2013/04/the-chartist/309271/; Kira Radinsky, *Data Monopolists Like Google Are Threatening the Economy*, Mar. 2, 2015, https://hbr.org/2015/03/data-monopolists-like-google-are-threatening-the-economy; Jonathan Tepper, *Why Regulators Went Soft on Monopolies*, THE AM. CONSERVATIVE, Jan. 9, 2019, https://www.theamericanconservative.com/articles/why-the-regulators-went-soft-on-monopolies/; John Mauldin, *America Has a Monopoly Problem*, FORBES, Apr. 11, 2019, https://www.forbes.com/sites/johnmauldin/2019/04/11/america-has-a-monopoly-problem/#49c756b52972.

[30] For example, he laments the effects of consumers' propensity to buy online for convenience's sake, thus feeding Amazon's rise and the decline of small neighborhood stores. Tim Wu, *The Life and Death of the Local Hardware Store*, N.Y. TIMES, Nov. 22, 2019, https://www.nytimes.com/2019/11/22/opinion/sunday/small-business-economy.html.

[31] Tim Wu, *The Supreme Court Devastates Antitrust Law*, N.Y. TIMES, June 26, 2018.

[32] Wu, *supra* note 29.

[33] *Id.*

a mockery of the 1950" Anti-Merger Act.[34] The solution is for antitrust to go beyond economics to become "a check against the political dangers of unaccountable private power."[35]

Giving his views fuller expression, Wu penned a short book, *The Curse of Bigness: Antitrust in the New Gilded Age*, in which he articulates his views in breezy and accessible form.[36]

Wu wastes no time diagnosing what he sees as today's competition problem. In his view, the point of antitrust is "to control the size of industrial giants."[37] By that measure, he views the law as an abject failure. The pharmaceutical, finance, media, airlines, and telecommunications industries receive mention, though tech platforms draw his greatest ire.[38] The problem is so severe, Wu argues, that we are going down the "road to fascism and dictatorship" – drawing a parallel to the conditions that produced Nazi Germany.[39] Indeed, Wu contends, "Hitler's rise and exercise of power were facilitated by the German Republic's tolerance of monopolies in key industries."[40]

One might find it farfetched to equate today's US antitrust laws with the conditions that produced the Nazi government. Wu, however, proceeds undeterred. In his view, "extreme economic concentration yields gross inequality and material suffering, feeding an appetite for nationalistic and extremist leadership."[41] Today's sad state of affairs is no accident, Wu tells us, because "mainstream antitrust economics" has "come to tolerate and even celebrate monopoly[.]"[42] Indeed, he has spoken of a "surrender of the government prerogative, which is to control monopoly at the behest not only of the consumer but of politics[.]"[43]

This is Chicago School thinking, Wu insists – a hollow school of thought that dressed up simplistic, but ostensibly intellectual, notions of price theory in the garb of consumer welfare. This effort by Robert Bork and his colleagues at the University of Chicago "was really laissez-faire reincarnated, without the Social Darwinist baggage, and with a slightly less overt worship of monopoly – but with much the same results."[44] Wu rejects as illusory the promised benefits of law and economics.[45]

---

[34] *Id.*
[35] Tim Wu, *Be Afraid of Economic "Bigness." Be Very Afraid*, N.Y. TIMES, Nov. 10, 2018, https://www.nytimes.com/2018/11/10/opinion/sunday/fascism-economy-monopoly.html.
[36] WU, *supra* note 11.
[37] *Id.* at 14.
[38] *Id.* at 21.
[39] *Id.* at 14; *see also* Wu, *supra* note 35.
[40] WU, *supra* note 11, at 80.
[41] *Id.* at 14.
[42] *Id.* at 83.
[43] https://www.c-span.org/video/?456021-1/communicators-tim-wu.
[44] Wu, *supra* note 11, at 91.
[45] *Id.* at 91 (arguing that Robert Bork took advantage of the fact that "despite the robes and bench, judges are still lawyers, and can become anxious when asked to decide complex and challenging cases" by offering "a calming remedy, with an appealing simplicity and apparent rigor" in the consumer welfare standard").

The Chicago method has not transformed competition policy into a scientific process because "economics does not yield answers but arguments."[46]

Brandeis was right, Wu argues, to champion antitrust as a check on private power.[47] The solution is to unwind the clock to an era before the Chicago School had worked its mischief. Wu envisions a competition policy that goes beyond economic analysis to incorporate political values.[48] For the past four decades, of course, mainstream antitrust thinkers have rejected the incorporation of any such values due to their incommensurability, subjectivity, and unpredictability. Wu waves off those concerns with the assertion that it "is not a good excuse."[49] In his view, concentration and corruption of the political process go hand-in-hand.[50] Hence, "the broad tenor of antitrust enforcement ... should be animated by a concern that too much concentrated economic power will translate into too much political power[.]"

Part of that reform effort, in Wu's opinion, should be to do away with antitrust's consumer-welfare mandate. That lodestar formed part of the Chicago revolution, which argued that the courts and agencies should administer antitrust in service of consumers through lower prices and higher output. The consumer-welfare standard ensured, among other things, that inefficient businesses could not usurp the antitrust process to seek shelter from competition. Like his neo-Brandeisian colleagues, however, Wu sees it as having "enfeebled the law" – promising "greater certainty and scientific rigor, it has delivered neither[.]"[51] In its place, he advocates for a "protection of competition" standard – one simpler than a welfare test, which courts cannot, in any event, accurately apply to complex transactions.[52] His preferred standard would protect a process, rather than a value.[53]

Wu never explains how his standard would apply. He is certainly wrong, however, to suggest that it is possible to enforce antitrust law responsibly without paying attention to values, which are another name for effects. In all likelihood, Wu would interpret the competitive-process standard to maximize the number of suppliers, to limit size, and to forbid low pricing or attractive consumer terms likely to produce a market leader.

Finally, Wu devotes considerable attention to merger reform, which he considers to be the "priority for Neo-Brandeisian antitrust[.]"[54] Championing tougher standards in the form of structural presumptions, Wu provides few specifics, though he does propose a per se rule against 4–3, 3–2, or 2–1 mergers.[55] The agencies routinely

---

[46] *Id.* at 135.
[47] *Id.* at 54.
[48] *Id.* at 55.
[49] *Id.*
[50] *Id.* at 58.
[51] *Id.* at 17.
[52] *Id.* at 136.
[53] *Id.*
[54] *Id.* at 127.
[55] *Id.* at 128–29.

demand remedies in such transactions, however, and block mergers to monopoly outright. It is therefore unclear precisely how such a per se rule would advance neo-Brandeisian goals. Here, Wu's argument seems oddly constrained. If one were truly to return to the 1950s and 1960s, before the Chicago School, then one would see rigid prohibitions against all or most horizontal and vertical mergers.

For Wu, perhaps, sources of inspiration go beyond America during the Warren Court era and the deconcentration pushes of the Roosevelt or Taft administrations. They include the European Union today. He calls for the US agencies to "borrow from Europe."[56] That jurisdiction, however, is characterized by the absence of rigorous due-process protections. EU competition law does not fully separate the investigative, prosecutorial, and adjudicative functions. It allows for no hearing before decision-makers, cross-examination rights, or discovery. The European Commission has also displayed a propensity to find violations without regard to effects.

No doubt, those qualities appeal to neo-Brandeisians keen to find antitrust problems with conduct or transactions that will not likely harm consumers. Still, although the European Commission has, without question, taken a more interventionist approach to competition problems than its US counterparts – especially with respect to technology platforms recently – it seems like an incomplete aspiration for neo-Brandeisians. The European Commission has exercised its broad mandate with care and discretion, and has never gone so far as to prohibit size on competition grounds. Perhaps for that reason, one of Wu's concluding proposals is to go further. Specifically, he would like the United States to adopt a no-fault administrative process through which to break-up overly consolidated industries.[57]

5.2.3.2 Lina Khan

If the neo-Brandeisian movement has a star, it is Lina Khan.[58] Exhorting a transformation, she has already driven the antitrust reform debate. Her heterodox vision is a reawakening – an anti-size movement that would return antitrust to its formative and long-neglected roots. She would deconcentrate industries, inhibit companies from operating marketplace platforms in which they also compete, and correct an imbalance in competition enforcement that has wrongly fixated on static price effects in downstream markets.[59]

---

[56] *Id.* at 131.
[57] *Id.* at 134.
[58] *See, e.g.*, Streitfeld, *supra* note 18; Robinson Meyer, *How to Fight Amazon (Before You Turn 29)*, THE ATLANTIC, July/Aug. 2018.
[59] *See* Lina Khan, *The End of Antitrust History Revisited*, 133 HARV. L. REV. 1655 (2020); Lina Khan, *The Ideological Roots of America's Market Power Problem*, 127 YALE L.J. FORUM 960 (2018); Lina Khan, *Sources of Tech Platform Power*, 2 GEO. TECH. L. REV. 325 (2018); Lina Khan, *The New Brandeis Movement: America's Antimonopoly Debate*, 9 J. EURO. COMPETITION L. & PRAC. 131 (2018).

Her greatest concern appears to be with mega-platforms. She thinks that free markets buttressed by contemporary antitrust principles are hopelessly ill-equipped to address the problems created by those networks. In tackling Silicon Valley, she is warmly disposed toward common-carrier solutions.[60] Her prescription calls for a siloing of activities – forcing certain integrated firms to divest up- or downstream businesses – and even price regulation. Hers is very much an anti-Chicago ideology. And it is has found traction. Op-eds, symposiums, articles, and even FTC hearings speak to her and other neo-Brandeisians' influence on the conversation. Khan has advised Democratic FTC Commissioner Rohit Chopra on competition policy, and apparently influenced his thinking.[61] She had the ear of Presidential candidate, Liz Warren, whose calls for a dramatic change in antitrust law echo neo-Brandeisian proposals. And it seems that the scope of her influence extends beyond the most progressive elements of the Democratic Party to influence the mainstream. At the time of writing, she had just been named Chairwoman of the FTC.

In 2016, while she was still a law student, Khan authored a pointed critique of the FTC, arguing that the agency was incapable of resolving the day's competition problems.[62] Hers was a scathing assessment. In her view, "the FTC is an agency adrift, squandering resources on trivial cases while failing to address the structural lack of competition that afflicts our economy."[63] She blamed the Chicago School's influence for allowing "a torrent of mergers and expansions" and producing an economy that "is in some respects more concentrated than it was during the Gilded Age[.]"[64]

Khan's signature paper, *Amazon's Antitrust Paradox*, argues that our competition laws are miscalibrated.[65] Targeting the vaunted consumer-welfare standard, she questions neoclassical antitrust's most essential premises. In her view, the agencies succumb to two grave errors. They look in the wrong place, and ask the wrong question. Economists tend to root their analysis in downstream effects, even if the restraint at issue occurs at the manufacturing or distribution level. They rarely worry if upstream distortions are unlikely to harm end consumers. To Khan, this is a gaping omission. And when the agencies do look at market outcomes, they tend to focus on price. Again, this is a function of neoclassical price theory, which economists use to

---

[60] Lina Khan & David E. Pozen, *A Skeptical View of Platforms and Commerce*, 119 COLUM. L. REV. 973 (2019).
[61] Rohit Chopra & Lina Khan, *The Case for Unfair Methods of Competition Rulemaking*, 86 U. CHI. L. REV. 357 (2020).
[62] Lina Khan, *How to reboot the FTC: The Agency's Antitrust Policy Isn't Up to the Challenge of the 21st Century. Here's How to Fix It*, POLITICO, Apr. 13, 2016, https://www.politico.com/agenda/story/2016/04/ftc-antitrust-economy-monopolies-000090.
[63] Id.
[64] Id.
[65] Khan, *supra* note 17.

model behavior's static effects. If price gravitates toward marginal cost, it is to be applauded.

To Khan, this is largely beside the point. The law and economics movement of the Chicago School, only moderately tempered by post-Chicago advances, has blinded enforcers to systematic losses of competition. Aggregations of buy-side power warrant condemnation, not celebration, and yet the agencies waved as digital platforms grew exponentially – their get-out-of-jail card's being that they charge consumers low or zero prices. Where defenders of the status quo see price theory as synonymous with rationalization and precision, Khan sees blindness and dogmatism. In her mind, price-theoretic models rid the antitrust calculus of many rich complexities. In pursuit of workability and scientific purism, neoclassical economists have sacrificed values that ought to have primacy of place.

Despite its titular role, Amazon was less the object of Khan's thesis as much as a vehicle for expressing it. To Khan, employing antitrust in service of consumers alone yields extreme and unwarranted implications. Chief among them was the Supreme Court's decision to eviscerate rules against predatory pricing and vertical integration – creating vulnerabilities that, she argues, Amazon has ruthlessly exploited. Observing that below-cost pricing is deeply rational in network industries in which scale is everything, Khan contrasts Amazon's "staggering growth" with "meager profits."[66]

To perfect its exclusionary drive, she contends, Amazon follows the tradition of monopolists of old – try to buy rivals at the outset, subject them to ruinous price competition if they refuse, and then acquire what remains – what one might call the John D. Rockefeller strategy. To Khan, Quidsi best exemplified the online retailer's strategy of killer acquisitions. In her telling, the company's successful foray into online baby care through Diapers.com floundered on Amazon's rocks. She contends that, after Quidsi rebuffed its 2009 purchase offer, Amazon sharply cut price and arrested Quidsi's ascent. Amazon then bought the company in 2011, following an in-depth investigation by the FTC. As of the time her note went to press in 2017, she claimed that Amazon led the online market for baby supplies with a 43 percent market share.[67]

Critics have questioned the completeness of Khan's account, noting not only that Amazon exited the space in 2017, but that Quidsi's founders used buyout money from Amazon to create a rival online retailer, Jet.com, which Walmart bought in 2016 for $3.3 billion and that sells diapers.[68] In the interim, such critics note, consumers benefitted from price competition between Amazon and Quidsi, while

---

[66] Id. at 713.
[67] Id. at 771.
[68] See, e.g., Jeffrey Eisenach, *Who Should Antitrust Protect? The Case of Diapers.com*, AEI BLOG, Nov. 5, 2018, https://www.aei.org/technology-and-innovation/who-should-antitrust-protect-the-case-of-diapers-com/.

the entrepreneurship underlying the Quidsi and Jet start-ups reflects the very acquisition opportunities that companies like Amazon present.[69]

Regardless, Khan's thesis culminates in two clear prescriptions. The law should address self-preferencing by dominant platforms, either by requiring vertical disintegration or subjecting them to common-carrier-style regulation. The key underlying this effort, she argues, is to "replace the consumer welfare framework with an approach oriented around preserving a competitive process and market structure."[70] That is a central tenet of the neo-Brandeisian prescription, and the object of Chapter 6 below.

5.2.3.3 Barry Lynn and the Open Markets Institute

If antitrust had a social-justice warrior, it would be Barry Lynn. A fiery champion for reform, he has devoted much of his career to tackling the "monopoly problem." Lynn trained not as an economist or lawyer, but as a journalist. Hostile to globalization and skeptical of capitalism – at least in its contemporary form – he has railed against both.[71] He would like to prohibit large technology firms from acquiring other companies, and has called for an absolute ban on future mergers and acquisitions by Facebook, Google, and Amazon.[72]

Lynn came to prominence through his work with the New America Foundation, a think tank for which he created and directed the Open Markets Initiative. In that role, he galvanized an influential movement against concentration in the US economy, organizing conferences attended by leading Democratic lawmakers, launching the Citizens Against Monopoly website, denouncing the Silicon Valley giants, and more besides. He burst to the forefront of the conversation on his firing in 2017. The ousting came after he applauded the European Commission's decision to fine Google $2.7 billion for alleging favoring its online shopping vertical search product. Commentators tied his ejection to Google's close ties to, and funding of, the New America Foundation – a causal link that Google denied.[73]

From there, Lynn launched the Open Markets Institute, which has proven to be a remarkably effective platform for advancing neo-Brandeisian views. The Institute has been a prolific publisher of industry studies, promoter of conferences, and nurturing community for talented young scholars and activists. To a degree, it has

---

[69] Id.
[70] Khan, *supra* note 17, at 803.
[71] BARRY C. LYNN, CORNERED: THE NEW MONOPOLY CAPITALISM AND THE ECONOMICS OF DESTRUCTION (2010); BARRY C. LYNN, END OF THE LINE: THE RISE AND COMING FALL OF THE GLOBAL CORPORATION (2005).
[72] Barry Lynn & Matt Stoller, *How to Stop Google and Facebook from Becoming Even More Powerful*, THE GUARDIAN, Nov. 2, 2017.
[73] See, e.g., Kenneth P. Vogel, *Google Critic Ousted From Think Tank Funded by the Tech Giant*, N.Y. TIMES, Aug. 30, 2017.

become synonymous with the neo-Brandeisian movement. Both he and the Institute have influenced a new generation of thought leaders, including Lina Khan.[74]

Lynn's views are not subtle. He sees monopoly in virtually every sector of the US economy. He rails against what he calls "super-giant corporations," but reserves his fiercest ire for large digital platforms. In his view, for example, "the business model of Google and Facebook... is to exploit the user. And what they do is capture information about you in order to exploit you better."[75] He sees those companies and Amazon as "the 21st century equivalents of the railroads, of AT&T" – and invokes their urgent breakup on antitrust grounds accordingly.[76] As with his neo-Brandeisian colleagues, he faults today's enforcers for following the Chicago School's law and economics approach, and calls for an urgent return to the anti-monopoly traditions of times past.[77]

It is de rigueur to oppose the consumer-welfare standard. Of course, Lynn obliges.[78] His larger vision, however, is quite radical. He does not wish to refine today's competition policies, but to discard them for something oppressive. He would forbid vertical integration – and especially dual distribution – although it consistently benefits consumers through lower prices and higher quality in the distribution chain.[79] So, too, he would prohibit "most price discrimination," even though it can enhance output.[80] None of this is surprising, for Lynn follows a well-trodden path associated with the far left. Indeed, he wants to clamp down on free trade in order to "[c]onfront foreign mercantilism."[81] Yet, free trade benefits all trading partners – and consumers, in particular – on account of comparative advantage.[82] This is economics 101.[83]

---

[74] Khan, *supra* note 17, at 710 (thanking "Barry C. Lynn for introducing me to these issues in the first place").

[75] *Communicators with Barry Lynn*, C-Span, Sept. 11, 2018, https://www.c-span.org/video/?451348-1/communicators-barry-lynn.

[76] *Id.*

[77] *See, e.g.*, Barry C. Lynn, *Antitrust: A Missing Key to Prosperity, Opportunity, and Democracy*, DEMOS, Oct. 2, 2013, https://www.demos.org/sites/default/files/publications/Lynn.pdf; Russell Brandom, *The Anti-Monopoly Case Against Google: A Conversation with Open Markets' Barry Lynn*, THE VERGE, Sept. 5, 2017, https://www.theverge.com/2017/9/5/16243868/google-monopoly-antitrust-open-markets-barry-lynn.

[78] Lynn, *A Missing Key*, *supra* note 77, at 15.

[79] *Cf. id.* at 16 with Daniel P. O'Brien, *The Antitrust Treatment of Vertical Restraints: Beyond the Possibility Theorems*, in The Pros and Cons of Vertical Restraints 72–74, 76 (2008) & Francine Lafontaine & Margaret Slade, *Exclusive Contracts and Vertical Restraints: Empirical Evidence and Public Policy*, in HANDBOOK OF ANTITRUST ECONOMICS 408–09 (2008).

[80] *Cf.* Lynn, *Antitrust: A Missing Key*, *supra* note 77, at 16 *with*, e.g., Dennis Carlton, Price Discrimination, OECD, ¶ 17, Nov. 2016 (citing Emek Basker, *Selling a Cheaper Mousetrap: Wal-Mart's Effect on Retail Prices*, 58 J. URBAN ECON. 203 (2003)).

[81] Lynn, *Antitrust: A Missing Key*, *supra* note 77, at 16.

[82] *See, e.g.*, Romain Wacziarg & Karen Horn Welch, *Trade Liberalization and Growth: New Evidence*, 22 WORLD BANK ECON. REV. 187 (2008); Jeffrey A. Frankel & David H. Romer, *Does Trade Cause Growth?*, 89 AM. ECON. REV. 379 (1999); Jeffrey D. Sachs & Andrew Warner, *Economic Reform and the Process of Global Integration*, in BROOKINGS PAPERS ON ECONOMIC ACTIVITY (1995); *see also* Council of Economic Advisers, *The Economic Benefits of U.S. Trade* (2015).

[83] *See, e.g.*, N. GREGORY MANKIW, PRINCIPLES OF ECONOMICS 47–59 (7th ed. 2015).

No matter the evidence or theory, economics is unlikely to move reformists like Lynn. The difference is one of principle. To neo-Brandeisians, proof that scale, integration, or trade reduces market-clearing prices and spurs economic growth does not answer the question. Theirs is not a utilitarian calculation in which net welfare gains dominate. For them, there is value – political in nature – to disintegrated, atomistic market structures. Hits to per capita GDP are worth the price.

5.2.3.4 Chris Sagers

Professor Chris Sagers is a leading progressive scholar of antitrust. He offers a bleak account of US competition policy. Lamenting "the death of antitrust," he has written of even the Obama "administration's failure to enforce" the law.[84] In his view, indeed, we do not "really have a competition policy at all" – not least because the courts and agencies have reduced merger policy to the point of challenging "only the most massively consolidating mergers."[85]

Merger policy, it seems, is where Sagers believes that our antitrust laws have gone furthest awry. The problem derives from an unfounded, but tenacious, belief that mergers yield efficiencies. In fact, Sagers concludes, "mergers don't do much good."[86] Indeed, he ventures, "there is in fact no meaningful proof that consolidation generates social benefits."[87] In his view, an unsubstantiated faith in the social value of merger activity has precipitated antitrust review standards that are remarkably permissive. In particular, he argues, a preoccupation with effects has led to a systematic failure to block harmful transactions. The solution is to adopt "some prospective, no-fault rule to control concentration for its own sake."[88]

Sagers does not hold himself out as a neo-Brandeisian.[89] He alludes to contradictions underlying proposed legislation infused with neo-Brandeisian thinking, pointing out that one cannot, for example, simultaneously protect "small businesses [and] suppliers, while fostering 'new innovative competitors.'"[90] He also has the intellectual honesty to make clear that protecting workers and small businesses "typically means higher consumer prices."[91]

Professor Sagers explores the issues with a more nuanced regard to evidence and trade-offs than others in the neo-Brandeisian movement. He is an elegant writer. And his thinking on the role of antitrust in preserving the competitive process is important.

---

[84] Chris Sagers, *Everyone Wants to Get Tough on Antitrust Policy, but Not Really*, N.Y. TIMES DEALBOOK, Apr. 29, 2016.
[85] Chris Sagers, *#LOLNothingMatters*, 63 Antitrust Bulletin 7, 26 (2018)
[86] *Id.* at 26.
[87] *Id.* at 5; *see also* CHRIS SAGERS, UNITED STATES V. APPLE: COMPETITION IN AMERICA 268 n.3 (2019) ("There is also growing evidence that mergers and acquisitions produce no significant benefits[.]").
[88] Sagers, *supra* note 85, at 7.
[89] *Id.* at 46 n.28.
[90] *Id.*
[91] *Id.*

Nevertheless, this book sees him as a proponent of neo-Brandeisian policies. Sagers worries about unchecked concentration, above all, and thus supports dramatic reforms to merger policy. He wants to rid prospective merger review of an effects-based inquiry, seeing it as unreliable and tailor-made to yield underenforcement. In championing a structural rule – albeit one yet undefined – he rejects the neoclassical antitrust tradition. He has criticized the agencies' practice of remediating partial overlaps in larger mergers through divestitures.[92] He is greatly encouraged by the rise of retrospective private merger litigation.[93] And he is a vocal advocate of bringing antitrust enforcement actions against the large Silicon Valley platforms.[94]

True, the basis for his argument sounds in consequentialist concerns. In particular, Sagers believes that antitrust's institutional framework simply cannot deal with problems of concentration-driven market power once that power becomes embedded. Hence, the answer is to nip the problem in the bud consistent with Section 7's founding vision. That justification arguably contrasts with the thinking of the larger neo-Brandeisian movement, which frames size as a problem in itself based on traditional progressive concerns for workers, small businesses, and resisting accumulations of economic power. Nevertheless, the changes that he envisions for competition policy go beyond refinement. His vision – the change that he thinks "is needed the most" – is "prospective, no-fault concentration control."[95]

There is much to applaud in Sagers' recent scholarship on reinvigorating antitrust by focusing on the role of competition itself.[96] Competition is messy, occasionally wasteful, and capable of yielding imperfect outcomes. Further, it is often most unclear how the competitive process will unfold, whether in terms of market structure, pricing, product qualities, or other attributes. Predicting the outcome of unbridled competition is famously difficult. But Sagers pays homage to this flawed process, rightly presenting competition as a critical social value worth preserving. The difficult question, of course, is how to blend preservation of the competitive process with anticipated effects. That is the question taken up in Chapter 8.

5.2.3.5 FTC Commissioner Rohit Chopra

Neither a lawyer nor an economist, FTC Commissioner Rohit Chopra has nevertheless become a thought-leader for progressive antitrust reformists. With a public-interest

---

[92] Chris Sagers, *The Limits of Divestiture as an Antitrust Remedy*, N.Y. TIMES DEALBOOK, Feb. 14, 2017, https://www.nytimes.com/2017/02/14/business/dealbook/the-limits-of-divestiture-as-an-antitrust-remedy.html.
[93] Chris Sagers, *Paging Don Qixote* [sic]: *The Last Hope for American Merger Law*, PROMARKET, Jan. 10, 2019, https://promarket.org/paging-don-qixote-the-last-hope-for-american-merger-law/?mc_cid=9bee2d788e&mc_eid=cb381d6019.
[94] *See, e.g.,* Chris Sagers, *Crack Down on Amazon*, SLATE, June 19, 2017, http://www.slate.com/articles/business/moneybox/2017/06/yes_there_is_an_antitrust_case_against_amazon.html.
[95] *Id.* at 24.
[96] CHRIS SAGERS, UNITED STATES V. APPLE: COMPETITION IN AMERICA (2019).

background dedicated to consumer protection, Commissioner Chopra brings a distinct viewpoint to the FTC. Joining the agency from the Consumer Financial Protection Bureau, he has used his position at the FTC to advance neo-Brandeisian perspectives.

Chopra has railed against the pharmaceutical industry, and chastised the Commission for pursuing long-established divestiture remedies meant to address horizontal overlaps between existing and pipeline drugs.[97] He would rather block such combinations outright, even if they are predominantly complementary. He has singled out private equity for harsh criticism, arguing that it has reduced competition in the financial sector by drawing capital out of public trading markets.[98] Although private equity funds are known to make the companies they acquire more efficient – often with an eye to resale – Chopra rejects that view, claiming that the funds simply curtail production in less profitable segments and lead their portfolio companies to take on more debt.[99] He also considers private equity funds to be unreliable divestiture buyers.[100]

He has called, among other things, for the FTC to engage in a rulemaking process for the purposes of antitrust law.[101] That proposal is heterodox. Modern antitrust is synonymous with competitive effects analysis, which guides the outcome as to every agreement, merger, or practice outside of a narrow band of hardcore restraints. The rule of reason is the vehicle through which adjudicators conduct that evaluation, the goal of which is accuracy. Chopra and his former advisor, Khan, would displace that standard – if only in part – with rules that identify certain restraints that constitute unfair methods of competition regardless of their effects.

Perhaps most notably of all, Chopra called for a moratorium on all non-bankruptcy-related merger and acquisition activity for the duration of the COVID-19 pandemic.[102] That proposal reveals how he thinks about M&A activity. Neo-Brandeisians see little or no social value in transactions in the market for corporate control – it is arguably one of their defining traits. For those who believe that voluntary contracts reallocate scarce resources to more efficient uses, it would be madness to block mergers and acquisitions during a severe recession, the likely effect's being to exacerbate the economic shock.

---

[97] See, e.g., In re AbbVie, Inc./Allergan plc, FTC File No. 191-0169, Dissenting Statement of Commissioner Rohit Chopra, May 5, 2020.
[98] Pallavi Guniganti, *FTC Commissioner Hits Out at Private Equity*, GLOBAL COMPETITION REV., Sept. 25, 2018.
[99] Id.
[100] Id.; see also Rohit Chopra, Prepared Remarks at FTC Hearings on Consumer Protection and Competition, Dec. 6, 2018, p. 3.
[101] Chopra & Khan, *supra* note 61; see also Comment of Federal Trade Commissioner Rohit Chopra, Hearing #1 on Competition and Consumer Protection in the 21st Century, Sept. 6, 2018.
[102] Rohit Chopra, Mar. 18, 2020, https://twitter.com/chopraftc/status/1240417656941023234; *Coronavirus & Concentrated Corporate Power: How We Got Here & Where We Need to Go*, AM. ECON. LIBERTIES PROJECT, https://www.economicliberties.us/event/coronavirus-concentrated-corporate-power-how-we-got-here-where-we-need-to-go-2/.

5.3 TESTING THE ANTI-MONOPOLY VISION

This section gives the neo-Brandeisian view its most workable expression, and then identifies the serious flaws associated even with that hypothetical implementation. It concludes by referring back to when the US government last mounted a serious effort to tackle the perceived problem of excessive concentration. That period marked a low point in the history of the federal antitrust authorities, and thus warrants careful reflection.

5.3.1 *How Neo-Brandeisian Antitrust Might Work*

Reduced to its essence, the anti-monopoly drive seeks to reignite structuralism. A push to deconcentrate industries in the near term, of course, would require legislative reform. Even if the agencies chased the Open Markets Institute's wish list, they would find little traction in the courts. Existing antitrust doctrine would not permit status-based monopolization offenses, no-fault compulsory divestitures, a crackdown on vertical restraints, or the abolition of all horizontal or vertical mergers and acquisitions.

For policymakers, however, a threshold inquiry is to optimize competition policy in the abstract. Normativity precedes practicality. For the purposes of this exercise, then, assume a compliant legislator and judiciary. The question thus becomes how one would best shape a US competition policy in pursuit of deconcentration. We can then evaluate the workability and prudence of that approach.

This exercise does not articulate the most extreme neo-Brandeisian vision. It does not, for example, treat consolidation as an intrinsic evil. Nor does it favor any one constituency over any other as deserving beneficiaries of competition. Similarly it does not construe scale-driven economies, whether in input or product markets, as a bad thing. Instead, it takes seriously the proposition that a structural loss of competition has occurred, and for which overly liberal antitrust enforcement is partially responsible. That is a hypothesis that warrants reflection, and – though the author disagrees with it based on the available evidence – there is a case to be made. This section undertakes that theoretical exploration.

5.3.1.1 The Principled Case for Reverting to Structuralism

One might state the case for broad structural reform as follows: the shift to an effects-based analysis brought with it prediction. Basing merger intervention decisions on anticipated effects, however, depends on a counterfactual than can merely be modeled and never observed. Two certainties follow. One is error. Despite their best efforts, the agencies (or courts) will bless harmful consolidating transactions that a structural rule would catch. The second is that, over time, such deals will incrementally – but inexorably – lead markets and industries to grow more concentrated unless entry dominates. What starts as an erroneously approved merger leading to price increases in an isolated market will spread. Like a malignant tumor, market power will creep into and infect all sectors of the economy. This outcome is especially pernicious because there is no good solution for concentrated industries in which market power has become entrenched. The point of the 1950 Anti-Merger Act was to nip consolidation in the bud through an incipiency standard. It is much easier to prevent the disease than to cure it.

Of course, there is value in allowing innocuous transactions to pass muster. On this score, an effects-based approach is superior because structural rules or heavy presumptions are, by definition, imprecise. But any value to be found here is meagre. Mergers often fail to realize productivities.[103] Efficiency-enhancing transactions appear to be the exception, rather than the rule. Further, horizontal combinations yield little or no social value. In differentiated products markets, the post-merger firm *always* has an incentive to raise price after buying a competitor. That is a mathematical fact. After closing, the buyer recaptures positive margins on sales that diverted to the target. That creates some incentive to exercise newfound market power. Yes, any sustained exercise of market power depends on customers' and competitors' responses, but those will not always cancel out the price effect. Further, economists have long expected rising concentration to make it easier for incumbents to coordinate on pricing. A voluminous literature bears out a positive intra-industry relationship between concentration and price – an association that exists across a broad swathe of settings.[104] And that is to say nothing about the countless inter-industry SCP studies that observed a positive correlation between concentration and market power.[105]

At this junction, a structuralist might appeal to contemporary realities and common sense. Industry after industry has become palpably more concentrated – a fact that depends not on sophisticated empirical work, but merely on opening one's eyes.[106] There has been no lack of approved blockbuster mergers. Antitrust has assumed newfound political urgency for a reason. People are alarmed. On top of this comes the formal work. The 2016 Council of Economic Advisors, *the Economist*, studies associated with the University of Chicago (of all places), and several other researchers find a trend of rising concentration within and across industries. Moreover, firm profits are tenaciously holding at historical highs, seemingly impervious to a competing away of rents. Further, consolidation seems to be outpacing new firm creation. This macro-level evidence combines with virtually all discernible data points in trending toward a common position: market power is on the rise.

That last conclusion remains controversial. To some progressive reformists, however, those who champion the existing law and economics approach are clinging to

[103] Chapter 2, § 2.2.
[104] Chapter 3, § 3.3.
[105] Chapter 3, § 3.2.
[106] Chapter 4, § 4.2.1.

dogma. If a strengthening of antitrust enforcement requires absolute proof, then nothing will change. Demonstrating a systematic loss of competition in the US economy would be an unimaginably vast and burdensome undertaking. Tying it to inadequate antitrust enforcement could be harder still. When anecdotal observations, macro-level evidence, theory, and an established paucity of merger efficiencies combine to point in one direction, we should act. Structuralists may acknowledge rigorous, evidence-based arguments to the contrary, but would likely say that conservative writers excel at explaining away unwelcome correlations and associations, without offering any evidence of over-enforcement of the antitrust laws. It is time, reformists would conclude, to do something.

The preceding argument captures the view not of the author, but of a putative structuralist concerned about the status quo. Some neo-Brandeisians would presumably go further, but we shall proffer a view of structural antitrust that is more measured. We will then critically examine that hypothetical implementation, and demonstrate why it would not be sound.

5.3.1.2 How a Reversion to Structuralism Might Take Form

A serious push in favor of deconcentration would have two components. First, merger-review standards would be revised in favor of structural rules and presumptions. Second, the government would seek to break-up the largest firms or subject them to behavioral obligations in order to facilitate the growth of rivals.

The first step would be easier than the second. The 1950 Celler–Kefauver Act already accommodates an incipiency standard. The Supreme Court has blessed enforcement directed at arresting a rising tide of concentration.[107] Even without going so far as to block transactions that give the post-merger firm less than 10 percent share of a fragmented market,[108] one could in theory ratchet up the antitrust inhibition of consolidating transactions under existing standards. The courts, however, are unlikely to embrace the standards underlying the Court's 1960s jurisprudence.

Moving past this framework, there are different ways radically to enhance the antitrust merger prohibition consistent with the structural vision. All would require legislative reform. A threshold change – popular among progressive reformists – may be to prohibit all 4–3 or worse combinations.[109] The government could make existing HHI thresholds binding. The 2,500 HHI threshold for "highly concentrated markets" could become a ceiling. In other words, the agencies would block any merger creating a level of concentration greater than that point. Further, the current

---

[107] Brown Shoe Co. v. United States, 370 U.S. 294, 317-18 (1962); *see also* United States v. Aluminum Co. of Am., 148 F.2d 416, 428 (2d Cir. 1945) ("[G]reat industrial consolidations are inherently undesirable[.]").
[108] *Cf., e.g.*, United States v. Pabst Brewing Co., 384 U.S. 546 (1966); United States v. Von's Grocery Co., 384 U.S. 270 (1966).
[109] *See, e.g.*, Wu, *supra* note 11, at 129.

HHI range for moderate concentration, 1,500 to 2,500, would become an area of presumptive illegality. Within that window, the parties would have to demonstrate that the transaction would enhance, rather than harm, competition. Otherwise, the transaction would be prohibited. An efficiencies defense – in the sense of justifying price increases based on productivities – would be officially abolished.[110]

Save for efficiencies, which seldom lead the agencies to clear transactions about which they otherwise harbor concerns, these changes would be significant. In practice, the agencies do not enforce the HHI thresholds with vigor. Their merger challenges invariably see HHIs far higher. That is because, consistent with the effects-based analysis imbedded in the Guidelines, concentration ratios merely serve as screens and proxies. Notably, the 2010 thresholds themselves marked a significant increases relative to 1997 guidelines, which defined high concentration at the 1,800 HHI level. The basis for the change was that, much like today's thresholds, they did not reflect agency enforcement practice.

Such revisions, of course, would transform merger review in traditional bricks and mortar industries. But what of digital platforms and the network industries in which they operate? Those spaces experience heavy dynamic competition. Displacement occurs unpredictably and suddenly – often from lateral markets – against a backdrop of steady incremental innovations. In that setting, technology is everything. Traditional horizontal merger review principles may not obviously apply to deals in which the competitive issue, if there is one, concerns the developmental trajectory of the target in a world but-for the transaction. And against that question, one must weigh the innovation-boosting effects of a healthy acquisition market for start-ups.

The anti-monopoly movement, as we have seen, views leading US technology firms as Exhibit A of our failed antitrust policies. If they are right, then structural reform of the antitrust laws must address this issue, too. HHI thresholds do not work if the acquirer and target do not presently compete in the same relevant market. Challenges would have to lie in the potential-competition doctrine. Such cases are notoriously difficult to win.[111] If structuralist policies were to achieve their sought goals in this new economy setting, then they would have to replace proof of effects with presumptions. One would have to fashion a standard that presumes competitive harm when a sufficiently dominant platform or technology company acquires a target operating in an adjacent space. Any such change, of course, would mark a dramatic departure from the status quo.

Merger reform, however, only answers half of the question. It would be equally important to address conduct. For reformists alarmed by largesse in Silicon Valley,

---

[110] The Horizontal Merger Guidelines do not recognize such a defense today. Rather, merger-specific efficiencies have to be of such a character as to neutralize the exercise of market power. U.S. Dep't of Justice & Fed. Trade Comm'n, Horizontal Merger Guidelines § 10 (2010).

[111] *See, e.g.*, Fed. Trade Comm'n v. Steris Corp., 133 F. Supp. 3d 962 (2015). *But cf.* United States v. Microsoft Corp., 253 F.3d 34, 58 (D.C. Cir. 2001) (per curiam) (en banc).

for example, a moratorium on future acquisitions in horizontal or adjacent spaces would be welcome, but incomplete, medicine. Such a change in the law would itself be radical, but structuralists – to say nothing of the more extreme neo-Brandeisians – want to deconcentrate industries. Here, one encounters a fork in the road. With carte blanche to rewrite the law, some self-proclaimed anti-monopolists would presumably seek a status offense in the form of a faultless monopolization standard. Breakups would ensue. Somewhat less radically, structuralists might preserve the existing requirement for exclusionary behavior in a Section 2 case, but instead magnify the scope of what counts as exclusion and potentially flip evidentiary burdens to help the agencies evade hard questions on effects.

To hasten implementation of these new policies, Congress might pass laws along the lines of bills previously introduced by Senator Klobuchar and others. The Anticompetitive Exclusionary Conduct Prevent Act, which she introduced in March 2020 with Senators Blumenthal and Booker, presents one such example.[112]

That bill addresses unilateral behavior. It would prohibit "exclusionary conduct that presents an appreciable risk of harming competition." It defines such conduct not as a practice that can exclude equally or more efficient competitors, but as one that materially disadvantages rivals or limits their opportunities. It does not exempt actions that exclude by making the implementing firm a more effective competitor. Hence, practices that enhance a dominant firm's efficiency or facilitate higher R&D or innovation would arguably come within the scope of prohibition. Hence, any unilateral practice that makes the firm's products more attractive to consumers than those of its competitors might exclude under the act. The bill goes further still, presuming that exclusionary conduct appreciably risks harming competition if the firm at issue had over 50 percent market share or otherwise has significant market power.

Such legislation would help the agencies challenge unilateral conduct in the digital economy and more broadly.[113] But it would mark a sharp departure from the modern focus on economic analysis and competitive effects.

Other legislation may target mergers and acquisitions. The Consolidation Prevention and Competition Promotion Act of 2019, introduced in January of that year, sought to do just that.[114] That bill would radically enhance the agencies' freedom to block transactions without proof of likely effects. It would eliminate the current "substantial" lessening of competition standard with a lesser material

---

[112] Anticompetitive Exclusionary Conduct Prevent Act, S. 3426, 116th Congress, 2d session, Mar. 10, 2020.

[113] Although monopolization cases poses significant litigation challenges, the government has a strong track record of success when it does sue. *See, e.g.*, McWane, Inc. v. Fed. Trade Comm'n, 783 F.3d 814 (11th Cir. 2015); United States v. Dentsply Int'l, Inc., 399 F.3d 181 (3d Cir. 2005); *Microsoft*, 253 F.3d at 58. *But see* Fed. Trade Comm'n v. Qualcomm Inc., – F.3d –, 2020 WL 4591476 (9th Cir. Aug. 11, 2020).

[114] Consolidation Prevention and Competition Promotion Act of 2019, S. 307, 116th Congress, 1st Session, Jan. 31, 2019.

lessening test, and shift the burden of proof in large or significantly consolidating transactions to the merging parties to show that their deal will not harm competition.

The next section evaluates a possible structural vision for antitrust reform. In doing so, it assumes that Congress has passed legislation of the preceding kind and that the agencies have decided both to make highly concentrated HHI thresholds dispositive and likewise to block 4–3s, 3–2s, and 2–1s. That universe fairly encapsulates the goals of some Democratic lawmakers, with the support of progressive reformists including neo-Brandeisians.

An even more radical change in the law would also be possible. The preceding draft legislation shies away from no-fault standards. It still allows merging parties to mount an evidentiary defense. One could imagine going further. The Neal Report of 1969, for example, recommended a Concentrated Industries Act under which the government could break up oligopolies.[115] That was the true zenith of the SCP vision for competition policy, and surely resonates with many structuralist reformists.

It seems outlandish for US antitrust policy today, but such powers are conceivable even within a market-based economy with a common-law tradition. The UK Competition and Markets Authority, for example, can conduct market investigations if it believes that various market features restrict or distort competition.[116] If the CMA identifies a structural problem – that is, not one tied to exclusionary practices by a dominant undertaking – then it can enforce no-fault remedies "aimed at making the market(s) more competitive in the future."[117] Its remedial toolkit includes divestitures.[118]

5.3.2 Structural Antitrust Examined: The Demerits of an Ideology

Free to enact policies of their choosing, determined structuralists would have many options. This section identifies two constructs, which represent two hypothetical implementations of increasing extremism. Both depart sharply from the status quo, and indeed would be radical. The former, however, has a defensible evidentiary foundation. We start there so as to engage with serious ideas in lieu of what some might perceive as a strawman position (albeit one ardently championed by some in the anti-monopolist movement). Having grappled with that "moderate" vision, we then touch on the most transformative imaginable reforms. Such proposals, which represent the core of the neo-Brandeisian movement, include no-fault divestitures, an effective ousting of the courts in favor of administrative enforcement, an outright ban of acquisitions by digital platforms with large market capitalizations, and so on.

---

[115] Phil C. Neal et al., *Report of the White House Task Force on Antitrust Policy*, reprinted in 2 ANTITRUST L. & ECON. REV. 11 (1969).

[116] CMA, Market Studies and Market Investigations: Supplemental guidance on the CMA's approach (2017).

[117] Id. §§ 3.3, 4.1–4.25.

[118] Id. § 4.19.

5.3.2.1 Why Even the "Moderate" Version of Structural Antitrust Is Problematic

A good-faith debate rages about antitrust's pivot away from structuralism in 1981.[119] Reformists who think that shift a mistake have evidence to support their convictions. The empirical literature connects price (and, in older studies, profit margins) to concentration. Critics discount statistical fallibilities in favor of the intuition that fewer sellers mean less competition. They see anecdotal evidence of consolidation in almost every industry of note. Reports of an economy-wide trend of increasing concentration and firm profits merely confirm the obvious. In structuralism, they see a principled and effective means for administering antitrust law. The Cournot-Nash model of oligopolistic competition provides direct theoretical support for the HHI framework. To be sure, strengthening the role of concentration ratios would mean a diminished role for effects, which would lead the agencies inadvertently to impede some procompetitive or competitively neutral mergers. For structuralists, however, that price is worth paying to fulfil antitrust's raison d'être.

Progressive antitrust reformists hold such views. It would be possible to realize their structural vision without abandoning certain core features of the US antitrust regime. On the less extreme implementation, courts would remain responsible for adjudicating antitrust cases. Section 2 liability would require exclusionary conduct, and never be a status offense. There would be no absolute ban on horizontal or vertical mergers. Outside of certain structural bands, firms could mount an evidentiary showing that their consolidation will not harm competition. Contested proceedings before independent adjudicators, with full rights to cross-examination, would remain fundamental in every case. A loss of competition would be the defining attribute of every antitrust violation.

Even such "moderate" structural reform would radically depart from today's approach. Drawing on existing proposals, including bills that progressive sponsors have introduced, assume the following attributes:

- Antitrust's organizing principle is the preservation of market structure, ensuring that relevant markets do not become concentrated. Whether a given delta in HHI, Cn, n-1 produces anticompetitive effects or not, a generalized connection exists between the two, meaning that antitrust is better off clamping down on concentration for its own sake.
- Critical concentration ratios are dispositive. Any 4–3, 3–2, or 2–1 transaction is illegal, as is any combination that creates a post-merger HHI above 2,500.

---

[119] As noted, 1981 was when Bill Baxter took control of the Antitrust Division. Even by the following year, merger review standards were remarkably different than those that had held sway even a year before. U.S. DEP'T OF JUSTICE, MERGER GUIDELINES (1982) (emphasizing a shift away from market-share considerations in favor of likely effects); Federal Trade Comm'n, Statement of Federal Trade Commission Concerning Horizontal Mergers (1982) (same).

- The law will presume that a merger creating a HHI between 1,500 and 2,500 will harm competition, just as it does with respect to a transaction that gives the post-merger firm a market share exceeding 30 percent (*Philadelphia National Bank*).
- The courts will presume that the relevant market definition alleged by the government is correct.
- For transactions valued over $5 billion – or ones in which a party has assets, net annual sales, or market capitalization over $100 billion – the parties will have the burden of proving that their merger will not harm competition.
- The Section 7 standard will no longer be a "substantial lessening of competition" but rather a material lessening.
- The agencies will disfavor divestitures, blocking consolidating transactions that would require more than a *de minimis* sale of one party's business in order to eliminate a problematic overlap.
- Efficiencies cannot justify a merger that creates problematic structural changes to a market.
- The law would prohibit unilateral practices by firms with monopoly power that materially disadvantage rivals or limit their opportunities.

Collectively, such reforms would give the agencies broad discretion to block transactions and police unilateral conduct. In this hypothetical world, their authority and evidentiary burden would remain somewhat bounded, but would be much relaxed relative to today. For structuralists, this toolkit would likely suffice to arrest further consolidation. Firms could clear modest horizontal combinations below structural thresholds and unlikely to be associated with effects.

For ardent reformists, however, a going-forward remedy may not suffice. The final element listed above, therefore, may be critical to those seeking a reversion to structuralist principles. By equating exclusion with mere disadvantage or limitation, the law would bring a broad sphere of unilateral conduct within the sphere of condemnation. This would allow the agencies to seek the breakup of dominant firms that they perceive to be entrenched. Such proposals, however, would be deeply misguided.

Each discrete element listed above warrants its own critique. There is, for example, no a priori basis in economics for a universal critical concentration ratio. Markets with at least four sellers and four buyers often reach competitive outcomes.[120] That is particularly likely where customers are sophisticated. This does not imply that every four-to-three merger, for instance, yields harms competition. Any structural threshold underlying a rule or presumption is arbitrary at the margin. That reality is of little concern when the threshold exists merely to guide

---

[120] *See* Martin Dufwenberg & Uri Gneezy, *Price Competition and Market Concentration: An Experimental Study*, 18 J. INDUS. ORG. 7 (2000).

further investigation. When it becomes an independent and conclusive basis for decision, however, then it becomes troubling.

Meanwhile, flipping the burden of proof upends the American tradition in which free contract is the default and the government must prove its case in order to enjoin private conduct. As described below, easing the agencies' need to establish harm to competition would usher forth diminished rigor of analysis and, in time, an abundance of unmeritorious cases. Separately, eliminating divestitures as a means for resolving horizontal merger issues – a neo-Brandeisian favorite[121] – is unworkable. Resource constraints pose a threshold problem. Suing to block every transaction that features, in some line, a problematic horizontal overlap would require a massive increase in staff and budget for the agencies. More fundamentally, however, the policy would be unsustainable. Sophisticated parties to a transaction could agree to sell an overlap unit as a precedent condition to their merger. The government would then face a *fait accompli*, and be left with trying to challenge a transaction that involves no competitive overlap – a case that, even on the proposals above – would likely be dead on arrival.

One could devote many pages to addressing individual recommendations for reform. Indeed, the next chapter does just that, evaluating each reform proposal imbedded in the Utah Statement – the most detailed prescription yet put forth by the anti-monopoly movement. With respect to the less extreme structuralist case outlined above, however, the real critique lies in four larger points.

First, the structuralist proposal above would represent a knowing abandonment of accuracy.

An effects-based standard asks the right question – whether, based on all available information, a particular merger, practice, or agreement will harm competition and hence consumers. It may not always yield the correct answer, but it strives to do so based on all information available about the relevant market. Structuralism does not even try to do so. One-size-fits-all rules and presumptions are, by definition, inaccurate when applied across dissimilar markets. They are also likely to be wrong even when formulated within a single industry. We *know* that concentration does not itself cause unilateral effects, save for the vanishingly rare case of quantity-based competition between identical firms selling homogeneous products in a market with perfect information (Cournot). Diversion and margins create unilateral price increases, not market shares or HHIs.

A competition policy that retreats to concentration ratios as the decision point does not seek to understand the realities of a given transaction in full context. Whether a HHI or Cn rule or presumption yields the wrong answer in a given case does not seem to matter to structuralists – they care whether it is directionally correct across many merger reviews. But if structuralists abandon informed decision-making in individual cases, then it is counter-intuitive to think that aggregating those

---

[121] Khan, *supra* note 62.

determinations will produce superior results than universalizing an effects standard that strives for precision.

Effects-based analysis has limitations, of course – especially when in predicting a market's future technological path. There are ways to control for those issues, however, while staying within a predictive framework. For example, in cases of indeterminism surrounding the effects of a consolidating merger between close rivals, the government should err on the side of impermissibility. But for all its limitations, however, they are neither as pervasive nor as deep as some reformists argue. The knowledge problem will never disappear, but it continues to erode. The past several decades have seen material advances in econometrics and industrial organization – the tools through which agencies inform their merger-clearance decisions. Structural rules and presumptions, by contrast, would be clumsy, imprecise, and overbroad.

This debate centers around error. An effects-based analysis should minimize the incidence of both Type I and Type II errors. The conventional approach to decision theory has overweighted the severity of a Type I error relative to Type II one – a mistake that has produced insufficient enforcement at the margin. Chapter 7 presents that important analysis. Structuralism, however, skews the calculus far from the optimal point. It accepts many Type I errors in order to minimize Type II mistakes. This disproportionate weighting may not matter if faults carry the same magnitude, but they do not.

At this point, progressive reformists would likely claim that mergers seldom generate productivities. On that telling, Type I errors inflict modest (or no) social costs. In fact, horizontal mergers are more likely to realize significant efficiencies than conglomerates ones.[122] True, horizontal combinations between firms with large market shares are less likely to realize scale economies – depending on the industry long-run average cost curve, they may have already been exhausted. But even mergers at high concentration levels can bring significant productivity gains, whether in distribution, managerial expertise, capital, technology, or more. In any event, many such transactions already encounter antitrust headwinds. The kinds of additional transactions likely to be caught by an expansion in the scope of the antitrust prohibition are the ones most likely to yield social value. In short, there is every reason to continue to strive for accuracy and to worry about false positives and false negatives alike.

Second, structuralism rests on a faulty premise – namely that preserving market structure is synonymous with protecting competition. That supposition falls prey to the same fallacy that led SCP researchers astray. Competition is not simply a function of structure. Rather, competition determines structure. Structural antitrust is therefore inherently flawed. By equating cause and effect, it guarantees perverse outcomes.

---

[122] *See* Chapter 2.

Consider a technology industry in which the principal (and most socially valuable) form of competition lies in R&D. Competition policy should instill strong incentives to innovate. Consumers will reward the most successful innovators with market share and larger margins, thus creating indicia of a competitive problem from the perspective of structure, when in fact the environment is optimized. High concentration ratios may reflect a healthy competitive space or the absence of one. The fact that the digital economy is ground zero for structurally minded reformists is thus particularly concerning. HHIs, Cns, and market shares provide limited insight into the competitive picture in such markets. An effects-based approach grapples with industry dynamics. Structuralists abandon such efforts, instead gauging a market's competitiveness by reference to numbers that may have dubious value.

More generally, markets tend to assume a structure that reflects their underlying cost and consumer-demand characteristics. Mature industries characterized by static competition, little innovation, and few scale economies will gravitate toward atomistic market structures. If large capital investments are not a requisite of entry or expansion, then low concentration may ensue. Professional services are a common example. By contrast, some industries experience long-run average-cost curves that decline over an extended range of output. Investment-based competition may feature heavily in such settings, leading firms to compete in infrastructure and quality, as well as in price. Telecommunications and other traditional network industries are good examples. Their optimal competitive structure will tend to be concentrated.

In short, the competitive pressures to which firms are subject depend on more than the mere number and relative symmetry of sellers in a market. Consolidation and pricing pressure may go hand in hand, if only to a point, in some industries. In other settings, high concentration may point to a competitive problem. Universal rules of thumb are thus unreliable. This reality makes a compelling case for an effects-based approach.

Third, relieving the agencies of the burden of proving their cases would bring unwelcome consequences over time. By design, structuralist reforms would make it easier for the government to block mergers and prohibit unilateral conduct. Suggestions include expanding the structural presumption of harm beyond today's *Philadelphia National Bank* standard, presuming the soundness of the government's alleged relevant market, flipping the burden of proof to force certain merging parties to prove that their deal is competitively neutral or better, and reducing the legal standard below its existing "substantial lessening of competition."

Those proposals, of course, assume that the agencies identify problematic transactions that they cannot block under existing law. That assumption may not be justified. It certainly was not the author's experience at the FTC. Many reformists presuppose a competition problem, and then point to the absence of enforcement as evidence of deficiencies in antitrust doctrine. This circular logic features throughout neo-Brandeisian scholarship. Nowhere is that phenomenon more obvious than with respect to Amazon and leading Silicon Valley firms, the existence and acquisition activity of which are themselves treated as proof positive of a loophole in the antitrust laws. Few pause to consider that the absence of antitrust challenge points to a virtue of today's law and economics approach, rather than a flaw.

Structuralist reforms would allow the government to prevent a broader swathe of deals. The immediate consequence, however, would not be more merger cases – the agencies today are not in the habit of blessing transactions that they expect to harm consumers – but more wins. The government has a strong litigation record, but the DOJ and FTC do lose occasionally. Recent examples include *Qualcomm*, *Sabre/Farelogix*, *Evonik/PeroxyChem*, and *AT&T/Time Warner*.[123] Insidious effects, however, would likely creep in over time.

In particular, the rigor of the agencies' internal evaluation and deliberations would erode in time. The prospect of going to court, facing a skeptical judge, and having to mount an impressive factual showing to discharge one's evidentiary burden imposes discipline. The agencies often savor litigating, but having to prove their case not only guards against overreach or exuberance, but forces staff to ask hard questions and bring thoroughness to their work.

That reality facilitates superior investigations, helping the agencies to reach correct intervention decisions. Flipping burdens, relieving the agencies of having to prove the relevant market, and adopting broad structural rules or presumptions would upend that environment. A softening of proof would follow. That has been the experience of other jurisdictions. Until the EU courts began to crack down, for example, the European Commission made more and more use of the "by object" restriction label to dispatch with agreements that it did not like without having to prove effects. The Commission even did so in complex cases for which simplistic conclusions were wholly unreliable.[124]

Eventually, the agencies would become comfortable with their de facto veto power. In time, they would prohibit some innocuous transactions and bring unjustified monopolization cases. Political expectations of reinvigorated enforcement would accelerate that phenomenon. Demands for the agencies to "do something" about Silicon Valley have already reached fever pitch. One could only imagine the expectations and pressure brought to bear on DOJ and FTC leadership in light of legal reforms of the kind discussed above.

Bad cases would be sure to result. This requires little conjecture. It was a hallmark of agency enforcement during the peak of the prior structuralist era in US

[123] Fed. Trade Comm'n v. Qualcomm Inc., – F.3d –, 2020 WL 4591476 (9th Cir. Aug. 11, 2020); United States v. Sabre Corp., – F. Supp. 3d –, 2020 WL 1855433 (D. Del. 2020), *vacated*, Trade Reg. Rep. ¶ 81,294 (3d Cir. July 20, 2020) (but clarifying that "this Order should not be construed as detracting from the persuasive force of the District Court's decision"); Fed. Trade Comm'n v. Rag-Stiftung, 436 F. Supp. 3d 278 (D.D.C. 2020); United States v. AT&T Inc., 916 F.3d 1029 (D.C. Cir. 2019).

[124] *See, e.g.*, C-67/13 P, Groupement de cartes bancaires v. Comm'n, 2014 E.C.R. 2204, [2014] 5 C.M.L. R. 22.

competition policy.[125] We have already discussed the debacle that was the DOJ's thirteen-year-long monopolization case against IBM – a meandering lawsuit filed in 1969 that squandered resources, achieved nothing, offered no coherent theory of competitive harm, morphed several times, and targeted a company for successfully out-innovating its rivals.[126] In short, it represented a perversion of the antitrust laws. It may also presage the kind of Section 2 case for which neo-Brandeisians clamor against today's leading digital platform and technology companies. Whether in the new economy or old, the hallmark of a meritorious monopolization case is exclusion that is not a byproduct of competition on the merits (including R&D, growth, meeting consumer demand, and product improvement), but of foreclosure or raising rivals' costs by investing in nonefficiency-enhancing ends. Even the "moderate" structuralist vision outlined above would move the needle away from the latter cases – which are principled and, for that reason, hard – to the former, which are neither.

The folly of pursuing deconcentration goals – in lieu of anticompetitive conduct – is plain in examples beyond the Justice Department. In the 1970s, an activist FTC endeavored to rework markets into more competitive structures, most notably the cereal industry. It proceeded under an aggressive "shared monopoly" theory, pursuant to which oligopolists violate Section 5 of the FTC Act even without agreeing with one another. On the FTC's view at the time, conscious parallelism that generated supranormal rents and deterred entry was actionable. Even under a doctrinal landscape that was far more accommodating of size-based antitrust intervention than today's law, the Commission failed to win or secure a remedy in *any* of those monopolization cases.

Those examples are telling because the FTC already enjoys broad authority under Section 5, which prohibits "unfair methods of competition."[127] In 1972, the Supreme Court observed that the Commission can proscribe an unfair competitive practice "even though the practice does not infringe either the letter or the spirit of the antitrust laws[.]"[128] The Commission's historical use of that authority is thus instructive as we think about how the agencies may act if granted broader powers today to block mergers, prohibit unilateral conduct, and arrest concerted restraints.

In 1972, the Commission sued Kellogg, General Mills, General Foods, and Quaker Oats, alleging a shared monopoly in which the respondents marketed some 150 cereal brands, used trademarks to deter competition, and refused to sell their products for private-label uses.[129] The case perfectly encapsulated SCP thinking, as it singled out as anticompetitive the firms' investment in product

---

[125] *See, e.g.*, William E. Kovacic, *Failed Expectations: The Troubled Past and Uncertain Future of the Sherman Act as a Tool for Deconcentration*, 74 IOWA L. REV. 1105 (1989).
[126] *See* Chapter 2, § 2.1.2.1.
[127] 15 U.S.C. § 45(a)(1).
[128] Fed. Trade Comm'n v. Sperry & Hutchinson Trading Stamp Co., 405 U.S. 233, 239 (1972).
[129] John D. Morris, *Cereal Monopoly by 4 Top Makers Charged by F.T.C.*, N.Y. TIMES, at 1, Jan. 25, 1972.

differentiation as a means for securing supranormal margins. The FTC further challenged shelf-allocation agreements and barometric price leadership. The Commission later dropped the case against Quaker Oats, but proceeded to administrative trial against the three remaining cereal makers. Ten years and $6 million after the Commission had authorized the complaint, the administrative law judge ruled against complaint counsel on every score, rejecting their effort to transform parallel conduct into actionable anticompetitive conduct.[130] In 1982, the Commission dismissed the complaint with prejudice, without hearing staff's appeal.

In a parallel to today's structural debate, FTC Commissioner Bailey observed, "From an economic perspective, I was troubled by a case which sought a remedy breaking up dominant firms in an industry simply because they had become dominant. Such an approach would be deleterious to effective competition."[131]

The FTC's cereal case was not the only debacle. The Commission devoted much of its attention in the 1970s to the oil and gas industry, given the energy crisis of the time. It sued the country's eight largest oil companies in 1973, alleging that they had perpetuated "a noncompetitive market structure in the refining of crude oil into petroleum products."[132] The theory of harm once again lay in oligopolistic interdependence. Like the cereal case, it failed. Eight years after approving the complaint, the Commission dismissed it.[133]

Another example lay in the FTC's lawsuit against the dominant publisher of flight schedules for disadvantaging commuter airlines in their efforts to compete against certificated air carriers. The respondent, of course, did not compete in the restrained market. That did not stop the FTC from finding an antitrust obligation to deal under its expansive Section 5 authority. That effort proved too much for the Second Circuit, which worried that "enforcement of the FTC's order here would give the FTC too much power to substitute its own business judgment for that of the monopolist in any decision that arguably affects competition in another industry."[134] The agency's last litigated vertical merger challenge also arose in this era – a case that the Commission lost at the Second Circuit in 1979.[135] The Commission also brought monopolization cases across a range of industries including bread, coffee, car rentals, and processed lemon juice.[136]

The thinking behind the enforcement efforts of that time bears remarkable parallels to today's neo-Brandeisian ideology. In 1977, for example, the FTC's

---

[130] Fed. Trade Comm'n v. Kellogg Co., 99 F.T.C. 8 (1982).
[131] Michael Decourcy Hinds, *U.S. Drops 10-Year Antitrust Suit Against 3 Largest Cereal Makers*, N.Y. TIMES, § 1, p. 1, Jan. 16, 1982.
[132] In re Exxon Corp., Trade Reg. Rep. (CCH) ¶ 20,388, at 20,269 (Dkt. No. 8934, July 17, 1973).
[133] Fed. Trade Comm'n v. Exxon, 98 F.T.C. 453 (1981).
[134] Official Airline Guides, Inc. v. Fed. Trade Comm'n, 630 F.2d 920, 927 (2d Cir. 1980), *cert. denied*, 450 U.S. 917 (1981).
[135] In re Fruehauf Corp., 603 F.2d 345 (2d Cir. 1979).
[136] See William E. Kovacic, *The Federal Trade Commission and Congressional Oversight of Antitrust Enforcement*, 17 TULSA L. REV. 587, 646 (1982).

Chairman gave an infamous speech in which he sought to infuse competition policy with such considerations as "resource depletion, energy waste, environmental contamination, worker alienation, [and] the psychological and social consequences of producer-stimulated demands."[137]

The FTC's experience speaks to the difficulties – not simply doctrinal – in basing antitrust on structuralism alone. As some of the Commission's leading and most experienced economists later observed in 2003, "There are probably few people today would defend those cases[.]"[138] Alas, that view no longer remains accurate.

Finally, structural antitrust risks incoherence. With unbounded authority, enforcement would become capricious. It was precisely that fear that led the US Courts of Appeals to reject each effort by the FTC in the 1970s to expand Section 5 far beyond the scope of the Sherman Act.[139] A cohesive theory with which to guide intervention would be difficult, if not impossible, to identify. An incommensurate set of factors would weigh on agency decision-making, meaning that the outcome of an investigation would turn on the decision-makers' predilection for certain values over others. Those values will differ between those responsible for competition policy, leading to sporadic and contradictory enforcement over time. And the lack of a clear objective may lead antitrust policy to meander, pursuing vagrant goals to the benefit of no particular constituency. That is the lesson of the Warren Court's antitrust jurisprudence and the agencies' misguided interventions through the late 1970s.

5.3.2.2 The Folly of More Extreme Neo-Brandeisian Proposals

Recently introduced bills approximate elements of the less extreme vision explored above. The changes envisioned by such draft legislation would be iconoclastic and ill-advised. To go yet further would magnify the error.

Some call for taking "antitrust policy-making away from the courts and rooting it back in Congress and regulatory agencies" as "a core part of neo-Brandeisian reforms."[140] Such proposals are unsupportable. Regulators that need not prove their case in front of a neutral arbiter in a contested proceeding will not hold themselves to optimal standards. They will adopt those that facilitate desired

---

[137] Michael Pertschuk, Remarks before the Annual Meeting of the Section of Antitrust and Economic Regulation, Association of American Law Schools, Atlanta, Ga. (Dec. 27, 1977).
[138] David Scheffman *et al.*, *20 Years of Merger Guidelines Enforcement at the FTC: An Economic Perspective*, 71 ANTITRUST L.J. 277, 278 (2003).
[139] E.I. du Pont de Nemours & Co. v. Fed. Trade Comm'n, 729 F.2d 128, 138-39 (2d. Cir. 1984); Boise Cascade v. FTC, 637 F.2d 573, 582 (9th Cir. 1980); *Official Airline Guides*, 630 F.2d at 927.
[140] Ganesh Sitaraman, *Unchecked Power*, THE NEW REPUBLIC, Nov. 29, 2018; *see also* Ganesh Sitaraman, *Taking Antitrust Away from the Courts: A Structural Approach to Reversing the Second Age of Monopoly Power* (2018), https://greatdemocracyinitiative.org/wp-content/uploads/2018/09/Taking-Antitrust-Away-from-the-Courts-Report-092018-3.pdf.

outcomes – that is, the easy path – rather than hold themselves to demanding burdens that lead to more accurate determinations over time.

Ousting the courts in favor of administrative enforcement would also do violence to due process, leading the United States down the same unbecoming paths that some other jurisdictions have followed. Even in the European Union, which has a mature and sophisticated antitrust system, firms accused of violating competition rules and facing potentially billions of euros in fines get no hearing in front of the ultimate decision-makers, no opportunity to present their case to adjudicators who are independent of the case team responsible for investigating and prosecuting the matter, and no right to cross-examination. Although the EU courts have thankfully become more demanding of late, traditionally the European Commission has enjoyed excessive deference in the event of party appeals. This is not a model to which US antitrust policymakers should aspire.

Others in the anti-monopoly movement want to sever the connection between antitrust and competition. In its modern conception, antitrust does not serve as a catch-all device for economic regulation or industrial policy. It exists in order to protect the competitive process. There is debate, of course, as to what preserving competition means in this context.[141] But it has not meant prohibiting transactions free of effects on competition simply because they are large.

Some neo-Brandeisians argue, however, for an outright ban on conglomerate mergers based on size alone, without any inquiry into horizontal overlap, vertical-access concerns, or any ensuing competitive effects.[142] Theories of harm in conglomerate transactions – in particular, the proposition that scope can have range effects that entrench market power through cross-subsidization and inhibiting entry – are controversial.[143] Some neo-Brandeisian authors dispense with the need to ground abolition decisions even on such flimsy grounds. They would simply adopt a prohibitory rule – in the case of one article, a ban on any merger in which both firms have assets greater than $10 billion.[144] In justification of this proposal, they observe that antitrust today would allow the first and third largest corporations, Apple and Exxon/Mobil, to merge. Indeed, it would because such a transaction would have no effect on competition. Rather than indict antitrust, the example reveals the opposite.

Antitrust can serve different roles, but is widely understood to preserve the social value associated with competition. It does not grant imprimatur to policymakers to reshape industries, inhibit free contract, or otherwise reconstitute markets to their liking. Modern antitrust presumes that markets, freed of unjustified restraints on

---

[141] See Chapters 1 and 8.
[142] Robert H. Lande & Sandeep Vaheesan, *Preventing the Curse of Bigness Through Conglomerate Merger Legislation*, 52 ARIZ. ST. L.J. 75 (2020).
[143] See, e.g., William J. Kolasky, *Conglomerate Mergers and Range Effects: It's a Long Way from Chicago to Brussels*, Nov. 9, 2001, https://www.justice.gov/atr/speech/conglomerate-mergers-and-range-effects-its-long-way-chicago-brussels.
[144] Lande & Vaheesan, *supra* note 142, at 79.

competition, will tend toward a more efficient structure. Consistent with the Coase theorem, merger activity is one way in which this process unfolds. Those who anticipate ruination visited upon us by unlimited conglomerate consolidation overlook efficiencies.

Large conglomerate mergers risk dissynergies, and thus encounter a natural business deterrent. The 1960s merger wave occurred principally through conglomerate transactions due to antitrust prohibitions on horizontal and vertical deals. Myriad studies in the decades that followed concluded that M&A activity of the time was not associated with productivity gains – a conclusion that some progressive reformists uncritically extend to horizontal mergers.[145] Neo-Brandeisians have also pointed to the near-$165 billion AOL/Time Warner merger as an example of how antitrust fails to arrest large conglomerate transactions.[146] It is an odd case study to bring up because it stands among history's most catastrophic M&A failures – hardly the kind of thing that prospective buyers would seek to emulate.

Beyond offering a solution in search of a problem, neo-Brandeisians offer few thoughts on how to wield vast regulatory power with direction and principle, and without overreaching and thus denying consumers the fruit of competition. That concern is acute, given the legislative and enforcement experience of the 1960s and 1970s discussed above. The absence of coherent principle arguably defined the period, which saw the enactment of anti-consumer policies. Indeed, this issue may present the most serious objection to the most extreme proposals for reform emanating from the left.

---

[145] See Chapter 2.
[146] Lande & Vaheesan, *supra* note 142, at 77.

6

Testing the Neo-Brandeisian Vision

In one respect, neo-Brandeisians are outspoken. They have much to say in diagnosing contemporary antitrust. On their account, the pivot from structuralism to effects has introduced the unwelcome art of prediction into competition law – an inquiry that neither courts nor agencies can reliably make. Creating the illusion of precision, they argue, this approach ensures that some anticompetitive transactions pass muster. Meanwhile, an obsession with price in administering the "consumer welfare" standard leads enforcers to overlook digital platforms that use free or low-cost offerings to achieve frightening rates of growth. Dominant control over infrastructure that is systemically important to the economy results. Presumed efficiencies in vertical integration provide carte blanche for further consolidation. For all of these reasons, reformists insist, we face a concentration crisis today. That is their critique, and – in that respect at least – they are clear.

Such reformists, however, are ultimately reticent. Yes, their criticism is as sharp as their prognosis is bleak. When it comes to the vital specifics of their championed reform, however, they are mum. What emerges is a general call to use concentration to decide merger cases. That structural approach is not merely to inform analysis, as it does today, but to end it. Yet, confusingly, they disavow a "strict" return to the structure-conduct-performance approach of the 1950s and 1960s.[1] More generally, low prices alarm the movement's scholars, who wish to see legal obstacles to predatory-pricing claims revoked. And they wish monopoly to become a condition that is, in itself, actionable.

These are hazy objectives – not specific reforms. If the movement is serious about reviving the anti-monopoly tradition, then it has to present its vision with granularity. It needs to do more than propose eliminating certain antitrust laws or enforcement policies. It must identify which rules or standards would stand in their place.

Such precision, however, is nowhere to be found. That deficiency speaks volumes. It is easy to render a broad critique, especially if one is loose with the empirical

---

[1] See, e.g., Lina M. Khan, Note, *Amazon's Antitrust Paradox*, 126 YALE L.J. 745 (2017) ("I am not advocating a strict return to the structure-conduct-performance paradigm.").

evidence, drawing firm conclusions from ambiguous data.² It is altogether more difficult, of course, to wrestle with the trade-offs that emerge in molding workable policies. Imperfect as it may be, neoclassical antitrust provides clear answers to hard policy questions, and has endured with broad bipartisan consensus for several decades as a result. Anti-monopolists, by contrast, have made virtually no effort on this front.

This chapter addresses the few specifics that neo-Brandeisians have mustered. It finds those prescriptions for reform to be inadequate.

6.1 THE UTAH STATEMENT

As noted, reformists have yet to lay out a progressive vision for antitrust with specificity. That failure has not escaped notice.

Responding to criticism, leading members of the neo-Brandeisian movement – specifically, Tim Wu, Lina Khan, and Marshall Steinbaum – purported to give the necessary detail in October 2019.³ In an apparent effort "to specify what, exactly, they mean, in concrete, legal detail" when neo-Brandeisians urge a revival of the antimonopoly tradition, they issued the "Utah Statement."⁴ The statement is worth reproducing in full, albeit broken down by constituent part in order to facilitate analysis.

The Utah Statement⁵

We believe that:
(1) Subjecting concentrated private power to democratic checks is a matter of constitutional importance;
(2) The protection of fair competition is a means to a thriving and democratic society and an instrument for both the creation of opportunity and the distribution of wealth and power;
(3) Excessive concentration of private economic power breeds antidemocratic political pressures and undermines liberties; and
(4) While antitrust is not an answer to every economic distress, it is a democratically enacted and necessary element in achieving these aims.

In reflection of these principles, we therefore call for the following reforms to current antitrust doctrine and enforcement practice:

This preamble recites neo-Brandeisian values. As abstract propositions, they are hard to refute. After all, political ideals inform antitrust.⁶ The authors were wrong to imply, however, that today's antitrust policies do not already serve those four goals.

---

² Neo-Brandeisians draw hard conclusions of entrenched and growing market power from industry statistics that do not support them. *See* Chapter 3.
³ https://unews.utah.edu/utah-statement/.
⁴ Tim Wu, *The Utah Statement: Reviving Antimonopoly Traditions for the Era of Big Tech*, ONEZERO, Nov. 18, 2019, https://onezero.medium.com/the-utah-statement-reviving-antimonopoly-traditions-for-the-era-of-big-tech-e6be198012d7.
⁵ *Id.*
⁶ *See* Chapter 1.

To be sure, some reformists disagree. The Utah Statement is a call to action, and signals that those values remain unfulfilled. In other words, it implies that private power has become concentrated to the point that it endangers democracy. And it burdens antitrust with some responsibility for that policy failure.

Today's antitrust laws, however, have not seen economic power accumulate to the point of risking our form of government. The contrary proposition is, to put it generously, alarmist. Attempted parallels between today's policies and those that accompanied the fall of the Weimar Republic, for example, do not withstand scrutiny. Today's antitrust framework would have prevented industrial conditions of the kind associated with the rise of Nazism.[7]

The DOJ and FTC employ sophisticated methodologies that are calibrated to protect competitive pressure, not arbitrary structural concentration thresholds. Neither agency is shy about litigating, and the discriminating nature of their interventions is grounds for praise, not condemnation. Yet, anti-monopolists now suggest that the same economists and lawyers who have incrementally refined competition policies over the past forty years have committed us to an industrial path that leads to fascism.[8] Neo-Brandeisians include talented scholars, deep thinkers, and gifted writers. They do their reform movement no favors in advancing such facially absurd propositions.

A separate inquiry might ask whether – separate and apart from competition – some firms control critical infrastructure on which the larger economy depends, and are vulnerable to instability. This phenomenon is likely to be sector-specific, and ought to be tackled outside of competition law. The classic example, of course, are financial institutions that "are too big to fail" because they operate as critical intermediaries in an industry prone to boom and bust cycles. Failures of regulation in such settings can necessitate subsequent state interventions in a manner that could arguably implicate the political concerns that animate neo-Brandeisians. But those concerns do not translate into a broader antitrust prescription.[9]

6.1.1 *Doctrine*

1. Vertical coercion, vertical restraints, and vertical mergers should enjoy no presumption of benefit to the public;
2. By rule or statute, non-compete agreements should be made presumptively unlawful;
3. The *Trinko* doctrine of implied regulatory preemption should be overruled;

---

[7] See Daniel A. Crane, *Fascism and Monopoly*, 118 MICH. L. REV. 1315 (2020).
[8] *See, e.g.*, TIM WU, THE CURSE OF BIGNESS: ANTITRUST IN THE NEW GILDED AGE 14, 18 (2018); Tim Wu, *Be Afraid of Economic 'Bigness.' Be Very Afraid*, N.Y. TIMES, Nov. 10, 2018, https://www.nytimes.com/2018/11/10/opinion/sunday/fascism-economy-monopoly.html.
[9] For the author's prior thoughts on this point, see Alan Devlin, *Antitrust in an Era of Market Failure*, 33 HARV. J.L. & PUB. POL'Y 557 (2010).

4. The *Brooke Group* test for predatory pricing and *Weyerhaeuser* test for predatory bidding should be overruled;
5. The *Berkley* [sic] *Photo* standard for establishing monopoly leveraging should be restored;
6. The essential facilities doctrine should be reinvigorated for dominant firms that deny access to critical infrastructural services;
7. Structural presumptions in merger review should be restored;
8. The *LinkLine* doctrine holding that price squeeze allegations fail as standalone Section 2 claims should be overruled;
9. *Noerr-Pennington* should be overruled and replaced by a First Amendment defense and appropriate statutory protections for workers; and
10. The Clayton Act's worker exemption should be extended to all who labor for a living, regardless of statutory employment status, for horizontal coordination, collective bargaining, and collective action in service of either.

These proposals mark the most detailed accounting to date of neo-Brandeisian reforms. Each one touches on weighty issues – questions that are variously doctrinal and steeped in the industrial-organization literature. Wu, Khan, and Steinbaum do not address those complications. Nor do they offer details about how the law would operate under their vision. The following pages consider the proposals in order.

6.1.1.1 "Vertical Coercion, Vertical Restraints, and Vertical Mergers Should Enjoy No Presumption of Benefit to the Public"

Vertical integration can eliminate double marginalization.[10] Economists have established this proposition time and again – it is an elementary part of the literature.[11] Firms set their boundaries at the point where in-house solutions are marginally cheaper than third-party contracting.[12] Save for situations in which vertical integration introduces risks of strategic conduct – a limited set of circumstances that the agencies are well positioned to identify[13] – an expectation of efficiencies naturally follows.

Of course, vertical mergers do not always remove double margins. Nor do they necessarily produce lower prices for consumers. The agencies must test for these characteristics in every investigation.[14] But such transactions can achieve benefits across a range of plausible scenarios. A general hostility to vertical mergers is therefore unsupportable as a matter of economics. Indeed, while hypotheses of

---

[10] *See, e.g.*, Roger D. Blair et al., *Analyzing Vertical Mergers: Accounting for the Unilateral Effects Tradeoff and Thinking Holistically About Efficiencies*, 27 GEO. MASON L. REV. 761 (2020).
[11] *See, e.g.*, DENNIS W. CARLTON & JEFFREY M. PERLOFF, MODERN INDUSTRIAL ORGANIZATION 417–18 (4th ed. 2005); *infra* notes 15 & 17.
[12] Ronald Coase, *The Nature of the Firm*, 4 ECONOMICA 386 (1937).
[13] *See* FED. TRADE COMM'N & U.S. DEP'T OF JUSTICE, VERTICAL MERGER GUIDELINES (2020).
[14] *Accord id.* § 6.

vertical foreclosure remain at best weakly supported, vertical integration is associated with falling prices and rising output.[15]

Vertical restraints can also benefit consumers. Although they inhibit competition within the distribution chain, that is not the end of the story. A manufacturer can induce its distributors or retailers to invest in its brand by promising to shield them from intrabrand competition. If the net procompetitive effect on interbrand competition dominates any diminished competition in the vertical chain, then the restraint will benefit consumers. Economists have developed models showing circumstances in which vertical restraints can promote or harm competition.[16] As a general matter, though, profit-maximizing firms will try to minimize the quality-adjusted cost of their distribution chains. Vertical restraints that emanate from producers – as opposed to those requested from downstream – are thus likely to be procompetitive.

Unsurprisingly, economists have found impressive evidence that vertical restraints benefit consumers.[17] A respected literature review concluded that "the present empirical evidence suggests that a fairly relaxed antitrust attitude toward restraints is warranted."[18]

These points are so well understood that it seems trite to revisit them. The Utah Statement, however, glides past the economics to reach an unsupported implication. Its authors believe that vertical integration often harms the public. The fact that it is their first policy prescription reflects a measure of urgency. And, although it is unclear what they mean by "coercion," the choice of word speaks volumes about how they perceive of vertical restraints generally.

Today's laws do not presume, in any event, that vertical arrangements benefit consumers. The law requires a plaintiff to *prove* that a particular restraint or merger is likely to harm competition. A defendant enjoys no legal presumption that its in-channel restraint or integration achieves efficiencies or will otherwise benefit consumers.

---

[15] See, e.g., Daniel P. O'Brien, *The Antitrust Treatment of Vertical Restraints: Beyond the Possibility Theorems*, in THE PROS AND CONS OF VERTICAL RESTRAINTS 72–74, 76 (2008); Ali Hortaçsu & Chad Syverson, *Cementing Relationships: Vertical Integration, Foreclosure, Productivity, and Prices*, 115 J. POL. ECON. 250 (2007); see also Francine Lafontaine & Margaret Slade, *Exclusive Contracts and Vertical Restraints: Empirical Evidence and Public Policy*, in HANDBOOK OF ANTITRUST ECONOMICS 408–09 (2008) (finding "surprisingly consistent" empirical evidence that vertical restraints not only benefit manufacturers, but "also typically allow consumers to benefit from higher quality products and better service provision").

[16] See, e.g., Carlton & Perloff, *supra* note 11.

[17] See, e.g., Lafontaine & Slade, *supra* note 15, at 408–09 ("While different theoretical models often yield diametrically opposed predictions as to the welfare effects of vertical restraints, we find that with manufacturer/retailer or franchisor/franchisee relationships the empirical evidence concerning the effects of vertical restraints on consumer well-being is surprisingly consistent. Specifically, it appears that when manufacturers choose to impose such restraints, not only do they make themselves better off but they also typically allow consumers to benefit from higher quality products and better service provision."); see also James Cooper et al., *Vertical Antitrust Policy as a Problem of Inference*, 23 INT'L J. INDUS. ORG. 639 (2005).

[18] Lafontaine & Slade, *supra* note 15, at 409.

Hence, on its terms, the Utah Statement's first policy proposal is mysterious. There is no doctrinal presumption to reverse. Perhaps its authors wish to reintroduce the per se rule for resale price maintenance and exclusive selling territories in the vertical chain.[19] There is no economic basis, however, for any such blanket prohibition. The evidence simply does not show (and theory does not imply) that such restraints generally harm competition or consumers. Or maybe the authors would like to presume competitive harm in vertical mergers that involve a share in some upstream or downstream market that exceeds a threshold – something akin to the *Philadelphia National Bank* presumption for horizontal transactions that give the post-closing firm over 30 percent market share.[20] Once again, however, there is no basis for such a presumption in a vertical setting.

In any event, the agencies have not systematically failed to block or remedy anticompetitive vertical transactions. Many such deals create efficiencies, but the government does not assume them.[21] Vertical mergers that create no efficiencies, but introduce a risk of strategic conduct over an important upstream asset, ought to be coolly received. When a transaction within the supply chain would create efficiencies, economists can evaluate the ability and incentive of a buyer to engage in input or customer foreclosure by estimating tradeoffs. The DOJ and FTC have often employed conduct remedies to preserve efficiencies that flow from disintermediation, whilst controlling any attendant risk to competition. Absent evidence that this approach has failed, there is scant reason to abandon it.

6.1.1.2 "By Rule or Statute, Non-compete Agreements Should Be Made Presumptively Unlawful"

Non-competes that arise in the employment and transactional settings differ in important ways.

The former warrant skepticism. The typical justification for non-competes in employment contracts is that, without them, employers will decline to invest in training their workers because other companies may free ride by hiring those skilled workers away.

Perhaps, but no one should accept that proposition uncritically. Companies have powerful incentives – born of competition and profit maximization – to hire skilled workers, invest in their development, and compensate them commensurately with their value in order to retain them. Non-compete agreements are not generally a but-for cause of hiring and training decisions at the firm level. To be sure, exceptions arise. Some positions require an unusual amount of specialized training, and free-riding opportunities may be abundant.

---

[19] *See* Leegin v. PSKS, 551 U.S. 877 (2007); State Oil v. Khan, 522 U.S. 3 (1997); Cont'l TV v. GTE Sylvania, 433 U.S. 36 (1977).
[20] United States v. Phila. Nat'l Bank, 374 U.S. 321 (1963).
[21] *See* Fed. Trade Comm'n & U.S. Dep't of Justice, VERTICAL MERGER GUIDELINES (2020), at § 6.

In general, though, competition on the sell side of product markets and on the buy side of labor markets will spur companies to train even high-skill employees. Laws guarding against appropriation of trade secrets provide further protection. And there is a significant reward at the larger policy level for enhancing competition in employment markets. Fluid labor markets ensure that human capital can flow to its highest value uses, allowing new entrants to find talent. California prohibits most non-competes in employment contracts – a factor that may have contributed to Silicon Valley's success.

Non-competes that accompany the sale of a business, however, are different. In buying a company, it is rightly part of the bargain that the seller not immediately re-enter the market. Doing so deprives the buyer of the value of its acquired assets. Of course, no sensible competition policy would allow a restraint on entry that either is perpetual or exceeds the scope of the business acquired. The FTC recently emphasized those principles, explaining that buyers cannot justify non-competes based on a "mere general desire to be free of competition following a transaction[.]"[22]

It is not clear whether the authors want non-competes accompanying the sale of a business to be presumptively illegal. That view would represent a radical change in the law.[23] And it would likely inhibit the market for corporate control, reducing asset prices. Long-established case law treats such restraints as enforceable if they are reasonable in duration and scope – a common-sense standard that ought to continue to govern.[24]

6.1.1.3 "The *Trinko* Doctrine of Implied Regulatory Preemption Should Be Overruled"

This proposal has much to commend it.

Given its reach, antitrust often encounters separate regulatory schemes. Questions of preemption naturally follow. Where legislation expressly precludes antitrust, then the inquiry obviously ends. Implied preemption is more controversial. Given the danger of inconsistent duties, superfluous enforcement, and confusion, should the Sherman Act yield in the face of a parallel legislative framework? The traditional view – one to which the author is favorably disposed – is that "[r]epeals of the

---

[22] *See, e.g., In re* DTE Energy Co., FTC File No. 191-0068, Analysis of Agreement Containing Consent Orders to Aid Public Comment, pp. 2–3, https://www.ftc.gov/system/files/documents/cases/07_dte-enbridge_aapc_redacted.pdf; *see also* Brian Telpner, *Just because it's ancillary doesn't make it legal*, Sept. 30, 2019, https://www.ftc.gov/news-events/blogs/competition-matters/2019/09/just-because-its-ancillary-doesnt-make-it-legal.

[23] *Cf. e.g.,* E.T. Prods., LLC v. D.E. Miller Holdings, Inc., 872 F.3d 464, 468 (7th Cir. 2017); Perceptron, Inc. v. Sensor Adaptive Machs., Inc., 221 F.3d 913, 919–20 (6th Cir. 2000).

[24] *See id.; see also* Kan Di Ki, LLC v. Suer, C.A. No. 7937, 2015 WL 4503210, at *19 (Del. Ch. July 22, 2015); *In re* Givens, No. 96-CV-13585, 2001 WL 34136695, at *5 (D.R.I. Mar. 16, 2001); Verson Wilkins Ltd. v. Allied Prod. Corp., 723 F. Supp. 1, 10–12 (N.D. Ill. 1989); Alders v. Afa Corp. of Florida, 353 F. Supp. 654, 657 (S.D. Fla. 1973); Syntex Labs., Inc. v. Norwich Pharmacal Co., 315 F. Supp. 45, 56 (S.D.N.Y. 1970).

antitrust laws by implication from a regulatory statute are strongly disfavored, and have only been found in cases of plain repugnancy between the antitrust and regulatory provisions."[25] Anyone favorably disposed toward competition policy ought instinctively to oppose revoking the antitrust laws.

The Supreme Court, however, has recognized the concept of "implied repeal" in unwarranted circumstances. In *Trinko* and later in *Credit Suisse*, it held the federal antitrust laws inapplicable in light of regulatory environments born of the Telecommunications Act and securities laws, respectively.[26] It did so notwithstanding despite the existence of express savings clauses.[27] Those holdings are problematic. The Court was unduly dismissive of antitrust's incremental value, and oddly trusting of regulation. Even the best designed regulatory systems suffer from omissions, information asymmetries, and lag.

This reality ought to be obvious. America's long regulatory experience tells a disheartening tale. Antitrust enforcement can fill regulatory gaps, and further deter strategic breach in circumstances loaded with anticompetitive potential. The Court's implicit-repeal doctrine, however, excludes this possibility. In light of *Trinko* and *Credit Suisse*, the DOJ may not be able to investigate anticompetitive conduct in many regulatory environments. That is a regrettable mistake. Indeed, scholars have pointed out that these decisions could have prevented the Antitrust Division's famous 1982 case against AT&T.[28]

The Court was especially worried about private litigation. Antitrust has already developed safeguards to defray such costs, however, from elevated pleading standards to demanding evidentiary requirements that stand between discovery and trial.[29] In part, the Court's worries may have stemmed from the nature of the issue presented in *Trinko*. The conduct at issue – refusal to deal with one's competitor – is a dubious source of liability.[30] It matches predatory pricing in threatening to turn antitrust on its head, giving a vehicle to those who cannot succeed by competing on the merits to punish those who can. That is not to say that strategic noncooperation with rivals, any less than sustained below-cost pricing, by a dominant firm should never yield liability. But it is to suggest that *Trinko* may have raised facts from which the Court was loathe to infer potential liability.

---

[25] United States v. Phila. Nat'l Bank, 374 U.S. 321, 350-51 (1963); *see also* Nat'l Gerimedical Hosp. & Gerontology Center v. Blue Cross of Kansas City, 452 U.S. 378, 388 (1981).
[26] Credit Suisse Sec. (USA) LLC v. Billing, 551 U.S. 264 (2007); Verizon Commc'ns, Inc. v. Law Offices of Curtis V. Trinko, 540 U.S. 398 (2004).
[27] *Credit Suisse*, 551 U.S. at 287–90 (Thomas, J., dissenting) ("A straightforward application of the saving clauses to this case leads to the conclusion that respondents' antitrust suits must proceed.").
[28] *See* Howard A. Shelanski, *The Case for Rebalancing Antitrust and Regulation*, 109 MICH. L. REV. 683, 684 (2011).
[29] Bell Atl. Corp. v. Twombly, 550 U.S. 544 (2007); Matsushita Elec. Indus. Co. v. Zenith Radio Corp., 475 U.S. 574, 594 (1986).
[30] The author doubts the merits of any expansive duty to deal. For a further discussion, see Michael Jacobs & Alan Devlin, *The Riddle Underlying Refusal-to-Deal Theory*, 105 NW. U. L. REV. COLLOQUY 1 (2010).

In one respect, however, *Trinko*'s reasoning was odd. As in *Credit Suisse*, the Court focused on the likelihood and severity of error in administering the Sherman Act. It was surely correct to identify a refusal to contract as an especially dangerous source of error. What the Court failed to credit, though, was that the Type I error cost of imposing liability in the circumstances presented was unusually low. The Telecommunications Act of 1996 already imposed a duty on the incumbent local exchange carrier to unbundle certain of its network elements and to offer them to entrants on "just, reasonable, and nondiscriminatory" terms.[31] The antitrust intervention is far more consequential where it finds a legal obligation to cooperate that does not otherwise exist. That is just one illustration of a broader point – the overlap between antitrust and the administrative oversight of a regulatory system is not exclusively a source of duplication. The threat of antitrust liability can magnify incentives to take procompetitive actions consistent with Congressional intent.

6.1.1.4 "The *Brooke Group* Test for Predatory Pricing and *Weyerhaeuser* Test for Predatory Bidding Should Be Overruled"

The Utah Statement repeatedly assails established doctrine. Too often, however, it fails to identify the standard that should govern instead. That was less significant in the previous proposal because revocation of *Trinko*'s implied-preemption rule would presumably reintroduce the governing standard under *Philadelphia National Bank*.[32] The issue is more problematic here.

Antitrust's most essential task is to spur merciless competition. Darwinian processes compel firms to strive ever harder to innovate, differentiate their products in ways that appeal to customers, find cost savings, and undercut their rivals on price. The prize – though seldom achieved – is monopoly. The cost is bankruptcy and potential market exit. The result is a race that few win outright, leaving a desirable (if imperfectly competitive) equilibrium in which consumers and larger society reap ample rewards.

That ecosystem is not for the faint of heart. Nor is it intrinsically fair. The market punishes bad luck as much as it does incompetence. Small or inefficient businesses may flounder in the face of at-scale firms that offer products, prices, and convenience that consumers value. And this process of competition will tend to create market structures that, given consumer demand, reflect underlying cost-demand characteristics. Those structures may not be to everyone's liking. But they reflect the outcome of a process that offers vast rewards.

It is hard to imagine anything more destructive of that process than broadly to forbid low pricing. *Every* firm unable to match its rivals has cause to sue if it can. As explained below, antitrust's modern preoccupation with avoiding Type I errors has

---

[31] 47 U.S.C. § 251(c)(3).
[32] United States v. Phila. Nat'l Bank, 374 U.S. 321 (1963).

gone too far.³³ But here that concern properly reaches its zenith. Price wars yield invaluable consumer benefits. To endanger the incentives to undercut one's competitor is to strike at the heart of sound antitrust policy itself.

A ban on excessively low pricing would nevertheless be justified if such conduct threatened competition. As a general matter, low pricing is not a rational means of exclusion unless the predator has lower costs than its rivals. If suppliers have equal costs, then the price cutter suffers far greater losses than its competitors, which would rationally reduce output during the period of attempted predation in order to reduce losses. The predator's implicit threat to keep prices at below-cost levels in this environment is not credible. And when the dominant firm ultimately raises price, as it must, then its equally efficient rivals may be able to rapidly increase output. Recoupment is unlikely.

Predation becomes more plausible, however, if the firm is more efficient than its rivals – a condition that reduces its interim losses and magnifies the exclusionary effect. Still, even in this situation, predatory pricing should be unlikely. No matter how efficient a firm may be, it cannot sustain below-cost sales indefinitely. Knowing this, one might expect its competitors to weather the period of attempted exclusion, whether by temporarily reducing output, drawing on the capital markets, or both. Again, because it cannot *sustainably* raise price after its below-cost pricing campaign, the firm would not see that strategy as a rational means of exclusion.

A firm may sometimes rationally price below cost, however, in order to exclude competition. The key is to convince rivals that the predator has lower costs than they do. If the firm can credibly signal that its pricing – though below cost in fact – is above its costs, then rivals may conclude that they cannot compete on the merits and must therefore exit. That possibility is magnified if prospective lenders cannot tell whether the targets of a predatory-pricing campaign are ineffective competitors or victims of temporary, subcompetitive prices. In those circumstances, access to capital on competitive terms may not be readily available.

There are, of course, realistic scenarios in which rivals cannot discern whether their low-pricing rival has relatively high or low costs. In such settings, a firm may signal that it has low costs by responding to competition with low pricing. In doing so, it may carve out a reputation as an efficient competitor that will respond to entry aggressively. Of course, the means by which it acquires this reputation – below-cost pricing – is extremely costly. But if the anticipated long-term benefit of supracompetitive rents discounted to present value is sufficiently large, then investing in a low-cost reputation may be justified.³⁴

In short, game-theoretic models show conditions in which such exclusion may be rational.³⁵ Those models, however, are possibility theorems – not general cases. And

---

[33] See Chapter 7.
[34] See generally CARLTON & PERLOFF, supra note 11, at 359.
[35] See, e.g., Bruce H. Kobayashi, *The Law and Economics of Predatory Pricing, in* ANTITRUST LAW AND ECONOMICS 116 (Keith N. Hylton ed., 2010).

they hold true only on strict assumptions, particularly on information asymmetries and conditions surrounding entry. That is not to present the models as mere abstractions never to materialize in the real world. There is some evidence, albeit modest, of real-life predatory pricing.[36]

Neo-Brandeisians see below-cost pricing as obvious, not irrational. They think it synonymous with leading digital platforms' business strategy. That critique begs the question, however, because it assumes that any unprofitable pricing by a firm is "predatory." In fact, below-cost pricing typically characterizes early-stage competition in network markets (or ones subject to learning by doing).[37] There, a firm's costs fall with rising output – and, hence, experience – incentivizing unprofitable sales in the short run.[38] In other words, low pricing is the expected form of competition in many settings. And those settings include digital markets of the kind assailed by neo-Brandeisians.

The Utah Statement, of course, directs its ire at the *Brooke Group* and *Weyerhaeuser* standards for price predation.[39] Under the relevant test, a firm's pricing violates Section 2 only if it both falls below the company's variable cost of production and creates a dangerous probability of recoupment.

There is reason to question not only that standard, but its underlying predicate. In the Court's view, "predatory pricing schemes are rarely tried, and even more rarely successful."[40] Though an apt characterization of the industrial-organization literature in 1986, that articulation now sits uncomfortably with the latest learning. Models imply that it may be an effective anticompetitive strategy. Further, although strategic below-cost pricing is not widespread, researchers have identified historical cases in which it likely occurred.[41]

One might justify the Court's inhibitory standard by invoking decision theory. The cost of erroneously forbidding low pricing is, of course, severe. But that does not answer the question, which also requires assessing the risk that effective price exclusion will go unaddressed. Economists increasingly accept that predatory pricing can be rational and may occur.[42] The *Brooke Group* standard, however, has all but eliminated Section 2 liability for below-cost pricing in the past three decades. That result may reflect the lack of meritorious cases. Or it may be a function of underdeterrence.

---

[36] *See, e.g.*, OECD, Predatory Pricing 14–18 (1989), https://www.oecd.org/competition/abuse/2375661.pdf.

[37] *See, e.g.*, Joseph Farrell & Michael L. Katz, *Competition or Predation? Consumer Coordination, Strategic Pricing and Price Floors in Network Markets*, 53 J. Indus. Econ. 203, 204 (2005).

[38] Carlton & Perloff, *supra* note 11, at 359.

[39] Weyerhaeuser Co. v. Ross-Simmons Hardwood Lumber Co., 549 U.S. 312 (2007); Brooke Grp. Ltd. v. Brown & Williamson Tobacco Corp., 509 U.S. 209 (1993).

[40] *Brooke Grp.*, 509 U.S. at 226 (quoting Matsushita Elec. Indus. Co. v. Zenith Radio Corp., 475 U.S. 574, 589 (1986)).

[41] *See, e.g.*, Predatory Pricing, *supra* note 36, at 14–18.

[42] *See, e.g.*, Patrick Bolton et al., *Predatory Pricing: Strategic Theory and Legal Policy* (2015), https://www.justice.gov/atr/predatory-pricing-strategic-theory-and-legal-policy.

Revising the *Brooke Group* and *Weyerhaeuser* standards would require great care. Price-driven exclusion happens, but it is not prevalent. EU competition law dispenses with a need to show likely recoupment of losses, and gives its principal enforcer, the European Commission, considerable regulatory power. Even there, however, predatory-pricing decisions are rare – the Commission imposed its first fine in sixteen years in 2019.[43] Any responsible legal standard must not impede price competition.

We thus arrive at a critical juncture. If we revoked *Brooke Group* and *Weyerhaeuser*, what standard should govern in their place? The Utah Statement does not say. This shortcoming deprives the authors' proposal of any real force. We have seen that, beyond merger review, anti-monopolists' biggest concern is with low pricing. Yet, they conspicuously dodge the hard question of defining the right standard.

Neo-Brandeisians' failure to specify a rule may reflect the incoherence of their critique, which blends quantifiable harms like price effects with such intangibles as "harm to the diversity and vibrancy of ideas[.]"[44] They likely disclaim having to show that below-cost pricing in a given case will have anticompetitive effects. If cognizable effects include not merely such incommensurate factors as price and ideas, but "lower income and wages for employees, lower rates of new business creation, lower rates of local ownership, and outsized political and economic control in the hands of a few," then a consequentialist standard would be utterly unworkable. Instead, neo-Brandeisians simply assume that such harms flow from below-cost pricing as a general matter, thus justifying a blanket prohibition. Specific proposals here are sorely needed.

Certainly, a ban on below-cost pricing would be reckless, whether by dominant firms or otherwise. It would prohibit many instances of efficient competition, and transform antitrust into a tool to deny consumers the benefits of Darwinian market processes. Even EU competition law, which dispenses with a need to show recoupment of losses, allows dominant undertakings accused of pricing below cost to objectively justify their conduct.

The real question is how much more the law should require than below-cost pricing. One might imagine a Section 2 monopoly-acquisition or -maintenance standard that would hold a firm liable for sustained pricing below average variable cost coupled with evidence of exclusionary intent (i.e., investment in a loss-making campaign not to introduce a superior product to market, but with the express goal of bankrupting smaller rivals or deterring entry).

Although the Utah Statement is mum on the details of a preferred standard, one of its authors has written more.

---

[43] European Comm'n, Press Release, Antitrust: Commission fines US chipmaker Qualcomm €242 million for engaging in predatory pricing, July 18, 2019, https://ec.europa.eu/commission/press corner/detail/en/IP_19_4350.

[44] Khan, *supra* note 1, at 767.

The greatest specificity to date comes from Lina Khan, an author of the Utah Statement, who wrote a thesis that Amazon has engaged in predatory pricing.[45] Even that lengthy treatment, however, omitted critical details. She invoked the term "predatory pricing" over ninety times in her paper, and criticized the modern rule time and again. Yet, rather than define the "correct" standard, she merely alluded to it in broad brushstrokes. Khan argued for "abandoning the recoupment requirement in cases of below-cost pricing by dominant platforms," though she holds out the possibility of a business-justification defense.[46] The vital cost metric to which one compares pricing, however, goes undefined.

Khan's proposal is troublesome for reasons beyond its abstraction. It excludes any evaluation of effects. That is uniquely problematic for predatory-pricing cases, where we worry about dampening incentives to compete on the merits. A standard that is indifferent to whether conduct ultimately harms consumers is ill-advised. If the law does not ask whether low pricing will likely yield net harm, then it will inevitably punish competition on the merits.

Second, Khan envisions different pricing liability standards for dominant platforms and other entities.[47] She would go so far as to *presume* that platforms with a market share of 40 percent or more engage in predatory pricing if they price below cost. This proposal would depart abruptly from conventional antitrust laws, which have general applicability and are agnostic about the identity or nature of an investigated firm. Whether by rule (e.g., naked horizontal price-fixing is per se unlawful) or by standard (e.g., the rule of reason governs vertical restraints), the law derives liability from conduct – not from a firm's characteristics. To be sure, the law often employs liability screens before evaluating effects. Only a dominant firm, for example, can unlawfully maintain a monopoly in violation of Section 2. But every firm with monopoly power is subject to the same standard, which determines liability by reference to likely effects.[48]

Khan's vision for predatory-pricing liability is thus problematic. It would subject dominant firms to different standards depending on whether their strength lies in platform (however defined). And it would render ultimate liability determinations without first analyzing effects. Instead, it would rest on an a priori assumption that predatory pricing is more likely to harm competition when undertaken in platform markets than by dominant firms elsewhere. That postulate, of course, flows from an intuition that low-price-driven scale is problematic notwithstanding overriding consumer benefits.

For neo-Brandeisians, however, these "flaws" are the whole point. Price-based competition is something to be celebrated only if a winner does not emerge. Digital platforms that rapidly scale are therefore objectionable, no matter how overwhelming

---

[45] *Id.*
[46] *Id.* at 791–92.
[47] The Utah Statement, which she coauthored, is silent on this point.
[48] United States v. Microsoft Corp., 253 F.3d 34, 58 (D.C. Cir. 2001) (en banc) (per curiam).

the benefits to consumers. Vanquishing this phenomenon requires more than refining today's predatory-pricing laws. It requires a status offense, which purges competitive effects from the liability standard. The traditional burden of proof hinders enforcement, so flip it and make it incumbent on the accused firm to overcome a presumption of harm. And, because even large digital platforms may have procompetitive incentives to price below total-average-cost, adopt a loose conception of cost for the purposes of a predatory-pricing standard. Khan's proscription follows each of these elements, and warrants rejection for the same reasons.

6.1.1.5 "The *Berkley* [sic] *Photo* Standard for Establishing Monopoly Leveraging Should Be Restored"

In *Berkey Photo*, the Second Circuit held that a dominant firm violates Section 2 if it uses its monopoly power to secure a competitive advantage in another market, even if, in doing so, it does not monopolize that adjacent market.[49]

That standard is problematic. In the author's view, antitrust is best understood as preserving constraints born of competitive market pressures. Harm to competition occurs when a merger, practice, or agreement lifts such a constraint. Anticompetitive effects follow through an exercise of market power – prototypically in the form of a price increase or output restriction, but also via reduced investment in technology and quality. Importantly, gaining "a competitive advantage" is not synonymous with harming competition. In its imprecision, the *Berkey Photo* standard would proscribe conduct that may even increase competition in the adjacent market. Indeed, the standard bears a disquieting resemblance with the principle of EU law that a dominant undertaking has a "special responsibility" not to distort competition.[50]

With good reason, then, several courts have rejected the *Berkey Photo* monopoly-leveraging standard.[51] The Ninth Circuit renounced it as too "loose" in 1991.[52] In 2000, the Federal Circuit dismissed outright the idea that a patentee could unlawfully leverage any market power imbedded in its intellectual property to other markets potentially within the scope of its patent.[53] And, in a powerful critique in 2006, the Seventh Circuit disclaimed monopoly-leverage theory in *Schor*.[54]

---

[49] Berkey Photo, Inc. v. Eastman Kodak Co., 63 F.2d 263, 275 (2d Cir. 1979).
[50] Case 322/81, Michelin v. Comm'n, 1983 E.C.R. 3461, ¶ 57.
[51] The Sixth Circuit followed *Berkey Photo* in Kerasotes Michigan Theatres v. National Amusements, 854 F.2d 135 136–37 (6th Cir. 1988) – at least insofar as recognizing that the extension of "dominance from one market into a second market" is actionable. Some courts have held open the question whether leveraging monopoly power to gain an unfair competitive advantage in another market can constitute a basis for liability under Section 2. See, e.g., Adv. Health-Care Servs. v. Radford Cmty. Hosp., 910 F.2d 139, 149 n.17 (4th Cir. 1990); Willman v. Heartland Hosp. E., 34 F.3d 605, 613 (8th Cir. 1994). Others have questioned a predicate of the *Berkey Photo* doctrine without expressly rejecting it. See, e.g., Enters. v. Venice Hosp., 919 F.2d 1550, 1567 (11th Cir. 1990).
[52] Alaska Airlines, Inc. v. United Airlines, Inc., 948 F.2d 536, 546 (9th Cir. 1991).
[53] *In re* Independent Service Org. Antitrust Litig., 203 F.3d 1322, 1326–27 (Fed. Cir. 2000).
[54] Schor v. Abbott Labs., 457 F.3d 608 (7th Cir. 2006).

Schor grounded its holding on the single monopoly mark-up theorem.[55] Derived from neoclassical price theory, it implies that a dominant firm can extract its supracompetitive rents only once. Should it bundle a monopoly product with a tied good sold in an otherwise-competitive market, for example, classic leverage theory suggests that the firm will then dominate both markets and enjoy monopoly profits in each one. The Chicago School showed that such an effort would reduce profit and thus be irrational. Charging a monopoly price for the tying product *and* a supracompetitive price for the tied good means charging an above-monopoly price. Based on that theory, and positing that exceptions would be so fleeting as to make the hunt for them unjustified, the Seventh Circuit rejected the *Berkey Photo* theory as "undisciplined."[56]

Schor was a thoughtful opinion, and its skepticism of leveraging theories was amply justified. Nevertheless, the panel overstated its case. The single-monopoly-profit theorem is valid, but holds true only in static models with fixed-ratio bundling.[57] It ought not to justify a blanket rule. Further, *Schor* revealed an obsession with avoiding Type I errors that goes too far.[58] The court adopted a rule of per se legality for conduct that employs monopoly power to ill effect in adjacent markets.[59] Antitrust policy should never categorically reject liability if economic analysis reveals likely harm to competition caused by a dominant firm. That is not the same, however, as defining a violation based on securing advantages in neighboring markets.

The Utah Statement's proposal to reinvigorate *Berkey Photo*'s monopoly-leveraging principle is thus ill-conceived. "Leverage" is an ambiguous concept with a troubling history. Often employed to forbid conduct perceived as coercive or unfair, leverage was a byword for antitrust analysis of old – conclusory and devoid of a rigorous economic theory for why a practice harmed consumers.

Nevertheless, the basic principle in *Berkey Photo* that a monopolist can violate Section 2 without monopolizing an adjacent market is right. The vital element missing from that opinion is harm to competition in the affected market. As per Chapter 6, such harm has a precise meaning. It is not one born of "leverage," "distortion," or "advantage" – concepts that are prone to mischief. Rather, it reflects the weakening of a market constraint, thus easing competitive pressures in the form of price, output, quality, or innovation.

If a firm that is dominant in one market engages in unilateral conduct that harms competition in another market, then Section 2 should prohibit it. The alternative is

---

[55] *Id.* at 611–12.
[56] *Schor*, 457 F.3d at 613.
[57] *See, e.g.*, Einer Elhauge, *Tying, Bundled Discounts, and the Death of the Single Monopoly Profit Theory*, 123 HARV. L. REV. 397 (2009). In his article, Professor Elhauge argues for an excessively strict liability standard for product tying, but his central critique of the single-monopoly-profit theory identifies material oversights in the conventional Chicago School narrative.
[58] *See* Chapter 7.
[59] *Schor*, 457 F.3d at 613.

a blind spot in antitrust policy, for – absent agreement – Section 1 provides no remedy. Importantly, however, there is no need for a standalone concept of "monopoly leverage" to employ Section 2 in useful service. Conduct that excludes rivals, forecloses them, or raises their costs with net anticompetitive effects in a relevant market should fall within that statutory prohibition. It is not labels, but the likely competitive effects of a unilateral practice, that matter.

6.1.1.6 "The Essential Facilities Doctrine Should Be Reinvigorated for Dominant Firms That Deny Access to Critical Infrastructural Services"

This proposal is unnerving, and not because refusing to deal should always be lawful. Rather, the law must set the parameters governing compulsory access with caution and precision – qualities that are conspicuously absent from the Utah Statement.

The Supreme Court has never recognized an essential-facilities doctrine. Still, it has recognized liability in some circumstances when firms refuse to cooperate with a competitor.[60] A famous Seventh Circuit case of 1983 gave that doctrine its ultimate expression.[61] In its 2004 decision in *Trinko*, however, the Court nearly eliminated the duty to deal.[62] From a policy standpoint, of course, an antitrust obligation to grant network access must be tightly cabined. Even so, *Trinko*'s sweeping renunciation of interconnection obligations went too far. Before addressing that point in further detail, however, some vital considerations warrant attention.

First, the need for limiting principles is self-evident. Unbounded access rights would subvert the free-market system. Capitalism works only if the state recognizes and enforces property rights. Private investment in infrastructure does not create free rights of access for third parties. That expectation fuels the capital flows that drive economic growth. Firms invest in physical or digital networks because the net present value, in light of opportunity cost, is positive. If firms piggyback on those capital expenditures, however, then they may dilute vital incentives.

Forced sharing can accelerate competitive pricing pressure. Consumers may thus benefit in the short run. Some commentators present this gain as part of a painful quid pro quo. But this need not be so. If investors' expected returns suffice ex ante, then compulsory dealing may even be optimal. But this is a dangerous game. No one can accurately gauge investors' minimum acceptable returns. Nor can one identify the access price below which mandatory interconnection diminishes long-term welfare. Myopic intervention may carry a heavy cost. Innovation is the most valuable form of competition. It is also singularly dependent on investment. Hence, a rush to

---

[60] United States v. Terminal R.R. Ass'n, 224 U.S. 383 (1912); Assoc. Press v. United States, 326 U.S. 1 (1945); Otter Tail Power Co. v. United States, 410 U.S. 366 (1973); Aspen Skiing Co. v. Aspen Highlands Skiing Corp., 472 U.S. 585 (1985).
[61] MCI Comm'cns Corp. v. Am. Tel. & Tel. Co., 708 F.2d 1081 (7th Cir. 1983).
[62] Verizon Comm'cns Inc. v. Law Offices of Curtis V. Trinko, LLP, 540 U.S. 398 (2004).

maximize static efficiency in the here and now may come at the expense of tomorrow. Property rights are the engines that propel competition. Diluting them may be destructive antitrust policy of the worst kind.

This line of thought yields a simple conclusion: do not recognize an antitrust duty to deal. If we need a bright-line rule, than that is clearly the best one. Yet, an absolute rule may be inferior to a demanding standard. Circumstances exist in which obligatory access on prescribed terms may enhance competition without stifling incentives. In that respect, property-right absolutists overstate their case. On certain assumptions, mandatory access at a prescribed fee is the socially optimal means of protecting ownership interests. In other words, an injunction will not always maximize social welfare. A volumetric literature addresses the law and economics of property, liability, and inalienability rules.

Although the insights are nuanced, some basic propositions emerge. In low-transaction-cost environments, the law should employ a property rule, granting the owner an injunction as a matter of right. Parties bargain in the shadow of law, and so the rule will induce the parties to negotiate. Because the parties know their reservation prices better than an adjudicator ever will, Coasean bargaining will result. Voluntary contracts reallocate scarce property rights more effectively than the state ever could directly.

When transaction costs become too severe, however, this process breaks down. Initial property allocations may become final, even though the owner's willingness-to-sell price is below others' willingness-to-buy price. In theory, liability rules can overcome this problem by awarding monetary damages equal to the cost of the incursion to the property owner. Such a rule gives third parties access to the relevant property, albeit at a price set by a third party (usually a court or regulator). Importantly, this possibility does *not* make liability rules superior to property rules when transaction costs are high. For damages to be preferable, the fee setter must be able to calculate damages accurately. Access to that information is typically imperfect and asymmetric. Thus, on realistic assumptions, property rules may surpass – or be no worse than – liability rules even when bargaining costs are high.

This problem emerges with special force in the antitrust setting. Courts do not operate as rate setters under Section 2, forcing dominant firms to open up their networks at a price to be determined through litigation. That is a regulatory undertaking. By contrast, the antitrust incursion is limited and blunt. Absent a remedial divestiture, compulsory access occurs only if a monopolist's refusal to deal unjustifiably excludes competition. The Supreme Court has narrowed the duty to deal not quite to vanishing point, but close enough as generally to make no difference.[63] It appears to be a requisite of liability that a dominant firm terminate a mutually beneficial course of dealing, thus forsaking short-term profits for an anticompetitive end.[64]

---

[63] *Trinko*, 540 U.S. at 409.
[64] *Id.*

That standard creates a property rule in most situations. Knowing this rule, parties have reason to negotiate access at mutually advantageous terms. If a network owner declines to contract at a price that the access seeker is willing to pay, then we should generally be cautious about foisting a rate on the owner. The exception arises in circumstances recognized in *Aspen Skiing* and preserved – however reluctantly – in *Trinko*. Specifically, if the dominant firm refuses to grant network access to its competitor at retail prices – that is, prices at which it *willingly* and profitably contracts with others – then a liability rule may become desirable.[65] In such a situation, the monopolist reveals vital information through voluntary contract in the market. We can be more sanguine about finding a duty to deal at a price that does not undercompensate the network owner.

Trinko erred in one respect. It treated a prior course of dealing as being indispensable to a duty to interconnect. That condition is too strict. To be sure, antitrust should impose access obligations only in narrow circumstances. It will be the rare case that provides the requisite confidence both that compulsory dealing will not deter investment and that the ensuing remedy is administrable. Among other things, liability premised on failure to grant access at a particular price will generally be unworkable. The exception, properly recognized in *Trinko*, arises when the monopolist has revealed its profitable wholesale or retail rates through voluntary contract in the market. Otherwise, courts cannot possibly hope to act as regulatory bodies that determine interconnection rates. One doubting that proposition need merely look at the FCC, which endured a near-decade of failed efforts to set lawful scope and terms of network access under the Telecommunications Act of 1996.[66]

Nevertheless, it is a mistake categorically to reject the possibility of antitrust duties to deal where no prior course of dealing exists. Specifically, Section 2 ought to reach a monopolist that flouts its statutory obligation to deal with rivals, where the course of conduct otherwise makes out a monopoly-maintenance claim. That is especially so if the statutory regime reflects a Congressional effort to increase competition in the relevant market. *Trinko* provided such a context, and the Court was wrong to go as far as it did.

In searching for an obligation to grant access, *Trinko* correctly distinguished its earlier liability decisions. *Terminal Railroad* and *Associated Press* involved *concerted* denials of access to infrastructure that rivals needed to compete.[67] In *Otter Tail*, a utility refused to sell electricity at wholesale to municipalities that created rival energy distribution systems – towns that were its former customers.[68] So, too, in *Aspen Skiing* a dominant firm discontinued a prior course of profitable dealing

---

[65] *Id.* at 409–10.
[66] *See* U.S. Telecom Ass'n v. FCC, 359 F.3d 554 (D.C. Cir. 2004); U.S. Telecom Ass'n v. FCC, 290 F.3d 415 (D.C. Cir. 2002); AT&T Corp. v. Iowa Utilities Bd., 525 U.S. 366 (1999).
[67] Associated Press v. United States, 326 U.S. 1 (1945); United States v. Terminal R.R. Ass'n of St. Louis, 224 U.S. 383 (1912).
[68] Otter Tail Power Co. v. United States, 410 U.S. 366 (1973).

without a valid business reason or being able to offer any efficiency justification for its behavior.[69] Indeed, the firm refused to sell to its competitors even at the retail rates that it otherwise made available to the public.[70]

Those characteristics were absent in *Trinko*, but the facts raised another plausible source of an antitrust compulsion to deal. Following the success of the 1984 break-up of AT&T in fostering long-distance competition, Congress passed the Telecommunications Act in 1996.[71] Seeking to inject competition into local telephone markets, the Act required the Baby Bells (incumbent local exchange carriers) to unbundle their network elements and to make them available to entrants (competitive local exchange carriers) at cost-based rates set by the FCC. Given the short- and medium-term infeasibility of facilities-based competition in the local market, CLECs needed access to the copper wire loops over the last mile in order to serve consumers. The carrot for an ILEC was that, once a state deemed the local market "competitive" on account of entry facilitated by forced network access, the ILEC could then enter the long-distance market.

In *Trinko*, an entrant alleged that Verizon, an ILEC, had failed to satisfy its network-sharing duties under the Act. Complaints led Verizon to enter into a consent decree with the FCC. The antitrust lawsuit followed on the heels of that decree, alleging that Verizon was unlawfully impeding competition in the local-telephone-service market.

In evaluating whether the plaintiff had stated a claim for monopolization, the Court honed in on mandatory interconnection obligations under the 1996 Act. Rather than support an essential-facilities claim, though, the statutory obligation detracted from it in the Court's view.[72] For an institution otherwise preoccupied with minimizing the cost of error, this was an odd interpretation.

Consider the risk that troubled the Court. Exclusion can maximize long-run welfare, typically by spurring facilities-based competition. To be sure, these benefits find form in preserving the first mover's incentive to invest in building a valuable network. But the gains from exclusion can go further. Facing the right cost-demand market characteristics, an entrant denied access to a dominant incumbent's network may build a rival system. This process introduces productive inefficiencies in the form of duplicative infrastructure, but – outside of natural monopolies – the gains from competition typically outweigh the costs. Compulsory dealing neuters the incentives for such facilities-based competition.

That is why the essential-facilities doctrine goes to critical infrastructure that rivals cannot economically recreate. And it is why antitrust law correctly requires a hook before imposing liability for a refusal to deal. That hook must give the courts comfort that the terms of compulsory access exceed those that the network owner would have

---

[69] Aspen Skiing Co. v. Aspen Highlands Skiing Corp., 472 U.S. 585 (1985).
[70] *Id.* at 593.
[71] Pub. LA. No. 104-104, 110 Stat. 56 (1996).
[72] *Trinko*, 540 U.S. at 411.

required ex ante in deciding whether to invest in the first place. Hence, *Trinko* was right to point to past contractual terms that were profitable for the owner before finding liability. But it was wrong to suppose that a terminated course of dealing is the only reliable means for making that determination.

In deciding whether to require owners to share their networks on particular terms, Congress faces the same difficult welfare calculus that antitrust wisely chooses to avoid in most cases. But when the legislature has made a determination – particularly in the name of increasing competition – then antitrust should pay homage to that assessment. The goals here are not antagonistic, but synergistic. That point brings us back to *Trinko*. Courts do not risk "getting it wrong" in finding an antitrust obligation to deal that is coterminous with a statutory obligation. If there is a mistake, then it is an error that Congress has already made in the name of promoting competition.

To be clear, this point would not make every breach of a statutory access obligation a Section 2 violation. A plaintiff must prove far more – the fact of monopoly power in a well-defined relevant market and likely anticompetitive effects, and also rebut legitimate procompetitive justifications for the refusal to deal, possibly using evidence of exclusionary intent. In this respect, to speak – as one often does – of a "duty" to deal is misleading. More accurately, the question is whether a refusal to deal can constitute exclusionary behavior if combined with the larger proof required to make out a claim.

Skepticism about antitrust's incremental value permeated *Trinko*. The author does not share that concern. Yes, antitrust litigation can be messy. But a simple fact remains. Dominant incumbents subject to statutory obligations to interoperate with rival networks will behave differently while under antitrust scrutiny than while free and clear of it. Monopolists are more likely to facilitate the competition that Congress desires if they know that refusing to contract on the requisite terms – or dragging their feet to achieve much the same end – will invite hard questions on the antitrust front. As explained in the implied pre-emption section above, it would be naïve to exaggerate regulators' ability to effect procompetitive outcomes. Antitrust can help.

In sum, we should disavow any expansive duty to deal. The law should respect property rights, and recognize incursions only in narrow circumstances. Qualifying situations are those in which systemic undercompensation of the owner and facilities-based competition are both unlikely. Typically, the former condition will be satisfied only if a prior course of dealing reveals terms on which the dominant firm is willing to contract with third parties (or previously with the plaintiff). But a congressional provision for mandatory access should qualify, too, and – in that respect, at least – *Trinko* got it wrong. Categorical exclusions are not the thing of optimal antitrust policy.

That discussion brings us to the Utah Statement's proposal to "reinvigorate" the essential-facilities doctrine. The recommendation is, of course, hopelessly ambiguous.

If revitalization entails paring *Trinko* back so that statutory access obligations can become cognizable antitrust duties consistent with the principles espoused in *Aspen Skiing*, then the proposal makes sense. One gets the impression, however, the drafters envision something bolder.

One point, above all, warrants attention. There is a world of difference between compulsory access as a *remedy* and as a source of *liability*. Neo-Brandeisians are correct that it is more effective to preserve competitive markets than to reintroduce competition in dominated ones. Nevertheless, firms can lawfully achieve monopolies by competing on the merits, and enforcers have no cause to intervene absent exclusionary conduct. When a firm maintains its monopoly through anticompetitive acts, however, then the law needs to employ an effective remedy with which to restore lost competition. That is a demanding task, and one for which mandatory dealing at prescribed rates for a time may be necessary.

6.1.1.7 "Structural Presumptions in Merger Review Should Be Restored"

Taken on face value, this recommendation is puzzling. Structural presumptions are alive and well.

In *Philadelphia National Bank*, the Supreme Court held that mergers creating firms with 30 percent or more of a relevant market are presumptively anticompetitive.[73] Such transactions create an inference of a substantial lessening of competition, which the merging parties can then try to rebut.[74] This remains the law of the land, and the agencies invariably rely on it in horizontal deals that they challenge in court. Further, their guidelines provide that mergers producing markets with HHIs over 2,500 with a delta exceeding 200 "will be presumed to be likely to enhance market power."[75]

Doctrinally speaking, it is unclear what the Utah Statement envisions here. More generally, the neo-Brandeisian movement wants to displace effects-based analysis with structuralism. The Statement, however, does not propose making the inference of harm to competition conclusive. Indeed, any such move would be inconsistent with the nature of a "presumption," which implies an opportunity for rebuttal. And since it is impossible to rebut a structural presumption by pointing to structural considerations, the counter-showing must involve an appeal to likely future effects. That after all, was the lesson of *General Dynamics*, a vital decision that progressive reformists nevertheless lament.[76]

Presumably, the drafters refer to how the agencies evaluate transactions and make enforcement decisions. There, it is true, structural presumptions play a secondary role. The FTC and DOJ use HHIs and other concentration indices as a screen meant to flag transactions that might harm competition, thus allowing the agencies

---

[73] United States v. Phila. Nat'l Bank, 374 U.S. 321, 364 (1963).
[74] *Id.* at 365.
[75] U.S. Dep't of Justice & Fed. Trade Comm'n, Horizontal Merger Guidelines § 5.3 (2010).
[76] United States v. Gen. Dynamics Corp., 415 U.S. 486 (1974).

to devote their limited resources to those deals. The staff who investigate transactions, however, never stop at structure alone. It would be embarrassing to present the DOJ's front office or FTC Commissioners with an enforcement recommendation based on little more than market shares and entry barriers. The only common exception is to justify a remedy.[77]

To replace effects with structuralism is to condemn antitrust to ignorance. Competition is not monolithic. The competitive process plays out in vastly dissimilar ways across markets. Nuances thus abound. An effects-based inquiry pays homage to those subtleties. Structuralism does not. The law should not blind itself, of course, to market shares and HHIs. Those factors have important roles to play. But effects-based antitrust analysis can – and does – heighten the accuracy of intervention decisions in ways that reduce error costs. In this respect, a presumption exists because it speaks to an underlying generality. But any generality lends itself to exceptions, and not all mergers in concentrated markets will produce anticompetitive effects. Hence, a desirable presumption guides analysis and focuses attention where it is needed most. The government lawyers and economists who are steeped in the workings of their overseen markets can then undertake a penetrating analysis, getting behind the numbers to understand how competition actually works and how the transaction will likely affect it.

There is another good reason not to grant structure alone dispositive weight beyond the monopoly scenario. In particular, it is sensitive to market definition. Depending on how one traces the contours of the relevant market, structural analysis may point in radically different directions. In the worst cases, the market-definition exercise becomes subjective and the structural analysis circular. This process obscures the more accurate methodology of examining unilateral effects, and then backing into the market definition if deemed necessary.

Neo-Brandeisians treat structuralism not as a guide, but as a rule. The Utah Statement's call to "reinvigorate" HHI-driven presumptions would thus cast a wide net, prohibiting mergers that are not only unlikely to harm competition, but apt to enhance it. A further overlooked consideration is that a blunt tool like structuralism may also bless some acquisitions that will likely produce harmful effects, notwithstanding the parties' modest share of a relatively unconcentrated market. As argued in the past two chapters, the weight of the evidence warrants

---

[77] The Commission will not issue a complaint alleging likely harm to competition – as it must to accept a remedy – without first finding "reason to believe" that a transaction would substantially lessen competition. Remedies often arise early in the review process. As a result, developing a robust effects analysis would subject parties to months of delay and expense when they would rather divest (or accept a behavioral constraint) and close their deal. In those circumstances, a structural justification often suffices. Even then, however, the practice has been controversial in some conservative quarters. See, e.g., In re Holcim/Lafarge, FTC File No. 141-0129, Statement of Commissioner Joshua D. Wright, Dissenting in Part and Concurring in Part, May 8, 2015 (dissenting from Commission determination that it had reason to believe a transaction would harm competition in portland cement markets by reducing the number of competitors from three to two, explaining that "the Commission's structural presumption is economically unfounded").

a heightened propensity to block deals in marginal cases. But, contrary to some progressive reformers' calls, the justification does not extend to inframarginal intervention decisions. The agencies should sharpen their tool kit, not discard it.

The point that competition differs between markets is critical, and worth exploring. A transaction will harm competition in bidding and transactional retail markets, for example, under different conditions. Consider a bidding market. There, a combination will have no effect unless customers prefer the merging parties over other RFP bidders. That holds true even if the parties' joint share is high.[78] In retail markets, by contrast, effects are a function of the diversion ratios between the merging firms' products and the margin on lost sales that the post-merger firm can "recapture" after closing. Absent marginal-cost savings realized by the merger, short-term effects are likely even under competition from several other firms. In both of these examples, it is unnecessary to define a market in order to determine the presence or absence of likely effects.

In mature "bricks and mortar" industries, competition typically occurs less in product quality or technology, and more in price or output. Static neoclassical models thus provide useful means of evaluation. Here, economists frequently use models of oligopolistic quantity competition to predict price effects. In markets that display Cournot-Nash competition, a merger-driven increase in concentration will typically lead to predicted price increases. Here, structuralism and economic modeling tend in the same direction, though the scope of the investigation obviously goes beyond those concerns alone.

Dynamic factors, however, complicate the analysis. Network industries often produce competition in technology, infrastructure, and quality. This raises several challenges. The principal source of consumer welfare lies in innovation. The market structure apt to produce optimal R&D-based competition is much less clear than in markets characterized by lower fixed-to-marginal-cost ratios. The economics literature has yielded an abundance of models, but few uniform or generally applicable rules about whether monopoly or competition – much less incremental movements between those two extremes – will best motivate innovation. The result is sensitive to model assumptions, meaning that there is no substitute for an in-depth investigation of the particular market at issue. For antitrust policymakers, of course, intuition typically cuts in favor of competition. But, even then, the optimal concentration level is far from clear.

Industries that feature large capital expenditures on infrastructure or technology tend to become concentrated. Network effects can exacerbate that effect. In such markets, oligopolistic structures are often competitively optimal and productively efficient.[79] Often, however, firms are not symmetrically positioned. An industry

---

[78] The agencies have explained that, under the right assumptions, a merger to even a 90 percent market share in a bidding market could yield no effects. U.S. Dep't of Justice & Fed. Trade Comm'n, *Quantitative Approaches to Competitive Effects in Bid Market Merger Investigations*, OECD Submission, Oct. 13, 2006.

[79] In the ultimate case of a natural monopoly – a market in which the industry long-run average cost curve is still declining when it intersects with the demand curve – the productively efficient result is to have a single firm meet all consumer demand. Such a situation, of course, creates well-known

leader may have scale, and in turn lower long-average costs of production. Reflecting Schumpeterian assumptions, it may be better positioned to invest in technology, while its relatively disadvantaged rivals struggle to grow.

Mergers in such markets tend to be difficult for antitrust enforcers, and produce controversial approval or blockage decisions. The challenge has several dimensions. First, acquisitions in concentrated markets may be associated with static price effects. Many investment-heavy markets yield differentiated products, which create market-definition challenges. Whether unilateral price effects will be material often turn on how closely positioned the merging products are to each other vis-à-vis other differentiated goods in the market. Coordinated effects may result if the loss of a competitor in an oligopoly meets other conditions favorable to parallel conduct.

Obviously, not every horizontal transaction in a concentrated, high-investment industry will give the post-merger firm an incentive to increase price. For example, marginal-cost efficiencies might offset such an incentive. Or customers may be sophisticated and have ample means at their disposal with which to discipline an attempted exercise of market power. Such buyers may not need several alternatives to the post-merger firm in order to force competitive outcomes.[80] Separately, in rare cases, the market may be subject to Bertrand oligopolistic price competition in selling homogeneous goods.[81] In general, though, such transactions create short-term price effects. Holding everything else constant (which we cannot do), they weigh against approving the merger.

Dynamic considerations, however, are all-important. In an investment-heavy market, changes in industry structure can have a significant impact on long-term outcomes. Suppose that an industry leader has a stronger position than its handful of rivals in such a concentrated market. There, a combination between #2 and #3 or between #3 and #4 may create a firm better positioned to compete with the industry leader or leaders. But while such a merger potentially creates scale efficiencies and technological improvements for the buyer, it also magnifies concentration. Unilateral effects may or may not be present.

The ensuing merger review thus involves difficult predictions about the future across multiples axes – long-term investment, merger-specific efficiencies, and static price effects. Here, structuralism is hopelessly inadequate as a standalone intervention guide. It cannot answer indispensable questions about incentives to innovate and disrupt the market. It would be naïve to suggest that an effects-based analysis can always answer those questions. But at least it asks the right question, and lends itself to ongoing empirical testing.

---

problems of allocative inefficiency associated with monopolistic pricing. The solution has traditionally been to regulate the monopolist or nationalize the industry, neither of which is ideal.

[80] For a classic decision recognizing this point, see United States v. Oracle Corp., 331 F. Supp. 2d 1098 (N.D. Cal. 2004).

[81] Bertrand price competition in markets for fungible goods with perfect access to information yield perfectly competitive outcomes, even in the situation of a duopoly.

A recent example of this dynamic lies in *T-Mobile/Sprint*. Before the merger, the mobile wireless industry was a four-firm oligopoly at the national level. Verizon was the largest carrier, followed by AT&T. T-Mobile and Sprint trailed the leaders by a significant margin. Nevertheless, T-Mobile had disrupted the market, including by forcing the industry leaders to offer unlimited data plans – an impact preserved by the DOJ's meritorious decision to block AT&T's attempted acquisition of T-Mobile in 2011.

In investigating the $26 billion merger between T-Mobile and Sprint, the DOJ acknowledged the likelihood of unilateral and coordinated effects.[82] The transaction was, of course, a 4–3. The Division approved the merger, however, subject to T-Mobile's divesting to DISH Sprint's prepaid retail wireless service business and various spectrum licenses, and giving DISH an exclusive option to acquire cell sites and retail stores decommissioned by T-Mobile after closing.[83] The goal was to induce DISH to build a fourth US-wide wireless network in competition with T-Mobile, Verizon, and AT&T.

Despite the Division's imposed remedy, standing alone it would likely have been insufficient to justify a merger that promised long-term anticompetitive effects. The government would not normally allow an incomplete divestiture in the case of a problematic horizontal acquisition – especially one that was not virtually guaranteed to replace the lost competition. But *T-Mobile/Sprint* was no such case. The DOJ implicitly accepted a key procompetitive justification for the acquisition – namely that it would magnify T-Mobile's ongoing disruption of the industry as an "Un-carrier" by accelerating its building out a 5G network, enhancing rural access, and exponentially growing its capacity.

Even with DOJ and FCC conditions, the *T-Mobile/Sprint* approval was controversial. Fifteen states and the District of Columbia sued to block the deal, notwithstanding the federal government's blessing.[84] The divide between how the Division and (some) state attorneys general viewed the transaction speaks to the complexity of tradeoffs associated with evaluating mergers with potentially offsetting static and dynamic effects. The state effort's thrust was quintessentially structural, alleging that the acquisition would reduce the number of nationwide competitors "from four to three[,]" and yield "an increase in market concentration" that "will result in diminished competition, higher prices, and reduced quality and innovation."[85] They also focused on static price effects associated with the loss of head-to-head competition. The DOJ filed a statement of interest against the state lawsuit.[86]

---

[82] United States v. Deutsche Telekom AG, Case No. 1:09-cv-2232, Competitive Impact Statement, Dkt. 20, p. 7 (D.D.C July 30, 2019).
[83] *Id.* at 8–12.
[84] State of New York v. Deutsche Telekom AG, No. 1:19-cv-5434, Dkt. 1, Compl. (S.D.N.Y. June 11, 2019).
[85] *Id.* ¶ 5.
[86] New York v. Deutsche Telekom AG, No. 1:19-cv-5434, Dkt. 348, Statement of Interest of the United States of America (S.D.N.Y. Dec. 20, 2019).

In the end, the district court ruled against the states.[87] Its reasoning, however, was an ode to the difficulty of effects-based analysis in dynamic markets. The judge lamented his role as "a fortuneteller" in encountering the "competing crystal balls" presented by the parties' proof.[88] In his view, the dueling economists "essentially cancel each other out[,]" yielding a "stalemate" that forced him to rely instead on "the plausibility and persuasiveness of particular witnesses' trial presentations" to decide the outcome – hardly the most rigorous ground for decision.[89] This outcome coincided with one state antitrust enforcer's bemoaning the centrality of economic analysis in merger review – a perspective that would engender much sympathy among the drafters of the Utah Statement.[90]

Ultimately, no flawless methodology for analyzing mergers in dynamic, investment-heavy markets exists. A consequentialist analysis may at some point become less scientific than intuitive, but it remains fact-based. Structuralism essentially gives up, and accepts the virtues and costs of a blunt instrument. That view, of course, becomes easier to accept if one thinks of unconcentrated industries as goals in themselves rather than as a means for preserving competitive pressures in a relevant market.

This discussion brings us to the ultimate question: What is structuralism good for? As Chapter 4 explored, structure and effects correlate. More specifically, rising concentration in a relevant product or service market is generally associated with price increases. Economists have observed that relationship across a swathe of industries. Exceptions exist, and not every increment in concentration will yield competitive harm – hence the need for nuance and a competitive effect approach. Nevertheless, structure remains an important piece of evidence. It illuminates competitive effects, yielding one rule and a larger guide. Specifically, mergers to monopoly should never be allowed. And, as concentration rises, enforcers should worry more about likely unilateral and coordinated effects. Further, if one wishes to diagnose the state of competition across a number of markets without getting into the weeds, structure is a useful proxy. Nevertheless, structuralism is far too blunt to facilitate accurate intervention decisions.

6.1.1.8 "The *LinkLine* [sic] Doctrine Holding That Price Squeeze Allegations Fail As Standalone Section 2 Claims Should Be Overruled"

This proposal appears reasonable, but masks propensity for mischief.

Price squeezes can emerge when a vertically integrated firm supplies its downstream competitors. Customer-rivals of this sort are obviously vulnerable. The

---

[87] New York v. Deutsche Telekom AG, 439 F. Supp. 3d 179 (D.D.C. 2020).
[88] *Id.* at 186–87.
[89] *Id.* at 187–88.
[90] Ben Remaly, *State enforcer questions economists' role in antitrust*, GLOBAL COMPETITION REV., Feb. 13, 2020.

integrated firm may not wish to supply its competitors at all. If it does so, however, then it will likely charge a wholesale price for the input that exceeds its internal cost of production. That cost differential gives the integrated firm a price advantage in the downstream product market. To complete the margin squeeze, it may choose to undercut its competitors' prices. In theory, equally efficient downstream rivals may have to exit if the input is necessary, they cannot procure alternative supply on competitive terms, it is not feasible to vertically integrate upward, and if the profits left downstream fall below their opportunity cost of capital.

Of course, whether this situation is desirable or problematic hinges on a crucial assumption beyond those just listed, which are necessary, but not sufficient for a competitive problem to emerge. Specifically, the integrated supplier's advantageous position may reflect superior investment and competition on the merits. In that situation, it may be best to allow the input supplier to refuse to deal in order to preserve incentives to invest in the first instance. If one firm developed a superior input, then it implies that others could do, too. Forced sharing encourages firms that might otherwise invest simply to enjoy access at a legally proscribed rate.

It will not always be desirable, however, to allow unfettered strategic behavior by the owner of a necessary input. The most obvious problem is transactional. A downstream competitor may come to own a critical input not organically, but through a strategic acquisition. There, the normative calculus is altogether different. The antitrust agencies try to prevent this problem from materializing in the first place by reviewing vertical acquisitions. Integrating upstream by buying an important or essential input can introduce incentives to foreclose downstream rivals or to raise their costs. The FTC and DOJ can sue to block such transactions, but more often impose behavioral conditions governing access.

Now suppose that conditions favorable to a price squeeze arise not by acquisition, but organic vertical integration. As noted, there are good reasons not to impose mandatory terms of contract on pain of antitrust sanction. But those reasons will not always hold. A vertically integrated firm could harm competition in ways that the antitrust laws should address. Fortunately, safeguards exist to address this possibility.

First, Section 2 prohibits below-cost pricing in a product market if it creates a dangerous probability of recoupment. That holds true whether the predator is an upstream supplier or not. Second, if an integrated firm terminates a profitable course of supplying its rivals, then it may violate Section 2 under *Aspen Skiing*. The same may be true if the firm refuses to contract with its nonintegrated rivals on wholesale or retail terms that it makes available to others. The Utah Statement concerns itself here with price squeezes not caught by those prohibitions.

Antitrust's existing sphere of protection is incomplete. On plausible assumptions, an integrated firm might exclude equally efficient rivals through a two-pronged approach. First, it would charge a supracompetitive price for an input to which there is no good alternative. Second, it would price just above its costs downstream. This is a variant of limit pricing, for which game theorists have shown exclusion to be rational on certain assumptions.[91]

Extending antitrust liability, however, requires more than an academic possibility of exclusion. In the first place, there is a world of difference between academic possibility theorems and demonstrable real-world harms that need correction. Above-cost pricing is seldom exclusionary in a manner that antitrust policy ought to recognize (prohibiting it would diminish an efficient firm's incentive to compete). Nor does refusing to supply on a buyer's preferred terms typically harm competition. Problematic exclusion residing in an antitrust "blind spot" will very much be the exception, rather than the rule.

Second, in order to expand antitrust's prohibitory scope, one needs to articulate a workable standard that will permit innocuous or procompetitive "squeezes," while correctly diagnosing the minority of cases that are genuinely harmful. Eliminating error is impossible. But sensible boundaries demarcating unlawful exclusionary behavior from hard competition are essential. Price squeezes implicate two of antitrust's most difficult problems – determining the scope and terms of mandatory access and scrutinizing the bounds of acceptable pricing. Courts and antitrust agencies are terribly positioned to perform these functions. We ought to be awfully careful about embracing imprecise standards.

The Statement identified no legal standard that ought to govern. Presumably, its drafters evoke *Alcoa*, which the Supreme Court effectively overruled in *linkLine*.[92] In 1945, Judge Learned Hand recognized price squeezes as a source of liability for dominant firms even if they did not monopolize a relevant market. "That it was unlawful to set the price of 'sheet' so low and hold the price of ingot so high, seems to us unquestionable, provided, as we have held, that on this record the price of ingot must be regarded as higher than a 'fair price.'"[93] He made clear that he did not look on that squeeze as a form of unlawful monopolization, but as a separate violation of Section 2.

Undeniably a profound concept in life and morality, "fairness" has no place in antitrust policy. Markets work best under punishing competitive pressures that create more losers than winners. A "fair price" lacks economic meaning. Such an indefinite and conclusory standard has no place in modern competition policy.

Recognizing a standalone cause of action for margin squeezes would introduce a sphere of liability that would be at once hazy and expansive. This might be justifiable if it corrected a substantiated problem. Yet, its principal function would be to punish low pricing that benefits consumers and is not below the seller's costs. Worse, it could reduce competition in two dimensions. First, it may deter owners of necessary inputs from voluntarily supplying their downstream rivals in the first place – lest a court later deem their terms unreasonable. Second, it would deter

---

[91] See CARLTON & PERLOFF, *supra* note 11, at 360–66.
[92] Pacific Bell Tel. Co. v. linkLine Comm'cns, Inc., 555 U.S. 438 (2009).
[93] United States v. Aluminum Co. of Am., 148 F.2d 416, 438 (2d Cir. 1945).

downstream rivals from building rival infrastructure and, in that way, suppress facilities-based competition. Ultimately, the Statement's proposal would turn courts into regulators, asking them to identify optimal access prices and monitor ongoing terms of supply.

6.1.1.9 "*Noerr-Pennington* Should Be Overruled and Replaced by a First Amendment Defense and Appropriate Statutory Protections for Workers"

Related to the First Amendment's Petitioning Clause, *Noerr-Pennington* exempts from antitrust liability genuine efforts to solicit favorable governmental action. It is a troubled doctrine. Lobbying the executive branch, propounding the passage of laws, and filing lawsuits all qualify for protection. In practice, however, it is hard to discern the boundaries of commercial action and lobbying. Some firms weaponize the petitioning process in a strategic effort to suppress competition. The law has narrowly limited the circumstances, however, in which petitioning becomes a sham that lacks protection. Yet that exception, narrow as it may be, remains doctrinally obscure. The law is particularly unclear with respect to a "whole series" of petitions.

Alas, a more fundamental problem has emerged. Courts often misconstrue the doctrine, carving out broader spheres of immunity than the underlying constitutional principles support. Relevant Supreme Court decisions succumb to logical inconsistency, adding to the confusion.

Those issues bring us to the Utah Statement. *Noerr-Pennington* is enormously complex as a doctrinal matter. Abolishing it in favor of constitutional immunity might alleviate the problem by refocusing courts' attention on the principles that the defense exists to serve. Difficult questions would remain, of course. As to those challenges, the Statement has nothing to offer. Chapter 8, however, analyzes how the courts ought to reform the *Noerr-Pennington* doctrine in order to enhance competition whilst respecting the First Amendment rights at issue.

6.1.1.10 "The Clayton Act's Worker Exemption Should Be Extended to All Who Labor for a Living, Regardless of Statutory Employment Status, for Horizontal Coordination, Collective Bargaining, and Collective Action in Service of Either"

The statutory labor exemption immunizes trade-union activities, subject to three common-sense limitations.[94] The union must be a bona fide labor group.[95] It must

---

[94] 15 U.S.C. § 17; H.A. Artists v. Actors' Equity Ass'n, 451 U.S. 704 (1981); Am. Fed. of Musicians v. Carroll, 391 U.S. 99 (1968); United States v. Hutcheson, 312 U.S. 219 (1941).
[95] H.A. Artists, 451 U.S. at 717 n.20; Am. Fed. of Musicians, 391 U.S. at 106.

act in its "self-interest" – meaning that it pursue labor market objectives.[96] And it must not combine with a nonlabor group.[97] The courts have expanded the scope of protection to certain reach agreements to which nonlabor groups are privy.[98] This nonstatutory exemption is directed at collective bargaining, and protects a broad swathe of conduct, including multi-employer bargaining.[99]

The Utah Statement does not explain how the existing scope of immunity for organized-labor activities is deficient. Consistent with the progressive impetus behind the neo-Brandeisian movement, a strong sympathy for workers shines through. The drafters clearly want to strengthen labor immunity. Given that existing limits on the scope of the statutory and nonstatutory labor exemptions serve to protect competition where labor market interests become attenuated, their proposed changes would almost certainly harm consumers. In this respect, it is odd for proponents of stronger antitrust enforcement to champion an expansion of policies that have as their express object the restriction of competition.

6.1.2 Method and Enforcement Practice

6.1.2.1 "It Is Not True That 'Congress Designed the Sherman Act As a 'Consumer Welfare Prescription'"

This recommendation captures the most dangerous ideology underlying the Utah Statement. The quoted interpretation of Congressional intent comes from a 1979 decision of the Supreme Court.[100] The proposition that antitrust exists to benefit consumers has since enjoyed broad bipartisan support. Recently, however, the consumer-welfare standard has become a banner item for the reform movement.

Neo-Brandeisians want to replace the law's focus on consumers with an expansive inquiry. They would consider the interests not merely of buyers, but of sellers. Not all sellers, however – they would focus on input providers in upstream supply markets (especially suppliers of labor). To that goal, they would add the interests of society more generally through the asserted benefits of industry deconcentration on values like democracy and income equality. The proposition that today's antitrust policies and existing market structures do violence to democratic norms is, of course, controversial. In the author's view, it is dubious at best. Tabling those concerns, the neo-Brandeisian proposal is deeply troubling. Not only would it upset the administrability of competition policy, it would lead to interventions that corrupt market

---

[96] *Id.* at 722.
[97] *Hutcheson*, 312 U.S. at 232.
[98] Connell Constr. Co. v. Plumbers & Steamfitters Local Union No. 100, 421 U.S. 616 (1975).
[99] Brown v. Pro Football, Inc., 518 U.S. 231 (1996).
[100] Reiter v. Sonotone Corp., 442 U.S. 330, 343 (1979) (quoting ROBERT BORK, THE ANTITRUST PARADOX 66 (1978)).

mechanisms in favor of an enforcer's predisposition toward preferred stakeholders. In this respect, it is worth addressing why there is much to like in the long-established consumer-welfare standard.[101]

Reduced to its essence, the consumer-welfare mandate has much to commend it.[102] To a sea of conflicting interests, it brings focus. The lodestar ensures that competition policy serves the consuming public, and will not be captured by those whose interests lie in restraining trade. Dangers abound. Public choice theory has much to say about how motivated stakeholders secure the passage of harmful laws and policies. Interest groups dominate the disorganized. We see those dynamics play out in all sorts of market settings. Public utilities tend to capture regulators, which struggle to prevent gold-plating and seldom – if ever – subject their wards to demands akin to true competitive pressures. Industries constantly lobby for protectionist laws.

Competition benefits consumers more than it harms sellers, but the effects are rarely felt equally. Modest price savings may be diffused over a great many buyers. Yet, they can net out to a consumer surplus that dwarfs the corresponding loss of producer surplus. The harm to sellers, however, may be localized. The few will thus try to deprive many of the fruits of competition.

Their efforts can find traction. Inefficient firms are often politically favored. Mom and pop shops, local companies, and small enterprises naturally elicit sympathy. Sometimes an entire industry becomes sheltered through hard government quotas on entry – taxis are a classic example. Evolutionary bouts of competition threaten to displace entire business models, as when ride-hailing services emerged or Tesla pioneered direct marketing in the automotive sector, bypassing traditional dealerships. The results are fierce and predictable – a no-holds-barred effort to preserve the status quo through efforts to pass anticompetitive legislation.

As discussed in Chapter 8, the consumer-welfare framework is descriptively inaccurate and normatively incomplete. Nevertheless, it has served a valuable role and is directionally laudable. Consumer welfare guides policymakers through the morass of conflicting interests. And it does so with a powerful utilitarian justification,

---

[101] This book agrees that consumers should be the only stakeholders whose interests ultimately "count" in the antitrust calculus, but argues that the measure of an antitrust violation should be distinct – specifically, where an agreement, practice, or merger eliminates a competitive constraint without offsetting benefit. *See* Chapter 6.

[102] To be sure, the consumer-welfare standard has never been entirely satisfactory. It is, among other things, ambiguous. Bork used the term as a proxy for aggregate welfare in the sense of how economists measure static efficiency – i.e., by combining producer and consumer surplus. The proposition that aggregate welfare ought to control – potentially allowing corporate efficiency savings to permit a merger likely to raise prices to consumers – has always been controversial, and does not reflect today's policies. But nor does the consumer-welfare standard receive a literal interpretation. Quite properly, antitrust prohibits buy-side conspiracies and exclusionary practices directed at upstream markets, where the beneficiaries of competition may be sellers. The mystery dissolves when one realizes that upstream monopsony ultimately restricts output in downstream product markets, too.

informed by economics. Focusing on other stakeholders ruptures the analysis, however, because offsetting values quickly emerge that are not obviously susceptible to quantification. Jobs raise the thorniest issues. Competitive displacement may be a source of major social value, but it comes at a terrible cost to the workers whose livelihoods disappear. So, too, competition on the sell-side of labor markets suppresses wages, potentially exacerbating wealth inequality.

Labor and competition policies come into obvious tension here. The economy generates wealth most effectively if jobs emerge to meet consumer demand – rather than be preserved as an end in themselves – and do so under competition on both the supply and demand sides. Unions can introduce bilateral monopoly in the absence of competition on the demand side, thus potentially improving efficiency, but otherwise restrain competition in ways likely to have harmful downstream effects. The political interests of workers are sufficiently fundamental, of course, that Congress and the courts have carved out broad exemptions from antitrust law for trade-union activity. Outside of that scope of immunity, however, competition policies ought to apply with full force. The consumer-welfare standard then helps to focus attention on the interests that should control.

It is no accident that, in the same breath that neo-Brandeisians call for a revolutionary expansion in the scope of antitrust liability, they urge its retreat on the supply side of labor markets. As noted above, they want to expand antitrust immunity so that workers can more freely eliminate competition between each other. And they want a new-founded skepticism of mergers and agreements between input buyers that lead to lower supply costs.

Especially telling was the widespread (though not universal) progressive opposition to the DOJ's case that Apple and five book publishers agreed to raise the price of e-books, thus increasing royalties for authors that Amazon's low-price business model had otherwise suppressed.[103] This is exactly the kind of confusion that emerges when one loses track of consumer welfare. If authors earn "unfairly low" compensation for their work, then coordination on the supply side could correct that "problem" whilst increasing prices in the downstream product market. But how to tell whether input pricing is monopsonistic as opposed to competitive? Whose interests should control? Losing sight of true north leads to undisciplined, conclusory analysis. It is much better to focus on competitive restraints that lead to effects, as opposed to beginning with existing market outcomes and asking whether they justify concerted action to "correct" market pricing. Absent evidence that a merger, practice, or agreement eliminates competition between input buyers, thus harming suppliers, it makes little sense to ask whether a correction is needed to improve upstream pricing. That line of thinking is exactly why focusing on consumers is so important.

---

[103] United States v. Apple Inc., 952 F. Supp. 2d 638 (S.D.N.Y. 2013), aff'd, 791 F.3d 290 (2d Cir. 2015), cert. denied, 136 S. Ct. 1376 (2016).

6.1.2.2 "Antitrust Rules Should Be Created through Case Development, Agency Rule-Making, and Legislation"

This is a terrible proposal. The courts have wisely discarded most antitrust "rules." Of those that remain, one is narrow and cost-justified. That is the per se rule against naked horizontal cartels. Others, like notification requirements under the HSR Act, are technical and similarly uncontroversial. Section 8's prohibition on director interlocks meeting particular criteria is rigid, but largely harmless due to the lack of monetary sanction. Certain antitrust rules, however, are widely seen as an anachronistic embarrassment.

The Robinson–Patman Act exemplifies this point. Its contradictory rules assume harm to competition in unwarranted circumstances, and prohibit a wide variety of price discounting that may benefit consumers. Such are its perversities that the agencies have refrained from enforcing the statute for the past several decades. Neo-Brandeisians, of course, want to resurrect it as an enforcement vehicle that can benefit suppliers at consumers' expense.

Rules do bestow legal certainty and minimize the costs of administering the law. In that respect, they have value. Indeed, in the right circumstances, they are preferable. Where the relative virtues and harms of a restraint are discernable ex ante, there is little need to rely on expensive ex post evaluation to make determinations that are only marginally more accurate. But rules are generally ill-suited to antitrust. Commercial behavior is complex, and its impact on a fluid marketplace even more so. Rules are inherently imprecise. They condemn what they should not, and permit what ought to be prohibited. The entire thrust of the effects era has been to find a better way. An ex post assessment that considers the rich context of a given restraint diminishes net error costs, producing a more accurate antitrust system.

Hence, the idea that the agencies should engage in rule-making is unsound. FTC Commissioner Rohit Chopra has recently championed that proposal, which the Utah Statement also supports.[104] In his view, the Commission would do well to enhance predictability and reduce enforcement costs – two advantages inherent in rules over standards. More dubiously, he would purport to enhance democratic participation by shifting ultimate adjudicative responsibility away from the courts and vesting it in the Commission, which would solicit public comment.[105]

Commissioner Chopra makes his case elegantly, and fairly observes limitations surrounding the administrability of the rule of reason. His mistake is to think indeterminism a general condition of antitrust adjudication. Further, the same difficulties that hinder accurate liability decisions under today's standard would equally afflict the identification of an optimal rule. He did not identify the specific

---

[104] Comment of Federal Trade Commissioner Rohit Chopra, Hearing #1 on Competition and Consumer Protection in the 21st Century, Sept. 6, 2018, https://www.ftc.gov/system/files/documents/public_statements/1408196/chopra_-_comment_to_hearing_1_9-6-18.pdf.

[105] *Id.*; *see also* Wu, The Curse of Bigness, *supra* note 8.

rules that he would envision forbidding as "unfair methods of competition" under Section 5 of the FTC Act beyond prohibiting pay-for-delay settlements and non-compete agreements. The devil is in the details, of course.

A final consideration warrants emphasis. The claim that firms endure acute legal uncertainty under today's antitrust standard is false. The vast majority of restraints are lawful under the rule of reason. Companies seek legal advice from counsel, who can confidently give the green light where the per se rule does not apply, the proposed restraint has a bona fide rationale, and the parties' plausible market shares do not exceed thirty percent. The true progressive objection to the rule of reason is not uncertainty, but permissibility. Rules would be far more inimical to business conduct. Neo-Brandeisians favor them for that reason, and because their enforcement does not require one to answer hard questions, such as the propensity of a restraint to produce anticompetitive effects.

6.1.2.3 "The States, the Laboratories of Economic Experimentation, Are a Critical Vanguard of Enforcement Efforts"

As members of a federal republic, the states have their own sovereignty. Without question, each has the constitutional right to enforce antitrust laws with its jurisdiction.

A distinct question is whether *national* antitrust policy is best served by encouraging more active intervention at the state level. It is true, of course, that the states are laboratories of economic experimentation. And there are questions of competition law uniquely suited to regional or local disposition. When a firm seeks to acquire assets within a state, the attorney general of that jurisdiction has every reason to intervene in order to protect consumers from a loss of competition. Transactions with localized competitive impacts are good candidates for prioritized state enforcement. Agreements, practices, and mergers of bounded impact are seldom deserving targets of the Justice Department's and Federal Trade Commission's attention. The federal antitrust agencies have limited budgets that ought to address matters of national significance. Meanwhile, the experience of state attorneys general can provide valuable insights for one another and at the federal level.

Laboratories, however, are self-contained. In some circumstances, active state intervention can disrupt effective competition policy. Problems emerge when the relevant geographic market is neither local nor regional, but instead national. Then, a patchwork of inconsistent antitrust policies may not advance enforcement in an accurate direction, but create a hodgepodge of inconsistent priorities. Deals in national or global relevant geographic markets are generally best resolved by the federal authorities. This is not to deny the possibility of incremental value of state intervention in some such cases. Antitrust policy benefits when federal courts scrutinize difficult matters, clarifying the scope of the law and crystalizing issues that will allow for more efficient disposition of similar matters in the future.

Nevertheless, there are real dangers if states too often second-guess the federal agencies in cases that affect competition in national or global markets. Beyond disrupting the administration of an efficient national competition policy and introducing the possibility of inconsistent policies, active state intervention in tension with federal enforcement brings other costs. For one, the depth of expertise in antitrust law is not uniform across the states. Although some jurisdictions have developed robust competition programs staffed by knowledgeable and experienced attorneys – California and New York are two prominent examples, though not the only ones – some others have more modest antitrust resources. More worryingly, certain state attorneys have, on occasion, displayed indicia of politically motivated antitrust enforcement. In that regard, one wonders if neo-Brandeisian calls for renewed vigor in state intervention reflect a hope that some jurisdictions will abandon the consumer welfare standard and law and economics in favor of an anti-size mandate.

In short, state enforcement is an important feature of US antitrust policy. Indeed, it is indispensable to protecting competition at the local and regional level, and an undeniable constitutional prerogative. It would be wrong, however, to encourage widespread intervention at the state level into mergers and practices that affect competition nationally or globally, and that lack any special nexus to particular states. The efficient disposition of notified mergers could suffer, and many parties would yield to the strictest jurisdiction's demands even if they exceed what the law requires – such being the cost of getting the deal done.

This concern is part of a larger emerging problem in global antitrust. As competition jurisdictions continue to proliferate around the world – there are now over 140 of them – fractured and overlapping interventions grow in kind. Extraterritoriality has become a real problem, as hold-out jurisdictions extract conditions beyond those already accepted elsewhere as conditions of approval. The most demanding regime sets the standard. And too often that standard reflects the country's industrial policy, rather than an attempt to preserve competition. This phenomenon undermines competition policy, and is not something that reformists ought to encourage within the United States, which is already unique in having two dedicated – and occasionally dueling – national antitrust enforcers.

6.1.2.4 "Private Enforcement Is a Critical Complement to Public Enforcement"

The US antitrust regime is unique. No other country builds its competition policy so centrally around litigation. In 1914, Congress made private actors principally responsible for enforcing the antitrust laws. Section 4 of the Clayton Act awards prevailing plaintiffs with treble damages, as well as their costs.[106] In an already-litigious society,

---
[106] 15 U.S.C. § 15.

it creates a burning incentive to seek out and challenge unlawful restraints of trade. That reality deters clear violations of antitrust law.

This system is hardly perfect. Burdensome, inefficient, and plagued by unmeritorious suits, it is nevertheless important. Federal and state competition authorities have limited budgets and, worse, restricted visibility into changing market dynamics. All government action suffers from an information problem, which justifies decentralization and hence market processes. Private litigation helps to solve that problem on the antitrust enforcement side. The first victim of exclusionary conduct is a competitor, not the state. The immediate casualties of a price-fixing conspiracy are buyers. The agencies cannot act on every meritorious complaint that they receive, and so inducing firms and consumers to vindicate their own legal rights ensures more robust enforcement of the antitrust laws. Private litigation is a natural complement to government enforcement. Indeed, beyond its hefty deterrent value, class action and B2B antitrust litigation has produced an abundance of valuable precedent. It has also facilitated an efficient use of government resources through amicus brief efforts to help develop the law in a preferred direction.

Seeing nuisance litigation directed at productive firms, conservatives tend to frown on private enforcement. They object to a real phenomenon. Defending even one lawsuit can cost millions of dollars. Discovery cost asymmetries can motivate plaintiffs with threadbare cases to litigate aggressively in pursuit of a settlement reflecting not an expected liability verdict, but foregone litigation costs. Worse, companies have every incentive to hijack the antitrust laws, turning them on their head as a weapon against their more effective competitors. Nothing wounds a firm more grievously than failing to keep up with its rivals.

Left unaddressed, these problems would kill the case for a litigation-centric antitrust policy. The courts have devised safeguards, however, designed to screen out misuses of the litigation system. Under the antitrust-injury doctrine, plaintiffs must show that their harm flowed from (or was the causal mechanism of) lost competition.[107] *Twombly* requires that a complaint allege sufficient factual content to make claimed antitrust violations plausible.[108] To proceed to trial in a conspiracy case, a plaintiff needs evidence tending to exclude the possibility of independent conduct.[109] The law imposes a host of other limitations on the scope of liability – from requiring proof of a dangerous probability of recoupment in predatory-pricing cases to cabining the scope of even a monopolist's duty to deal.[110] Many of those exclusions are controversial in neo-Brandeisian eyes. Viewed in the

---

[107] Brunswick Corp. v. Pueblo Bowl-O-Mat, Inc., 429 U.S. 477, 489 (1977); *see also* Blue Shield of Va. v. McCready, 457 U.S. 465 (1982).
[108] Bell Atlantic Corp. v. Twombly, 550 U.S. 544, 545-46 (2007).
[109] Matsushita Elec. Indus. Co. v. Zenith Radio Corp., 475 U.S. 574, 588 (1986) (citing Monsanto Co. v. Spray-Rite Serv. Corp., 465 U.S. 752, 764 (1984)).
[110] Brooke Grp. v. Brown & Williamson Tobacco Corp., 509 U.S. 209, 222 (1993); Verizon Commc'ns, Inc. v. Law Offices of Curtis V. Trinko, 540 U.S. 398, 409 (2004).

context of treble-damage-fed private litigation, rivals' incentives to use the threat of liability to free-ride on others' investments, and larger error costs, however, they generally make sense.

6.1.2.5 "The Markets for Labor – and in Particular Problems Caused by Labor Market Monopsony – Should Be Subject to Robust Antitrust Enforcement, and Enforcers Should Treat Business Structures That Restrict Alternatives For or Coerce Working Americans As Suspect"

This statement has two components. The first proposition is axiomatic – so much so that one might think it unworthy of mention. *Of course* labor markets warrant robust antitrust enforcement. No mainstream antitrust thinker denies the benefits of competition in input markets. Nevertheless, this point does warrant emphasis because it has received insufficient attention from the agencies.

First, the economics: market power on the buy side distorts markets in the same way that it does on the sell side. In a competitive labor market, the equilibrium wage equals the marginal revenue product of labor (MRP). In other words, compensation equals the extra revenue that a firm earns by hiring one additional worker. Monopsonistic combinations force input prices below MRP. In the extreme case of a single employer in a relevant labor market, the company will set wages at the point where MRP meets the firm's marginal factor cost. The result is a subcompetitive wage, which reduces the output of labor below the optimal point. Not only does this phenomenon reduce employment, it has counterintuitive downstream effects.

Some intuit that lower wages benefit consumers because they make products or services in the downstream market cheaper. That is not true when compensation falls below the competitive level. Just as rising prices in a goods market induce firms to increase supply, so falling wages in a labor market will – over time – reduce supply. Suppressed wages dissuade marginal workers from entering that work space, accelerate retirement, and induce substitution toward other careers. Economists would also expect the quality of work supplied to fall. The drop in output in the labor market will force buyers – that is, firms that hire workers to help them build products or offer services – to substitute the labor-capital input mix. That substitution will be inefficient, and hence more costly. The ensuing increase in the marginal cost of production will lead employers wielding monopsony power to *raise* price, thus harming downstream consumers.

The law and economics of monopsony are well established. Horizontal conspiracies are equally illegal on the buy and sell sides.[111] Since 2016, the agencies have prioritized investigating no-poach and no-hire agreements between employers as

---

[111] *See, e.g.*, Weyerhaeuser Co. v. Ross-Simmons Hardwood Lumber Co., 549 U.S. 312, 321–22 (2007).

per se violations.[112] And their horizontal merger guidelines devote an entire section to transactions that combine "competing buyers."[113]

The DOJ and FTC thus seem well attuned to the potential for anticompetitive effects on the buy side of labor markets. To the best of the author's knowledge, however, the agencies have never sued to block a merger solely because it endangered competition between firms to procure employees. The lack of such intervention would be appropriate if transactions seldom endangered competition in labor markets. This has indeed been a widely held view. Economists have long seen such markets as competitive, fluid, and not subject to long-term entry barriers. Outside of a few specialized areas, the supply side is unconcentrated to the point of being atomistic. Certainly in the early stages of their careers, workers have many options. Relative to assets or infrastructure, labor is mobile. No intellectual property inhibits movement or switching. Combined, these factors can make it difficult for employers sustainably to exercise market power in labor markets.

That seems to be a fair approximation across various employment markets, but it is not universally true. Enforcers may have uncritically assumed that some labor markets are competitive when they are not. Employers can exercise market power. No-poach agreements in Silicon Valley revealed that sophisticated companies found it profitable to restrain competition. For positions of unusual skill, labor supply may be limited. That condition will spur prospective employees to compete by offering more generous compensation and perks. As competition on the hiring side grows, so does the private benefit to employers of suppressing that competition. Even in low-skill jobs, employers have incentives to avoid competing. Non-compete agreements are hard to justify in the absence of specialized and investment-heavy training on the part of an employer that is susceptible to free-riding. To invoke one example, the practice of certain sandwich chains imposing non-competes on their workers raised a red flag.

To their credit, the agencies moved quickly to clamp down on no-hire and no-poach agreements.[114] The FTC held a workshop in 2020 on the competitive effects of non-compete covenants.[115] This is all encouraging, but a major question remains unaddressed – what of the effects of mergers in concentrated markets on employment? This is no mere academic question. Antitrust thought leaders are beginning to call for a renewed focus on buy-side power in employment markets on the merger side.[116]

---

[112] See, e.g., DEP'T OF JUSTICE & FED. TRADE COMM'N, ANTITRUST GUIDANCE FOR HUMAN RESOURCE PROFESSIONALS 4 (2016).
[113] HORIZONTAL MERGER GUIDELINES, *supra* note 75, at § 12.
[114] See *supra* note 112.
[115] Fed. Trade Comm'n, Non-Competes in the Workplace: Examining Antitrust and Consumer Protection Issues, Jan. 9, 2020, https://www.ftc.gov/news-events/events-calendar/non-competes-workplace-examining-antitrust-consumer-protection-issues.
[116] See, e.g., Ioana Elena Marinescu & Herbert Hovenkamp, *Anticompetitive Mergers in Labor Markets*, 94 IND. L.J. 1031 (2019); Suresh Naidu et al., *Antitrust Remedies for Labor Market Power*, 132 HARV.

Some calls for merger reform vis-à-vis labor markets are iconoclastic. Herbert Hovenkamp has characterized the implications of scrutinizing mergers for lost competition between employers as "staggering."[117]

Some reformists envision using structural screens to identify mergers that harm competition in labor markets. That is far too blunt an instrument. The requisite analysis will be difficult. It is easy to tell whether two merging firms sell overlapping products. A given company may hire employees for all sorts of dissimilar positions, and the breadth of the relevant labor market for each such role may not be at all obvious. Further, companies may compete in labor markets regardless of whether they do so downstream. The inquiry is not obviously bounded. It thus points to the potential for a resource-intensive, searching investigation into many mergers that otherwise raise no competitive issues.

All of this warrants caution. In the author's view, the issue screams out for dedicated study by the FTC, perhaps in the form of a Section 6(b) retrospective study. In the meantime, and consistent with the guidelines, the agencies should watch out for transactions that bear indicia of close head-to-head competition on the hiring front, while continuing their good work on no-poach and non-compete agreements in labor markets.

To conclude this section where it began, the Utah Statement's proposal about antitrust in labor markets has two components. As discussed, the first has much to commend it. The second is uselessly abstract. It is unclear to which "business structures" the drafters refer, much less what they mean by coercion or restricting alternatives. Neo-Brandeisians obviously advance traditional progressive polices favoring labor – and to do so in this instance through competition policy. There is every reason to be wary of this effort. Antitrust should remain firmly rooted in economic analysis and competitive effects, with labor markets being no exception.

6.1.2.6 "The Broad Structural Concerns Expressed by Congress in Its Enactment of the 1950 Anti-Merger Act, Including Due Concern for the Economic and Political Dangers of Excessive Industrial Concentration, Should Drive Enforcement of Section 7 of the Clayton Act"

This misguided proposal lies at the heart of the neo-Brandeisian movement.

It is true, of course, that competition policy hinges on a threshold societal choice about which values antitrust law ought to serve.[118] It is not possible to "disprove" a political value, such as a predilection for atomistic markets as an end in itself. It is

---

L. Rev. 536 (2018). For less measured accounts, see Sandeep Vaheesan, *How Contemporary Antitrust Robs Workers of Power*, L. & Pol. Econ., July 19, 2018, https://lpeblog.org/2018/07/19/how-contemporary-antitrust-robs-workers-of-power/; Open Markets Institute, *Monopoly Basics: Workers & Monopoly*, https://openmarketsinstitute.org/explainer/labor-and-monopoly/.

[117] Marinescu & Hovenkamp, *supra* note 116, at 1031.
[118] See Chapter 1.

possible, however, to question the premises on which a claimed virtue rests. To the extent that some reformists justify deconcentration efforts on consequentialist grounds – lower prices for consumers, better worker compensation, reduced income inequality, enhanced democratic participation, and the like – one may contest those predicates on factual grounds. To these considerations, one should also add the contradictions of a competition policy focused on structure alone. Its administration is apt to be erratic, and have unwelcome effects on investment incentives.

Structuralism should be neither the principal means nor goal of antitrust analysis.[119] That conclusion is doubly urgent if the measure of concentration derives not from an economically defined relevant market, but from broader industry.[120] Whatever their value to tracing competition trends at a high level, *industrial* concentration statistics provide no means for administering the antitrust laws.

The interested reader can turn to Chapters 3 and 5 for a detailed treatment given structure referred to in the two preceding footnotes. For now, it will suffice to write that a return to the merger policies of the 1950s and 1960s would harm consumers, disrupt socially valuable business activity, and tear up the past half century's economics literature. That is not a responsible vision for antitrust reform.

6.1.2.7 "Anticompetitive Conduct Harming One Party or Class Should Never Be Justifiable by Offsetting Benefits to Another Party or Class. Netting Harms and Benefits across Markets, Parties, or Classes Should Not Be a Method for Assessing Anticompetitive Effects"

The first sentence of this proposal is circular. Whether conduct is "anticompetitive" can hinge on its net effects – a calculus that weighs offsetting costs and benefits. Every vertical restraint, for example, inhibits competition within a manufacturer's supply chain. Retailers thus lose the opportunity to make profitable extra sales, and some consumers pay elevated prices. Many such restraints, however, are procompetitive. That is because, by inhibiting competition in one narrow channel, they can promote it at a larger level – the classic intra- versus inter-brand competition trade-off.

A more interesting question is cross-market effects – a controversial proposition within the agencies. Almost by definition, mergers between firms that do not (and would not) go head-to-head for the same consumers are not horizontal. Recent economic models, however, show that such mergers might reduce competition when a common intermediary bundles the merging parties' non-direct-substitute goods.[121] This literature focuses on health-system and hospital combinations in

---

[119] *See* Chapter 4.
[120] *See* Chapter 3.
[121] *See, e.g.*, Leemore Dafny et al., The Price Effects of Cross-Market Hospital Mergers, 50 RAND J. ECON. 286 (2019).

different geographies that bargain to be part of a common insurer plan.[122] Because neither party is a substitute for the other, their merger should not relieve a competitive constraint. A developing literature, however, suggests that a merger between in-plan but geographically distant hospitals could enhance their leverage vis-à-vis a mutual payer to the extent that the insurer requires broad geographic coverage. Much work remains to be done here before the theory is sufficiently substantiated and subject to appropriate limiting principles such that it can propel enforcement decisions.

Neo-Brandeisians enthusiastically support greater intervention to prevent health-system consolidation.[123] Hence, one would expect them naturally to embrace theories like cross-market effects. Yet, the Utah Statement's proposal here would expressly foreclose that possibility.

The drafters oppose netting effects because they see it as a means for blessing practices and mergers with which they take issue. The 2018 *AmEx* decision epitomizes the point.[124] There, the Supreme Court threw out a trial verdict against American Express, which had imposed antisteering clauses on merchants that accept Amex cards. Those restraints allow Amex to preserve elevated merchant fees by prohibiting vendors from offering point-of-sale discounts to buyers who used a card with lower fees. The inflated fees flow back, in part, to Amex cardholders. To prove its case, the DOJ showed that the antisteering provisions had actual anticompetitive effects on the merchant-side of the platform. The Supreme Court reversed for failure to prove harm to competition in a relevant market. In doing so, it held that credit cards are platforms that facilitate a single, simultaneous transaction.[125] In that setting, the Court found, evidence that Amex's agreements raised merchant fees was insufficient because it did not show that harm netted out across both sides of the platform – specifically that antisteering provisions raised "the cost of credit-card transactions above a competitive level, reduced the number of credit-card transactions, or otherwise stifled competition in the credit-card market."[126]

Progressive antitrust reformists reacted with alarm. Tim Wu, one of the authors of the Utah Statement, characterized the opinion as a "chillingly efficient assault on America" and a "hard march backward to laissez-faire economic policies of a sort not seen since the 19th century."[127] As a practical matter, demonstrating harm to competition netted out over both sides of a simultaneous transaction platform

---

[122] *See id.*; see also Robert W. McCann & Kenneth M. Vorrasi, *Cross-Market Effects in Hospital Mergers: A Collision of Economic and Legal Theory*, 30 HEALTH LAW HANDBOOK 215 (2018).

[123] *See, e.g.*, Open Markets Institute, *The Role of Hospital Monopolies in America's Health Care Crisis*, Dec. 2, 2019, https://openmarketsinstitute.org/wp-content/uploads/2019/12/191105_OMI_Hospital_Monopolies-v21.pdf.

[124] Ohio v. Am. Express Co., 138 S. Ct. 2274 (2018).

[125] *Id.* at 2286.

[126] *Id.* at 2287.

[127] Tim Wu, *The Supreme Court Devastates Antitrust Law*, N.Y. TIMES, June 26, 2018.

would pose significant evidentiary difficulties for a plaintiff. Even if the Court had properly conceived of the relevant market, the decision may illustrate how pursuing economic purity in antitrust can reach a point of diminishing returns. Trying too hard to reduce Type I errors (false convictions) eventually yields disproportionately costly Type II errors (false acquittals).

As a former antitrust lawyer and professor of regulation, Justice Breyer is one of the Court's more knowledgeable jurists on matters of competition policy. He wrote a stinging dissent in *AmEx*, describing as "'economic nonsense'" the fusion of two sides of the platform into a single market.[128] Merchants and shoppers both use card services, but their uses are complementary. A merchant that faces a transactional fee increase can avoid it by choosing to decline the relevant card in favor of other cards – a substitution effect. What it cannot do is become a cardholder itself. Doing so would not help its escape an excessive transactional fee, and thus would not discipline any exercise of market power.

There is much to criticize in the Court's opinion. The cross-relationship between two sides of a platform is one of complementarity – a phenomenon that is by no means unique to transactional networks. Whenever raising the price of one good suppresses demand for another – for ice cream and cones as between merchant fees and consumer demand for credit cards – separate ownership brings with it negative externalities. We do not typically think of this price-demand interconnection as bringing complements within a single market.

Why did the Court engage in such gymnastics? It was likely reacting to a problem born of the legal ramifications of market definition itself. The law prevents a defendant from justifying harm to competition in a relevant market by pointing to offsetting benefits in another market.[129] Hence, the doctrinal limitation on cross-market effects may have led the Court to adopt such an awkward conception of the relevant market. Ironically, the concept that bothers neo-Brandeisians so much – summing harms here and costs there – may itself have been the basis for *Amex*, a decision that they loathe.

Indeed, this seems likely. There is no question that the antisteering provisions at issue in *Amex* suppressed merchant-fee-based competition between credit-card issuers at the point of sale. Cabined within that zone of inquiry, the challenged restraints were clearly anticompetitive. But restricting one's view to the point of sale alone ought to leave any thoughtful antitrust thinker uncomfortable. Just as clear as restrained competition in merchant fees were benefits that flowed to cardholders, fueling quality-based competition between issuers. Now, one might think that the harms outweigh plausible offsetting effects on the issuing side, but that determination requires a utilitarian calculus that a market limited to the merchant side of the

---

[128] *Am. Express*, 138 S. Ct. at 2295–96 (Breyer, J., dissenting).
[129] *Id.* at 2302 (Breyer, J., dissenting).

platform would foreclose. Even Justice Breyer in dissent struggled on that point, acknowledging the implications of his preferred market definition exercise:

> American Express might wish to argue that the nondiscrimination provisions, while anticompetitive in respect to merchant-related services, nonetheless have an adequate offsetting procompetitive benefit in respect to its shopper-related services. I believe that American Express should have an opportunity to ask the Court of Appeals to consider that matter. American Express might face an uphill battle. A Sherman Act § 1 defendant can rarely, if ever, show that a procompetitive benefit in the market for one product offsets an anticompetitive harm in the market for another.[130]

As discussed in Chapter 8, the law would do well to revisit market definition's role in antitrust. Its binary nature is unbefitting the nuanced evaluation that the complex realities of marketplace behavior demand. Rigid share thresholds may inoculate harmful restraints or point to market power that is, in fact, illusory. The incorporation of economics remains incomplete in this space. The result is tensions of the kind so plainly on display in *Amex* – accept a sensible market definition and then risk condemning a restraint under partial ignorance, unable to account for procompetitive effects felt nearby (though outside the market), or magnify the bounds of the market itself to make it coterminous with the scope of offsetting effects at cost to the coherence of the market definition exercise itself. Contrary to the Utah Statement's proposal above, the law would do well to consider the full universe of stakeholders impacted by a restraint, and not cabin its purview to actors within markets that are likely to be imperfectly calibrated.[131]

6.1.2.8 "False Negatives Should Not Be Preferred Over False Positives, and the Costs of Erroneous Lack of Enforcement Should Not Be Discounted or Assumed Harmless, But Given Appropriate Weight When Making Enforcement Decisions"

Antitrust error is profoundly important. Decision theory is a useful tool that lends itself to pro- and anti-intervention considerations depending on the facts presented. Some free-marketeers have captured error-cost analysis, however, and turned into an unjustified weapon against merger and conduct challenges in close cases. A correction is overdue.

The Utah Statement is correct on this point, at least as expressed. As ever, though, the ultimate disposition of this question requires a great deal of nuance. Chapter 7 provides an in-depth treatment of decision theory in antitrust. It remains a vital issue for meaningful reform.

---

[130] *Id.*
[131] *See also* HORIZONTAL MERGER GUIDELINES, *supra* note 75, at § 10, n.14.

6.1.2.9 "Structural Remedies Are to Be Preferred"

In cases involving lost head-to-head competition, the agencies have long favored structural remedies in the form of divestitures. That preference is well founded.

In acting to preserve competition, the DOJ and FTC guard the process by which firms try to capture sales from each other. Anything that consumers value yields a potential channel of rivalry. Outside of the digital realm, price is typically the principal and most salient means of luring buyers away from alternatives. But it is by no means the only one. Quality, attractive terms (like warranties), brand, data privacy, and even social responsibility may be – to varying degrees – avenues of competition that warrant protection. That is why behavioral remedies seldom work in horizontal cases. A contractual promise not to raise price, for example, is not merely simplistic; it is incomplete. The pressure to compete remains. When firms cannot compete on price, they switch focus to quality – as the piano bars on 747s in the late 1970s exemplified.

Hence, if a merger creates market power, a behavioral remedy may limit the buyer's ability to raise price (though imperfectly because price caps cannot respond in real time to changing demand and cost conditions). But all nonprice-based means of competition between the merging parties would be lost, and for that the conduct remedy would fix little or nothing. It is extraordinarily difficult to reduce all material dimensions of competition to writing in an enforceable contractual remedy. The proper fix is to block the merger or – if the injury to competition is limited to a subset of markets in which the parties compete – require the buyer to divest its or the seller's overlap business. If the divestiture buyer is well positioned and incentivized to compete as the parties did, then the remedy would preserve the full range of incentives born of competition.

The agencies' preference for structural remedies has continued to harden over time – in part because *reliably* correcting lost competition is difficult, even with divestitures. Illustratively, in 2017 the FTC published a case study of 46 horizontal mergers in which it had imposed remedies between 2006 and 2012.[132] Of those transactions, the Commission had required structural fixes in forty of them.[133] Yet, only two-thirds of those remedies successfully maintained the competitive market structure that had preceded the merger.[134] Many lessons flowed from that merger retrospective, perhaps the leading one of which was that divestitures of ongoing businesses (as distinct from partial-asset-package divestitures) were more likely to succeed.[135]

The Utah Statement adds nothing new here, though its failure to specify the purported sphere of application introduces concerns. As explained, horizontal issues

[132] Fed. Trade Comm'n, The FTC's Merger Remedies 2006–2012: A Report of the Bureaus of Competition and Economics (Jan. 2017).
[133] *Id.* at 13.
[134] *Id.* at 18.
[135] *Id.* at 1.

demand structural remedies. That is seldom the case for vertical acquisitions. Such transactions do not eliminate head-to-head competition, and thus do not introduce the grave (and typically unsurmountable) difficulties of crafting a conduct remedy to account for the full scope of lost competition. Objectionable vertical mergers introduce the ability and incentive for the buyer to engage in input or customer foreclosure. When access is the issue, contractual fixes are more suitable. Importantly, vertical acquisitions usually bring with them valuable double-marginalization efficiencies. A well-crafted conduct remedy facilitates those benefits, while protecting downstream rivals against strategic conduct.

Under the Trump Administration, the Justice Department unveiled an unprecedented opposition to behavioral remedies, even in the vertical setting. In *AT&T/Time Warner*, it sued to block a transaction largely analogous to prior deals that earlier administrations had blessed with conduct remedies – most notably, *Comcast/NBCU*. In light of the disposition of that case, it seems unlikely that vertical merger challenges will follow when the parties are willing to agree to a suitable contractual remedy.[136]

6.1.2.10 "Harms Demonstrated by Clear and Convincing Evidence or Empirical Study Should Never Be Ignored or Discounted Based on Theories That Might Predict a Lack of Harm"

This principle is correct.

Theories allow economists to form hypotheses about causal relationships, which they can in turn test empirically. The more closely a theory predicts outcomes, the more useful it becomes. Economic models necessarily rely on simplifying assumptions – the full panoply of true causal factors is far too complex to capture. Many of those assumptions are unrealistic, neoclassical assumptions of constrained optimization among them. Such simplifications, however, are essential to a workable model. And, even though they may be inaccurate as to many individual actors, over an entire population of firms and consumers, departures from rational profit and utility maximization may cancel out and revert to the mean.[137]

Across the broad spectrum of applications of neoclassical law and economics, firm behavior often stands out as most reliably in line with predicate assumptions – namely, profit maximization. But it is still an abstraction. Firms cannot maximize profits as models envision because, in practice, they cannot define the marginal cost of incremental production. Business judgment, reputational factors, anticipated customer reactions, brand differentiation, and countless other factors beyond equating marginal cost and marginal revenue (or rivals' expected reaction in oligopolies) drive real-life pricing decisions. In no way do those complications, however, impugn

---

[136] United States v. AT&T, Inc., 916 F.3d 1029 (D.C. Cir. 2019).
[137] There is an entire field in the form of behavioral economics dedicated to understanding the circumstances in which people and companies consistently deviate from rational behavior.

the value of microeconomics. Price theory is a powerful tool for predicting firm behavior and market outcomes.

Competition law has thus drawn on the industrial-organization literature to infuse doctrine with economic content. Pleading standards, the evidence required to proceed to trial on a conspiracy claim founded on parallel conduct, the treatment of vertical restraints, the law governing predatory pricing and bidding claims, and more all reflect antitrust law and economics. Economic theories are equally influential in helping the agencies understand the likely effects of practices, agreements, and mergers.

Antitrust entices many lawyers because of its rich theoretical content. Some say that, while many attorneys spend their days with their heads in books, competition lawyers spend their days with their feet on the desk. Thinking is a wonderful feature of antitrust practice, but it creates a danger. A beloved theory can obscure counter-intuitive evidence. That is a dangerous propensity. Theories predict effects. When economists can observe effects directly, then the need for a predictive theory evaporates. Unsurprisingly, this outcome is limited to consummated mergers and past restraints or practices. And, even then, economists use models to project outcomes in the but-for world in order to estimate the magnitude and direction of price effects. Nevertheless, evidence of competitive harm can emerge that displaces the need for abstract models or theories.

In that respect, numerous features of the agency toolkit go to incentives, not guaranteed outcomes. For example, GUPPIs calculated using diversion ratios and margins estimate an incentive to raise price post-closing. They do not, in themselves, predict that prices will rise – let alone by the percentage of the GUPPI. Vertical integration often creates an incentive to cut price and expand output, but there is no guarantee that this will actually happen. Those and many other insights from law and economics rationalize antitrust policy, and properly guide agency decision-making. But every theory requires ongoing fact-checking, substantiation, and refinement.

These considerations reduce to a common-sense proposition: if facts and theory conflict, the former should control. That pecking order is obvious, but people sometimes become so immersed in the intellectual purity of the governing theory that it blinds them to contrary evidence. A good example lay in neoclassical antitrust thinkers' dismay when the Supreme Court decided *Kodak*.[138] There, a firm sold cameras in a competitive market, but allegedly quashed competition in aftermarket parts and service by withholding spare parts in order to charge elevated prices. Price theory would suggest that it is impossible to exercise market power in a sustained fashion in an aftermarket because consumers in the principal market would factor post-sales costs into the upfront price, adjusting it accordingly and thus abandoning the expensive firm in favor of its rivals. The plaintiffs had

---

[138] Eastman Kodak Co. v. Image Tech. Servs., Inc., 504 U.S. 451 (1992).

introduced evidence, however, that consumers did not fully internalize later costs at the point of original purpose. The Supreme Court acknowledged that the evidence may bear out the vaunted theory that "the equipment market does discipline the aftermarkets so that all three are priced competitively overall[.]"[139] But it refused at the summary judgment stage to hold that such theory would dominate contrary evidence as a matter of law.

6.1.2.11 "Clear and Convincing Evidence of Anticompetitive Intent Should Be Taken As a Presumptive Evidence of Harm"

Antitrust poses great demands of those who employ it. It was not always so. Comprised of rules hostile to vertical restraints, mergers of all non-conglomerate varieties, and perceived coercion, it once prohibited broad swathes of conduct. Little or no appeal to effects was necessary. Today, the law has abandoned rules in pursuit of greater accuracy through searching inquiries. Its administration has grown more exacting in kind. The economic analysis of business conduct is formidably complex – so much so that some doubt the federal judiciary's ability to apply it.[140]

Confronted with esoteric questions of demand elasticities, GUPPIs, and SSNIPs, courts and enforcers search for more digestible criteria. Intent emerges as the ultimate simplification. Business documents are the delivery vehicle.

Suppose that the parties to a merger advance a broad market definition that, if accepted, would suggest an inability to exercise market power. Economics offers a rigorous means by which to resolve that question. Dueling economic testimony on the marginal consumer's propensity to substitute away from a product in response to a 5 percent price increase, however, may paralyze overwhelmed decision-makers.[141] But what if the buyer's deal documents proclaim that the transaction will allow the post-merger firm to raise price? Does that end the matter, rendering the market definition question academic? And what if business executives in their emails and presentations frame "the market" in narrower terms than their attorneys and economics later advance?

To the uninitiated, these questions barely survive their asking. *Of course* documentary evidence should control. What businesspeople write among themselves in the ordinary course is reliable. Their later efforts to explain away such references smack of opportunism. Best of all, this adjudicative process seems administrable. In lieu of dueling experts and nuanced arguments artfully crafted by lawyers to

---

[139] *Id.* at 486.

[140] *See, e.g.*, Michael R. Baye & Joshua D. Wright, *Is Antitrust Too Complicated for Generalist Judges? The Impact of Economic Complexity and Judicial Training on Appeals*, 54 J.L. & Econ. 1 (2011).

[141] For a recent case in which a district judge readily acknowledged this phenomenon, see New York v. Deutsche Telekom AG, 439 F. Supp. 3d 179, 187–88 (D.D.C. 2020).

advance their client's preferred position, documents emerge as objective and straightforward.

This line of thinking is intuitive, but misguided. Documentary evidence of intent is seldom reliable.[142] Inevitably, both parties can find snippets that support their positions. Companies that enter into large transactions often have many employees, and an individual's intent – even if accurately captured in an email or memo – seldom represents that of the "company." Indeed, as a legal fiction that represents the input of potentially myriad actors, a firm may not be susceptible to having intent akin to that of a person. The real question is whether the person or people driving the deal – or the knowledgeable businesspeople providing inputs into financial modeling and the like – expect the transaction to have certain effects based on their experience and reduce those expectations to writing. At that point, at least, one asks the right question.

Economists and businesspeople employ terminologies that overlap in words, however, but seldom in meaning. What a salesperson thinks of as "the market" may radically differ from what emerges from the SSNIP test's application. Bankers, especially on the sell side, have a notorious disposition toward hyperbole. Their grandiose claims about the business's value may range from the absence of meaningful competition to the prevalence of entry barriers. They cause no lack of angst for counsel, who frequently instruct their clients at the early stages of a deal to think carefully about how they characterize the business and the competitive space in which it operates. Many businesspeople succumb to imprecision in their day-to-day emails. Anyone who has spent time in transactional work can attest to the occasional executive's and banker's propensity for poor word choice in framing a deal.

What emerges is a case not for ignoring "hot" documents, but for contextualizing them and treating them with the level of skepticism that they deserve. Under that standard, if truly convincing evidence of anticompetitive intent emerges from the record, then it ought to weigh on the government's decision whether to intervene. The agencies have not been shy about doing so.[143] But it would be a mistake, as the Utah Statement proposes, to presume harm to competition from evidence of intent alone. There is no substitute for rigorous economic analysis meant to predict competitive effects. Simplifications born of documentary admissions provide only the illusion of accuracy. Done properly, antitrust policy requires agencies and courts alike to ask the hard questions and grapple with the complexities that result.

---

[142] *Accord* Geoffrey A. Manne & Marc Williamson, *Hot Docs vs. Cold Economics*, 47 ARIZ. L. REV. 609 (2005).

[143] *See, e.g.*, United States v. Bazaarvoice, Inc., No. 13-CV-0133, Compl., Dkt. 1 (N.D. Cal. Jan. 10, 2013) (challenging an unreported, consummated deal in the face of unusually bad documents that characterized the goal of the acquisition, among other things, as being to "[e]liminat[e] [Bazaarvoice's] primary competitor" and "provide 'relief from price erosion.'").

6.1.2.12 "Mergers Should Be Subject to Both Prospective and Retrospective Analysis and Enforcement Practice"

Prospective merger review is the norm – the HSR Act requires it for signed transactions that surpass certain thresholds. The FTC is studying whether to expand notification requirements for acquisitions by technology and platform companies with large market capitalizations.[144] Otherwise, disputes concerning prospective merger review focus on whether the agencies ought to employ tougher standards on the merits. That question is the object of sustained discussion elsewhere in this book.

The real weight of this neo-Brandeisian proposal falls on retrospective analysis. Ex post merger review is undeniably important, and in many respects uncontroversial.

Nonreportable transactions can still harm competition. Hence, the agencies investigate and, if necessary, challenge mergers that closed without advance review.[145] On occasion, the government announces concerns after the HSR waiting period has expired, but before closing. In those circumstances, there is no statutory bar to closing, but the parties assume the risk of a subsequent lawsuit and divestiture if they do so.[146] A more controversial – and globally unusual – feature is that the DOJ and FTC may revisit transactions that they have previously blessed. This may occur because the parties had omitted problematic item 4(c)/(d) materials from their HSR, and later made a corrective filing.[147] Customer complaints may lead the agencies to identify issues that had previously eluded them.[148] Or, as a recent case illustrates, a private party may disagree with the government's antitrust review and bring its own action.[149]

That set of outcomes is not exhaustive. In outlier situations, the passage of time, a change of enforcement ideology, and market developments may combine to induce the DOJ or FTC simply to change its mind.

Progressive reformists have honed in on the last category, which likely motivated the Utah Statement. A troubling quirk of antitrust implies that no consummated acquisition can ever be definitively clear of antitrust risk. Every merger closes with

---

[144] Fed. Trade Comm'n, Press Release, *FTC to Examine Past Acquisitions by Large Technology Companies*, Feb. 11, 2020, https://www.ftc.gov/news-events/press-releases/2020/02/ftc-examine-past-acquisitions-large-technology-companies.

[145] *See, e.g., In re* Otto Bock HealthCare N. Am., Inc., Dkt. No. 9378, Opinion of the Commission (F.T.C. Nov. 6, 2019); United States v. Bazaarvoice, Inc., Case No. 13-cv-133, 2014 WL 203966 (N.D. Cal. Jan. 8, 2014); *In re* Evanston Nw. Healthcare Corp., FTC Dkt. No. 9315, Opinion of the Commission (F.T.C. Aug. 6, 2007). The government does not always succeed in bringing such cases. *See, e.g.,* Fed. Trade Comm'n v. Lundbeck, Inc., 650 F.3d 1236 (8th Cir. 2011).

[146] *See, e.g., In re* Chicago Bridge & Iron Co. v. Fed. Trade Comm'n, 534 F.3d 410 (5th Cir. 2008).

[147] *See, e.g., In re* Automatic Data Processing, Inc., FTC Dkt. No. 9282, Compl. (Nov. 13, 1996); United States v. Automatic Data Processing Inc., No. 1:96-CV-606 (D.D.C. Mar. 27, 1996); *In re* Tops Markets (2010); *In re* Airgas (2001).

[148] *See, e.g.,* United States v. Parker Hannifin Corp., No. 1:17-cv-1354, Compl. (D. Del. Sept. 26, 2017);

[149] *See* Steves & Sons, Inc. v. Jeld-Wen, Inc., 292 F. Supp. 3d 656 (E.D. Va. 2018) (appeal pending at the Fourth Circuit).

an asterisk next to its status under Section 7 of the Clayton Act. To be clear, the risk is vanishingly small for all but the most significant transactions. Significance can be measured, however, either at closing or at any time in the future. The latter possibility introduces a risk, albeit one that rarely materializes.

This idiosyncrasy traces to a 1957 Supreme Court decision, *E.I. du Pont*.[150] Under that standard, the government may sue to unwind an acquisition that was innocuous at closing if the transaction risks harm to competition at the time of suit.[151] That standard holds even if the acquisition preceded the lawsuit by several decades.[152] Indeed, on a plausible reading of the decision, lack of foreseeability has no legal significance. This feature of merger law should concern anyone who opposes retroactive liability, including in the form of ex post facto prohibitions.

Consummated merger review remains important. When new facts reveal a loss of unique competitive constraint, antitrust enforcers should act. Intervention is easiest to justify for unreported or incompletely notified deals. There are good reasons, however, to permit the agencies to revisit previously approved transactions. Error is inevitable, and consumers pay the price. The rigor of review employed is, of course, significant. Decisions to close in the initial waiting period may arise under imperfect information. By contrast, the agencies should not casually revisit decisions made after an exhaustive investigation pursuant to a Second Request. In all cases, however, should the post-merger firm exercise newfound market power after closing, then it may imply that the DOJ or FTC got it wrong.

How to reconcile this policy with the problematic implications of *E.I. du Pont*? The answer is that the universe of previously cleared mergers subject to retrospective merger challenges should be limited to horizontal transactions that foreseeably endangered competition *at the time of closing*. In some deals, it will be clear to all involved that the merger will eliminate some measure of competition. Whether the agencies permit the merger on the front end reflects a prediction – one founded on an assessment whether the parties are sufficiently close competitors within the context of the relevant market's dynamics and any substantiated efficiencies that a sustainable exercise of market power will result. If the government gets it wrong, then a subsequent challenge founded on demonstrable anticompetitive, post-closing effects is justified. It is an altogether different proposition if – years later – the agencies revisit a previously approved transaction that, at closing, had no foreseeable effect on competition. Should market dynamics evolve to create a market structure not to the government's taste, then the solution does not lie in some form of backward tracing to undo past transactions that had no obvious competitive issues at the time of closing.

---

[150] United States v. E.I. du Pont de Nemours & Co., 353 U.S. 586, 607 (1957) (acquisition of 23 percent of General Motor stock between 1917 and 1919 violated Section 7 because at time of suit, almost forty years later, it was likely to create a monopoly).
[151] *Id.*
[152] *Id.*

Fortunately, the agencies have made little use of *E.I. du Pont*, which might allow them to undo all sorts of antique transactions that trace, however circuitously, to likely competitive issues today. Moving against good-faith acquisitions that were both innocuous and devoid of foreseeable risk to competition at the time of closing would undermine the rule of law and disrupt business expectations. To the extent that neo-Brandeisian reformists envision widespread after-the-fact reexamination of previously vetted mergers, that would be troubling.

On a final – but important – point, nothing in this section pours cold water on the value of retrospective merger studies, which are indispensable to understanding the efficacy and calibration of the agencies' review standards. The agencies should systematically study past transactions more often than they do, focusing on ones that they cleared in marginal cases. That is where the most useful insights reside, informing the agencies' toolkit going forward.

6.1.2.13 "The Determination by the Antitrust Agencies of Relevant Market Definitions Should Receive Judicial Deference"

The agencies house superior expertise in antitrust law and economics than the courts that oversee them. Federal courts sometimes get it wrong, and reject meritorious cases.[153] Those yearning for a more robust and interventionist competition policy often see courts as part of the problem. In such critics' view, though the agencies are disinclined to bring enough cases, the courts whittle down the universe of successful challenges further. In the process, they might deter the DOJ and FTC from bringing marginal cases, and instill a sense of unwelcome risk aversion within the agencies' halls. The courts already recognize the agencies' horizontal merger guidelines as persuasive in overseeing merger cases. Why not go a step further, and formally defer to relevant market definitions advanced by the government?

That would be a mistake. A cherished US tradition, robust due-process protections are worth preserving. The reviewing agency operates as investigator and prosecutor. Formally deferring to its conclusions introduces an adjudicative dimension to its process. That is a classic violation of fundamental procedural safeguards. The fact that the institutional design of most competition law regimes outside of the United States flouts those bulwarks is no reason to follow suit.

The goal is not merely to preserve judicial review. It requires that a neutral decision-maker apply the law after determining facts in a contested proceeding in which the government bears the burden of proof.[154] To be sure, these protections

---

[153] For two recent examples in which federal district judges fundamentally misconstrued the economics of market definition, for example, see FTC v. Penn State Hershey Med. Ctr., 185 F. Supp. 3d 552 (M. D. Pa. 2016), *rev'd*, 838 F.3d 327 (3d Cir. 2016) and FTC v. Advocate Health Care Network, 162 F. Supp. 3d 666 (2016), *rev'd*, 841 F.3d 460 (7th Cir. 2016). In each case, the appellate court served its function and corrected the lower court's error.

[154] The U.S. antitrust system does not always realize this ideal. The FTC's administrative litigation mechanism, known as "Part III," blurs the line between prosecutorial and adjudicative functions by

make life difficult for the DOJ and FTC, and allow some mergers to close unimpeded that the agencies wanted to block. Recent examples include *AT&T/Time Warner*, *Evonik/PeroxyChem*, and *Steris*.[155] The case for preserving these safeguards is not one of abstract principle. They guard against real dangers.

The DOJ and FTC have remarkably talented staff. No matter how exceptional their lawyers and economists, however, they remain vulnerable to the full swathe of human foibles. Impressions form early in an investigation, and can harden. Bayesian inference requires dispassionate objectivity that can be hard to maintain in the throes of a heated and time-sensitive investigation. Confirmation bias may lead staff attorneys to filter out or discount evidence in tension with their initial view of the relevant market, repositioning, likely entry, and the like. Enthusiasm can overwhelm reason. The agencies employ numerous internal processes to counter such phenomena, ensuring separate tiers of review and vigorous debate. Suitably introspective case teams guard against the dangers, but the risk underlies all of the agencies' investigative efforts because it reflects human nature.

A diminished burden would introduce unwelcome incentives. Over time, an enforcer relieved of its obligation rigorously to prove harm to competition would build its cases differently. Such an agency would naturally gravitate toward standards that make its work easier – not harder. Consider the proposal at hand, namely that Congress require the courts to defer to the agencies' market definitions. Confident in its diagnosis of how a merger will affect competition, an agency may be tempted to bolster its case by adopting a unnecessarily narrow market.

Proving unilateral effects within a differentiated product market, for example, may be difficult because it requires showing that the parties are positioned closely to one another relative to other suppliers. Defining a market limited to product traits unique to the merging parties, by contrast, would allow the DOJ or FTC to sidestep the effects question by effectively "proving" its case through market definition alone. As explained in Chapter 9, that is already a problem.

---

instilling within the same Commission the authority to approve the filing of a complaint and later to decide whether a violation occurred. For the authoritative study on the FTC's Part III process, see Maureen K. Ohlhausen, *Administrative Litigation at the FTC: Effective Tool for Developing the Law or Rubber Stamp?*, 12 J. COMPETITION L. & ECON. 623 (2016). One possible solution to the Part III issue would be to make the director of the Bureau of Competition responsible for authorizing the filing of an administrative complaint, preserving the independence of the Commission and making that body accessible to the respondents to file a motion to dismiss, for example, that would be more likely to receive neutral scrutiny.

[155] United States v. AT&T, Inc., 916 F.3d 1029 (D.C. Cir. 2019); Fed. Trade Comm'n v. Rag-Stiftung, 436 F. Supp. 3d 278 (D.D.C. 2020); Fed. Trade Comm'n v. Steris Corp., 133 F. Supp. 3d 962 (N.D. Ohio 2015). As another example, the DOJ lost its effort to enjoin Sabre's acquisition of Farelogix, though the deal ultimately fell through after the CMA prohibited it. United States v. Sabre Corp., – F. Supp. 3d –, 2020 WL 1855433 (D. Del. 2020), *vacated*, Trade Reg. Rep. ¶ 81,294 (3d Cir. July 20, 2020) (but clarifying that "this Order should not be construed as detracting from the persuasive force of the District Court's decision").

This is no abstract concern. Subject to deferential judicial review, the European Commission long made liberal use of "by object" restrictions in order to prove violations by assertion rather than by proof. Such unrestrained enforcement undoubtedly facilitates "stricter" policy – and attracts praise from neo-Brandeisians for that reason – but it comes at the cost of accuracy and due process.[156]

---

[156] Thankfully, the European courts have started reigning in some of these excesses. *See, e.g.*, C-67/13 P, Groupement de cartes bancaires v. Comm'n, 2014 E.C.R. 2204, [2014] 5 C.M.L.R. 22.

PART III

Antitrust Reform

7

Taking a Finger Off the Scale

Revisiting Decision Theory

How should antitrust change? The answer lies in how we decide hard cases.

For decades, an odd proposition has held sway. That is, we are better off permitting anticompetitive conduct than to prohibit efficient or neutral behavior. One might find that principle doubly strange – perplexing in that we should allow neither and irregular because ties should cut in favor of competition. In fact, agencies and courts often decide antitrust matters within a penumbra of uncertainty. Incorrect decisions are thus guaranteed, and especially so in investigations that yield close calls. But why tolerate, or even endorse in relativistic terms, harm to competition?

The answer lies in a clever article written by then-Professor Frank Easterbrook in 1984.[1] He argued that mistakes are not created equal. If anticompetitive conduct escapes review or finds welcome in a miscalibrated rule, then harms will ensue. Such effects, however, wear away. Supranormal rents spur entry and expansion, eroding inflated margins and restoring competitive equilibrium. That outcome, imperfect as it may be, contrasts favorably with mistaken prohibitions. If we ban efficient conduct, then its benefits are lost forever. Doctrine is immune to market pressures. This asymmetry informs the intervention calculus. Much as we increase the burden of proof in criminal cases, knowing that we will set more guilty people free, so antitrust enforcers should refrain from intervening in unclear cases. This approach displays humility, limiting the agencies and courts to prohibitions in which they can be confident, while refraining from possible misadventure. And it bears a quasi-scientific quality – because we can weight Type I and Type II errors differently, the social optimum does not minimize the raw numbers of mistakes. It minimizes the weighted sum of such errors.

That logic has long resonated with the antitrust community and especially with those on the right. It also arrived on scene when the costs of wayward competition policy were still painfully apparent. The Warren Court's antitrust jurisprudence and the agencies' enforcement policies of the 1960s and 1970s had been a masterclass in the dangers of undisciplined and far-reaching intervention. Consistent with

---

[1] Frank H. Easterbrook, *The Limits of Antitrust*, 63 TEX. L. REV. 1 (1984).

Chicago School views on decision theory, fear of false condemnation has influenced the Supreme Court time and again. On occasion, it had led the Court to marginalize antitrust exposure in a regrettable way.

Although the DOJ and FTC seldom address uncertainty in their merger reviews head-on, an aversion to Type I errors has influenced their thinking. The phenomenon is apparent under some Republican administrations, which have occasionally cleared major consolidations in surprising circumstances. It is most obvious, however, in how some conservative thinkers at the agencies and elsewhere approach Section 2 cases. Indeed, Easterbrook's views found their most extreme manifestation in the Justice Department's 2008 report on monopolization standards.[2] There, the government parted company with the FTC (an independent agency) and embraced an intervention calculus so skewed toward inaction as effectively to abandon public scrutiny of unilateral conduct.

We have already burrowed into a wealth of information about market self-correction, merger efficiencies, the illuminative value of structuralism, and more. Merger retrospectives, observed firm profits, prevailing industry-level data, and historical experience with prior approaches complete the picture. This effort yields helpful insights, even if few hard truths of universal conclusions emerge. One inference, however, plainly follows – the views emanating from both extremes of opinion are wrong.

First, a structural revolution would strip antitrust of precision, discarding reliable analysis for unfounded rules and presumptions. The theoretical premise behind structuralism is absent. There is no general causal relationship between changes in concentration ratios and harm to competition. Claims of a systematic loss of competition across the US economy do not follow from the data. Anti-monopolists insist that dominance endures without governmental intervention. But that assertion, no matter how emphatic, is hard to square with reality.

Beyond lacking supporting evidence, structuralists advance policies sure to harm consumers and the larger economy. The agencies' experience of the 1970s was a debacle not to be revisited. A modern incarnation would fare little better. Breaking up technology firms with large capitalizations would accomplish little in enhancing static competition, but would destroy integration-related productivities and dilute incentives to invest in innovation at scale. That is especially so if effected through a no-fault monopolization of the kind championed by some reformists. Similarly, prohibiting most horizontal and vertical mergers would deprive consumers of plausible benefits. Empirical claims that M&A activity lacks social value cherry-pick some studies at the expense of others. In fact, productivities are most likely to arise in the kind of transactions that currently hover at the edge of permissibility today. In short, neo-Brandeisians and other proponents of radical change to antitrust policy have not made their case.

---

[2] U.S. Dep't of Justice, Competition and Monopoly: Single-Firm Conduct Under Section 2 of the Sherman Act (2008), *withdrawn* (2009).

Second, free-marketeers who criticize today's enforcement standards for being too strict do so against the tide. The evidence does not imply excessive public antitrust intervention today. Many industries are consolidating (albeit more modestly than reformists claim), firm profits remain high, the modern law and economics is permissive by historical standards, the courts impose real hurdles in the way of government enforcement, and the digital economy's rising importance magnifies accelerative trends in leader scale beyond what one encounters in traditional bricks and mortar industries. And, to cap it off, a wide range of studies find negative price effects from mergers allowed to clear at the margin. The sensible response is to increase scrutiny at the margin.

Heightened enforcement in close cases is thus on the agenda. But how to effect such change? Generalities offer little help because they flounder in the presence of matter-specific complexities. Anecdotal observations that an agency overestimated supply-side responses in clearing a borderline investigation are helpful, for example, but only prove so much. What may have been a miscalculation in one market may be right on the money elsewhere. And any one retrospective may or may be right. Counterfactual modeling to gauge effects is sensitive to available data and assumptions, so it would be a mistake to view any transaction flagged in a study as associated with price increases as necessarily having been anticompetitive. This makes drawing broader inferences from specific case studies a precarious exercise.

In short, antitrust has properly evolved into a precision instrument that predicts effects based on evidence flowing from in-depth investigations. That feature is its strength. But it makes lofty abstractions of little value to the responsible enforcers struggling with whether to clear a transaction, require conditions, or sue to block it.

Error stands out as a towering exception. The agencies already strive for precision. They investigate matters exhaustively and employ precision tools in pursuit of their mission. As the next two chapters explore, they could profitably recalibrate certain of their methodologies, including market definition. Federalism, the Supreme Court, and Congress limit the DOJ and FTC's ability meaningful to expand the scope of the US economy subject to their scrutiny. The real question for the agencies, however, is how they deal with vexing questions of the kind associated with our hypothetical enforcers referenced in the preceding paragraph. When the facts weigh, however slightly, in favor of permitting unconditional clearance, then they should do so. When they point toward divestitures, behavioral remedies, or an outright blockage effort, then that is the direction in which the agency should go. But what if it is a wash? What if real substantiated evidence of harm to competition meets indicia of likely market correction, and the government simply does not know which is right? This is where meaningful reform will happen. It will not yield the revolutionary, iconoclastic changes desired by some, but it will be meaningful and keep antitrust within its proper effects-based framework.

The agencies should revisit their toleration for false negatives over false positives. The contemporary default in favor of inaction in uncertain cases turns the thrust of antitrust policy on its head. It denigrates the very harms that Congress passed the antitrust laws to address. Its counterdirectional thrust is an unforced error. In fact, Type II errors are more serious than commonly supposed. Type I errors remain serious, but the conservative prescription goes too far. Doctrinal errors do erode, based in no part on the federal antitrust agencies' dedication to advancing the state of industrial economics and moving enforcement in ever-more-enlightened direction. What this amounts to should be neither shocking nor controversial. It is simply a call to focus on getting it right, and not to put the thumb on the scale in favor of laissez faire.

Going forward, enforcers should not skew error analysis by weighting Type I errors more heavily than Type II mistakes. Instead, they should minimize the raw number of errors of all kinds. This proposal sounds technical, but it would have real significance and could be realized almost overnight. This chapter begins by explaining the role of error in antitrust law

7.1 THE GENESIS (AND INEVITABILITY) OF ERROR

Antitrust can be an uncertain business. Prospective merger review, by definition, predicts the future. Even retrospectives must compare observed outcomes with the but-for world. Monopolization litigation implies that the market would have been more competitive without the impugned conduct. Rule-of-reason cases allege that the contracting parties could have achieved the same outcome in a less restrictive manner. Counterfactuals define the antitrust violation, but they are almost never observable.

Every agency move – be it action or inaction – obscures what might otherwise have been. It is the antitrust analogue to Heisenberg's uncertainty principle. Challenge a dominant-firm practice, and you risk depriving the world of a competitive response that may not only have cured the problem, but made consumers better off. Stand back, and the monopolist may endure without challenge. Block a merger and the buyer may pursue a second best course that provides greater efficiencies and competition over time. Or perhaps the transaction would have given the buyer a unique launching pad with which to invest in and develop industry-leading innovations. An erroneous prohibition decision would extinguish those benefits, leaving all but the post-merger firm's competitors worse off. Even after the fact, it is hard to tell whether some merger or conduct review decisions were right. Beforehand, it is more vexing still.

Lest there be any misimpression, competition law is infrequently a walk into the unknown. The agencies make thousands of decisions each year. Few are close calls or unreliable. We have a robust understanding of how market events and industry conditions fuse to create effects. Hence, the agencies confidently approve transactions that pose little threat, and similarly allow the myriad restraints of trade imbedded in contracts throughout the economy proceed without hindrance.

Of course, enforcers do not always get it right. They might approve a merger without full appreciation of the facts. And they bring unmeritorious cases from time to time. But whether they close or sue after an in-depth investigation, the decision reflects an exhaustive fact- and data-gathering exercise, considered debate, numerous layers of independent review, and stakeholder input, including advocacy from the parties. Industrial economics has come far, illuminating the causal determinants of competitive effects and helping enforcers to understand the market impact of various transactions, restraints, and practices. Advanced econometrics allow the agencies to make better informed decisions than ever before.

Given these impressive advances, why all the talk of error? The answer is twofold, going to mission and margin.

First, much depends on antitrust's mandate. If it were an exercise in optimization, intervening in order to maximize social welfare, then it would be unworkable. Take vertical restraints. They generally benefit consumers by aligning incentives within the supply chain. Tradeoffs exist, however, between investment-related benefits to be achieved in interbrand competition and softened price competition in the intrabrand channel. Generally good, sometimes bad, vertical restraints are susceptible to general conclusions at a policy level and determinations as to net harm or benefit in a given case. But we cannot define the optimal restraint. No one can compute which specific minimum resell price, for example, is exactly right in a particular instance.

So, too, the law generally allows dominant firms to decide whether to deal with their rivals. A standard might, in theory, require such a firm to license its competitors on terms that make society best off – terms that might sometimes involve dealing at a certain (infinitely variable) price or not at all. Again, economics identifies tradeoffs. Mandatory dealing may enrich static competition at the possible expense of incentives to invest. How that calculus works out with respect to a specific firm and refusal, however, is difficult to say. Identifying the optimal access price, which may range from zero to infinite, is likely impossible. Neither the adjudicators nor objects of the law could answer the question.

One can extend that analysis to antitrust's full remit. Directional evaluations are workable. Precise delineations of optimality are not. We have no a priori basis with which to identify each market's most efficient structure. Indeed, we cannot even discern universal associations between deltas in concentration and market power.[3] Antitrust thus preserves existing competitive pressures. It does not try to maximize competition. This is a matter of feasibility. Venturing beyond the evaluative capabilities of antitrust law and economics means indeterminism. So antitrust policymakers work within the art of the possible. This is another way of saying that error sets the parameters of competition policy. Extending the antitrust frontier would make intervention decisions ill-informed and, ultimately, arbitrary. Absent compelling evidence that protecting competition is not enough (e.g., natural monopoly),

---

[3] *See* Chapter 3.

then it seems unthinkable to go further. It is only when we give up on markets that we accept price and access regulation, an optimization effort that never works perfectly and seldom works at all.

Second, even within today's preservation-of-competition framework, error looms large. That is not to deny the bountiful insights made possible by modern economics. It simply observes that marginal, but unavoidable, decisions often encounter unknowns. Time-dimensional questions are a classic example. Resolving many antitrust questions requires at least implicitly weighing short- and long-term effects that may point in opposing directions. Quantification is infeasible, and hence so is an informed utilitarian social welfare calculus. Sometimes the future is so uncertain and the magnitude of the long-run effect sufficiently attenuated that we can discount it and make a well-informed intervention decision focused on static effects. But that is not always the case. When predictable benefits and indeterminate costs (or vice versa) offset one another in magnitude, a dilemma results. Monopolization cases that focus on unilateral practices alone most often encounter that problem.

More generally, even exhaustive investigations leave questions lingering about the market's likely evolution. Hard cases invite questions of judgment. This is not the typical case, but nor is it rare. Every year brings intervention decisions that rouse debate and disagreement within the responsible agency. Indeed, the FTC and DOJ have themselves taken diametrically opposed positions to the same problem or case. For example, the DOJ intervened in opposition to the FTC's monopolization case against Qualcomm in 2019, while the FTC refused to sign onto the DOJ's report on Section 2 standards in 2009.[4] Such incidences arise despite both agencies' deep expertise and experience, revealing the limits of knowledge and the role of priors and intuition in navigating uncertain waters.

In short, error will remain a critical feature of competition policy, no matter how dedicated it is to empiricism and economics or how disciplined it may be in bounding the scope of its inquiry. Choosing one course obscures the path not taken. Uncertainty and tradeoffs are thus staples of the antitrust diet. What to do in the presence of uncertainty? Facing the unknown, throwing one's hands into the air may appeal. Yet, for competition policy, inaction bring consequences just as surely as does intervening. There is no escaping hard choices, and there are real costs to getting them wrong.

Navigating the unknown is the domain of decision theory. The core insight is that errors differ not by probability (by definition, under uncertainty probabilities are unknown), but potentially by severity. Wrongly prohibiting a restraint, practice, or merger snuffs out gains in the matter at hand. The ensuing precedent, however, does far worse. It universalizes the harm across all such future cases. Firms staring at an inhibitory rule cannot proceed, no matter how efficient the desired path. By

---

[4] See Kadhim Shubber, *US Regulators Face Off in Court Tussle over Qualcomm*, Fin'l Times, Feb. 9, 2020; Press Release, FTC Commissioners React to Department of Justice Report, Competition and Monopoly: Single-Firm Conduct Under Section 2 of the Sherman Act, Sept. 8, 2008.

contrast, should anticompetitive phenomena unfold without challenge, then prices will rise. The ensuing welfare loss is unwelcome, of course, but it is also transient. Ferreting out opportunities for superior margins, firms gravitate toward supranormal rents. As entry causes excess returns to dissipate, the market will see competitive equilibrium restored. The period of transition represents a true harm. But being isolated and ephemeral, it inflicts costs that appear modest relative to wrongful prohibition. As noted, this reasoning has led antitrust law to attach greater weight to false condemnation than wrongful endorsement. Type I errors dominate Type II errors.

That view brings extraordinary implications for competition policy. It represents a conscious decision to restrict antitrust's scope – to put one's thumb on the scale in favor of standing idly by. This is not a focused directive. It is a commitment to underenforcement that extends across antitrust, not to idiosyncratic circumstances seldom encountered. Yes, error may be of scant concern in the majority of issues investigated by the federal antitrust authorities. In fiscal year 2018, for example, they cleared 97.8 percent of the 2,111 notified transactions without a Second Request.[5] They were informed determinations, and virtually all were surely correct. But the long tail is not where antitrust policy matters. It is the margin that counts, and for the past thirty years or more we have approached those important questions with an openness to inaction.

It is important to acknowledge what the traditional antitrust position on error means. It suggests nonintervention where the weight of evidence implies harm to competition. Conservative administrations have at times wholeheartedly embraced fear of Type I errors. The fact that they have sought to formalize a predilection for Type II errors into policy suggests that this philosophy has real-world implications for how the agencies (and courts) make vital decisions, especially in close cases.

Evidence of rising industry-level concentration and stubbornly high firm profits over time coincide not just with the shift from structuralism to effects in 1981 – an evolution that ought to be celebrated for moving antitrust into the precision era – but with a widespread view in the enforcement community that Type I errors are more serve than Type II mistakes. Whether the conventional view on antitrust error is correct stands among the most urgent questions of reform. In fact, as explained below, the traditional conservative position on embracing more false negative over false negatives is wrong. Properly understood, decision theory supports greater intervention at the margin than proponents of error analysis have typically conceded.

To be sure, the federal antitrust authorities intervene sparingly. The DOJ and FTC issued forty-five second requests in 2018 in order to conduct an in-depth review. Thirty-nine of those investigations resulted in merger-enforcement challenges, which the agencies resolved via consent decree or by outright litigation.

---

[5] Fed. Trade Comm'n & U.S. Dep't of Justice, Hart-Scott-Rodino Annual Report: Fiscal Year 2018.

7.2 ERROR COSTS LEAD THE COURTS AND AGENCIES TO NARROW ANTITRUST'S REACH

Fear of overenforcement has left an indelible mark. The Supreme Court, in particular, has fixated on antitrust's propensity for error. The result has been a narrowing of scope, not only as to the elements that define a claim, but of the Sherman Act's application, too. Along the way, the Court has couched its analysis expressly in terms of error costs.

"The cost of false positives counsels against an undue expansion of § 2 liability."[6] While embracing that view, the Court has been less contemplative about false negatives. Indeed, on occasion, it has denigrated the "benefits of antitrust intervention" as "slight[.]"[7] This asymmetric balancing reflects a conservative bent regarding competition policy. Many thinkers on the pro-business side tend to associate antitrust with nuisance litigation (of which there is, to be sure, no lack). In fixating on the costs of a vigorous competition program, however, such commentators underestimate offsetting value. Analysis more attuned to the tradeoffs would still accommodate safeguards against overenforcement – *Twombly* on minimum pleading requirements is a good example[8] – but would reject efforts to eject antitrust outright or impose hurdles likely to frustrate effective enforcement. At times, the Court has shown itself attuned to the appropriate tradeoffs, albeit with dissents from the more conservative Justices.[9] More often, however, fear of getting it wrong has led antitrust to recede. That phenomenon warrants attention at this time of possible reform.

Credit Suisse, for example, found that federal securities law implicitly preempted antitrust scrutiny of joint underwriting activity pursuant to an IPO.[10] Remarkably, it did so notwithstanding a Congressional savings clause. Error concerns drove the Court's reasoning. It observed that "antitrust courts are likely to make unusually serious mistakes" in evaluating securities marketing activity. Acknowledging that this "kind of problem exists to some degree in respect of other antitrust lawsuits[,]" the Court worried that joint marketing of IPOs makes "mistakes unusually likely" for those tasked with resolving Sherman Act claims.[11]

The majority doubted antitrust's value and administrability. That is regrettable. Competition is chaos. It spurs duplicative investment, bankruptcies, and at times concentration. It punishes the unfortunate as severely as the incompetent. Yet it is a source of immeasurable value. Efforts to oversee that turbulent process, of course, may succumb to misjudgment. Modelling dynamic competition in all its rich complexity poses intractable difficulties. But antitrust is a vital policy tool for

---

[6] Verizon Comm'cns Inc. v. Law Offices of Curtis V. Trinko, LLP, 540 U.S. 398, 414 (2004).
[7] *Id.*
[8] Bell Atl. Corp. v. Twombly, 550 U.S. 544 (2007).
[9] *See* N. Carolina State Bd. Dental Exam'rs v. Fed. Trade Comm'n, 574 U.S. 494 (2015); Fed. Trade Comm'n v. Phoebe Putney Health Sys., 568 U.S. 216 (2013).
[10] Credit Suisse Sec. (USA) LLC v. Billing, 551 U.S. 264 (2007).
[11] *Id.* at 282.

preserving the competitive process. Impediments to its clean application ought not to inhibit its robust enforcement. *Credit Suisse* missed that point, thinking that "an antitrust action in this context is accompanied by a substantial risk of injury to the securities markets[.]"[12] That decision saw an ousting of the federal antitrust laws, against the wishes of the DOJ's Antitrust Division.

To be clear, the Court has not always been wrong to consider false positives in cabining liability. The law on predatory pricing (or bidding) is an apt example. There seems no better way to turn competition policy on its head than to adopt a standard that endangers aggressive pricing. Even after the fact, it is difficult to identify a suitable measure of cost, much less to gauge whether prices fell below it. For the company, it is harder still to predict the outcome of any such future inquiry. The Court was thus exactly right to observe that "cutting prices in order to increase business is the very essence of competition. Thus, mistaken inferences in cases as this one are especially costly because they chill the very conduct the antitrust laws are designed to protect."[13]

Other judicial applications of error analysis, however, have taken us in an unfortunate direction. As the next chapter discusses, today's law shows an unhealthy preoccupation with market definition. One reason is that courts have sought to limit false positives by categorically excluding from liability practices by firms that lack a particular share of the market. Such decisions have embraced Easterbrook's work on decision theory.[14] As addressed below, the cut-offs chosen are, at the best of times, arbitrary. Worse, they create incentives to distort market definition with an eye to triggering certain thresholds.

More generally, the language of error analysis has fueled skepticism about antitrust enforcement. Courts observe, with an eye to false positives, that "overly zealous application of antitrust law can halt procompetitive behavior."[15] Others discount short-term harm to competition because "practices that exclude or harm rivals ... which appear at first glance to be restrictive" may benefit competition.[16] Such observations are not strictly wrong. Rather, they evince a mindset skewed that accepts underenforcement in order to avoid erroneous intervention. Some decisions go further still, belittling antitrust as "an imperfect tool for the regulation of competition."[17]

---

[12] *Id.* at 284.
[13] Matsushita Elec. Indus. Co. v. Zenith Radio Corp., 475 U.S. 574, 594 (1986); *see also* Weyerhaeuser Co. v. Ross-Simmons Hardwood Lumber Co., 549 U.S. 312 (2007).
[14] *See, e.g.*, SCFC ILC, Inc. v. Visa USA, Inc., 36 F.3d 958, 965 n.9 (10th Cir. 1994) (citing Easterbrook, *supra* note 1, at 17); United States v. Microsoft Corp., 253 F.3d 34, 69 (D.C. Cir. 2001) (en banc) (per curiam) (citing Easterbrook, *supra* note 1, at 21–23).
[15] RDK Truck Sales & Serv. Inc. v. Mack Trucks, Inc., Civ. No. 04-4007, 2009 WL 1441578, at *14 (E.D. Pa. May 19, 2009) (citing Easterbrook, *supra* note 1, at 2).
[16] JetAway Aviation, LLC v. Bd. of County Comm'rs of Country of Montrose, Colo., 754 F.3d 824, 853 n.21 (10th Cir. 2014) (Holmes, J., concurring) (citing Easterbrook, *supra* note 1, at 8).
[17] SCFC ILC, Inc. v. Visa USA, Inc., 36 F.3d 958, 962 (10th Cir. 1994) (citing Easterbrook, *supra* note 1, at 39).

The agencies likewise worry about error. In a 2008 report, the DOJ urged the importance of error costs in formulating monopolization standards.[18] In doing so, it rejected the profit-sacrifice test for identifying exclusionary conduct because it "raises serious concerns of enforcement error[.]"[19]

7.3 EASTERBROOK'S MISTAKE

Decision theory has left a firm imprint on antitrust. Given its impact, one might presume it to be well calibrated. It is not.

Modern thinking on antitrust error traces to Easterbrook's work, *The Limits of Antitrust*. Despite its enduring force, his essay hinges on critical assumptions that no longer withstand scrutiny. An impressive piece of scholarship, it is best understood as an indictment of what came before, rather than as an accurate diagnosis of the present and future. The period leading up to 1984 was of a different kind than modern enforcement. The judiciary's and executive's overreach in pursuing structuralist competition policies is now plain for all (or many, perhaps) to see. What remains true is the variety of dangers that await antitrust decision-makers. Information deficits grow more severe as one moves from company to lawyer to judge. Historically, a tendency to condemn what is not understood tells a cautionary tale. And Easterbrook was spot on in encouraging "the lure of the model of atomistic competition and more on the making and testing of predictions."[20]

Easterbrook's key point, however, was that "judicial errors that tolerate baleful practices are self-correcting, while erroneous condemnations are not."[21] Everything follows from that point. It drove his prescriptions for reform. It informs decision theory to this day. On scrutiny, however, the hypothesis dissolves. Not only does it lack substantiation – it is just plain wrong.

Begin with the proposition that Type I errors do not self-correct. Easterbrook spilled much ink speculating why infirm rules might endure, venturing that firms seldom admit to breaking laws and thus rarely devote their efforts to challenging them, and so on. No matter his intuition, he was off-base. There has been no lack of bad law in antitrust, but it has been reversed left and right. The Court rejected the per se rules against minimum and maximum resale price maintenance.[22] It jettisoned the ban on exclusive territorial division within the vertical chain.[23] It did away

---

[18] SINGLE-FIRM CONDUCT, *supra* note 2, at 9.
[19] *Id.* at viii.
[20] Easterbrook, *supra* note 1, at 9.
[21] *Id.*, at 3.
[22] Leegin Creative Leather Prods. v. PSKS, Inc., 551 U.S. 877 (2007) (overruling Dr. Miles Med. Co. v. Park & Sons Co., 220 U.S. 373 (1911)); State Oil Co. v. Khan, 522 U.S. 3 (1997) (overruling Albrecht v. Herald Co., 390 U.S. 145 (1968)).
[23] Cont'l TV, Inc. v. GTE Sylvania, Inc., 433 U.S. 36 (1977) (overruling United States v. Arnold, Schwinn & Co., 388 U.S. 365 (1967)).

with the unsound presumption that patents convey market power.[24] It has softened the illogical per se rule against product tying.[25] It backed away from the rigidities of its earlier structuralism in evaluating mergers.[26] So, too, it rejected the perverse implications of literally construing the rule against price fixing.[27] And even where bad law remains – the Robinson–Patman Act is the prime example – the federal antitrust authorities follow sound economics and deprioritize unjustified enforcement efforts. The agencies have not brought a price-discrimination case in decades. In fact, the FTC's last public intervention in this space was in 2015, when it encouraged the Seventh Circuit to construe the Robinson–Patman Act narrowly.[28]

The history of antitrust jurisprudence speaks to the common-law statute that underlies it. Congress left it to the courts to interpret the law, recognizing that our understanding of how business practices affect competition will continuously grow more refined. To put it bluntly, stare decisis has a weak gravitational pull in antitrust.

True, some bad law endured for a long time. The rule in *Dr. Miles* against vertically imposed minimum resale prices endured from 1911 until 2007. But reacting to the exigencies of the situation it had created, the Court gutted the rule in 1919 in *Colgate*.[29] The reasoning may be tortured – it is illegal to agree with a distributor on a minimum price, but okay to announce the same price in advance and refuse to deal with anyone who refuses to abide by it – but the effect was to facilitate a good workaround. Firms must still endure the same nonsense today with archaic state laws against resale price maintenance, but the same fix applies. Private-ordering solutions can make short work even of ill-guided jurisprudence.

Easterbrook was also too quick to conclude that erroneous antitrust laws impose stifling costs. As he himself was at pains to point out, firms experiment with various strategies, practices, and restraints in order to test consumer preferences and achieve efficiency gains.[30] No doubt, inartful antitrust rules cause problems, and they are to be avoided. But they also open doors. A firm unable to merge might find in-house solutions or partnerships that are not only workable, but potentially better. This is not to cast Type I errors as costless. But the theory of the second best reminds us that ultimate costs are hard to discern. It is thus wrong to presume every act of antitrust overreach to be a perennial source of social harm.

In short, Easterbrook's thesis depends on a critical premise – specifically, that incorrect prohibitory rules endure and impose significant costs. Given the Court's

---

[24] Illinois Tool Works v. Independent Ink, Inc., 547 U.S. 28 (2006) (abrogating Int'l Salt Co. v. United States, 332 U.S. 392 (1947)).
[25] *Cf.* Jefferson Parish v. Hyde, 466 U.S. 2 (1984) *with* Std. Oil Co. of Cali. v. United States, 337 U.S. 293 (1949) (observing that tying "agreements serve hardly any purpose beyond the suppression of competition").
[26] United States v. Gen. Dynamics Corp., 415 U.S. 486 (1974).
[27] Broadcast Music, Inc. v. CBS, Inc., 441 U.S. 1 (1979).
[28] Woodman's Food Market, Inc. v. Clorox Co., No. 15-3001, Brief of Amicus Curiae the Fed. Trade Comm'n in Support of Defendants-Appellants and Reversal (7th Cir. Nov. 2, 2015).
[29] United States v. Colgate & Co., 250 U.S. 300 (1919).
[30] Easterbrook, *supra* note 1, at 5, 8–9.

willingness to revisit flawed antitrust rulings and the role of economics in guiding enforcement, mistakes in antitrust are more fleeting than permanent. So, too, the costs of false positives are not always severe. In some cases, they may be negative. Business can work around some bad precedent. Although one can generally presume preferred business practices to be more efficient, and thus infer harm from overbroad antitrust prohibitions, there is no basis for thinking every Type I error more harmful than a given Type II error.

The thornier question is market self-correction. Well, yes, capital markets and incentives to profit draw firms to supranormal rents. The problem lies in the blanket nature of the argument. Easterbrook presented self-correction as a universal phenomenon. That is more an article of faith than a substantiated fact.

For one thing, exclusionary practices by definition inhibit market self-correction. Indeed, presuming monopoly power to be ephemeral as a basis for nonintervention begs the question. A predicate question in a monopolization case is whether the market will self-correct faster than the government can remediate any harms inflicted. The answer does not lend itself to generalizations. One must discern whether, in the presence of the exclusionary conduct, market forces will still addresses the problem faster than the agencies could do. Even absent foreclosure or exclusion, it is very much an open question how durable market power may be in one industry to the next. Indeed, there is some concern that strategies to build "moats" around various industry leaders' product positions – whether through intellectual property or heavy product differentiation – have increased profits without triggering an effective competing away of profits.

For another, a Type II error that becomes imbedded in law creates a sphere of permissibility. Firms find it profitable to limit competition, and will thus take advantage of gaps in antitrust coverage. Hence, a false negative does not merely create one instance of harm. It creates a recurring series of injuries – ones that may outpace the self-restorative nature of market forces. This is a critical point, and yet one that Easterbrook and countless others who preach the virtues of accepting many Type II errors in order to avoid fewer Type I errors overlook.

More generally, markets vary by difficulty, and in particular *risk*, of entry. The agencies rightly scrutinize the history of entry and expansion in relevant markets when scrutinizing mergers, practices, or restraints. Observations dominate theory. Markets in which the principal competitive asset is people – such as professional services industries – tend to see rapid self-correction. In those settings, Type I errors are apt to be mild. By contrast, infrastructure-heavy network industries that require massive upfront investment may be less quick to remediate. These are mere generalities, though. The devil is in the details, and the entry question must be tailored to the nature of possible competitive harm at issue. Ultimately, blanket assertions of market self-correction are an insecure foundation on which to construct antitrust policy.

In all, Easterbrook oversimplified a complex problem and made unwarranted assumptions. Standing alone, his essay remains a terrific piece of scholarship. But it is good time to revisit the uncritical proposition that antitrust should always err on the side of minimizing false positives.

To return to timing, the world really has changed since Easterbrook wrote in 1984. He observed that "suits against mergers more often than not have attacked combinations that increased efficiency, and the dissolution of mergers has led to higher prices in the product market."[31] That was almost certainly true of enforcement during the 1950s through 1970s. It is not true of the modern era. By the same token, the proposition that "the costs of other enforcement efforts have exceeded the benefits"[32] is well founded vis-à-vis the structuralism of the SCP era, but not the case today.

One point, however, warrants emphasis. Error analysis requires greater sensitivity to case-specific nuances than categorical rules of thumb allow. A common situation of uncertainty revolves around the likely net effects of a unilateral practice by a dominant firm. The fact of exclusion is unremarkable, and standing alone provides no basis for antitrust liability. After all, the most effective means of exclusion is to develop a superior product than one's rivals. The real question is whether the unilateral practice represents a form of competition on the merits, meaning an investment or choice by the monopolist in improving the quality, price, or efficiency of its offerings. Documentary evidence of intent is notoriously unreliable.[33] But if sufficiently pervasive (i.e., not cherry-picked), contextually supported (e.g., the product of informed analysis rather than gratuitous assertion), and not meaningfully contradicted by other contemporaneous evidence, then it can illuminate the picture. Evidence that a monopolist sought to eliminate a rival as an end in itself, rather than as a byproduct of winning over consumers based on superior terms or quality, means something. It should be rightly incumbent on a monopolist in such a situation to explain the efficiency-enhancing basis for its impugned conduct. Famously, Microsoft was unable to articulate *any* justification for certain of its actions directed at Netscape.

Easterbrook argued, however, that one should attach little or no weight to a defendant's inability to proffer a legitimate rationale for its challenged conduct. That is remarkable, and thankfully not the law.[34] In the context of trying to minimize error, it is inexplicable, giving safe harbor to literally indefensible conduct. Such an approach would not minimize the sum of error costs, but maximize the severity and number of false negatives. It seeks to eliminate Type I errors outright by ousting Section 2 enforcement. As explained above, despite the demonstrable failure of some cases, responsible monopolization actions are a key part of effective competition policy.[35]

[31] *Id.*
[32] *Id.*
[33] *See* Geoffrey A. Manne & Marc Williamson, *Hot Docs vs. Cold Economics*, 47 Ariz. L. Rev. 609 (2005).
[34] United States v. Microsoft Corp., 253 F.3d 34, 66-67 (D.C. Cir. 2001) (per curiam) (en banc).
[35] *See* Chapter 2, § 2.1.2.2–2.1.2.3.

7.4 A BETTER WAY TO THINK ABOUT ERROR

Antitrust once neglected analysis for binarism. The structuralist era paid little attention to market dynamics. Rather than grapple with complexity, it set hard thresholds that were sure to be miscalibrated in a great many cases. The SCP period saw the agencies embark on far-ranging deconcentration efforts between the 1950s and 1970s. The methodologies employed were crude, inflexible, and arbitrary at the margin.

If we somehow had to operate so rigidly, employing rules in lieu of standards, then error analysis may cut as Easterbrook so elegantly advised. Today's approach, thankfully, is far more refined than the SCP policies of old. The law and economics revolution properly brought focus to bear on competitive effects. In lieu of inartful structural thresholds, the agencies embraced a harder question – how will the restraint, merger, or practice at issue affect the relevant market? The task may be more demanding, but the prize is accuracy. Indeed, the competitive effects revolution sharply reduced the aggregate number of errors. The impact was asymmetric, of course. Type I errors fell by a lot, while Type II errors increased, albeit to a smaller degree.

Now that we have structured analysis to minimize the raw number of mistakes, where does that leave decision theory? First, it displaces binary propositions of the kind that Easterbrook championed. The question is not whether the government should blindly weigh false positives more heavily than false negatives. Rigor and fidelity to the facts at hand characterize analysis today. We should think about error no differently. This means engaging with the potential consequences – upside and down – that may conceivably flow from the investigation at hand. Few errors of any kind are equally severe, let alone across different industries and investigations. Some errors are fleeting; others cause harms that linger tenaciously. One-size-fits-all approaches to uncertainty do not mesh with the competitive effects approach.

If a first-order principle is useful, though, then it is this: equalize false positives and negatives in the first instance. Antitrust policy must abandon its across-the-board preference for inaction over intervention. Under uncertainty and holding everything else constant, failure to prevent harm to competition is as serious as prohibiting innocuous restraints. In other words, decision-makers should not try to minimize the weighted sum of errors by setting a standard or rule of general application. Rather, their default position should be to minimize the raw number of errors.

In danger of stating the obvious, this proposal does not mean that the agencies should ever sued based on guesswork, supposition, or speculation. Responsible antitrust intervention is not the thing of coin tosses. Rather, when the government encounters a gap in knowledge touching on an important component of an otherwise-meritorious case, it should not stop in its tracks. Perfection would stop the DOJ and FTC in their tracks. Exhaustive factual investigation, econometric analysis, theory, industry experience, and judgment go a long way – and often all the way – in building a virtuous case. But uncertainty is no stranger to this process, and ties should not cut in favor of inaction.

If the starting point is to treat Type I and Type II errors as equally serious, then it is by no means the final step. Fact-specific considerations properly come to the fore. Specifically, can we make a more informed decision about the tradeoffs at hand? This effort gleans insights about the severity of possible error costs associated with the relevant decision. This is not a question of assigning probabilities to various outcomes – if that undertaking becomes possible, then we are no longer in the domain of uncertainty. It is a question of assigning magnitudes to various outcomes and thus discerning whether a prohibition or clearance decision bears the greater danger. In answering this question, the agency should be mindful of evidence suggesting that marginal decisions are cutting systematically in one direction.

In short, the error inquiry should be attuned to the matter presented. It is not simply a question of avoiding false positives by erring on the side of nonintervention. Any list will be non-exhaustive, but consider the following possibilities.

7.4.1 The Zero-Efficiency Vertical Acquisition

Even small risks or benefits to competition can tip the balance of a merger review under uncertainty. Consider a standalone asset of value to downstream competition. A retailer vertically integrates upward by acquiring the asset, which was previously owned by an independent firm – that is, one with no downstream presence. The parties claim no efficiencies, but the transaction does not appear *likely* to lead to input or customer foreclosure. It does, however, introduce a risk that did not previously exist of strategic pricing or access behavior. There are foreseeable circumstances in which enhanced downstream profits from foreclosure would dominate the foregone upstream profits. Whether such an event will occur cannot be determined.

On these facts, the Type I error cost is trivial (the acquisition did not create productivities). The Type II error cost, though modest, is larger. Preserving the independence of the competitively important asset may or may not protect downstream competition – we cannot know for sure – but it could do so in a non-outlier scenario. No less importantly, if the basis for decision carries over in recurring fashion to other such acquisitions, then potential harms become certain ones. Here, decision theory favors blocking the transaction. A behavioral remedy would also be justified, but may be disfavored in the absence of efficiencies worth preserving.

7.4.2 Procompetitive Effects That Require Predicting the Future Path of the Industry

Suppose that a transaction eliminates close head-to-head competition between the parties, extinguishing a unique competitive constraint that the seller posed on the buyer. The post-merger entity would have the largest share of the market. The reviewing agency thus predicts significant unilateral effects, providing a static rationale for blocking the merger. Standing alone, this conclusion would justify a prohibition decision.

The parties claim, however, that the market is on course to deliver subpar innovation for consumers. Those results, they argue, would be suboptimal relative to the outcome under the merger. There is no way to predict whether inadequate investment in R&D will occur without the transaction. In other words, dynamic effects require understanding how the market will develop and there is no evidence, in the hypothetical, about the path of that development.

Error analysis warrants blocking the merger. The Type II error cost is significant. The merger is likely to be associated with strong upward pressure on price. If the market is inhospitable to entry or incumbent expansion, it may take considerable time for the government-blessed merger to a dominant position to erode. A Type I error would inflict harm, too, of course, but it may be more transient than the false negative. An initial block decision would reveal information previously unavailable to the relevant agency – the actual innovation profile of the industry under the existing industry structure would come into focus. When those facts crystalize, it would allow the government to make an informed decision about the benefits of any future consolidation.

But change the hypothetical slightly, and the result flips. Suppose that there is a widely recognized need in the industry to solve intractable problems through innovation. In other words, the need for innovative solutions is not hypothetical, but much discussed. The parties show that the merger would allow them to draw on complementary solutions and capabilities in order to create new products and hasten innovation. Whether such benefits are merger-specific, however, is unclear. Nevertheless, clients largely support the merger on account of the superior offerings that they anticipate from the post-merger firm. The question is whether static price effects exceed dynamic efficiencies. On the facts at hand, it is impossible to quantify those offsetting consequences and thus reduce them to a utilitarian calculus. Uncertainty rears its head. If it appears that the transaction could provide a unique accelerant of R&D or quality, however, then error costs weigh in favor of approval. Dynamic efficiencies are larger sources of consumer benefit than price or output effects.

7.4.3 Mergers and Concentration

Long-run average cost curves differ between markets. In general, however, they display U-shaped characteristics. This fact informs how the agencies should approach mergers. In particular, concentration in a well-defined relevant market can provide a useful shorthand for the potential scale economies implicated by a transaction.

As a general matter, a consolidating merger is more likely to realize scale economies at low to moderate concentration levels. For good reason, the agencies typically approve horizontal mergers in such circumstances. Type I error costs (i.e., the consequences of blocking low-concentration transactions) may be high due to the extinction of such efficiencies. Conversely, Type II error costs (i.e., failing to arrest the rare transaction in an unconcentrated market that harms competition) are apt to be low. If unilateral effects result, then they are likely to be short-lived. These factors point toward approval.

By contrast, mergers at extremely high market shares are less likely to realize certain efficiencies. Specifically, the firms may have already exhausted (or nearly exhausted) scale economies.[36]

Of course, there is more to productivity than scale alone. Efficiencies in the distribution channel may reduce merging firms' marginal cost of production, pushing prices downward. Human capital, whether in the form of labor or management or both, can have transformative effects. Intangible assets, information technology infrastructure, superior access to capital, and far more besides can affect efficiency.[37] Even within the same industry, companies often differ tremendously in terms of total factor productivities.[38] It thus follows that, even at high scale levels, horizontal mergers can produce significant efficiency gains. Absolutes concerning the relationship between market shares and efficiencies are thus unreliable, and there is no substitute for a merger-specific analysis of likely productivity gains.

Nevertheless, at high levels of market concentration, the risk calculus shifts. False positives may impose milder costs if few scale economies remain untapped at the buyer's pre-merger state and the transaction otherwise does not promise significant productivities. False negatives may be large because, depending on the market's characteristics, supply-side responses could be slow to erode harmful effects given the paucity of remaining sellers and the scale enjoyed by incumbents. Consistent with those factors, the antitrust laws already block many transactions at high concentration levels. This a function not of structuralism per se or error analysis. Rather, it reflects the fact that mergers between close competitors in heavily consolidated industries tend to see diversion ratios and margins that are likely to create harmful price effects. Decision theory may buttress that conclusion if it appears that the buyer is already close to minimum efficient scale and non-scale-based sources of productivities from the merger are found wanting.

Those insights support contemporary merger review. But they also illuminate today's proposals for change. Realistically, merger reform would expand the net to envelop the moderately concentrated landscape where many horizontal deals today get through. Consistent with the focus on competitive effects, those incremental transactions warrant fact-specific analysis. Such transactions, though, are likely to be

---

[36] The exception would be in markets that have cost characteristics that resemble natural monopoly.
[37] See, e.g., Chad Syverson, *What Determines Productivity?*, 49 J. ECON. LIT. 326, *passim* (2011).
[38] *Id.* at 326-27.

associated with scale economies in many industries. Hence, calls to make horizontal merger review stricter implicate greater Type I error costs than those associated with today's standards. Against this lies evidence that some clearances at the margin have been associated with harmful effects. In other words, observed Type II error costs warrant taking a harder line in close investigations going forward. How those errors net out depends on a granular evaluation of the potential magnitude of benefits and costs that may flow from the merger at hand.

To wrap up, none of this detracts from the need for case-specific inquiries. It is a rule of thumb meant to guide error analysis. Further to that point, scale economies are not the only source of potentially important merger productivities.

7.4.4 Exclusionary Conduct by a Dominant Firm

Error analysis has distinguished merger review and monopolization cases. If we wrongly prohibit a merger, the thinking goes, then the disaffected parties can achieve their efficiencies the old-fashioned way – through organic growth. But wrongly prohibit unilateral conduct, and you cripple the incentive by dominant firms to compete hard on the merits, innovate, and experiment. A takeaway has been that we should take a hard line with consolidating mergers, while treading carefully in dominance cases.

This line of thinking is valid, but incomplete. Type II errors in exclusionary-conduct cases may be unusually severe. The traditional Section 2 narrative errs heavily on the side of nonintervention because monopolization offenses supposedly create transitory effects. By contrast, Section 2 cases are cumbersome and ineffective.

Chapter 2 explored those questions, yielding two insights. First, there is no substitute for effective agency leadership, which ferrets out unmeritorious actions and does not bring (or maintain) public monopolization actions without a discernible and attainable objective. But where the facts point to harmful exclusion, then governmental intervention may be vital. The fact of competitive market cycling is undeniable, but it is contingent on effectively policing restraints and practices that serve principally to exclude competition. The core insight is that Type I errors may see exclusionary conduct expand and become perpetuated. The result will be an erosion of the very market forces on which noninterventionists rely.

Few doubt the complexity of monopolization cases or the difficult questions of judgment that await enforcers considering them. Erroneous condemnation is a real fear. US antitrust law goes a long way to addressing the greatest dangers by not making monopoly power a status offense. Such a rule would compromise the incentives that underlie capitalistic market systems, diluting vital incentives in pursuit of myopic structural gains. Neo-Brandeisian proposals to reject that feature of existing law are ill-advised. Staying within today's framework, though, the agencies should not shy away from bringing cases where they conclude that a dominant firm is excluding competition on a basis that does not enhance efficiency. Some uncertainty will always accompany Section 2 cases, but as Chapter 2 observed, some such matters carry great merit. A traditional and incomplete conception of antitrust error should not stand in the way.

7.4.5 Using Retrospectives to Diminish Error Costs in Merger Review

With superior resources, the agencies could reduce error costs by more often scrutinizing transactions that they previously cleared. This approach would bring two benefits, albeit at a price.

First, more retrospectives of "close call" merger decisions may help the agencies to test the hypotheses that led them to approve transactions, improving the accuracy of their methodologies and assumptions. Second, a greater propensity to allow transactions to close, but monitor their effects, may reduce Type I errors while diminishing associated Type II errors. It would be irresponsible to bring that philosophy to an extreme conclusion, but – wielded with restraint – it may be an effective tool in the event of insufficient evidence to make an informed determination about likely effects. This approach would be particularly valuable for heavily consolidating transactions that are nevertheless plausibly associated with procompetitive disruption or innovation. It would help society to clear some of the most potentially valuable mergers at the frontier of permissibility, while diminishing the risk that harmful consolidations will take root without challenge.

After-the-fact investigations, alas, harm legal certainty. Investors need confidence in order to devote capital to business expansion (and hence greater competition). A fear of second-guessing based on transactions reviewed years before may have deleterious effects on incentives. For that reason, the agencies should wield a "wait and see" selectively.

7.5 CAN WE IMPROVE OUTCOMES WITHOUT SACRIFICING PRECISION?

Investigations often bring the merits into focus. Where they do not, it is because a material fact remains unknown (or is unknowable). Matters lying on the threshold of an enforcement action typically involve highly concentrated relevant markets and evidence of close head-to-head competition. The hallmark of a marginal decision, of course, is offsetting considerations. Typically, an enforcement choice becomes difficult when the parties contrast what they could achieve together relative to a but-for world claimed to be inferior. Predicting the future is famously difficult, and a likely source of error. It is here that predilections about the efficacy of market-self correction through entry, repositioning, and incumbent expansion – as well as the likelihood and significance of merger efficiencies – make the difference. Since the early 1980s, Republican administrations have been more likely to clear mergers in such marginal circumstances, but such clearance decisions have not been within their exclusive province. Mergers allowed through on the cusp of a merger challenge often generate price increases. This fact warrants greater intervention at the margin.

This discussion brings us to some initial principles that the agencies should follow going forward.

First, the Justice Department and Commission must scrutinize claimed efficiencies. A material loss of competition should control the outcome unless the proposed deal will likely yield significant benefits, either by enhancing the buyer's ability to compete going forward or by realizing merger-specific productivity gains that will benefit consumers. Absent convincing evidence to that effect, then there is little or nothing to balance against the elimination of a competitive constraint in the target. A merger challenge properly follows. Conversely, powerful evidence of merger-specific efficiencies would signify the potential for a significant Type I error. As many transactions fail to produce their claimed benefits, the agencies should construe asserted justifications with an appropriate degree of suspicion.

Second, when the agencies encounter claims that a merger will not harm competition because of how the market will likely develop in years ahead, they ought to be similarly hesitant. It is difficult to substantiate predictions about an industry's future development. Absent confidence in a market's future trajectory – whether it be technological progress or evolving consumer demand – the Antitrust Division and the FTC should put their faith in the competitive process. Hence, if a merger demonstrably harms competition today, then the agencies should be loath to approve it based on speculative claims about how that loss of rivalry will generate benefits tomorrow.

Here, decision theory points toward enforcement. The market will eventually undo the mischief of a Type I error that blocks a procompetitive combination – as the future comes into focus, and the benefits of a combination become more compelling, transactions may then become permissible and firms will have incentives, independent of acquisitions, to grow organically. By contrast, a Type II error that allows an anticompetitive merger to close based on mistaken presumptions about the industry's future development harms consumers in ways that may take years for the market to erode. As noted, though, where evidence gives the government confidence about the industry's direction and that the transaction may be a unique accelerant of innovation, then error analysis points in the other direction, even in the presence of uncertainty.

Third, the agencies should not be afraid to bring hard cases in front of skeptical judges, as long as they can develop a robust case that reflects sound economics. The judiciary does not always evolve as quickly as would be ideal in the face of our evolving understanding of how competition works, and some judges simply get it wrong. But, over time, the common-law system has shown itself to be remarkably adapt at developing in directions consistent with the FTC and DOJ's thinking – albeit with a lag. Truthfully, the agencies should probably lose more cases than they presently do. That is especially true given the demanding evidentiary standards that US law (rightfully) imposes on them.

8

Rethinking the Consumer-Welfare Standard

8.1 INTRODUCTION

Reformists have zeroed in on antitrust's consumer-welfare standard.[1] Defenders of the status quo see this as a hallowed norm – the true north that guides enforcers through a maelstrom of conflicting interests to ensure that their efforts serve buyers.[2] It guards against regulatory capture by those who would benefit from diminished competition. It brings unity of purpose to analysis, cleansing it of incommensurate value judgments about whose interests ought to dominate in any one matter.

Some reformists, however, view a single-minded focus on buyers as the root of today's problems.[3] On their account, it obscures economic phenomena that matter to sound antitrust policy. They argue that a laser-focus on consumers blinds enforcers to the harms of zero-price, exponentially scaling platforms, and misdiagnoses accumulations of buyer power as efficiencies rather than phenomena that distort supply markets. Indeed, for those in the anti-monopoly movement, low prices are the enemy. Hence, they champion a normative benchmark more in tune with their vision of atomistic market structures that limit scale economies.

A robust debate has followed. The FTC devoted an afternoon of hearings to whether it should refine, preserve, or reject the consumer-welfare standard.[4] For the Commission's Office of Policy Planning even to float that possibility was itself remarkable. It heard from a spectrum of voices, from those who staunchly defend the status quo to leading progressive voices like those of Timothy Wu, Maurice

---

[1] *See, e.g.,* Marshall Steinbaum & Maurice E. Stucke, *The Effective Competition Standard: A New Standard for Antitrust*, Roosevelt Institute 11, 22, 29–41 (2018), https://rooseveltinstitute.org/wp-content/uploads/2018/09/The-Effective-Competition-Standard-FINAL.pdf.

[2] *See, e.g.,* Herbert Hovenkamp, *Is Antitrust's Consumer Welfare Principle Imperiled?*, 45 J. CORP. L. 101 (2019).

[3] *See, e.g.,* Tim Wu, *The "Protection of the Competitive Process" Standard*, FTC Hearings on Competition and Consumer Protection in the 21st Century, Nov. 1, 2018; Barry Lynn, FTC Hearings on Competition and Consumer Protection in the 21st Century, Tr., Nov. 1, 2018, p. 168.

[4] FTC Hearing #5: Vertical Merger Analysis and the Role of the Consumer Welfare Standard in U.S. Antitrust Law, Nov. 1, 2018, https://www.ftc.gov/news-events/events-calendar/ftc-hearing-5-competition-consumer-protection-21st-century.

Stucke, and Barry Lynn, who railed against today's benchmark. Op-eds have proliferated, many of them tracing the perceived evils of today's competition policy to the choice of underlying norms.

In fact, this debate is both overblown and misdirected. In the first place, antitrust enforcement is principally a doctrinal matter. Although the theoretical lodestar informs doctrine's evolutionary path, it does not define it at a point in time. If reformists want a quick solution to inadequate enforcement, forcing a change in parlance will not get them there. The courts are the ultimate arbiters of antitrust mergers and litigation, and antitrust doctrine is now quite mature. Immediate changes that matter include error analysis, as discussed in the preceding chapter, and working to correct miscalibrated doctrine, which is the object of the next chapter.

In short, neo-Brandeisians imply that burning the consumer-welfare flag will somehow bring about revolutionary change to antitrust law. Such is not the case. Nevertheless, there is a case for revisiting competition policy's long-held banner. With reform afoot, now is the perfect time to take a critical look at sacred cows. It turns out that change is indeed warranted, though neither of the kind that neo-Brandeisians seek nor for the reasons that they espouse. Ultimately, three facts concerning antitrust's guiding standard govern the reform debate.

First, "consumer welfare" is descriptively inaccurate. Neither economic analysis nor antitrust doctrine turns on whether consumers are better off. The law never compels businesses to improve buyers' well-being. Nor does not it find behavior anticompetitive simply because it harms purchasers. The defining quality of an antitrust violation lies elsewhere – namely, in the weakening of a competition-generated constraint on firms' choices. We should correct the inapt characterization for good reason, as to wit:

Second, the mislabeling has consequences for antitrust's long-term development, even if less so for immediate policy. For example, despite the consumer welfare standard's inapt framing, antitrust remains concerned with restraints that harm competition between buyers in dealing with sellers. Yet, if a consumer-focused framework deflects attention from the correct locus of antitrust analysis – the fact of competition – to focus disproportionately on downstream buyers, then it may create blind spots or points of diminished attention over time. It may also invite "creative" antitrust theories where none belongs or lead to the denigration of theories that warrant attention. For instance, the controversy surrounding exotic conceptions of antitrust liability may reflect confusion about what antitrust does.[5] It is not a consumer-protection statute. It exists to preserve competitive market constraints on firm behavior. Hence, whether the law ought to recognize privacy, data

---

[5] *See, e.g.*, Maurice E. Stucke, *Looking at Monopsony in the Mirror*, 62 EMORY L.J. 1509, 1548 (2013) ("No consensus exists in the United States or globally on what *consumer welfare* actually means, who the consumers are, how to measure consumer welfare (if it is indeed measurable), or how to design legal standards to further this goal.") (emphasis in original).

security, algorithmic coordination, and other controversial topics as antitrust problems is a function of competition, not consumers' interests.

Third, in clarifying antitrust's objective, we should tie it to protecting the competitive process. Neo-Brandeisians ostensibly agree.[6] Contrary to their views, however, that clarification does not mean preserving an unconcentrated market structure. It refers to guarding market-generated competitive pressures. The fact of overlapping terminology with diametrically opposed meanings reinforces the problem. Terms of art routinely aired to capture the goals of antitrust are imprecise to the point of being near-useless.

This chapter explains how the federal antitrust authorities should reframe the consumer-welfare standard. Chapter 9 then wraps up Part III on antitrust reform by identifying specific doctrinal issues that warrant revisiting.

8.2 CONCEPTUALIZING THE ANTITRUST FRAMEWORK

Antitrust is imbued with values.[7] One might thus describe the field as political. Not in the sense that the executive branch interferes with the administration of competition policy. The federal antitrust authorities prize their independence. Any normative expression in antitrust, however, requires resolving (however implicitly) contested questions. We can see this in the reform debate. Neo-Brandeisians and neoclassicists are ships passing at night. They disagree on virtually every premise that underlies competition policy.

The threshold question is the most divisive. It concerns the role of the state. Some think capitalistic market systems inherently exploitative, and would thus have the government run the economy. When the executive controls the economic means of production (socialism) or extinguishes all private property rights (communism), it displaces competition and hence antitrust policy. Such economies perform disastrously on account of lost incentives and information asymmetries, among other problems. By contrast, the evidence for building a liberal market-based economy is overwhelming. Competition flourishes in countries characterized by property rights, freedom of contract, the rule of law, a state that does not crowd out private investment, effective capital markets, and judicial enforcement of private rights. In its purest form, antitrust exists to protect the rivalrous market pressures created when firms vie for mutually exclusive contracting opportunities.

This is all well and good, but it does not settle the role of the state. The vital issue concerns market efficacy. If antitrust prevents harmful restraints, policies, and mergers – and if the government enforces suitable consumer-protection regulations to enhance access to information – will the economy produce desirable outcomes?

---

[6] See, e.g., Lina M. Khan, *The Ideological Roots of America's Market Power Problem*, 127 YALE L.J. F. 960, 971 (2018); Steinbaum & Stucke, *supra* note 1, at 29–41.

[7] See Chapter 1.

Or will markets left free to evolve tend toward unpalatable outcomes, even if antitrust enforcers successfully preserve competitive pressures?

Commentators disagree. For the past fifty years, the United States has followed the belief that markets freed of artificial hindrances to competition grow increasingly efficient. Neo-Brandeisians insist, however, that such markets yield excessive concentration, income inequality, reduced access to opportunity, abuses both of workers and consumers, and distortions of democracy. They wish for the state to intervene. Such reformists want antitrust to be about far more than preserving competitive market pressures. They envision controls on competition itself – the imposition of hard structural boundaries that leave less space for unilateral practices, free contract, and organic growth at the firm level.

Those who trust markets reject such proposals outright. They recoil from the track record of natural-monopoly regulation in the United States and nationalization elsewhere. Free markets expose firms to merciless Darwinian pressures that spur efficiency and innovation, and force companies to respond to consumers' interests. According to many free-marketeers, when the state takes the reins, bureaucracy, incompetence, regulatory capture, and inefficiency ensue.

The right point between these extremes remains ever debated, but some facts are clear. Among them is that the state cannot recreate the rich incentives fostered by competitive markets. The question for policymakers, then, is not whether markets are perfect or government control ineffective, but whether and when the state can incrementally improve outcomes by stepping in to limit firm behavior. The antitrust reform debate is really about whether we need to do more than preserve existing competition.

Some people certainly think that we do. One might thus imagine an antitrust policy goal tied to *maximization*. On that view, regulators would not accept the status quo in concentrated or dominated markets. If they believe that market power endures, then merely preventing anticompetitive practices would not deliver competition's full benefits to consumers. At that point, however, the lines between competition law and regulation blur. If an agency undertakes an optimization exercise, then it assumes the full information problem that frustrates effective governmental control of economic activity elsewhere. This is a problematic exercise, even apart from the weighty rule-of-law issues associated with no-fault liability. As previously discussed, the relationship between industry structure, market power, and efficiency is murky. A regulator may decide that a market's present and likely future constitutions are undesirable relative to a structure preferred by the government. That undertaking, however, is at best precarious.

For that reason, as well as the limited-government tradition that honors freedom of contract, the United States has eschewed such an approach. Not everyone does. The United Kingdom's CMA, for example, can require no-fault divestitures in order to refashion markets into more competitive market structures.[8] The European Union and myriad jurisdictions that draw inspiration from it allow enforcers to go beyond harm to competition to prohibit exploitation, including in the form of monopolistic pricing.

Among its many difficulties, the maximization concept is most vulnerable to a lack of limiting principle. Unbounded, it would undermine market forces as the state becomes responsible for continuously evaluating and, if necessary, refining market structures. Brought to the extreme, it would become inconsistent with a free-market economy. In practice, most jurisdictions not content to preserve existing competition selectively choose their interventions. The European Commission has been commendable in this regard, showing more restraint in wielding its power to prohibit "unfair" pricing than some countries, which have employed pricing laws as tools of industrial policy.

Neo-Brandeisians want to create and maintain unconcentrated market structures. Their views are distinctly maximalist, and they reject any suggestion of limiting antitrust to preserving market pressures.

8.3 THE CONSUMER-WELFARE STANDARD

This is the context in which the consumer-welfare debate arises. Distinct interpretations notwithstanding, policymakers generally use "consumer welfare" to refer to the buyer surplus associated with neoclassical price theory. It is thus a static measure, which demarcates the area below the demand curve and above the market-clearing price. To employ antitrust in service of this benchmark requires intervening to arrest business conduct likely to restrict output and raise prices relative to the status quo ante. In other words, this framework defines as "anticompetitive" conduct that will likely injure consumers.

In practice, however, the technical definition fades into the background. Commentators use the term more loosely. In the vernacular, it captures the proposition that antitrust serves consumers' interests, not those of competitors. For the past forty years, US antitrust enforcers have pushed that one simple message around the world. It is hard to overstate the value of that effort. Over 130 competition regimes are now active around the world. Those entities are of varying sophistication. Some of them are disinclined toward rigorous economics, while others are fond of industrial policy. The potential for mischief is high. In times past, even the European Commission stood accused of protecting EU companies from mergers likely to create more effective competitors – *GE/Honeywell* stands out as an infamous example. Today, the pro-consumer push is so engrained that it would embarrass an enforcer to disclaim it.

---

[8] See CMA, Market Studies and Market Investigations: Supplemental Guidance on the CMA's Approach (2017).

Focusing on consumers has much to commend it. Every economic transaction implicates interests beyond those of the contracting parties. Firms have an incentive to shield themselves from competition. Their interests are localized, while those of consumers are dispersed. Protectionist impulses can lead governments to extinguish competition. Populists accuse corporations of suppressing local businesses and of undermining democracy. This can put pressure on a sympathetic, vulnerable, or captured regulator to impose rules and market structures at odds with the interests of the larger consuming public. Within this sea of conflict, a clear guiding star is invaluable. The consumer welfare standard focuses on revealed preferences – a nonabstract expression of choice by buyers through their voluntary transactions. By placing consumers' interests above those of others, antitrust can screen out noise that threatens to derail sound enforcement. In doing so, it protects consumers against proposals that would deprive them of the low prices and higher quality associated with competition. Political efforts directed at suppressing disruptive innovation by startups from Uber to Tesla speak to the danger that a consumer welfare helps to avoid. We worry about the many, not the few.

Consumer welfare thus lies at the heart of modern US antitrust policy. The Supreme Court famously observed that the Sherman Act serves a consumer-welfare prescription.[9] The 2010 Horizontal Merger Guidelines take as their goal the prevention of mergers likely to "harm customers as a result of diminished competitive constraints or incentives[.]"[10] Although consumer welfare is less firmly engrained within E.U. competition law, the Commission has embraced the concept several times.[11] And a host of scholars have passionately defended antitrust's hallowed consumer-focused framework.[12]

Yet, several deficiencies plague the consumer-welfare standard. It lacks explanatory power, deviates from the static efficiency metric that economists use in their modeling, and omits the dynamic measures of welfare that matter most. Confusing matters, some writers use the term as a shorthand for a different normative benchmark, namely aggregate welfare.[13] That metric is synonymous with the allocative

---

[9] Reiter v. Sonotone Corp., 442 U.S. 330, 343 (1979) (quoting ROBERT BORK, THE ANTITRUST PARADOX 66 (1978).

[10] U.S. Dep't of Justice & Fed. Trade Comm'n, Horizontal Merger Guidelines § 1 (2010).

[11] Joaquín Almunia, *Competition and Consumers: The Future of EU Competition Policy*, Madrid, May 12, 2010 ("Consumer welfare is at the heart of our policy and its achievement drives our priorities and guides our decisions."); Neelie Kroes, *European Competition Policy Delivering Better Markets and Better Choices. European Consumer and Competition Day*, London, Sept. 5, 2005 ("Consumer welfare is now well established as the standard the Commission applies when assessing mergers and infringements of the Treaty rules on cartels and monopolies.").

[12] *See, e.g.*, Elyse Dorsey et al., *Consumer Welfare & the Rule of Law: The Case Against the New Populist Antitrust Movement*, 47 PEPPERDINE L. REV. 861 (2020); A. Douglas Melamed & Nicolas Petit, *The Misguided Assault on the Consumer Welfare Standard in the Age of Platform Markets*, 54 REV. INDUS. ORG. 741 (2019); Makan Delrahim, Ensuring the Legacy of the Consumer Welfare Standard, Nov. 14, 2019, https://www.justice.gov/opa/speech/file/1222866/download.

[13] Steven C. Salop, *Question: What Is the Real and Proper Antitrust Welfare Standard? Answer: The True Consumer Welfare Standard*, 22 LOYOLA CONSUMER L. REV. 336 (2010).

efficiency that economists use in static modeling.[14] It has benefits relative to a true consumer welfare standard, including eliminating an artificial distinction between sellers and buyers because economic actors act in both capacities across markets.

A consumer-welfare standard can nevertheless invite controversy because of the value judgments that its invocation implies. If one defines an antitrust violation by its impact on downstream pricing alone, then it excludes upstream price distortions, industry concentration, income and opportunity equality, employment, and dispersion of political power as goals of competition law. For neoclassical economics types, of course, those traits are features, not bugs. Anti-monopolists, however, see the value judgments embedded in the consumer-welfare standard as emblematic of everything that is wrong with today's antitrust policies.[15] For them, salvation lies in an altogether different standard – one that preserves unconcentrated market structures and is indifferent to effects in particular cases.

The neo-Brandeisian critique is not, however, on all fours with the standard that it assails. Anti-monopolists hold it up as a norm that praises low pricing and thus perversely celebrates, rather than condemns, digital platforms that achieve exponential growth. Such reformists further contend that the prevailing benchmark excludes (or diminishes) non-price dimensions of competition, thus overlooking labor market distortions that harm writers, artists, gig-economy workers, and employees whom, the critics say, neo-classicists view as commoditized inputs into a system that exists to serve consumers only.

Whatever the merits of that broader critique, it misconstrues the standard that *actually* governs competition policy today. It is past time to jettison the misleading consumer-welfare terminology in favor of an accurate description. Properly understood, the existing orthodoxy neutralizes many criticisms pressed by neo-Brandeisians. It does not grant carte blanche to firms wishing to distort upstream markets or to monopolize via low-price-fueled growth. The *sine qua non* of an antitrust violation is harm to competitive market constraints. To be sure, one can quibble with the doctrine that gives expression to antitrust's lodestar, but that is distinct from critiquing the normative goal itself.

8.4 A CONSUMER-WELFARE STANDARD LACKS DESCRIPTIVE POWER, AND IS ANALYTICALLY MISPLACED

Competition brings a host of benefits. It forces companies to set price closer to their costs, reducing economic distortions and elevating industrial output. Markets – and,

---

[14] Daniel A. Crane, *Rules Versus Standards in Antitrust Adjudication*, 64 WASH. & LEE L. REV. 49, 81 (2007) (It is "generally assumed today" that "allocative efficiency is the goal.").

[15] See, e.g., Tim Wu, *After Consumer Welfare, Now What? The "Protection of Competition" Standard in Practice*, CPI ANTITRUST CHRONICLE, Apr. 2018; Marshall Steinbaum, The Consumer Welfare Standard is an Outdated Holdover From a Discredited Economic Theory, Roosevelt Institute, Dec. 11, 2017, https://rooseveltinstitute.org/consumer-welfare-standard-outdated-holdover-discredited-economic-theory/.

by extension, economies – grow as they become more competitive. Pricing pressure makes firms chase cost savings, adopt efficient manufacturing processes, and move toward optimal scale, all of which reduces waste and enhances the availability of scarce inputs to others. Competition holds inflation in check. Most importantly, competition can spur firms to invest in R&D-driven technology races, potentially accelerating innovation that can deliver benefits to society far surpassing the static efficiency gains envisioned above.

Antitrust protects that process. Or at least it should. Between the 1950s and 1970s, the courts and agencies implemented a structuralist agenda that interfered with efficiency-boosting restraints, practices, and mergers. In the 1930s, Congress passed the Robinson–Patman Act in order to protect small businesses from competition. The FTC enforced that anticompetitive legislation with gusto through the 1970s. That was an era in which antitrust policy lost its way. The Chicago School revolutionized the field by observing the perversities of the period. The genius of the consumer-welfare conceptualization was to impress on enforcers and judges alike the importance of thinking about the beneficiaries of competition. That anchor helped decision-makers to weed out antitrust lawsuits, often filed by struggling rivals, that sought shelter from competition itself. Chicago's enduring influence has been to convince policymakers of the dangers of turning antitrust policy against the beneficiaries of competition.

Intuitive and digestible, the consumer-welfare framework has dominated antitrust thinking ever since. Yet, it has never been strictly correct. Its proponents sacrificed accuracy in pursuit of simplicity. It implies that antitrust begins with the beneficiaries of competition, rather than with competition itself. That gets the analysis backwards. Consumer impact does not define the antitrust violation. In evaluating a merger, restraint, or practice, we do not begin by asking whether consumers stand to lose or gain. We start by evaluating the significance of competition at issue, determining whether a unique competitive constraint would be lost. In a horizontal case, it is the loss of such competition that violates the antitrust laws. Such an event tends to cause sustained anticompetitive effects, but not always. And when harms do materialize, it is usually – but not always – consumers who suffer.

To tease out the distinction between consumer harm and injury to competition, it helps to consider idiosyncratic circumstances that sever the causal link between the two. Suppose that firms bid to run infrastructure or a franchise that faces no competition. In other words, imagine a competitive process that awards a monopoly. This scenario may disconnects consumer impact and harm to competition. If one took the consumer-welfare standard literally, then the antitrust question would not survive its asking. Buyers would face a monopolist no matter who wins, so antitrust has nothing to say. Hence, bidders for the opportunity would be free to collude or rig the process, harming competition without (at least obviously) harming customers. Some strict adherents to the Chicago School have incorrectly gravitated toward that view.

Such was Judge Easterbrook's dissenting opinion in *Fishman*.[16] There, two groups submitted dueling bids to purchase the Chicago Bulls, which was the sole NBA team in the city. An investor in the losing bidder owned the only suitable stadium in Chicago, and refused to let it. The losing bidder successfully convinced the NBA to disqualify the winner for its failure to have procured a stadium, and then took over the contract. The excluded competitor sued under the antitrust laws. Judge Easterbrook, a leader in the antitrust law and economics movement, had little time for the claims presented. If the team were a natural monopoly and the stadium an essential facility, as the district court had found, then the competition at issue was for a monopoly and no effects would transpire. In his view, "only injury to consumers violates the antitrust laws."[17] Seeing none, he saw no case.

Writing for the panel, the late Judge Cudahy took an altogether different approach. In his view, the Sherman Act protects competition in all of its forms, including to acquire a natural monopoly.[18] He agreed that "the enhancement of consumer welfare is an important policy – probably the paramount policy – informing the antitrust laws."[19] He did not think it a condition of an antitrust claim directed at harm to upstream competition, however, to identify injury to consumers downstream. The Seventh Circuit's opinion stressed the distinction emphasized in this chapter: "The antitrust laws are concerned with the competitive *process*, and their application does not depend in each particular case upon the ultimate demonstrable consumer effect. A healthy and unimpaired competitive process is presumed to be in the consumer interest."[20]

Judge Cudahy worried about courts' ability to gauge the true costs associated with lost competition. His opinion was an ode to the value of competition itself. On the facts at hand, he thought there "no way of telling whether IBI or CSPC would be a 'better' owner from the perspective of basketball fans. But we think the Sherman Act requires that the choice between them result from unconstrained competition on the merits."[21] On his reading of the Supreme Court's jurisprudence as it then was, "the Court has never given us [reason] to believe that anything save unfettered competition is the key to consumer well-being."[22]

Embracing the competitive process over consumer welfare, however, implicates a serious objection. How should we define harm to competition for the purposes of sustaining an antitrust violation? Competition is gelatinous. It has myriad dimensions and brings consequences variously obvious and subtle. Its full results may take time to materialize. Though an undoubted source of social value, competition also brings with it costs. Most importantly, being multifaceted, competition is

---

[16] Fishman v. Estate of Wirtz, 807 F.2d 520, 563–85 (7th Cir. 1986) (Easterbrook, J., dissenting).
[17] Id. at 569.
[18] Id. at 533.
[19] Id. at 535.
[20] Id. at 536 (emphasis in original).
[21] Id. at 537.
[22] Id. at 537.

difficult to quantify. A traditional measure is market structure, which is an unreliable barometer and at best a rough proxy for static competitive pressure. Concentration ratios are necessarily imprecise because they treat every seller as indistinguishable from all others, save for their share of sales. They shed little light on the competitive process, which, in its abundant richness, goes far beyond n-1 or HHI statistics.

One might be tempted to describe competition for the purpose of antitrust analysis as the degree of rivalry implicated by a merger, restraint, or practice. If, as this books argues, one should define a violation by harm to the competitive process rather than harm to consumer welfare, then it might seem to follow that any weakening of competition falls within the crosshairs. But that would be both unworkable and unwise. *Every* contract restrains competition in at least one dimension, while often promoting it in others. Even the most innocuous (and, indeed, most efficient) horizontal mergers extinguish competition between the parties. It is no answer to suggest such transactions are illegal because they eliminate competition – they do, but only in the narrowest dimension and not in broader context. Unless they are to retreat to structuralism, antitrust decision-makers need some means for identifying harm to competition.

Here is where the consumer-welfare terminology stops fraying and comes apart. The question is not whether "consumers" at the bottom of the vertical chain are worse off. Rather, we care about anticompetitive *effects*, which may take the form of higher prices, but could be lower prices upstream (from reduced competition on the buyer side), reduced quality, or diminished incentives to innovate. The law and economics approach offers a clever solution for diagnosing allegedly anticompetitive behavior: will it likely produce harmful effects? Price-theoretic models are tailormade for this exercise, at least for static purposes.

Predicting competitive effects is fundamental to antitrust. Nevertheless, no more than consumer welfare, effects do not themselves define a Sherman Act violation. Those effects flow from something else – an act that dilutes or eliminates a constraint. The antitrust laws guard competition-generated suppression of market power. Its removal or weakening leads to cascading effects of the kind that economists capture in their models and observe in the data. The injury associated with such effects gives impacted victims standing to sue. Yet, the antitrust question is never whether conduct led to elevated prices, diminished output, or throttled innovation. It is whether the conduct was, in the first instance, anticompetitive. The two differ. Fraudulent or tortious business behavior, for example, may extract higher prices. A firm may renege on its contract in order to exploit the promisee's vulnerability. Whether the antitrust laws prohibit such strategic opportunism depends on whether the conduct eliminates a competitive constraint, not simply whether it led to higher prices.[23]

---

[23] *See, e.g.*, Rambus, Inc. v. Fed. Trade Comm'n, 522 F.3d 456 (D.C. Cir. 2008).

Defining antitrust as an exercise only in predicting or measuring effects mischaracterizes the law, both conceptually and doctrinally. In practice, the distinction rarely matters – lifting a constraint often facilitates an exercise of newfound market power. But, as the next section explores, the difference bears significance for the long-term development of competition policy.

We thus return to question, if we do not define conduct as "anticompetitive" by its effects, then how should we define it? Of the restraints that do not harm consumers, how to tell which ones are lawful and which are illegal? Every restraint inhibits competition to some degree. The categorization question thus stands among antitrust's greatest difficulties.

The answer lies in evaluating the nature of the conduct itself, the quantum of competition implicated by it, and the capacity of the market quickly to replenish any lost rivalry. A shorthand is to ask whether the agreement or transaction eliminates a unique competitive constraint.

Effects play a critical role here, but *only* if they are tied to lifting a competitive constraint. Suppose that a utility defrauds the industry regulator, tricking it into authorizing higher rates. Reprehensible and apt to produce harmful effects as it may be, such conduct is not the stuff of antitrust.[24] The actions do not implicate any rivalrous process, and thus have no bearing on competition. Now consider a horizontal acquisition between two of many similarly situated firms in a competitive market. The transaction eliminates competition between the parties, and thus comes within the purview of antitrust. No sustainable effects could follow, however, due to an abundance of choice enjoyed by buyers, other sellers' incentive to expand, and plausible efficiencies associated with the deal. Although the transaction reduces competition in one dimension – rivalry as between the parties – it does not harm competition at the market level, which remains vibrant, undiluted, and (if the post-merger firm attains desired productivities) even potentially increased.

As a practical matter, then, competitive effects are the right way to think about antitrust problems. But they represent the second step – the threshold inquiry's being to identify an act that dilutes or eliminates a competition-generated constraint on a firm's behavior. Only when effects trace to such an event do they become a sufficient, though unnecessary, means for identifying harm to competition.

8.5 LOOKING BEYOND CONSUMERS TO COMPETITION

Antitrust's welfare debate is not merely semantic. True, lax conceptions of the law's goals often go unnoticed. That is because candidate frameworks – consumer welfare, total welfare, protecting competitive market pressures, or promoting an unconcentrated market structure – yield the same or similar answers across many scenarios. After all, one need not unlock antitrust's inner secrets in order to condemn

---

[24] *Cf.* NYNEX Corp. v. Discon, Inc., 525 U.S. 128, 136 (1998).

naked price-fixing conspiracies, mergers to monopoly, and the like. But easy cases only go so far. The specifics matter because some important cases implicate irreconcilable values. Imprecision about antitrust's goals then impedes analysis and evaluation.

Whenever a scrutinized practice implicates divergent interests, the relevant benchmark is important. This goes beyond the core neoclassical/neo-Brandeisian divide about how to treat scale that brings efficiency, lower price, and greater market concentration. Recent years have seen an abundance of exotic antitrust theories. From digital platform scale to data privacy shortcomings, commercial behavior perceived as troubling has spurred calls for antitrust intervention. This approach conceives of competition law as a tool of broad economic policy – something that the government should use to prevent distortions based on size or to prohibit opprobrious conduct. Such calls blur the lines between antitrust, consumer protection, and regulation. Diagnosing them has proven to be controversial.

The consumer-welfare standard bears some responsibility here. It invites the question whether scrutinized conduct may harm consumers or otherwise produce effects. As explained, that approach skips the essential threshold inquiry, which requires connecting the act to a competitive market constraint. If one jumps right to a welfare evaluation, then it is easy to make antitrust issues out of behavior that may not impact the competitive process. We have seen that scenario play out many times, as various commentators blame antitrust for allowing banks to become too large to fail or for failing to intervene to arrest platforms from scaling rapidly. Much of the time, such calls trace either to a confused understanding of what antitrust is or a fundamental (but rarely articulated) disagreement about what antitrust should be.

Looking beyond consumers to the preservation of competitive pressure unlocks the key to proper antitrust analysis. To illustrate the point, consider a few seldom-encountered scenarios. Can an act of violence, for example, expose the wrongdoer to criminal sanctions as well as antitrust liability? Generally, of course, the answer is no because most crimes have no bearing on competition-generated constraints on firm behavior. The fact that the vast majority of crimes make society worse off under almost any welfare calculus has no bearing on antitrust. Yet, there is no categorical bar on antitrust considerations. Suppose, for example, that the owner of one firm set his competitor's factory ablaze. It would obviously be a matter of criminal law, and expose the wrongdoer to civil liability in tort and property law. We might be content from a policy perspective to leave deterrence and remediation to those areas of law, but they do not crowd out an otherwise meritorious antitrust claim. If the arsonist were dominant in a relevant market, the act would also be one of monopolization. So, too, if a monopolist threatened a prospective entrant with physical violence should she compete, that would sound in antitrust.

Similar principles apply to other, less-outlandish scenarios. A breach of contract in itself is typically not an anticompetitive act, even between rivals. The *Colgate* doctrine has long given companies flexibility as to with whom they contract and on what terms. But a promisor can simultaneously breach its contract and expose itself to antitrust liability if, on the facts at hand, the Sherman Act imposed a duty to deal.

In such scenarios, it is easy to confuse the analysis by asking whether the act harms consumers or whether other legal mechanisms are better placed to resolve the issues. Antitrust stands alone, however, and the proper question always focuses on the nature of the action at issue. Did it weaken a competitive constraint on firm behavior? If so, did it plausibly bring with it the potential to increase competition in another dimension? Should the behavior weaken competition, then effects come to the fore. But the first question always focuses on the nature of the conduct at issue itself, and specifically how it relates to rivalrous market pressures. Likely consequences in terms of market outcomes come next, but we must take care not to become absolutist. The causal path of effects may not always be clear.

So oriented, consider some prominent and divisive antitrust questions. Writers have called on antitrust to solve perceived issues concerning data privacy and security, algorithmic collusion, digital platform integration, and more besides. To address any, let alone all, of these in detail would consume a chapter. But take briefly the question of data – a recurring topic *de jour*. Is big data an antitrust problem? Should Section 7 block transactions between firms that would combine large datasets? What if the buyer plans to relax data-privacy guarantees that the seller had previously pressed? To some commentators, there is a common and obvious answer to those questions. In the digital economy, users typically pay with their data rather than money. Hence, a transaction that facilitates greater access to and usage of users' data should run afoul of the Clayton Act. So, too, pooling data may give a large firm an advantage over rivals. And the list goes on. Many critics of today's policies view data aggregation practices and privacy limitations as antithetical to consumers. They thus dress up these phenomena in antitrust garb, making Section 7 and Section 2 issues out of them.

Principled analysis, however, begins not with whether a data practice or merger plausibly harms consumers – that inquiry comes later. Instead, it asks whether data constitute a focal point of competition. *They may*. As before, there is no categorical exclusion. Antitrust reaches as far as rivalrous market pressures extend.

Suppose, for example, that two of many digital platform providers uniquely differentiate themselves by offering unusually generous privacy terms to their users. Many users, enthused about the privacy guarantees and principles, flock to that duo. That is a non-price form of competition that the antitrust laws would protect. If their merger would eliminate the buyer's only close rival in offering those terms, and if consumers valued those terms in choosing with whom to contract, then Section 7 ought to apply in full.

By contrast, if a transaction merely joined two firms' respective complementary datasets, then there is no lost competition. Unless the combination reinforced a monopolist's dominant position without offsetting efficiency justification or created an incentive and ability to foreclose downstream competition from an essential or important input, then antitrust has nothing to say. Even if users disliked the transaction or buyer, and the deal resulted in a welfare loss for consumers or others, that is not in itself a competition law issue. Understanding why is indispensable to informed antitrust policy. It is why questions surrounding big data are not inherently antitrust problems, but can be in the right circumstances. For example, in particular markets, they might represent a channel of competitive pressure that the Sherman Act protects. Hence, conservative observers who reject any role for antitrust in this setting go too far.

One might ask why this matters. Competition for natural monopoly is a rare event. In practice, even under this book's proposal to conceive of antitrust's mandate as protecting the competitive process, effects usually determine whether a restraint is anticompetitive or not. Hence, this might appear to a fuss about very little. In fact, two considerations warrant revising the consumer-welfare standard.

The first lies in misadventure. Stray from a consumer-welfare or other effects-based standard, and aggressive theories become easier to justify. In the ultimate case, in which one defines an antitrust violation as any conduct, agreement, or transaction that contributes to an unwanted economic condition, then analysis collapses into one's normative outlook. Antitrust then become a conclusory exercise in value judgment. As discussed previously, neo-Brandeisians want antitrust to protect the competitive process. By that, they mean fostering unconcentrated markets and, if necessary, deconcentrating existing markets into atomistic structures. Their goal is to increase market pricing both upstream and downstream in order to create a fairer system of wealth distribution and opportunity. In the abstract, this vision is appealing. In practice, it would entail reducing competition itself at consumers' expense. For reformists of the neo-Brandeisian persuasion, any business conduct seen to fuel consolidation or reduce prices by too much is ripe for antitrust condemnation. Status offenses will loom. In such an environment, theories of antitrust liability would quickly become unmoored. Well-intentioned, but harmful, interventions would follow. The market incentives that drive competition in the first place are most vulnerable.

The second consideration involves the opposite danger. Reframing the consumer-welfare standard will not simply guard against overenforcement. In time, today's confusing nomenclature may also yield *under*enforcement.

Some advocates for change blame "[e]conomists obsessed with 'efficiency' theory" for rising concentration, deepening income inequality, and the failure to rein in Silicon Valley.[25] On that account, today's consumer-welfare standard has blinded the agencies not only to harms associated with upstream distortions, but to larger social ills associated with concentration. The latter critique goes beyond economics to implicate socio-political questions of the kind addressed in Chapter 2. But the

---

[25] Rana Foroohar, *Antitrust Is Changing from the Ground Up*, Fin'l Times, July 27, 2020.

former criticism goes to the heart of things. It is the view that embracing consumers means ignoring sellers. That diagnosis is overstated. The agencies worry about harm to competition, including on the supply side of input markets.[26] They do not literally construe consumer welfare.

Nevertheless, a valid concern does lurk within this picture. The consumer-welfare movement has been synonymous with the pursuit of competitive effects. For the most part, the trend has been wholly laudatory. There comes a point, however, at which insisting on such proof as effectively to remove the possibility of a false conviction harms social welfare by allowing too much anticompetitive conduct to pass muster. It is at this juncture that taking competition seriously on its own terms has much to offer. The path by which suppressed competition visits harms on society is not always clear and, yes, can go beyond the price effects that (properly) capture most attention in the typical antitrust case. To require a robust effects case in every case, however, may go too far. Instead, the question should be whether the challenged merger, agreement, or conduct loosens competitive pressure. If it does, then it satisfies the necessary condition of an antitrust violation. Sufficiency requires more, but may not demand a complete demonstration of likely unilateral or coordinated effects, though they would certainly suffice. Rather, the presence or absence of offsetting benefits is key. That is why we dispense with competitive effects in per se cases. And it is why competition to acquire a natural monopoly should be cognizable.

That insight is more significant than may first appear. A plaintiff should be able to make out an antitrust claim based on anticompetitive conduct (i.e., an act that weakens a competition-generated constraint on firm behavior) that *either* will likely carry unilateral or coordinated effects *or* is not likely to be associated with ancillary benefits. The question achieves peak importance when the interplay between the all-important future and the conduct at issue is obscure. An important example may involve innovation. There remains a great deal of uncertainty in the economics literature about whether monopoly or competition presents the optimal conditions in which R&D will flourish. The famous Arrow-Schumpeter debate has yielded countless models, each one dependent on specific assumptions. Suppose that parties with a history of R&D races wish to merge to monopoly, arguing that together they will have incentives to invest more than when they are apart. In such a setting, ties cut in favor of competition. Absent convincing evidence to the contrary, antitrust enforcers should trust that rivalrous pressures – and that is especially so when there is evidence that competition with the other party spurred past innovation efforts. It would, in the author's view, be a mistake to insist in such a case that the agencies prove likely competitive effects in such circumstances.

To be sure, one could dispatch such hypotheticals by appealing to the consumer-welfare standard. The benefit of embracing the competitive-process framework,

---

[26] HORIZONTAL MERGER GUIDELINES, *supra* note 84, at § 1 ("Enhancement of market power by buyers ... has adverse effects comparable to enhancement of market power by sellers.").

however, lies in treating rivalrous processes as valuable in themselves. That is not a function of structure alone, as neo-Brandeisians suggest, but of market-generated incentives that the antitrust laws ought to protect. To invoke consumers is to embrace the need to show how a restraint will harm them. It is the intuition that led Judge Easterbrook astray in *Fishman*. As discussed, an act of violence on competition can itself invoke antitrust condemnation.

8.6 CONCLUSION

Consumer welfare remains Chicago's most persistent edifice.

Its success is partially a function of ambiguity. Agreeable and intuitive, the framework offers something for almost everyone. Reformists of the 1970s and 1980s wrested control of the antitrust machine from structuralists, and pointed it toward competitive effects. In doing so, they remade competition policy into its present form. Their cause enjoyed overwhelming empirical and intellectual support, as advances in industrial organization undid the prior era's learning. The antitrust revolution's depth, reach, and duration were truly remarkable, however, and ought to have been more controversial than they were. Consumers – presented as sacrosanct and as the lone beneficiaries of antitrust intervention – played less an analytic role than a marketing one in that revolution. They covered what is, at heart, a neoclassical position. To invoke the consumer-welfare standard today is thus to pay homage to the law and economics approach. Scant wonder that neo-Brandeisians loathe it and free-marketeers recoil when anyone calls it into question.

Antitrust has not seen a debate like today's in half a century. Everything is up for grabs, and nothing is free of scrutiny. Anti-monopolists take issue with virtually every feature of today's effects-based analysis, and stake out absolutist positions based on inconclusive evidence. This book takes seriously claims of antitrust failure. It finds the case to be overblown, but supports ratcheting up scrutiny in close matters within a framework tied to preserving competitive pressure. In their quest to right perceived wrongs, reformists have seized onto the consumer-welfare standard as the key to reform. As noted, that effort is misjudged. Antitrust enforcers do not construe the term literally. They worry about buyers, sellers, and anyone else injured by, or as the means of effecting, reduced competition. And even if they won the battle for nomenclature, neo-Brandeisians' preferred articulation of antitrust's goal – preserving the competitive process – would not cure the ills to which they are reacting. Sherman Act doctrine is mature, and reminding the agencies that all beneficiaries of competition matter would not yield transformative change.

What anti-monopolists really pine for is structuralism. Their objection is less with the substance of the consumer-welfare standard as it is with the effects-based approach associated with it. The attacks on today's framework thus have an artificial flavor. In neo-Brandeisians' view, only atomistic market structures would achieve superior outcomes over time. It is amusing to observe, then, that their critique would fit comfortably within the framework that they assail. They argue that predicting effects is unreliable, serves to bless harmful consolidations, and gets us little in return because few mergers are efficient. If they are right, then structural merger policies would benefit consumers. So, too, low-price-driven growth by digital platforms would harm consumers if the distortions and entrenchment that anti-monopolists fear come to pass. The debate has little to do with consumers, and everything to do with the role of neoclassical price theory and the importance of preserving incentives to invest. In this way, the consumer-welfare standard finds itself at the heart of a shadow war.

Although some defenders of the status quo may consider the proposal heterodox, we should revisit the consumer-welfare standard. Once valuable, the conceptualization has exhausted its purpose. For Chicagoans, the goal was never to maximize the well-being of buyers alone – rather it was (and remains) to maximize the joint surplus of buyers and sellers. In other words, it reflects the allocative and productive efficiency goals of neoclassical price theory. Such a framing is true to normative economic conceptions of static efficiency. Yet, it hardly resonates with a larger audience, much less captures the public or judicial imagination. To call it a ruse would be to go too far, but those who invoke it rarely mean what the term implies.

Consumer welfare has nevertheless played a valuable role. It helped to inject much-needed coherence into a previously confused space. It penetrated a noisy spectrum of inconsistent stakeholder interest to focus attention on the beneficiaries of competition. It has achieved this at the price of accuracy. Descriptive shortcomings might be forgivable, even after this much time, but they threaten to impede further refinement of antitrust policy. This moment of reform bursts with opportunity. It is therefore right to ask whether we should persevere with a miscalibrated framework.

As noted, fixing the issue will not yield transformative changes overnight. Nor should it because today's US antitrust policies are fundamentally sound. What is clear, however, is that the economy is heading in a direction that will test competition law's rationality, mission, and political content. One would have to blind not to see trends toward digitization, data-driven analytics, and a shift in key business infrastructure away from physical assets in favor of intellectual property and technology. Exponential growth, disruption, and displacement will be key features of the network economy.

These developments bear great promise, but they will exert pressure on our competition laws. Issues of first impression will proliferate, and observers will query whether antitrust's premises are well suited for the twenty-first century. The FTC itself held a multitude of hearings on that very topic. The problem with the consumer-welfare articulation is that it turns every policy question into a potential antitrust issue. Any perceived shortcoming in how markets operate or how firms behave will implicate consumers, thus giving cover to those who would employ antitrust against behavior having little or nothing to do with competition.

Opportunism, business torts, breaches of contract, violated regulatory commitments, size, or the imposition of unpopular user terms will invite the heavy apparatus of antitrust. Determining when such phenomena sound in antitrust requires looking not to consumers, but to competition. They sometimes do, but they often do not.

Some doubt corporate motives, question free-market principles, discount the value of efficiencies, and trust state intervention. For those so inclined, making antitrust issues of business practices that harm consumers has everything to commend it. Why, they might ask, should we make preservation of competitive pressure the litmus test for antitrust intervention? Doing so, they may argue, would serve only to facilitate business ills that the antitrust laws might fruitfully suppress. The answer lies in two considerations.

First, antitrust enforcers are good at discerning harm to competition. They are horribly positioned to identify optimal market structures a priori. This goes to the foundation of the free-market system itself, which reflects the information and incentive problems that stymie government control of the economy.

Fleshing this point out further, competition is by far the superior vehicle for directing economic activity. That is why we focus our antitrust laws on protecting it. If we go further, prohibiting other forms of seemingly opprobrious conduct or recognizing a status offense, then we risk suppressing market responses that would yield superior outcomes than regulatory intervention. The game is not worth the candle. That is especially so when the law already provides recompense for wronged parties through civil actions for tort, breach of contract, and the like. But it is also true when the state action deprives stakeholders of what the market might otherwise have provided.

Consider a Section 2-driven breakup of a large company premised not on exclusionary behavior, but on a judgment that divestitures will create a superior market structure. Put aside the potential inefficiencies associated with such an order, as well as the poisoning of incentives to invest, compete, and win occasioned by faultless liability intervention. Such a remedy would also deprive consumers of a world in which the market could have seen dominance erode or the incumbent produce spectacular innovations to stave off potential displacement. The absence of exclusionary conduct makes such outcomes entirely plausible. If antitrust were employed in this way, enforcers would inevitably get it wrong.

Second, if antitrust became an unconstrained consumer-protection tool, then it would do tremendous damage through overdeterrence. Commercial behavior that had no effect on competition may come within the crosshairs, making executives question any business decision that an enforcer (or private plaintiff) might later say hurt consumers. Antitrust as a free-wheeling liability machine ought to repel anyone who thinks through the details. The antitrust laws cast an imposing shadow, allowing potentially catastrophic treble damages if applied not only to anticompetitive conduct, but any business decision later deemed injurious of some consumers' interests.

There seems no principled way to cabin the analysis without reverting back to what this book recommends – namely, preservation of competitive pressure – or to today's effects-based standard.

Evolving away from a consumer-welfare framework to one founded on preserving competitive pressure would not merely stave off unintended harmful consequences. It will also help the agencies and courts more accurately diagnose novel forms of anticompetitive conduct that find little direct precedent, but threaten to suppress incentives to compete or weaken constraints on the exercise of market power. The requisite analysis of such an issue, of course, can be complex and beyond the confines of this chapter. But no manner of penetrating examination will yield the right answer if it is not directed at the correct question. The next phase of antitrust enforcement will encounter issues more nuanced than ever before. As always, industrial organization will help to illuminate the problems at hand. There would be great value, however, to the agencies' being more particular about precisely what goal animates their analysis. For the reasons discussed here, the framing should lie not in consumer welfare, but in preserving competitive pressure.

9

The Antitrust Evolution

9.1 COMPETITION LAW'S ECONOMIC PROGRESS ENCOUNTERS A FORK IN THE ROAD

Cries for revolution fill the air. The structuralism for which anti-monopolists pine, however, would bring antitrust to a regrettable place. For all its flaws, the competitive effects era has striven for accuracy. Modern analysis hones in on the causal determinants of unilateral static effects – diversion ratios and margins – and contextualizes them in light of the fluidity and dynamism of the market at issue. It does not stop there. Customers' expectations about the merger or practice weigh heavily on the analysis. Probable efficiency gains, anticipated seller responses, and customers' ability to discipline attempted exercises of market power complete the picture. That canvas bestows the richest possible basis for inferring the presence or absence of tractable harm. Neo-Brandeisians would abandon that exercise in favor of something rigid and imprecise. In their preferred world, market shares and concentration ratios would not guide the analysis, but dispose of it.

Anti-monopolists thus champion dogmatic policies. They would reject illuminative evidence in favor of hard thresholds. It is hard to understand how abandoning economists' hard-won insights over the past half-decade would yield superior antitrust enforcement. Nevertheless, some reformists urge categorical rules that would indiscriminately condemn all mergers, for example, that surpass critical ratios. They would prohibit many innocuous transactions knowing that effects are unlikely. So, too, they would condemn deals that create more effective competitors or accelerate innovation. They would accept such harms because they believe that preserving atomistic market structures would, in the end, yield net benefits. The mystery is how an approach that eschews the most informed merits-based decision in each matter would surpass one that always tries to get it right.

It would be wrong, of course, to suppose the competitive-effects approach free of cost. Just as structuralism casts an unduly expansive sphere of condemnation, so, too, consequentialist analysis unintentionally lets some harmful practices and mergers slide by. At times, the more exuberant proponents of law and economics have ventured uncritical laissez faire dogma. Passionate calls for reform thus bear value. Refinement is the hallmark of evidence-based antitrust, and yet it is all too easy to immerse ourselves in the apparatus of modern competition law without scrutinizing the big picture. While the evidence does not support neo-Brandeisian claims of systematic antitrust failures – let alone of pervasive monopoly – the full context raises unsettling questions for guardians of the status quo. This is the right time to revisit questions long thought settled, and to reflect on how we might improve competition policy as we move deeper into the twenty-first century.

On scrutiny, the record yields two principal conclusions. First, the agencies have a solid record in bringing meritorious cases and screening out bad ones, though it appears that the enforcement margin is associated with failures to intervene in circumstances that warrant it. This is not true of every close decision, of course, but appears indicative of the universe of such calls. That insight reasonably follows from the retrospective literature. The solution, as per Chapter 7, lies principally in decision theory.

The second conclusion is that not everyone likes where consumer-driven policies lead. This point is vital, and yet underappreciated. US antitrust is not an apparatus of market control. Enforcers serve a deferential role. The government may have views about the best product, optimal technology, or ideal market structure, but it matters not. Antitrust preserves competitive market pressure.[1] As a result, the DOJ, FTC, and state attorneys general are along for the ride. If consumers see fit to reward an innovator with a monopoly of breathtaking scale, then antitrust agencies have nothing to say absent exclusionary practices. The digital network economy, however, has brought the implications of free-market antitrust policies into full view – arguably in a way that we have not seen before. For those convinced that market-deferential polices are sound, then claims of antitrust failure ring hollow. The agencies' decision not to arrest innovation- and low-price-driven platform growth is a feature, not a bug. Others judge competition policy not by its underlying principles, but by the market structures that ensue. Whether a function of consumer choice or not, they recoil from the dominance that they perceive across various technology industries.

Hence, a common theme underlies neo-Brandeisian calls to revert to structuralism, abandon the consumer-welfare standard, suppress competition by vertically integrated platforms, relieve downward pressure on prices, ease competition in labor markets, and so on. They view with distaste the business offerings and industry structures that have formed in response to consumers' purchasing decisions. They want to take that control away from buyers, and replace it with their own preferences. In essence, the anti-monopoly movement seeks to impose its own preferred vision for American enterprise. This fact explains much of today's controversy. Calls for an antitrust revolution do not reflect a judgment that the agencies have misapplied

---

[1] *See* Chapter 8.

economics at the margin. They would hold with equal passion even if the DOJ and FTC never erred at all.

For reasons explained throughout this book, there is every reason to reject the neo-Brandeisian position. Simply put, the competitive-effects approach is orders of magnitude better. It does not follow, however, that today's antitrust policies are optimally calibrated. Far from it – there is room to improve, and that is the object of this Part III.

The single most important reform is to think about error differently. Uncertainty about a market's long-term trajectory or efficiencies should not deter the agencies from bringing cases founded on a serious loss of competition. The government should agonize about closing a borderline investigation as much as some conservative policymakers fret that they might inadvertently bring an unmeritorious one. The agencies should strive to reach the correct answer in every case, of course, and remain committed a rigorous analysis of effects. But they (and the courts) should abandon an uncritical overweighting of false positives across the universe of decisions. Whether Type I or Type II errors ought to dominate turns on a nuanced assessment of the matter at hand. As a general matter, though, errors matter in both directions.

This book's substantive recommendations for reform conclude with this chapter, which explores antitrust doctrine that most warrants revision.[2] Many such changes will not take form overnight, but they represent fruitful areas for long-term development in the law.

The issue most in need of revision is market definition. That such a foundational tenet of the law needs adjustment is itself telling. The agencies, courts, and academics have spilled no lack of ink on the topic. Ironically, the problem is partially a function of the DOJ and FTC's pursuit of economic rigor. The result has been a tendency to define markets too narrowly. The courts, for their part, have too often gone the opposite direction. The Supreme Court's controlling law on market definition is too broad. Neither of these phenomena would be troublesome except for related doctrine that can make or break an antitrust case. The courts recognize market-share cutoffs that often make defining a market to be dispositive. The law's refusal to credit cross-market effects is similarly a function of incomplete market definition. Neither feature of the law is properly calibrated. Only now are commentators beginning to appreciate the dangers of narrow market delineation by the agencies.[3] Plaintiffs have long sought to constrict the scope of the market in order to get the benefit of big shares. One unintended consequence may be to place

---

[2] Chapter 8 progressed the reform discussion by urging enforcers to come clean about antitrust's normative framework, and to move beyond the useful, but inaccurate, consumer-welfare standard.
[3] See, e.g., Christine S. Wilson, *The Unintended Consequences of Narrower Product Markets and the Overly Leveraged Nature of Philadelphia National Bank*, Address at the Antitrust Enforcement Symposium, University of Oxford, June 30, 2019.

important competitive alternatives in separate markets, inoculating their combination from antitrust challenge.

Other systematic issues are worth tackling. *Noerr-Pennington* remains dangerously expansive. Born of the First Amendment, it immunizes conduct that petitions the government for redress. The doctrine, however, has become unmoored from its constitutional foundation. Some lower courts have misconstrued the immunity. In particular, certain decisions inoculate commercial behavior that harms competition simply because market impact occurs through threatened or filed lawsuits. This form of reverse immunization perversely absolves marketplace actions that directly affect competitive constraints, and have nothing to do with bona fide petitioning of the government.

Next, the agencies should redouble their efforts to scrutinize private and quasi-public regulatory bodies that issue licenses or competitively significant certifications. Many of the most significant harms to competition flow from governmental action. Market forces cannot erode such restraints, and federalism prevents the agencies from intervening where states act as sovereigns. Nevertheless, the FTC and DOJ have done tremendous work investigating quasi-state action that does not meet the requirements for immunity. They should aggressively continue those efforts, and do everything within their power to lobby all levels of governments about the virtues of competition-enhancing laws and policies.

Separately, the law on compulsory dealing requires incremental refinement, as does the law on predatory pricing.[4] The Supreme Court should also revisit its holdings on implied regulatory preemption.[5] Realistically, of course, there is little that the agencies can do in the short term to ameliorate these holdings. But they can advocate for changes in the law, bring deserving cases on the liability frontier, and lay the evidentiary and theoretical framework for developing the law in that direction. Work by the agencies' economists features prominently in that final respect. Finally, the FTC can employ its Section 6(b) authority to study industries with an eye toward understanding anticompetitive conduct that would evade liability on today's law. Over time, the law tends to respond to evidence-based competition policy of this sort, as the FTC's modern hospital-merger-review program born out of a Section 6(b) study shows.

9.2 MARKET DEFINITION

The relevant market stands among antitrust's foundational concepts. Done properly, it facilitates structural analysis in the form of concentration statistics. Useful as a screen, it points to the absence or presence of significant market power and sheds light on one factor bearing on the likelihood of coordinated effects. In terms

---

[4] Chapter 6, §§ 6.1.1.4, 6.1.1.6.
[5] *Id.* at § 1.3.

of its economic function, it can serve to illuminate the price elasticity of demand facing the relevant firm (at the competitive price point in a monopolization case, and at prevailing prices in a horizontal merger investigation).

Market definition features in almost every case not advancing a per se claim.[6] No merger challenge may proceed in its absence.[7] Every action under Section 2 requires proof of the relevant market.[8] Indeed, even with direct evidence of competitive effects, a plaintiff must establish such a market in challenging a vertical restraint.[9] Being dispositive, the relevant market obviously matters. Accuracy unleashes the power of insight. Blunders point decision-makers in the wrong direction.

As one of antitrust's core policy levers, market definition risks upsetting competition enforcement if misapprehended. Unfortunately, that problem has come to pass. Difficulties inherent in the market-definition exercise – and attendant upon its interpretation – are distorting otherwise sound policy.

Two elements of the market-definition exercise are crucial. Absent their satisfaction, the inquiry loses illuminative force. First, the market must be defined with precision. Second, to the extent that the law ascribes significance to various market shares, then those thresholds must have a sound basis in economics. Each task brings with it imposing difficulties. Delineating the scope of effective competition is as much art as science, and yet carries with it the possibility of error and misdirection. Assigning presumptions and rules to market shares is harder still. While calculating the outer bounds of a market draws on data, no such empirical anchor underlies the ascription of doctrinal value to a structural number. It is on the latter facet of market definition where antitrust has gone most seriously awry.

9.2.1 Defining the Market: A Task in Pursuit of a Purpose

Several factors conspire against market definition. Its roots lie in structuralism. As the predicate underlying any concentration measure – be it HHI, C4, C8, n-1, market shares, or otherwise – the relevant market must capture, but not exceed, the universe of material competitive constraints. Delicate and vulnerable to miscalibration, the process yields a precarious basis for analysis. Worse, the exercise routinely fails on its own terms. A direct causal relationship between market concentration and static effects exists only under quantity-based Cournot competition involving the sale of homogenous products between sellers with identical costs.[10] Those characteristics seldom, if ever, materialize. This is not to deny

---

[6] Within the universe of non-per se claims, the exception is limited to cases in which a plaintiff challenges a horizontal restraint and demonstrates evidence of actual adverse effects on competition. In those circumstances, the need to define the market with precision is relaxed. See Fed. Trade Comm'n v. Indiana Fed. of Dentists, 476 U.S. 447 (1986).
[7] See, e.g., Brown Shoe Co. v. United States, 370 U.S. 294, 335 (1962); 15 U.S.C. § 18.
[8] See, e.g., United States v. Grinnell Corp., 384 U.S. 563, 570 (1966); 15 U.S.C. § 2.
[9] Ohio v. Am. Express, 138 S. Ct. 2274, 2285 n.7 (2017).
[10] See Chapter 3 supra.

observed correlations between price and concentration. Nor is it to doubt that computed shares of a well-defined market are an important data point for antitrust analysis. Rather, anticompetitive effects lies not in HHI or market share deltas, but in something else. That something else is diversion ratios and margins, as to which concentration ratios (built around market definition) are at best rough proxies.

Few markets display the product homogeneity that underlies the classic Cournot model. Rather, most industries witness heavy product differentiation as sellers vie for niche positions and build brand loyalty in pursuit of sustainable market power. It is here, in the most common of situations, that the exercise of defining the market flounders. Structuralism is rooted in the supposition that competitors differ only by size. The most rudimentary concentration ratio, Cn, jettisons even that detail. And the best available concentration index, HHI, ignores the proximity of offerings between sellers and the strength of customer preferences. Yet, those qualities determine effects.

When analyzing heterogeneous goods, the agencies face a predicament. Consistent with the foundational case law, they could define the market to include all competing products. Doing so, however, produces misleading concentration measures that assign equal weight to every seller, potentially as adjusted for size. Consumers may see various substitutes, however, as close or distant alternatives – a crucial distinction that imputed concentration ratios and market shares would overlook. The alternative confines the market to only those products that buyers see as close alternatives. This is the more economically rigorous approach, and the one that finds favor today at the agencies. Products are in if buyers would switch to them in order to defeat a small price increase, and otherwise out. Yet, today's preferred approach is intellectual dishonest. Enforcers present thinly populated markets that exclude substitutable products that clearly compete with in-market goods.

For that reason, market definition has grown in tension with the modern focus on competitive effects. Devised in a less sophisticated era, and sustained by an archaic doctrinal framework, the inquiry threatens to hinder effective policy. The problem is the law continues to attach real – often dispositive – significance to market shares that flow from the definitional process. That doctrine creates an alluring prize for the determined plaintiff, who has every incentive artificially to narrow (or even to gerrymander) the market in order to achieve share thresholds. Even the most upstanding plaintiff has incentives to hit targets. The DOJ and FTC worry about losing high-profile litigation matters, and seldom allege market definitions in horizontal merger challenges that do not yield a market share over 30 percent for the post-merger firm. That threshold, of course, represents the structural presumption of anticompetitive effects set by *Philadelphia National Bank*.[11] At best, the marker presents an unwelcome incentive for narrow market segmentation.

---

[11] United States v. Phila. Nat'l Bank, 374 U.S. 321, 364 (1963).

At the level of federal enforcement, however, the trend toward confined markets is principally a function of effects. The agencies define the outer bounds of the relevant market as the narrowest set of substitutes over which a hypothetical monopolist could profitably increase price by 5–10 percent. In industries characterized by differentiated products, shockingly constricted market definitions result. This approach can extinguish the difference between delineating the scope of competition and the ultimate question on the merits. In other words, competitive effects analysis and market definition can become one and the same. This approach is not strictly wrong. In fact, it speaks to the superfluous nature of the relevant market, which is a remnant of structuralism and ought to play a subservient role. Doctrine, as we shall see, has yet to catch up.

The exercise can thus assume a circular quality in which a merger expected to have harmful effects must arise in a narrow market in which the parties have a large share. In such circumstances, the agencies may dismiss evidence of a broader market. Doing so begs the question unless effects are sufficiently clear as to make the definitional exercise redundant. In that case, the agencies may reject a broad market as inconsistent with expected price effects. The distinction between the market's scope and effects dissolves completely if a market comprised of the two merging parties alone would support a SSNIP.

Of course, the agencies have to define a market. They thus labor with a redundant definitional exercise. In a market for differentiated goods, two or few products in a much larger competitive space may support a SSNIP if buyers see the candidate goods as relatively close alternatives. Razor-thin markets thus proliferate. Markets defined more organically – that is, by the existence of competitive pressure driven by reasonable interchangeability – tend to encompass a broader product set more in line with business expectations. The modern approach, however, yields slender markets distinguished from the larger competitive space by idiosyncratic product features. To the cynical eye, the defined market may appear to be a charade.

Bizarre "relevant markets" thus emerge, some flirting the line with self-parody. Consider the following examples as alleged by the FTC:

- "Superpremium ice cream" occupies a separate relevant product market than "premium or economy ice creams."[12]
- Branded canola and vegetable oils lie in a separate relevant market from private label canola and vegetable oils.[13]
- "Shelf-stable pickles are not in the same market as ... refrigerated pickles[.]"[14]
- A market for "premium natural and organic supermarkets" does not include "conventional supermarkets."[15]

---

[12] *In re* Nestlé Holdings, Inc., FTC Dkt. No. C-4082, Compl. ¶ 11 (June 25, 2003).
[13] *In re* J.M. Smucker Co., FTC Dkt. No. 9381, Compl. ¶ 31 (Mar. 5, 2018).
[14] Fed. Trade Comm'n v. Hicks, Muse, Tate & Furst Equity Fund V, L.P., Compl. ¶¶ 13, 15 (D.D.C. Oct. 23, 2002).
[15] Fed. Trade Comm'n v. Whole Foods, Compl. ¶ 35; *see also* Fed. Trade Comm'n v. Whole Foods Market, 548 F.3d 1028 (D.C. Cir. 2008).

- "Branded seasoned salt products" form a relevant market that excludes "private or store label" salt products.[16]
- Loose leaf tobacco and moist snuff are in different markets.[17]

These counterintuitive markets reflect price-demand relationships, not functional interchangeability. Even perfect substitutes can lie in different markets. The agencies and some courts have concluded, for example, that generics can occupy a separate relevant market than a bioequivalent branded drug.[18] From the perspective of functional interchangeability, of course, this makes no sense. In performing a SSNIP test or evaluating cross-price demand elasticities, however, one may find indicia of a weak competitive constraint. For example, a hypothetical monopolist of generic drugs that are on market may find it possible to raise price by 10 percent without suffering a critical loss of sales to the pioneer drug. Oddly narrow market definitions follow.

Despite the underlying economic logic, such granular markets are facially unappealing. As adjectives pile up in order to exclude interchangeable goods, resulting markets look increasingly suspect. Whether they are problematic for antitrust policy, of course, is a distinct question. In fact, they are. As the next section explains, artificially circumscribed markets threaten to inhibit the sound administration of competition law.

9.2.2 Narrow Markets Create Real Problems

The trend toward narrow markets has gone too far. This is not a question of optics, though inferences of gerrymandering do antitrust few favors. Rather, bringing cases around hyper-focused relevant markets introduces unnecessary dangers.

First, a sparsely populated market helps the government (or other plaintiff) only if the court accepts it. But the agencies sometimes flounder at this first hurdle, and are more likely to do so if they venture beyond what the evidence or common sense supports. Such foot faults may allow some harmful consolidations to pass – ones that would have succumbed to a more robust case on the merits. Of course, occasionally the agencies bring unmeritorious cases – for example, challenging horizontal mergers in which harmful effects are unlikely. And, in some such cases, they may mask weakness behind a structural case built on an artificial market definition. Should those cases fall at the first hurdle, then that is the right outcome. This will not always or generally be the case, however. Getting greedy on market definition may sabotage an otherwise deserving case.

An unfortunate dynamic facilitates narrow market definition – namely, the proliferation of consent orders. The agencies frequently define markets, but are seldom put to their proof. Most contested mergers are resolved through voluntary

---

[16] *In re* McCormick & Co., Inc., FTC Dkt. No. C-4225, Compl. ¶ 8 (July 29, 2008).
[17] Fed. Trade Comm'n v. Swedish Match, 131 F. Supp. 2d 151 (D.D.C. Dec. 14, 2000).
[18] *See, e.g.*, Geneva Pharms. Tech. v. Barr Labs., 386 F.3d 485, 497 (2d Cir. 2004).

divestitures. Companies rarely have the appetite to delay their transactions in order to litigate with the DOJ or FTC. For this reason, the government can allege the existence of dubious markets of the kind explored above – ones that exclude interchangeable, competitive products that differ only by branding, perceived quality, customer preference, price differences, or (most questionable of all) customer type. This creates a soft precedent, from which the agencies struggle to back away in later investigations. Such precedent, however, does not flow from contested proceedings presided over by an independent decision-maker and illuminated by cross-examination.

Past consents thus lend credence to narrow markets. They make it easy for staff to justify continuation of the status quo, but all the harder to recommend broader market definitions in tension with prior agency-blessed positions. A dangerous momentum ensues. It can lead the DOJ or FTC to allege markets that may not survive judicial scrutiny. This is no academic possibility. The government has been burned in the past. Certain of those failures surely allowed harmful consolidations to pass. It would be better if the agencies brought challenges built on more realistic groupings of substitutes, and then focused their effects case on proximity of competition between the merging parties (the kind of analysis that they now partially shoehorn into the market definition inquiry).

The following discussion ventures no view about the merits of each underlying case. With that important qualification, matters in which the FTC or DOJ tripped up on the relevant market reinforce the point.

First, the government has lost cases because it alleged too narrow a market. It is hard not to begin with the classic example.

In 2004, the DOJ sued to block Oracle's acquisition of PeopleSoft.[19] The space at issue was enterprise resource planning (ERP) software. The government zeroed in, however, on a narrow subset of such software. It charged a loss of competition in HR and financial management ERP software products, further limited to those that "meet the needs of large and complex enterprises with 'high functional needs.'"[20] In the market so limited, it saw a three-to-two transaction. In a sophisticated opinion, Judge Vaughan Walker rejected the government's alleged market. He reasoned that customer preference is not the issue, but rather what buyers "could do in the event of an anticompetitive price increase by a post-merger Oracle."[21] The government's case fell due to an overly narrow market definition.

Not much has changed. In 2020, the DOJ lost its challenge to Sabre's $360 million acquisition of Farelogix in the travel technology space.[22] Airlines sell roughly half of

---

[19] United States v. Oracle Corp., 331 F. Supp. 2d 1098 (N.D. Cal. 2004). Latham & Watkins LLP represented Oracle in the case.
[20] *Id.* at 1102.
[21] *Id.* at 1131.
[22] United States v. Sabre Corp., 452 F. Supp. 3d 97 (D. Del. 2020), *vacated*, Trade Reg. Rep. ¶ 81,294 (3d Cir. July 20, 2020) (but clarifying that "this Order should not be construed as detracting from the persuasive force of the District Court's decision").

their US tickets on their own proprietary websites.[23] Much of their revenue, however, flows through indirect channels. Such sales occur overwhelmingly via global distribution systems (GDSs) – transaction platforms that connect airlines, hotels, car rentals, and the like for a booking fee.[24] Sabre is the largest GDS provider. Farelogix came into partial competition with GDS by offering its Open Connect product, a new distribution capability (NDC) that links technology systems to an airline's passenger services system. Farelogix's NDC led to partial disintermediation, helping airlines shift functionalities away from GDSs.

The Antitrust Division sued, portraying Farelogix as a disruptive innovator that had elicited pro-customer competitive responses by Sabre.[25] The DOJ pointed to incriminating documentary admissions about the deal. Rather than allege a market in which Sabre and Farelogix directly competed, however, the government averred two separate downstream markets into which the parties were input providers. Specifically, it identified markets for booking services for airline tickets sold through (1) traditional bricks and mortar travel agencies and (2) online ones like Travelocity and Expedia.[26]

The district court saw those markets as doctored. "'No can expect to gerrymander its way to an antitrust victory without due regard for market realities.'"[27] Courts seldom venture such views about public antitrust cases. The market segmentations championed by the government, however, struck the district judge as far too narrow. In selling its GDS services, Sabre faced competition from airlines that could (and often did) choose to go direct, in part or whole.[28] The DOJ's market excluded the direct channel, and thus omitted a key competitive constraint. More fundamentally, Sabre did not itself sell "booking services" in the averred market. Sabre's GDS services were far broader.[29] In the court's view, "the correct interpretation of the record is that the subset of Sabre services DOJ labels 'booking services' are not a separate product but, instead, have 'no independent economic significance.'"[30]

Again, this discussion offers no judgment on the underlying merits of these cases. Such examples, however, speak to a market-definition exercise that carries unwarranted independent significance. To be sure, it is a legal requirement. But there is something unsettling about merger challenges that turn on whether the evidence bears out the particulars of the alleged market. The inquiry exhibits all the signs of form over function. If a transaction eliminates a unique competitive constraint, then it warrants prohibition under Section 7. The DOJ and FTC cannot avoid defining

---

[23] *Id.* at 23.
[24] *Id.* at 5–6.
[25] United States v. Sabre Corp., Compl., Dkt. 1, No. 19-cv-1548 (D. Del. Aug. 20, 2019).
[26] *Id.* at ¶¶ 44–46.
[27] *Sabre*, 452 F. Supp. 3d at 139-40 (quoting It's My Party, Inc. v. Live Nation, Inc., 811 F.3d 676, 683 (4th Cir. 2016)).
[28] *Id.* at 125–26.
[29] *Id.* at 140.
[30] *Id.*

the relevant market. They can advance markets, however, that are true to the universe of close substitutes and lack indicia of manipulation.

Second, to such examples, we should add close calls that ultimately broke for the government, but that may not have. Such incidents speak to the danger associated with advancing unnecessarily narrow relevant markets.

For example, the FTC lost two hospital merger challenges in the past five years at the trial court level – both times because the district judges found the alleged geographic markets to be implausibly localized.[31] Each market excluded hospitals in the same city or locale, reflecting application of the SSNIP test. In each case, more economically sophisticated panels at the US Courts of Appeals reversed.[32] Similarly, in the *Whole Foods* example cited above, the district court rejected a market limited to organic supermarkets, only for the DC Circuit to reverse it.[33] This tendency, however, speaks to the worrisome reality that (i) market definition has become infused with competitive effects, yielding counterintuitive relevant markets that (ii) are apt to lead generalist judges astray. Over time, some meritorious merger challenges will fail as a result.

A recent case further illustrates the point. In 2020, the DOJ brought its first merger challenge to resolution through arbitration – an alternative dispute mechanism limited in that instance to a single issue, market definition.[34] The transaction between Novelis and Aleris combined two manufacturers of aluminum used in car manufacturing. Vehicle makers use steel and aluminum in automotive body sheet (ABS), switching their proportions of each based on design choices that consider weight and cost. The two metals, of course, are not homogenous. Steel is cheaper, while aluminum is lighter. The dispositive question presented for arbitration was whether aluminum ABS sold to automakers in North America represented a relevant market. The government based its market definition on a SSNIP test. The parties argued that the alleged market excluded interchangeable products, observing that car makers routinely (indeed invariably) substituted between the two in the regular course.

The government won, but the case is instructive. Step back from the idiosyncrasies of market definition. The real antitrust question had little to do with whether aluminum and steel are substitutes for car manufacturers. They plainly are. It concerned unilateral effects. The merger arose between two sellers of comparable goods in a differentiated products market. The analysis should have focused on diversion ratios and margins (the determinants of static price effects), customers' ability to discipline attempted exercises of market power, likely seller reactions, and

---

[31] Fed. Trade Comm'n v. Advocate Health Care Network, 841 F.3d 460 (7th Cir. 2016); Fed. Trade Comm'n v. Penn State Hershey Med. Ctr., 858 F.3d 327 (3d Cir. 2016).
[32] Id.
[33] Fed. Trade Comm'n v. Whole Foods Mkt., 548 F.3d 1028 (D.C. Cir. 2008).
[34] United States v. Novelis, Inc., No. 1:19-cv-2033, Dkt. 1, Compl. (N.D. Ohio, Sept. 4, 2019). Latham & Watkins LLP represented Novelis in that matter, though the author did not file an appearance in the case.

likely efficiencies. To resolve the matter through a market-definition inquiry was to force the effects question into an ill-fitting structuralist inquiry. Was it a Pyrrhic victory?

The case for going broader in market definition centers on substitutability. Various brands of ice cream are substitutes, even if some carry a price premium, are more exclusive, or have superior flavor. Private label and branded consumer goods are near-carbon copies of each other. Trademarks and patents may help their protected goods command a price premium, but that is the stuff of product differentiation – rarely market separation. *Novelis/Aleris* merely continues an unfortunate theme.

Third, the move toward a more economically rigorous conception of market definition can also cause problems by combining goods that are not substitutes on the demand side, but may be substitutes on the supply side. There, as elsewhere, this book would rather see the agencies tackle effects outside of the market definition inquiry. Problems have recently emerged from aggregating products that have separate uses and between which buyers cannot switch.

That was the FTC's shortcoming in *Evonik/PeroxyChem* in 2019.[35] There, the Commission lumped together all forms of non-electronics hydrogen peroxide. It did so, even though uses depended heavily on distinct customer needs (not preferences). The Commission's rationale was that supply-side "swinging" capabilities allowed producers quickly to change from making one kind hydrogen peroxide to another.[36] Such an ability, however, should go to competitive effects rather than market definition.

The federal judge in *Evonik* saw the product-type aggregation as "an important misstep" in the FTC's market definition.[37] That result underscores the problem addressed in this section. The district court rejected otherwise-solid evidence of unilateral effects because the FTC failed to substantiate the claimed relevant market.[38] The FTC's expert did not base his economic model on the relevant market, which makes sense because GUPPIs and merger simulation are not a function of market definition. The court's ruling highlights the danger of market definition, which should illuminate the competitive analysis, not become a dogmatic threshold obstacle to a sound case. Form over substance is not a defining characteristic of sound antitrust policy.

Finally, market definition remains precarious, of course, even when the proffered market is facially plausible. In *Lundbeck*, the FTC tried to undo the company's acquisition of two drugs that treated the same heart condition for prematurely born babies.[39] It defined the product market as "the sale of drugs approved by the FDA to

---

[35] Fed. Trade Comm'n v. Rag-Stiftung, 436 F. Supp. 3d 278 (D.D.C. 2020).
[36] *Id.*
[37] *Id.* at 287.
[38] *Id.* at 319.
[39] Fed. Trade Comm'n v. Lundbeck, Inc., 650 F.3d 1236 (8th Cir. 2011). Latham & Watkins LLP represented Ovation/Lundbeck, for which the author appeared in the case.

treat PDA" – one in which only two drugs existed and both belonged to the defendant.[40] Suing after a large, post-acquisition price increase, the FTC sought disgorgement in a case that the bar widely expected the Commission to win.

The company prevailed, however, by showing the absence of cross-price demand elasticity between the products. The Eleventh Circuit affirmed, triggering an explosive reaction by Commissioner Rosch, among others.[41] In his view, the absence of pricing pressure between the two drugs should not have hindered their combination in a relevant market. Perhaps, but, as discussed, the point of the exercise is to illuminate the sphere of competition. If there is no competition between two goods – that is, no rivalrous pressure exerted by one product on another – then it makes little sense to include them in the same market. Even if one did, the requisite loss of competition required to sustain a horizontal antitrust violation would be absent. One may need to consider nonprice dimensions of competition, too, of course, before reaching this conclusion. But the absence of competitive pressure should be dispositive.

Ultimately, *Lundbeck* reinforces the importance of sound market definition. It is reasonable – indeed, generally correct – to collect functional substitutes in a market. As argued below, it would serve competition policy well to adopt a more holistic approach to market definition than one laser-focused on the hypothetical-monopolist test. The government stumbled in *Lundbeck*, however, even without insisting on an implausibly narrow market. This presages the dangers associated with the modern approach, as the agencies routinely pursue markets so narrow as to appear manufactured. The solution is to broaden the exercise, while reducing the doctrinal weight given to market shares. As *Lundbeck* teaches, however, going broader only makes sense if one includes products that competitively constrain the sale of other goods in the candidate market. Otherwise, the chosen market isn't capturing effective competition.

9.2.3 A Better Way: Relax Market Segmentation Based on Product Differentiation, But Moderate Its Legal Implications

The preceding critique is not an indictment of the government's enforcement efforts. Some economists would prefer to dispense with market definition. The agencies, however, face a legal obligation. And while some staff may sympathize in the abstract with defining broader markets and proving effects through proximity of competition, in practice the courts stand on market share thresholds. One could hardly expect the government to doom meritorious cases by alleging expansive markets that encompass all substitutes, no matter how distant, and thus surrender low market shares that may be dispositive. Over time, the goal should be to push

---

[40] Fed. Trade Comm'n v. Ovation Pharma., Civ. No. 08–6379, Compl., ¶¶ 26, 27 (D. Minn. Dec. 16, 2008).
[41] Statement of Commissioner J. Thomas Rosch, Fed. Trade Comm'n v. Lundbeck, Inc., FTC File No. 081-0156, Jan. 20, 2012.

evolution in the law itself, relaxing the implications of various market share thresholds. In the near term, the agencies ought to move incrementally away from hyperfocused market definitions. Product heterogeneity is not, in itself, a basis for market division. In tandem, the government should work to move the courts away from dogmatic positions on shares and HHIs.

This effort is overdue. Market definition is a *structural* inquiry. But its function is to help illuminate *effects*. This creates a painful matching exercise. If one defines structural parameters through an effects lens, then market definition loses independent significance. But ignore the relative competitive pressure exerted by candidate substitute products, and then one risks distorting the implications that flow from market shares and concentration ratios. The latter shortcoming flows from problems associated with structuralism itself.[42]

One answer is to jettison the relevant market, and commit purely to effects.[43] The relevant market, however, is worth preserving. Predicting effects is a time-consuming, data-driven, and expensive undertaking. Although structural statistics are imperfect proxies for likely effects, they remain proxies nonetheless. Businesses, the antitrust counsel who advise them, and the agencies tasked with making threshold determinations need workable means for drawing directional insights about competition. Structuralism fits the bill.

Market definitions tied principally to product characteristics and functional interchangeability do not require econometrics. They are intuitive, and flow from understanding how the industry works. Collecting substitutes into a market, and excluding products with a distant or nonexistent competitive relationship, is holistic. It also resists charges of gerrymandering. And it is true to founding doctrinal principles.[44] That process is not scientific, but nor is structuralism generally. Precision lies in effects. Concentration ratios provide a first pass. When based on a properly calibrated market, they provide decent means for inferring whether serious antitrust issues are probable, a close call, or tenuous. Further economic analysis will yield the ultimate answer.

For this to work, we need a relevant market inquiry that is tailored to its structural role, but carries reduced doctrinal significance. The result would be a more humble undertaking. Rather than a dispositive conclusion, the relevant market would serve merely a framing role – a contextual snapshot in which one should construe the restraint or merger at issue, but one that is deeply subservient to evidence of competitive effects. Such a reality would mark a radical deviation from litigated cases today.[45] Most importantly, the law would have to becomes less rigid in

---

[42] See Chapter 3.
[43] Accord Louis Kaplow, Why (Ever) Define Markets?, 124 HARV. L. REV. 437 (2010). But cf. Gregory J. Werden, Why (Ever) Define Markets? An Answer to Professor Kaplow, 78 ANTITRUST L.J. 729 (2012).
[44] See United States v. E. I. du Pont de Nemours & Co., 353 U.S. 586, 649 (1957) (quoting Std. Oil Co. of Cal. v. United States, 337 U.S. 293, 299 n.5 (1949)).
[45] The change would be less severe at the agencies, which have all but disclaimed a meaningful gap between the determination of the relevant market and competitive effects. U.S. Dep't of Justice & Fed. Trade Comm'n, Horizontal Merger Guidelines § 4 (2010).

attaching significance to various market shares. Examples include rules that market shares above 70 percent constitute prima facie evidence of monopoly power, attempted monopolization claims require at least 50 percent market share, and liability in rule of reason cases under Section 1 often necessitates markets shares over 30 percent.[46] Shares are merely a function of the outer bounds of the relevant market determination – a binary "in or out" inquiry between imperfect substitutes. Viewed in that light, humility is the order of the day.

A less rigid inquiry would result. Courts would have to be open to finding or rejecting liability in circumstances where imputed shares would seem to point in the other direction. A merger between two firms with low shares of a broadly defined market for differentiated products, for example, may harm competition if customers (i) significantly prefer their products over other, more distant offerings and (ii) lack effective mechanisms for defeating an attempted exercise of market power. And the converse may be true. A post-merger firm with a large share of the market may accelerate innovation or exert downward pressure on price.

This is not the stuff of overnight fixes. But the relevant market's role today – hybrid and tortured – is not sustainable. The agencies ask it to be a vessel of economic analysis, a purpose for which it is ill-suited. The tension inherent in market definition has come to light in ways that hurt the agencies' enforcement mission. The government has lost some cases and almost lost some others for want of a broader relevant market.

The relevant market's role today also highlights the division between how the agencies employ twenty-first century economic analysis internally and litigate cases using mid-twentieth century legal principles publicly. This is far from optimal. To take but one example, agency staff have never in the modern era justified a merger challenge in court simply because they calculate a post-merger share exceeding 30 percent of the market and thus triggering the *Philadelphia National Bank* presumption. And yet that presumption is invariably the first thing that the agencies cling to when they go to court. Antitrust's economic evolution remains incomplete.

The agencies can only do so much, but they can start improving things immediately. In the short term, it means shying away from hyper-segmented product markets of the kind that strict SSNIP tests might make tempting. Lengthy product market definitions ought to invite suspicion. Efforts to break relevant product markets apart by branded and private label goods, patented and nonpatented products, separate buyer characteristics, and the like are emblematic of the problem. Going forward, the

---

[46] See, e.g., United States v. Dentsply Int'l, 399 F.3d 181, 187 (3d Cir. 2005) (a market share hovering between 75 to 80 percent is "more than adequate to establish a prima facie case of power"); M & M Med. Supplies & Serv., Inc. v. Pleasant Valley Hosp., Inc., 981 F.2d 160, 168 (4th Cir. 1992) (market shares over 50 percent usually required for an attempted monopolization claim); Jefferson Parish Hosp. Dist. No. 2 v. Hyde, 466 U.S. 2, 26 (1983) (30 percent market share was insufficient to support finding of market power for purposes of product tying claim under Section 1).

agencies ought to resist them. Doing so will require building up stronger effects cases and having the confidence to stand behind them. They are entirely up to the task should they choose to embrace it.

The Tenth Circuit may have put it best after wrestling with the problem that "[t]here is no subject in antitrust law more confusing than market definition." It concluded simply that, by "defining the relevant market, ... we identify the firms that compete with each other." *SCFC ILC, Inc. v. Visa USA, Inc.*, 36 F.3d 958, 966 (10th Cir. 1994). Imprecise as it may be, that functional inquiry ought to dominate over SSNIP tests that can produce implausibly narrow markets in differentiated products markets.

9.3 NOERR-PENNINGTON: RECONCILING COMPETITION WITH THE FIRST AMENDMENT

Antitrust fosters competitive markets. Reform-minded critiques ask whether, in light of that goal, existing policies are miscalibrated. As this book makes clear, that inquiry is hazy. Optimization is a phantom concept because important economic relationships remain obscure. The connection between market structure and effects, to draw on one foundational example, is achingly complex. That difficulty alone infects applied policy at every turn. As discussed in the past several pages, market definition is a victim of that very ambiguity. It plays a tortured role as a result. It feeds structural analysis and yet has become a vehicle for competitive effects, all the while cabined by outdated case law.

Difficult as the evaluative process may be, clear policy shortcomings occasionally emerge. The paradigmatic example arises when the government ousts antitrust. In its absence, competitive pressure evaporates. Past experiences with direct industry regulation tell a sorry tale. Governmental price, access, and quality controls are no substitute for market pressures. But, imperfect as they may be, they at least try to replicate competitive forces. At times, however, the government simply exempts portions of the economy from antitrust and foregoes any effort to recreate competitive outcomes.

Chapter 6 criticized the Supreme Court's implied regulatory immunity holdings despite Congressional savings clauses, and recommended against expanding labor immunities beyond their existing scope. Historical oddities, including baseball's antitrust exemption, are hard to justify. And overexpansion of state action immunity warrants special pushback on account of local state-affiliated boards' and others quasi-state actors' vulnerability to regulatory capture.[47] If you believe in competition, then you should instinctively oppose steps to crowd out – or outright eject – antitrust law.

[47] The FTC has taken commendable steps in this regard. *See* N. Carolina State Bd. Dental Exam'rs v. Fed. Trade Comm'n, 574 U.S. 494 (2015); Fed. Trade Comm'n v. Phoebe Putney Health Sys., 568 U.S. 216 (2013).

This chapter wraps up by addressing an important limit on antitrust's reach. Some cabining is inevitable, of course. In the case of the state action doctrine, for example, federalism compels it. The *Noerr-Pennington* doctrine is similar. The First Amendment's Petitioning Clause guarantees one's right to request that the government take desired action. And so antitrust obliges. A firm cannot violate the Sherman Act by asking the state to quash competition on its behalf.

While it is difficult to criticize the constitutional foundation of a petitioning-based immunity, as far all exemptions, we should endeavor to preserve antitrust's reach to the greatest extent possible. The impetus carries special weight in this context because lobbying carries special competitive dangers. Competition is a painful and unwelcome reality for the businesses subject to it. They have every reason to seek shelter. The antitrust laws prevent them from doing so through private agreement – indeed, hardcore cartels lead to jail time – exclusionary practices, or anticompetitive mergers. But concerted restraints only go so far. Conspirators have incentives to cheat, agreements only bind those privy to them, supranormal returns attract entry, and even accords to limit rivalry cannot capture every dimension of competition (e.g., a price fix incentivizes the firms to chase extra sales through higher quality). The safest harbor from competition lies in the state. The government can extinguish competition altogether because market forces cannot overcome the force of law. We see this phenomenon play out time and again.

The government's capacity to arrest competition is severe. Public choice theory explains that the state is vulnerable to regulatory capture.[48] What this boils down to is that petitioning – the act of lobbying the executive, legislative, or (less obviously) judicial branches – for relief from rivalry stands among the most harmful forms of conduct from a competition perspective. Yet, on account of the First Amendment, it is largely outside of antitrust's capacity to address. But largely is not entirely.

This section addresses the *Noerr-Pennington* doctrine, a judicial construct that immunizes nonsham petitioning from antitrust liability.[49] It stands among the most troubling features of contemporary doctrine because it has grown overbroad. Having separated from its constitutional mooring, it now immunizes conduct that has an attenuated relationship to First Amendment principles. Confused and confusing, the doctrine has led some courts to immunize larger courses of anticompetitive conduct if the instrument of harm involves threatening or filing lawsuits. The result has been an unjustified restriction of the Sherman Act's ambit. If not addressed, it threatens to inflict real harm on the antitrust mission, particularly as it relates to intellectual property.

---

[48] *See, e.g.*, R. DOUGLAS ARNOLD, THE LOGIC OF CONGRESSIONAL ACTION (1992).
[49] Eastern R.R. Presidents Conf. v. Noerr Motor Freight, Inc., 365 U.S. 127, 129–31 (1961); United Mine Workers v. Pennington, 381 U.S. 657 (1965).

9.3.1 Noerr's *Cryptic Underpinnings*

The two seminal decisions that created the *Noerr-Pennington* doctrine concerned lobbying of the legislative and executive branches, accordingly.[50] The antitrust question seems less urgent in that setting, if only because the invocation of the political machinery of government is so clear. *Noerr* saw railroads hire a firm to launch an aggressive publicity campaign aimed at securing the passage of laws to inhibit truckers.[51] *Pennington* involved a concerted effort by a union and some companies to induce the Secretary of Labor to establish a higher minimum wage.[52] As the Court observed, "*Noerr* shields from the Sherman Act a concerted effort to influence public officials regardless of intent or purpose."[53]

Few would suggest exposing lobbying of the executive or legislative branches to liability under the Sherman Act. The analysis gets more complicated when it comes to litigation. Mistruths, omissions, prevarication, and worse surround the lawmaking and lobbying processes. The law cannot countenance such behavior in the judicial setting.[54] The rough and tumble of politics, to say nothing of the liberties with truth that fill legislative chambers, contrast with the fact-finding and adjudicative function of the judicial branch. Higher standards must prevail in the courts, which remain vulnerable to abuse and thus represent a potential weapon for those seeking to harm competition.

No one should doubt the constitutional influences that underlie *Noerr-Pennington*. Whether it is a creature of the First Amendment, however, is less clear. In *Noerr*, the Court did not expressly invoke the Petitioning Clause, though it appealed to activity that touches upon it.[55] Rather, it construed the Sherman Act as being directed only at private restraints and practices.[56] In doing so, it avoided grappling with "important constitutional questions."[57] The opinion thus categorically distinguished "the result of valid governmental action" from the effects of "private action."[58] In the former setting, the Court decided, "no violation of the Act can be made out."[59] In other words, "mere attempts to influence the passage or enforcement of laws" is outside the scope of prohibition.[60] At no point since has the Court equated the *Noerr-Pennington* doctrine with the First Amendment. To the

---

[50] *Id.*
[51] *Noerr*, 365 U.S. at 129–35.
[52] *Pennington*, 381 U.S. at 660.
[53] *Id.* at 670.
[54] *See, e.g.*, Calif. Motor Transp. Co. v. Trucking Unltd., 404 U.S. 508, 512–13 (1972); Grip-Pack, Inc. v. Illinois Tool Works, Inc., 694 F.2d 466, 470–73 (7th Cir. 1982).
[55] *Noerr*, 365 U.S. at 139 (referring both to the "right of the people to inform their representatives in government" and the "right to petition").
[56] *Id.* at 135–36.
[57] *Id.* at 138.
[58] *Id.* at 136.
[59] *Id.*
[60] *Id.* at 135.

contrary, it has inserted "breathing room" between the Petitioning Clause and possible liability.[61]

It would be unsustainable, of course, to make *Noerr* immunity coterminous with the First Amendment. In the first place, it is not clear that filing a lawsuit is itself a constitutionally protected act of petitioning. Certainly, availing of the litigation process implicates the Petitioning Clause differently than lobbying the legislative or executive branch.[62] Indeed, the Supreme Court has never held that suing in court constitutes petitioning for the purposes of the First Amendment.[63] But even if filing in court were clearly so protected, there are actions incidental to suing that are clearly not acts of petitioning, but that could not practically be exposed to antitrust. A good example involves demand letters that threaten litigation. By no stretch of the imagination does private correspondence from one company to another amount to petitioning the government. Yet to immunize litigation while exposing threats of suit to antitrust scrutiny would make a mockery of the law.

Mathematical identity between the Petitioning Clause and the *Noerr-Pennington* doctrine is neither accurate nor desirable. As explained below, however, the courts would do well to bring the two principles closer together.

9.3.2 Noerr *Exceeds Its Proper Scope in the IP Space*

The Supreme Court has not built *Noerr-Pennington* immunity expressly on the First Amendment. Rather, it began with the premise that the government can freely harm competition, meaning that the Sherman Act brings no liability when restraints of trade materialize through that channel alone.

That principle bears strong explanatory power. The railroads in *Noerr* did not themselves agree, or otherwise take action themselves, to increase prices, reduce output, or exclude rivals truckers. They asked the legislature to do it for them. So, too, in *Pennington* unions and partner companies asked members of the administration to adopt policies that would allegedly harm nonunion rivals. In both cases, any harm to competition was a function of state action. The matter is altogether different when competitors elect to limit rivalry between themselves. Such conduct represents private marketplace behavior, and produces anticompetitive effects independently of any state action. The fact that, in eliminating competition in this manner, conspirators genuinely aim to induce legislative or executive action is no defense. That was the holding of *Trial Lawyers Association*, where some DC lawyers agreed not to represent indigent defendant absent an increase in pay by the government.[64] The Court distinguished restraints of trade sought as "the intended *consequence* of

---

[61] BE & K Const. Co. v. NLRB, 536 U.S. 516, 531 (2002).
[62] Borough of Duryea, Pa. v. Guarnieri, 564 U.S. 379, 402–03 (2011) (Scalia, J., concurring in the judgment in part and dissenting in part).
[63] Id.
[64] Fed. Trade Comm'n v. Superior Court Trial Lawyers Ass'n, 493 U.S. 411 (1990).

public action" from the case in hand where "the boycott was the *means* by which respondents sought to obtain favorable legislation."[65]

9.3.2.1 *Noerr*'s Focus on Public Action Is Ill-Suited to IP

Vexing issues arise, however, when these principles encounter intellectual property. Standing alone, a patent commands no intrinsic value. It is a piece of paper. It finds meaning only because the law allows its owner to sue for unauthorized practice of the claimed invention. In other words, it is a ticket for accessing the judicial system. It follows that any market impact associated with the procurement, use, or assertion of a patent necessarily ties to the government. The state creates and enforces the property right. In acquiring a portfolio, negotiating a license, threatening to sue, or filing an infringement complaint or ITC proceeding, a patentee invokes the power of the state.

Blunt application of *Noerr*'s basic principle threatens to oust antitrust entirely from the patent space. If we start from the premise that no Sherman Act liability derives from harm to competition inflicted by the government (including the courts), then even stunning acts of anticompetitive conduct by patentees may be immune. Suppose that two competitors agree to sue their mutual rival in order to exclude it from the market. That is a paradigmatic case of collusion. Yet, their arrangement does not touch on product pricing, manufacturing levels, sales territories, or other aspects of direct commercial activity. It is an agreement to enforce presumptively valid intellectual property rights. The scheme could harm competition only if the courts found the asserted patents to be valid and infringed or if the accused infringer's expectation of that outcome led to market exit or reduced market presence. A literal reading of *Noerr*'s foundational case law surrenders a clear conclusion – the agreement is exempt. The collusion cannot harm competition independent of the judicial apparatus.

This is merely one example. There are others. Facing antitrust scrutiny for their acquisitions, firms may argue that creating a patent monopoly – whether by canvassing an industry's technology space or acquiring substitute technologies within a narrow technology market – is outside the scope of the Sherman Act. Why? Because no patent acquisition affects competition until it is enforced. Any market exclusion would flow from the threat or act of filing suit, and thus under *Noerr* would be "the result of valid governmental action" rather than the effects of "private action."[66] Or suppose that a member of a standard-setting organization fraudulently conceals its patent holdings and then steers the committee toward its proprietary technology in lieu of others. It later holds up its rival standard-implementers by suing to enjoin them from using a patented technology that the SSO would not have

---

[65] *Id.* at 424–25 (emphasis in original).
[66] *Noerr*, 365 U.S. at 136.

adopted but-for the concealment. It could argue that judicial findings of infringement and award of injunctive relief harm competition – its earlier nondisclosure having no such effect. If accepted, antitrust immunity follows. Or a group of SSO members could agree to rig a vote so that the organization chooses its technologies over others. The same immunity argument would remain open to them.

Hence, the doctrinal underpinnings of the *Noerr-Pennington* doctrine threaten to render antitrust a nullity in the patent space. Sound judgment ought to direct courts away from such extremes. In interpreting the relationship between the antitrust and patent laws, they have generally avoided the extreme implications of applying *Noerr* principles literally. But not always – several prominent decisions have gone the wrong way. The underlying rationale is readily discernible – quasi-constitutional immunity presents an appealing way to get rid of antitrust-patent cases that may stretch, or exceed, the capabilities of some courts. Even as the courts have typically gravitated toward workable interpretations, however, the jurisprudence that has emerged, however, has been far from ideal. The judicial principles espoused are clouded, and at times logically contorted.

This matters because the shift from hard assets to IP is among the most pronounced features of modern economy. The future lies in technology, and patents will continue to grow in importance. The antitrust laws play a critical role in ensuring that technology industries remain exposed to competition. Policing the procurement and use of patents will feature heavily in executing that function. An overbroad interpretation of *Noerr-Pennington* thus poses grave dangers, threatening not merely to weaken – but to expel – antitrust from issues of core importance to competition in the new economy.

The following discussion explores where the case law has gone wrong. It commends the agencies for intervening to reinforce vital interpretive principles needed to preserve effective antitrust oversight. To preview the conclusion, however, the key missing ingredient in the jurisprudence surrounding Noerr lies in the Petitioning Clause itself. Instead of asking whether the courts inflict the relevant injury to competition in a patent case, the courts should look at the impugned conduct and ask whether it implicates concerns embedded in the First Amendment. Doing so would quickly elucidate the relevant analysis. It is difficult to argue that arm's length patent acquisitions involving two private firms, for example, sufficiently touches on petitioning or lobbying the government as to justify immunity. The same holds true for the standard-setting and collusive-agreement examples mentioned above.

9.3.2.2 The Courts' Interpretation of *Noerr-Pennington* Immunity in the Patent Space Remains Nettlesome

The Supreme Court has arrived at some common-sense conclusions. In *Singer*, for example, two competitors settled infringement litigation by pooling their patents and agreeing to enforce them against a mutual Japanese competitor.[67] Viewing those facts, it found a clear Section 1 violation. Despite coming two years after *Noerr*, at no moment did the Court reference that opinion or suggest in any way that a cartel agreement focused on patent enforcement could somehow escape antitrust scrutiny on account of public action or First Amendment-related petitioning.

In *Allied Tube*, the Court encountered a conspiracy to rig the voting of a private SSO the recommendations of which the government relied upon in adopting industry standards.[68] Avoiding the extreme implications of its own reasoning in *Noerr*, it found no immunity. No one disputed that the "ultimate aim" of the vote-rigging was "to influence governmental action."[69] And the agreement could not harm competition in any market without such state action. For that reason, the Court thought it "a case close to the line."[70] It should have been no such thing. The reasoning that fed the Court's correct decision should have made it easy – "the context and nature of petitioner's activity make it the type of commercial activity that has traditionally had its validity determined by the antitrust laws themselves."[71] That same hesitancy has perhaps helped to feed overbroad interpretations by the lower courts. Finally, we have already touched on the sound holding in *Trial Lawyers Association*.[72]

Alas, the Court has fallen short in two key respects. First, it has failed to ground *Noerr-Pennington* immunity squarely in the Petitioning Clause – a clarification that would help the lower courts focus antitrust scrutiny where it belongs while respecting First Amendment principles. Instead, its decisions take a mish-mash approach and, at times, appear ends-focused rather than analytically driven.[73] The problem is that decisions like *Allied Tube* and *Noerr* are quite difficult to reconcile doctrinally. Conversely, the Court's subsequent conception of sham as use of litigation (or other forms of petitioning) as a weapon in itself rather than a means to a sought end was helpful.[74] Alas, it did not endure in meaningful form beyond 1993.

Second, in a 1993 opinion, the Court adopted a definition of sham that is far too restrictive.[75] There, in *Professional Real Estate*, it held that sham litigation requires objective baselessness and intent to interfere with the business relationships of a competitor.[76] It calibrated that standard practically to eliminate antitrust counterclaims founded on IP lawsuits directed at competitors. If one takes seriously the proposition that firms can harm competition by suing not in the pursuit of relief, but

---

[67] United States v. Singer Mfg. Co., 374 U.S. 174 (1963).
[68] Allied Tube & Conduit Corp. v. Indian Head, Inc., 486 U.S. 492 (1988).
[69] *Id.* at 504, 512.
[70] *Id.* at 507 n.10.
[71] *Id.* at 505.
[72] *Trial Lawyers Ass'n*, 493 U.S. at 411.
[73] For a more detailed analysis by the author, see ALAN DEVLIN, ANTITRUST AND PATENT LAW (2016).
[74] *See, e.g.*, City of Colum. v. Omni Outdoor Adver., Inc., 499 U.S. 365, 380 (1991) (holding that the "sham" exception to *Noerr* "encompasses situations in which persons use the governmental *process* – as opposed to the *outcome* of that process – as an anticompetitive weapon") (emphasis in original).
[75] Prof'l Real Estate Investors v. Colum. Pictures Indus., 508 U.S. 49 (1993).
[76] *Id.* at 60–61.

to inflict cost through use of the legal apparatus alone, then the PRE standard is a terrible mistake. Even the most powerful evidence of anticompetitive intent and effect go nowhere if the merits of the IP claim, though faltering, edge past frivolity. And, conversely, proof that the IP plaintiff filed the world's most hopeless suit against competitors with the naïve, but genuine, hope of securing relief would likewise enjoy immunity. These are the things of extreme policy, not optimal calibration. A cost-benefit standard of the kind championed by Judge Posner in *Grip-Pak* would make much more sense.[77]

The Court's shortcomings in this space have produced two phenomena – one welcome, the other less so. The first derives from that a separate and earlier definition of sham litigation enunciated in *Trucking Unlimited* in 1972.[78] There, the Court recognized as a sham the filing of repeated lawsuits "with or without probable cause, and regardless of the merits of the case."[79] Although the *PRE* decision referenced that prior decision and did so without criticizing it, the authoritative nature of its definition of sham has led some to think it the final word. Others believe that *PRE* defined sham for the purposes of a standalone lawsuit. Regardless, a standard based on objective baselessness is poorly equipped to deal with abuses of the judicial process that involve bringing numerous actions. Coupled with the fact that *PRE* adopted an overly narrow definition on its own terms, there are compelling reasons to recognize a different standard tied to *Trucking Unlimited*. A circuit split presently exists on the question.[80] The agencies should lend their voices to the debate in favor of that broader standard, which the weight of case law to date supports.

Unfortunately, the Court's opaque jurisprudence has led lower courts to construe *Noerr* too broadly. For example, in 2012, a court held that filing a patent-infringement lawsuit retroactively immunized the patentee's prior conduct surrounding the use of a standard-essential patent.[81] That holding realized the perversities of an overly literal interpretation of *Noerr*, as discussed above. The low point, however, arose in Capital One's antitrust claims against Intellectual Ventures based on aggregating, concealing, and enforcing thousands of patents in the financial-services space. In 2017, the district court found sufficient evidence to bring the antitrust claims to a jury, but found *Noerr-Pennington* immunity because the patent acquisitions and concealment had no market effect

---

[77] Grip-Pak, Inc. v. Illinois Tool Works, Inc., 649 F.3d 466, 472 (1982), *cert. denied*, 461 U.S. 958 (1983).
[78] Calif. Motor Transp. Co. v. Trucking Unltd., 404 U.S. 508 (1972); *see also* Otter Tail Power Co. v. United States, 410 U.S. 366, 380 (1973).
[79] *Id.* at 512.
[80] *Cf.* Puerto Rico Tel. Co. v. San Juan Cable LLC, 874 F.3d 767 (1st Cir. 2017), *cert. denied*, 138 S. Ct. 1597 (2018) *with* Hanover 3201 Realty, LLC v. Vill. Supermarkets, Inc., 806 F.3d 162, 179–80 (3d Cir. 2015); Waugh Chapel S., LLC v. United Food & Comm'l Workers Union Local 27, 728 F.3d 354, 364 (4th Cir. 2013); Primetime 24 Joint Vent. V. Nat'l Broad. Co., 219 F.3d 92, 100–01 (2d Cir. 2000); USS-POSCO Indus. v. Contra Costa County Bldg. & Const. Trades Council, 31 F.3d 800, 811 (9th Cir. 1994).
[81] Apple, Inc. v. Motorola Mobility, Inc., 886 F. Supp. 2d 1061, 1066–67, 1075–77 (W.D. Wis. 2012).

independent of litigation.[82] That holding would immunize all patent acquisitions, no matter how harmful or anticompetitive, from antitrust review. The agencies intervened on appeal through an amicus brief in order to highlight the judicial error.[83] The Federal Circuit did not address the matter, deciding instead to affirm on a narrow, technical ground of issue preclusion.[84] For that reason, the lower court ruling thus stands uncorrected and may be relied upon to ill effect elsewhere.

The substantive merits of antitrust theories in the patent space tend to be divisive. Regardless of one's take, however, immunities are not the right way to resolve them. Antitrust reform invokes competition anew. We can debate which policies best advance investment and other constituent elements of competition. It seems clear, however, that expansive immunities serve to hinder the proliferation of competitive markets that antitrust policy champions.

---

[82] Intellectual Ventures I LLC v. Capital One Fin. Corp., 280 F. Supp. 3d 691 (D. Md. 2017). The author represented Capital One at various points during the litigation.
[83] Intellectual Ventures I LLC v. Capital One Fin. Corp., Case No. 18-1367, Brief for the United States of Am. and the Fed. Trade Comm'n as Amici Curiae in Support of Neither Party (Fed. Cir. May 11, 2018).
[84] Intellectual Ventures I LLC v. Capital One Fin'l Corp., 937 F.3d 1359 (Fed. Cir. 2019).

Conclusion

Key Recommendations

Antitrust will never be perfectly calibrated. No matter the consensus (or lack of it) about the goals of competition policy and the role of economics, enforcers face a formidable challenge. Accuracy requires predicting the but-for world, which no one can observe. Economic modeling and econometrics hone the image, but it often remains blurry. The repository of knowledge about industrial organization is impressive, but incomplete. For antitrust policymakers, missteps are endemic because certain facts are unknowable.

Trying to get it right inevitably means getting it wrong, typically by allowing some harmful transactions and practices to slip through the net. The stark alternative is to retreat to structuralism in pursuit of inhibitory rules and presumptions that will catch harmful acts of consolidation at the expense of overenforcement. This dilemma lies at the heart of antitrust policy. Trade-offs are inescapable. Competition law is not, of course, an exercise in binary choice between extremes. One may commit to the pursuit of accuracy, whilst acknowledging the limits of knowledge. It is there, at the frontier of knowledge, where most refinement has occurred over the past forty years.

For that reason, reform is a constant. Evolution is baked into antitrust's DNA. A devotion to competitive effects means committing to economic analysis and evidence-based policy. Bayesian updating may be par for the course, but some moments invite a fundamental rethink beyond testing priors. This is such a time. A plausible hypothesis now bears examination. In embracing consequentialist analysis, did enforcers overthink the details and miss the big picture? Some people have grown alarmed about the growth of digital platforms, technology companies, and traditional enterprises alike. A perceived loss of competition is now a salient political issue. Industry-level data point to rising concentration and firm profits. No one can doubt that, for all its intellectual richness, modern antitrust is far more accommodating of consolidating practices and mergers than the regimes of old. Have the data-focused gurus of the DOJ and FTC been too clever by half?

The answer lies in the best available evidence and theory. Too many critics of the status quo, however, hold certain dubious propositions as self-evident. They see dominant firms as entrenched, and deny the tendency of markets to cycle. They reject the prospect of merger-generated efficiencies. So, too, they see consolidation and consumer gains as mutually exclusive. They think it obvious that an environment in which world-class innovators in digital markets rise to prominence, fuel start-up R&D around them, and bestow vast benefits on consumers is broken. They see competition from vertically integrated platforms as socially destructive. And, above all, they equate rising concentration in some industries as synonymous with lost competition in relevant markets across the US economy.

In fact, none of those propositions is obviously true. Some reformists have declared certain truths and demanded extraordinary changes to fix the status quo. They have done so on the most infirm of foundations. This is, perhaps, not surprising. Theirs is not an evidentiary dissection, but a movement. We can do better. In fact, there is evidence that enforcement is suboptimal. But determining why and, just as importantly, crafting the appropriate policy response require introspection and objectivity.

That is why Part I examined the nature of market self-correction, the potential value of monopolization cases to spur competitive displacement, the frequency and magnitude of merger-generated efficiencies, and above all the relationship between structure and competition. These are not matters of mere technical interest. Their resolution sets competition policy's foundation. Of inestimable importance, they stand among antitrust's most difficult questions. Free-marketeers and neo-Brandeisians alike tend to use priors to construct a background set of assumptions with which to inform (starkly different) visions of antitrust policy.

On examination, however, the evidence does surrender useful insights. What emerges is a complex picture at odds with the extreme characterizations of the left and right. Markets are not frail creatures prone to systematic failures at every turn, thus requiring deep governmental intrusions through structural or price regulation. The intuition that pervades neo-Brandeisian thinking about market efficacy is hard to square with reality. By the same token, though, capitalistic processes are not so forceful and antitrust intervention so blundering as to warrant laissez faire policies. Few industrial economists today would agree with the free-market impulses of the Chicago School's founding proponents like Robert Bork, who correctly diagnosed the frailties of the Warren Court's antitrust jurisprudence, but carved out rather extreme views about the nature of market self-correction and the infeasibility of exclusionary strategies.

TAKING STOCK OF THE EVIDENCE

Nonstate-protected monopolies erode over time. Even seemingly impervious firms founder when they fail to anticipate a technological shift or neglect consumers. That dynamic is especially pronounced where some reformists' fears of entrenched monopoly are most acute – in digital network markets. But this is merely to say that markets are reasonably receptive to consumer demand, thus justifying an implicit premise underlying the US antitrust system, namely that markets freed of artificial restraints of trade produce good, if imperfect, outcomes. In that respect, antitrust serves a vital purpose in liberating markets and hastening the competitive cycling process. That value includes the most controversial element of antitrust policy, monopolization cases. Practices that impede market self-correction stand among the highest priorities of enforcement – the catch being that they are generally the most difficult to diagnose.

Merger-generated efficiencies are important. Some reformists dismiss the concept wholesale, thinking them a figment of conservatives' imagination. Meanwhile, those predisposed toward limited government and free contract see transactional productivities everywhere. Again, the reality lies in-between. Studies following the 1960s merger wave revealed that conglomerate deals of the era produced few, if any, efficiencies. Exceptions were sporadic. Indeed, many such transactions appear to have yielded dissynergies. Ensuing divestitures in the 1970s were associated with productivity gains, but these may simply have reflected the undoing of past inefficiencies. The evidence since then has been mixed.

Nevertheless, horizontal transactions are more likely than other combinations to create efficiencies. Further, those benefits seldom materialize in the short term. That timing point is critical, and may explain why some studies find no, or few, efficiencies from horizontal mergers. Some work that considers the time dimension finds powerful evidence of merger-generated productivities.[1] More generally, economists have found evidence of horizontal deal-driven productivities in industries like beer,[2] manufacturing,[3] paper,[4] and retail grocery.[5] Even in the banking industry, which has seen weak evidence of merger-created efficiencies, some transactions appear to have provided such benefits.[6]

---

[1] Orley C. Ashenfelter et al., *Efficiencies Brewed: Pricing and Consolidation in the US Beer Industry*, 46 RAND J. ECON. 328 (2015); Dario Focarelli & Fabio Panetta, *Are Mergers Beneficial to Consumers? Evidence from the Market for Bank Deposits*, 93 Am. Econ. Rev. 1152 (2003).

[2] Victor J. Tremblay & Carol Horton Tremblay, *The Determinants of Horizontal Acquisitions: Evidence from the U.S. Brewing Industry*, 37 J. INDUS. ECON. 21 (1988).

[3] Vojislav Maksimovic & Gordon Phillips, *The Market for Corporate Assets: Who Engages in Mergers and Asset Sales and Are There Efficiency Gains?*, 56 J. FINANCE 2019, 2020 (2001); Robert H. McGuckin & Sang V. Nguyen, *On Productivity and Plant Ownership Change: New Evidence from the Longitudinal Research Database*, 26 RAND J. ECON. 257 (1995).

[4] Martin Pesendorfer, *Horizontal Mergers in the Paper Industry*, 34 RAND J. ECON. 495 (2003).

[5] Daniel Hosken et al., *Do Retail Mergers Affect Competition? Evidence from Grocery Retailing* 30 Fed. Trade Comm'n Bureau of Econ., Working Paper No. 313 (2012), https://www.ftc.gov/sites/default/files/documents/reports/do-retail-mergers-affect-competition%C2%A0-evidence-grocery-retailing/wp313.pdf.

[6] *See, e.g.*, Allen N. Berger & David B. Humphrey, *Megamergers in Banking and the Use of Cost Efficiency as an Antitrust Defense*, 37 ANTITRUST BULL. 541 (1992).

Claims that mergers seldom create efficiencies are thus wrong. But it would be equally incorrect to suggest that most transactions bestow productivities. Many buyers fail to achieve the synergies that they anticipated through the deal. The evidence does suggest, however, that M&A activity overall is a source of social value *to the extent that* the antitrust laws prevent transactions that create market power. In terms of reform, the key insight is that the mergers and acquisitions most likely to come within the crosshairs under an expansion of Section 7 would be those most likely to create efficiencies. Those are horizontal transactions that arise in settings of moderate concentration.

Economic self-correction, antitrust enforcement's acceleration of market processes, and the (limited) propensity of mergers to spur efficiencies warrant a robust, but discriminating, competition policy. The agencies should strive to reach the right decision in each matter, permitting socially valuable practices, agreements, and mergers, while clamping down on those likely to harm consumers. That is the competitive effects approach. The goal is the most accurate possible decision in each case. The merits of that approach may seem obvious, but they elude many critics of the status quo. The alternative to competitive effects lies in structuralism.

The relative merits of these polar opposites – effects versus structure – drive the reform debate. "Anti-monopolists" see effects as an ode to free-market ideology: a naïve pursuit of accuracy that is illusory because the necessary counterfactuals elude prediction. It would be much better, they argue, to abandon the pretense in favor of something that actually works. Structuralists draw a hard line in the sand based on various concentration ratios, and need little or nothing more to condemn a merger or firm that crosses them. Whether this approach is justifiable turns, in the first place, on how closely deltas in market structure relate to anticompetitive effects – that is, how often an increase in HHI leads quality-adjusted prices to rise. And it turns on the severity of social costs associated with mistakenly prohibiting transactions or practices that do not harm competition.

Chapter 3 found the link between structure and effects wanting. To be sure, concentration and price correlate in numerous industries. Any causal relationship, however, is indirect and bidirectional. Concentration indices remain useful if tied to an accurately defined relevant market. Structuralism informs the competitive picture, yielding a rudimentary static snapshot of the competitive space. And no one can declare structure irrelevant across applications. Increments in concentration will eventually be associated with harmful effects. An exhaustive competitive effects analysis is hardly necessary, for example, to oppose a merger to monopoly.

Nevertheless, structuralism has little to offer at the margin and, hence, in resolving close investigations. No critical concentration ratio applies across markets. It may not exist in some settings, and would be difficult or impossible to identify even if it did. Ultimately, HHIs and Cns are flawed proxies for competitive effects. There is enough there to use them for big-picture impressions, to guide analysis, and perhaps as justification for accepting remedies. But, other than in extremes, they should not dictate whether to enjoin a merger or practice. We have better tools for predicting effects – diversion ratios, margins, proximity of competition between the next most preferred seller after the parties, likely customer and supplier response, and so forth. The economics literature certainly does not support a blanket ban on, for example, all five-to-fours, four-to-threes, HHIs over 2,500, and so on. And, as described above, we should not be cavalier about the social cost of banning competitively innocuous mergers. The transactions likely to be caught up in a structural expansion of antitrust are horizontal ones at moderate levels of concentration – the kinds of deals that are most likely to produce efficiencies.

The economics of market structure inform whether competition in the US economy has declined over time. Cries of a monopoly crisis fill the air, sounding the alarm over perceived consolidation. Formal work has lent credence to these worries, as voices like those of the Council of Economic Advisors under Obama, *The Economist*, and a host of scholars observe that concentration and firm profits have risen in synch. In fact, based on available data, it is impossible to determine whether modest national industry-level trends toward consolidation point to a loss of competition in relevant antitrust markets. Indeed, plausible factors beyond competition may explain the macroeconomic trends observed.

WHAT NOT TO DO

Structuralists urge reforms of varying immoderation. Less extreme proposals include reversing the burden of proof for transactions that exceed certain financial metrics, a flat-out prohibition of mergers exceeding critical concentration ratios, stronger structural presumptions, making the government's alleged market presumptively correct, and relaxing Section 7's requirement for a plaintiff to demonstrate a "substantial" lessening of competition.

Such changes, of course, would mark an extraordinary departure from the status quo. They would also be ill-advised. Abandoning the accuracy engendered in today's competitive effects approach would move antitrust from an enlightened state to one of knowing imprecision. It would not simply mean additional Type I errors and fewer Type II ones, but a great many more errors combined. And this is to say nothing of the truly outlandish proposals that some reformists have raised – ideas like ousting the courts in favor of administrative litigation and blocking mergers based not on competition but dollar amounts. Discarding foundational principles of due process is no way to improve merger review. Meanwhile, severing the link between harm to competition and antitrust liability would allow the government to impose its preferred industry structures and limits on commercial behavior untethered to injury to the competitive process. These are not the things of responsible reform.

To their credit, neo-Brandeisians and other reformists have a few good ideas. The Utah Statement examined in Chapter 6 represents a diligent effort to articulate changes directed at solving perceived shortcomings. The issue of perception, however, is vital because many of the "problems" are misdiagnosed or undiagnosable based on existing information. Many prescriptions are thus off base, and in some cases simply advance long-running progressive goals that go beyond competition policy. Nevertheless, certain suggestions are well founded. These ideas include the primacy of evidence over theory and a legal preference for structural over behavioral remedies, at least in resolving horizontal issues.

THE CASE FOR STRENGTHENING ENFORCEMENT AT THE MARGIN

Antitrust reform does not require burning the house down and starting anew. Today's framework is analytically sophisticated, built off of decades of empirical learning, reflects the latest insights from industrial economics, and – above all – endeavors to reach the right answer. The evidence does not point to a systematic failure of US competition enforcement, and certainly not of the kind that would justify undertheorized and empirically unsound reversions to structuralism of the 1950s–1970s persuasion.

The competitive effects approach is sound. That defense, however, is not a call for inaction. At various times since 1981, antitrust has been too permissive. Judge Easterbrook's work on the danger of false positives relative to false negatives is largely responsible.[7] Error analysis has lent intellectual cover to those favorably disposed toward limited government. But it has also influenced how principled enforcers decide close calls. In fact, Type II errors are more severe than conservative writers have granted. Better informed analysis suggests action when faced with a significant loss of competition and market-power-neutralizing buyer or seller responses are not clear. The agencies have sometimes blessed major consolidations where circumstances point to unilateral effects. Numerous retrospective studies attest to this fact.[8] Horizontal transactions between close competitors have been associated with post-merger price increases, and they warrant careful scrutiny for that reason.

Those findings do not stand alone. No one has yet established a loss of competitive pressure across the US economy. Nevertheless, trends of rising concentration and firm profits match with diminished competition. This point is easy to misconstrue. There is *insufficient* evidence to bear out the hypothesis that market power has increased in any systematic way across the economy. Hence, those who claim that national industry-level statistics and accounting profits demonstrate rising market power venture unsubstantiated opinion. Simply put, we lack data tied to relevant antitrust markets that could cast light on competitive dynamics. The limitations baked into NAICS statistics, however, do not make them irrelevant – especially when read in light of larger context.

[7] Frank H. Easterbrook, *The Limits of Antitrust*, 63 TEX. L. REV. 1 (1984).
[8] See Chapter 5.

The combination of data points – retrospective studies suggesting that various mergers cleared in close cases produced harmful effects, an overarching philosophy of underenforcement in such investigations founded on decision theory, readily observable indicia of consolidation across many industries, sustained near-record high firm profits, and firm death rates that exceed birth rates – points in the same direction. This picture, limited and opaque as it may be, makes it prudent to ratchet upward antitrust scrutiny in close cases.

PROPOSALS FOR REFORM

Antitrust is about unleashing the power of competition. The question is how best to do that. Some reformists suggest that only unconcentrated market structures provide an environment in which competition will flourish. Though true of some markets, however, that is not universally the case. Antitrust policy must stoke incentives not merely to preserve the status quo, but to invest in the hope of achieving disruptive innovations. Industries' optimal form is a function of competitive dynamics, underlying cost conditions, and consumer preferences. No one size fits all, suggesting that an effects-based analysis sensitive to the characteristics of the market at issue remains optimal.

We can, however, take competition yet more seriously.

Broad Efforts Aimed at Reinvigorating Competition

First, regulatory barriers to entry are a real problem. The US economy is awash with them. State licensure on professional entry is the chief culprit.[9] It inhibits competition in a vast range of professions ranging from those that require university degrees – for example, law, medicine, dentistry, and education – to those with less specialized skills like barbers, hair-braiding, and massage therapy. This web of restraints is beyond the influence of market forces, for they flow from the power of the state. It deprives consumers of price competition and workers of mobility. The common justification for licensure is public safety. That is a legitimate goal surrounding the purchase of credence goods or services, though its significance varies. There is, after all, a world of difference between a bad haircut and botched heart surgery.

Incumbents have every incentive to pull the ladder up behind them, ratcheting up the difficulty of licensure beyond the needs of public safety. Federalism magnifies the problem. There is, for example, no good policy reason why states should maintain separate requirements to practice law, medicine, or other any other profession. Meanwhile, regulatory systems to oversee business activities protect

---

[9] See, e.g., *The Effects of Occupational Licensure on Competition, Consumers, and the Workforce: Empirical Research & Results*, A Roundtable Organized by the FTC's Economic Liberty Task Force, Nov. 7, 2017, https://www.ftc.gov/system/files/documents/public_events/1252903/empirical-roundtable-all_slides.pdf.

consumers, but in many cases have grown bloated, serving chiefly to inhibit new business creation and expansion.[10]

This phenomenon frustrates antitrust enforcers because federalism and state action immunity tie their hands. But a national conversation is underway about competition in America. The topic is politically salient for the first time in a generation. It provides an opportune moment to approach this issue with zeal. State and local governments need to drive such changes, which are challenging because they typically clash with special-interest groups aligned with incumbents. The federal antitrust authorities have an important role to play here in advocating for a sensible paring back of harmful restraints. The FTC's Economic Liberty Task Force represented a promising move, and, to their credit, some states have begun taking steps to liberalize the practice of certain professions.[11]

America will not soon be free of unwarranted regulatory impediments to entry, but the web of such restraints strangles competition across sectors, hurting low-income workers worst of all. This is not an issue of antitrust law, but of broader competition policy. Any reform effort cannot overlook what may be the single largest outstanding impediment to greater competition across US markets.

Second, the courts and agencies should reframe (or clarify) their normative framework to focus on preserving competitive pressure. The current shorthand – namely that the Sherman Act serves a consumer welfare prescription – has been net helpful, but is descriptively inaccurate and normatively incomplete. Worse, it may distract focus away from competitive effects that materialize in upstream markets. The acquisition of monopsony power, whether by agreement or through unilateral exclusionary practices, is every bit as deserving of attention as its analogue on the selling side of a market. Although the consumer-welfare framework does not lead the agencies to reject the value of competition elsewhere, over time it may distort analysis and focus attention away from where it belongs.

This does not make every upstream effect worthy of antitrust intervention. In evaluating the effects of upstream conduct, economists often trace the extent to which, if at all, the behavior affects price or output in the downstream product market. There is often good reason for this. It prevents isolated changes in the price of an asset from itself determining the existence or absence of an antitrust violation. Rather, harm to market outcomes is required.

For example, in analyzing a vertical merger and concluding that the buyer of an upstream input may have an incentive to raise price to its rivals, thus raising their costs, economists would usually determine whether price increases will likely follow

---

[10] See, e.g., *The Best and Worst States for Small Business, Red Tape Blues*, THE ECONOMIST, July 3, 2014; *Red Tape in California: Beware of the Yogurt*, THE ECONOMIST, May 19, 2011.

[11] See FTC Economic Liberty Task Force, *State-Based Initiatives: Selected Examples*, https://www.ftc.gov/policy/advocacy/economic-liberty/state-based-initiatives.

downstream.[12] This makes sense because the focus is on the impact to market-generated competitive pressure. If some downstream sellers' costs go down and others rise, but the net effect is downward pressure on price in the downstream market, then competition has increased. In that way, downstream effects keep the intervention calculus trained on the relevant question. It should not be a requisite of an antitrust violation, however, that harm to competition materialize in a downstream product or service market. The agencies should move against such harm in any relevant market, regardless of whether it is one in which consumers transact. The metric should be a loss of competitive pressure apt to produce effects in a relevant market.

Third, Congress should appropriate larger sums to federal competition enforcement. The Antitrust Division and Commission account for an imperceptible fraction of the US budget. Yet, they bestow disproportionate value on society. Staff do heroic work with the resources made available to them, but they face real constraints. The federal agencies lack the personnel and budget to investigate anywhere close to the full universe of potentially harmful restraints and transactions in the economy. They prioritize the most significant ones, coordinate with state attorneys general on matters of local concern, and tackle the more prosaic matters as they come to attention. But this simply means doing the best that they can, and they could do better with more. Today, staff labor under antiquated and inadequate IT systems. The agencies lack the capacity to run systematic retrospectives in the regular course – econometric work that would do more than almost anything else to improve merger review. Proper funding, combined with the right leadership dedicated to responsibly expanding the sphere of review, would produce benefits far exceeding the cost to taxpayers.

That the DOJ and FTC nevertheless boast an enviable track record is testament to the many exceptional lawyers, economists, and other professionals who comprise their ranks. A sense of public interest and opportunity motivates hundreds of credentialed applicants every year. Nevertheless, the pay disparity between the public and private sectors in the antitrust bar is excessive. Congress should increase compensation within the DOJ and FTC at least to match the higher pay scale available to attorneys who work at the SEC. Doing so would entice yet stronger applicants to the agencies, thus further improving their work.

One reform that is sadly gaining traction would limit the opportunities available to agency lawyers who wish to move to private practice. That is a cynical and misplaced proposal. It falsely supposes that a "revolving door" breeds favors. Some reformists charge that agency lawyers eyeing a move in-house or to a firm go easy on companies under investigation. They further imply that agency alumni use their prior relationships with staff to extract concessions that would otherwise be

---

[12] *See, e.g.*, United States v. AT&T, Inc., No. 1:17-cv-02511, Compl., ¶¶ 4 (D.D.C. Nov. 20, 2017) (alleging downstream product market effects that would harm consumers).

unavailable. That narrative is alien to anyone who has spent time at the agencies. Staff hold themselves to the highest standards, and no one receives a deeper grilling than advocates who used to work at the agency.

In fact, the tradition of movement between the public and private antitrust bars is a source of immeasurable strength. It enriches the talent pool available to the agencies. It draws in rising stars and leading industry figures alike who would otherwise find a long-term career in government economically unworkable. And, far from being a source of corruption, the presence of agency alumni in private firms and companies helps them understand the DOJ's and FTC's procedures, expectations, and means of analysis. It can facilitate a mutual trust between investigating staff and attorneys in the private bar representing companies before the agency, facilitating more open, efficient, and transparent review. Meanwhile, on both sides, hiring cycles help to erode an "us versus them" mentality that can otherwise take hold. Perspective is valuable, and in less supply in a world in which professionals are largely siloed in one place or another. This is one of the greatest advantages that US antitrust enforcers enjoy over competition agencies in most other countries, where the choice between the public and private sectors tends to be a long-term one.

We now move beyond larger policy levers of reform to consider specific doctrinal changes.

Revisiting Antitrust Doctrine

First, we should pare back doctrinal limits on antitrust's reach. The Supreme Court has wrongly found implicit preemption of the Sherman Act, despite the presence of a savings clause.[13] Fears of exposing industries, sectors, or activities to antitrust scrutiny are generally overblown, and reflect fear of the disruption associated with competition itself. That association may indeed hold true, but unbridled rivalry – for all its messiness – usually benefits society. Immunities are especially harmful when they crowd out not only private litigation, but agency action. Of course, reversing Supreme Court decisions on implied preemption in the near term will require Congressional action. But the agencies can help make the case for such changes, which would reflect a broader endeavor to reignite competition in the US economy.

Unfortunately, the issue goes beyond preemption. Some lower courts interpret *Noerr-Pennington* too broadly, immunizing commercial practices simply because they find ultimate effect through petitioning conduct. This problem has become especially pronounced with respect to patents, which have little significance divorced from the fact or threat of suit. The agencies have recently filed amicus briefs to address the problem, but the law remains both unsettled and confusing.[14]

---

[13] Credit Suisse Sec. (USA) LLC v. Billing, 551 U.S. 264 (2007); Verizon Commc'ns, Inc. v. Law Offices of Curtis V. Trinko, 540 U.S. 398 (2004).

[14] *See, e.g.*, Intellectual Ventures I LLC v. Capital One Fin'l Corp., No. 18-1367, Brief for the United States of America and the Federal Trade Commission as Amici Curiae in Support of Neither Party

Further, *Noerr* immunity is anchored to the Supreme Court's *PREI* decision, which defined sham litigation so narrowly as almost to eliminate it.[15] That ruling should be revisited. Meanwhile, a circuit split is growing about how to treat a "whole series" of proceedings, as distinct from an isolated act of petitioning.[16] A flurry of dubious lawsuits against a rival is apt to inflict competitive harm. *PREI*'s objective baselessness threshold is ill-suited to evaluating such proceedings, justifying a relaxed standard for establishing sham. As ever, the law should narrowly limit carve-outs from antitrust scrutiny.

Further to this effort, the agencies should continue aggressively to limit efforts by state-affiliated entities to claim state-action immunity.[17] Other broad exemptions from antitrust scrutiny, whether historical oddities like those applicable to (certain aspects of) professional baseball or otherwise, warrant reexamination.

Overbroad antitrust immunities are especially destructive of sound policy. Freed of antitrust scrutiny, firms have every incentive to limit competition. This is not the stuff of marginal decisions in close merger reviews. Exemptions carve-out entire swathes of the economy. Although parallel systems of regulation often fill the void, there is every reason to doubt their efficacy relative to the DOJ and FTC's policing.

Second, market definition has outgrown its proper function. The law should relax the significance of various market-share thresholds, which introduce perverse incentives when delineating the relevant market. Plaintiffs invariably tighten the arc to, or sometimes beyond, the bounds of reason. Single-brand product markets, ones broken down by product characteristic (or, worse still, customer type), and narrow geographies are *de rigueur* in many complaints. For their part, the agencies have effectively collapsed the distinction between competitive effects and the relevant market. They are not wrong to do so, technically speaking, but it renders market definition redundant. The whole undertaking reflects the legal ramifications of markets in which the parties have a modest share. And though defensible on the basis of economics, markets defined pursuant to the hypothetical monopolist test and related inquiries sometimes take on a caricatured quality. This might only be a quirky feature of contemporary antitrust, but it carries real costs.

It is time to drop the charade, and get honest about market definition's proper role. When the agencies advance markets in which shelf-stable pickles do not compete with refrigerated pickles, branded seasoned salt lies in a different competitive space than private or store label salt, and superpremium ice cream occupies a separate area of competition than premium or economy ice creams, something has

---

(Fed. Cir. May 11, 2018), https://www.ftc.gov/policy/advocacy/amicus-briefs/2018/05/intellectual-ventures-i-llc-et-al-v-capital-one-financial-corp.

[15] Prof'l Real Estate Investors, Inc. v. Columbia Pictures Indus., In., 508 U.S. 49 (1993).
[16] *See supra* Chapter 9, note 80.
[17] N. Carolina State Bd. Dental Exam'rs v. Fed. Trade Comm'n, 574 U.S. 494 (2015); Fed. Trade Comm'n v. Phoebe Putney Health Sys., 568 U.S. 216 (2013).

gone wrong.[18] The phenomenon is not merely peculiar. It bears hidden dangers. Defining markets too narrowly risks overlooking harms to competition that appear to be out-of-market. And straining to prove a sparsely populated markets risks a judge, even in an otherwise-meritorious challenge, throwing out the case. The agencies have lost cases, almost lost others, and will continue to do so on that very ground. Product differentiation itself is seldom reason enough to place otherwise good substitutes in different markets.

As explained throughout this book, the answer to any purported loss of competition in the US economy does not lie in reverting to structuralism. Rather, we should rededicate ourselves to effects, push back on antitrust immunities and exemptions, liberalize markets, and above all abandon the uncritical occupation with minimizing Type I errors. The constant, however, lies in trying to get it right and thus cabining any use of simplistic structural triggers. Within that modern vision, there is little place for conclusive legal rules that defeat an attempted monopolization claim if the firm's market share is less than 50 percent. And why should an actual monopolization claim require a ~70 percent share? And is it really the case that an agreement between firms with a share of 30 percent or less cannot harm competition for the purposes of the rule of reason? This is to say nothing of the 30 percent presumption embedded in *Philadelphia National Bank*.

These are artificialities – arbitrary thresholds that have scant relationship to the likelihood of harmful effects. And yet they apply universally across markets of unrecognizably divergent competitive conditions. Accurate competition analysis eschews such shortcuts, and embraces holistic analysis of the transaction, practice, or restraint at issue. The seminal cases on market definition do not collapse the inquiry into an economic analysis of competitive effects. They envision a relevant market defined by the reasonable interchangeability of sold products, recognizing that homogeneity is a rarity and that differentiated goods compete with each other.[19] Enforcers should not have to shoehorn market definitions to meet requisite market share thresholds. Rather, they should embrace descriptively accurate markets characterized, as the Supreme Court has told us with an eye to geographic bounds, by the "area of effective competition."[20] Within that setting, plaintiffs should then prove their cases by explaining why anticompetitive effects are likely to occur, without the help or hindrance of shares that are themselves derivative of the chosen market.

---

[18] *In re* McCormick & Co., Inc., FTC Dkt. No. C-4225, Compl. ¶ 8 (July 29, 2008); *In re* Nestlé Holdings, Inc., FTC Dkt. No. C-4082, Compl. ¶ 11 (June 25, 2003); Fed. Trade Comm'n v. Hicks, Muse, Tate & Furst Equity Fund V, L.P., Compl. ¶¶ 13, 15 (D.D.C. Oct. 23, 2002).

[19] Brown Shoe Co. v. United States, 470 U.S. 294, 325 (1961) ("The outer boundaries of a product market are determined by the reasonable interchangeability of use or crosselasticity of demand ... between the product itself and substitutes for it."); United States v. E.I. du Pont de Nemours & Co., 351 U.S. 377, 395 (1956) (analyzing whether products are "reasonably interchangeable by consumers for the same purpose").

[20] United States v. Phila. Nat'l Bank, 374 U.S. 321, 359 (1963) (Tampa Elec. v. Nashville Coal Co., 365 U.S. 320, 327 (1961)) (emphasis omitted).

Finally, this is not some wonkish issue with limited impact on real-life competition enforcement. The problem is growing more severe, and warrants immediate correction. The Supreme Court has recently embraced market definition more closely than ever before and simultaneously worsened its implications for competition enforcement.

The *Amex* opinion may be the Court's most economically illiterate modern antitrust decision.[21] Progressive thinkers, in particular, recoil from the decision based on the potentially insurmountable hurdles that it imposes on plaintiffs trying to challenge anticompetitive conduct on a two-sided platform for simultaneous transactions.[22] The Court inexplicably required plaintiffs to define a market in a vertical restraints case notwithstanding evidence of direct effects. It then pieced together a tortured market definition, forcing two complementary offerings into a unitary whole without evidence that the combination represented a set of interchangeable products or services. Many economists have denigrated the decision, which may limit antitrust enforcement in the digital economy.

Amex's disjointed reasoning and odd result, however, are partially a function of the importance attached to the relevant market itself. The majority properly worried that effects-based evidence limited to one side of a two-sided platform would generate false positives. The solution ought to lie in *how* we prove direct effects. Instead, the Court seized on market definition. If it found a market limited to one side of the credit-card network, then law disqualifying out-of-market effects from the rule-of-reason evaluation would mean finding a violation notwithstanding plausible offsetting procompetitive effects elsewhere. Even Justice Breyer, whose dissenting analysis was far more cogent than the Court's opinion, displayed some discomfort on this ground.[23] It was that quirk of the law, which consciously excludes relevant evidence of effects, that helped to drive this conclusion.

These tortured machinations speak to an underlying problem. The solution is to move more resolutely toward competitive effects and away from doctrinal rigidities of the kind encapsulated in market definition and the myriad structural inferences that flow from it.

Significant Policy Changes That the Agencies Could Enact in Short Order

Changes of the preceding kind would be terrific, but they would take political will and time. Further, although most competition policymakers would agree with

---

[21] There is a flurry of commentary on this issue, but *see, e.g.*, Herbert J. Hovenkamp, *Platforms and the Rule of Reason: The* American Express *Case*, COLUM. BUS. L. REV. 35, 46, 49, *passim* (2019).

[22] *Ohio v. Am Express*, 138 S. Ct. 2274 (2018); Tim Wu, *The Supreme Court Devastates Antitrust Law*, N.Y. TIMES, June 26, 2018.

[23] *Ohio*, 138 S. Ct. at 2302 (observing that, although "American Express should have an opportunity" to show offsetting procompetitive effects, it "might face an uphill battle" because "Sherman Act § 1 defendant can rarely, if ever, show a procompetitive benefit in the market for one product offsets an anticompetitive harm in the market for another").

paring back overly burdensome licensure requirements, those restraints tend to inhibit competition in professional-services markets that are already atomistic or otherwise reasonably competitive. Similarly, antitrust exemptions tend to be limited to certain segments of the economy. What should the agencies do immediately in order to realize meaningful and helpful changes to antitrust policy?

First, the agencies should rethink error. This is, perhaps, antitrust reform's most fundamental issue. The DOJ and FTC should commit to weighting false positives and negatives equally in the first instance, and thus strive to minimize the raw number of errors. Their starting position ought to weigh anticompetitive practices the same as false condemnations. A weighting exercise should follow based on a searching examination of the possible costs of getting it wrong in the market at hand.

This recommendation sounds technical. But it goes to the very heart of competition policy and how agencies decide investigations. This change would be significant, particularly if fully internalized within the agencies. It would be easy to adopt because, at least with respect to internal deliberations, it requires overcoming no doctrinal impediments. There is likely no other reform that would realize an immediate recalibration across the full swathe of close matters overseen by the agencies. And it would achieve those benefits while leaving untouched the vast majority of restraints, practices, and notified mergers, which pose little or no risk to competition.

By definition, this fix would have teeth only for those matters that straddle the line between permissibility and illegality – investigations the resolution of which requires deciphering unknowable facts. This does not describe the typical matter investigated at the FTC or DOJ, but it captures all or most close calls. It is there, at antitrust's great unknown, where mistakes are most likely, most serious, and presently slanted in favor of nonintervention.

For too long, US enforcers and courts have accepted an intuitive, but wrong, proposition about uncertainty. Everyone agrees that mistakes are inevitable. But the view has somehow become engrained that failing to enjoin an anticompetitive practice (Type II error) is less harmful than condemning a competitively neutral or procompetitive one (Type I error). The reasoning behind this fallacy is incomplete. Many believe that markets erode the effects of anticompetitive conduct, while incorrect legal prohibitions are impervious to market forces and thus likely to endure.

In fact, a rule (or standard) that permits anticompetitive conduct ensures its recurrence. Harmful acts may outpace restorative market processes. Indeed, exclusionary conduct has as its very goal and effect the preservation of monopoly power, thus inhibiting the market's curative forces. No less importantly, every failure to stop anticompetitive conduct represents a failure of the antitrust mission, which is to protect the market-generated competitive pressures that usher forth countless benefits to consumers and larger society alike. Meanwhile, US antitrust institutions have shown themselves to be adept at revisiting prohibitory standards, rules, and priorities that subsequent advances in economics revealed to be erroneous. The agencies' views on vertical restraints and priorities toward enforcing the backward provisions of the Robinson–Patman Act stand out as clear examples. This phenomenon suggests that Type I errors are not, as often claimed, likely to endure indefinitely.

In short, decision theory represents the book's principal recommendation for change. It offers the great benefit of universality. Delving into the particulars of close cases inevitably leads to divisive interpretations of conflicting evidence – the very qualities that make the matters difficult to decide in the first instance. Monopolization actions often meet this description. It is hard to discern valuable lessons from anecdotal case studies, particularly when the merits remain obscure. And any insights nevertheless garnered may not be generalizable. By contrast, rethinking how the agencies – and, in time, the courts – treat error suffers no such deficiency. In many ways, this recommendation embraces the value of competition itself. Close calls should cut in favor of preserving competitive pressure. It is entirely possible, and indeed necessary, to combine that prescription with a full-throated commitment to competitive effects and empiricism as the means of antitrust analysis.

Finally, and related to several recommendations above, the agencies should be less risk averse in approaching litigation when the evidence shows a substantial lessening of competition. They win too often. In part, the agencies' preference to build up near-ironclad records before suing reflects efficient use of limited resources. When Congress limits their ability to litigate, the agencies must pick their battles and strive to win. In an optimal system, however, they would sue and lose more frequently than they do. To be clear, the agencies are not scared of litigating. Anecdotally, the author never saw the FTC shy away from a tough fight that it thought was justified and at least potentially winnable. But the ideal state would be more litigious.

When agencies lose, their enforcement effort still typically benefits society. Courts decide the law. The DOJ and FTC do not. When the judiciary rules against the government, it clarifies the law's outer bounds. Meanwhile, an unsettling practice sees the agencies mold soft precedent via untested consent decrees. The principles thus enunciated may deviate from what is socially optimal – a phenomenon that litigation would address. Further, a willingness to litigate deserving cases even on a challenging record means that the government will sometimes win when it might otherwise have stood still.

For that reason above all others, this moment of national reflection on antitrust policy justifies a rededication to the value of competition, a discarding of preoccupation with false positives, and a commitment to evidentiary analysis.

Index

abuse of dominance cases, 45
Amazon, 25–26, 151–52
   breakup of, 33–34
Amazon's Antitrust Paradox (Khan), 150–51
ancillary-restraint doctrine, 9–10
anticompetitive conduct, 213–16
   cross-market effects, 213–14
anticompetitive effects, 105–7, 259, 260
Anticompetitive Exclusionary Conduct Prevent Act, U.S. (2020), 161
anticompetitive mergers, 142–43
Anti-Merger Act, U.S. (1950), 158
   in Utah Statement, 212–13
anti-monopoly movement. *See also* neo-Brandeisian movement
   Brandeis and, 137
   competition policy and, 4
   consumer-welfare standard and, 256
   declining economic competition and, 119
   natural monopolies, 11
   political antitrust and, 28
   testing of, 157–73
antisteering clauses, 214–16
antitrust law and policies. *See also* anti-monopoly movement; Chicago School; market structure; political antitrust
   through agency rule-making, 206–7
   capitalism and, 14, 15
   through case development, 206–7
   conceptualization of, 252–54
   consumers as stakeholders under, 204
   development of, 80–82
   as doctrine, 302–5
   economic content of, 2
   efficiencies through mergers and acquisitions influenced by, 71–72
   expansion of, 34
   Federal Trade Commission hearings on, 5, 20
   goals and purpose of, 9, 11–12
   horizontal equity and, 16
   idealism as influence on, 2
   market efficacy and, 252–53
   maximization approach to, 253–54
   political content of, 13–21
      competition increases as part of, 17–18
      expanded federal role as result of, 20
      regulatory dimensions in, 19–20
      through restraint of trade, 18–19
   price theory and, 2
   public debate on, 1–5
   recommendations for, 293–307
      competitive effects approach, 298
      for enforcement, 298–99
      evidentiary stock, 294–97
      pitfalls in, 297–98
      policy changes, 305–7
   Robinson-Patman Act and, 206
   under Sherman Act, 9
   in Silicon Valley, 36
   social-welfare criterion for, 16
   wealth maximization and, 16
antitrust mandates, 233–34
antitrust reform. *See also* consumer-welfare standard; neo-Brandeisian movement
   proposals for, 299–302
   public monopolization cases and, 44–47
   theoretical approach to, 229–32
antitrust rules, efficiencies through mergers and acquisitions
   error-cost analysis and, 57
   frequency of, 57–58
   under Hart-Scott Rodino Act, 58
   significance of, 57–58
AOL, 36–37
Apple, 25–26
Arnold, Thurman, 81–82

asset rationalization, 23
AT&T case, 49–50
authoritarianism, 29
Autor, David, 130–31

Bain, Joe, 81, 83–85
  on structure-profit hypothesis, 85–86
Baker, Jonathan, 143
banking industry, mergers and acquisitions in, 63–65
bargaining. *See* collective bargaining
Baxter, Bill, 89, 163
Bell, Alexander Graham, 49
below-cost pricing, 44, 183–84
Berkley Photo standard, 187–89
Bessen, James, 132
bidding. *See* predatory bidding; *Weyerhaeuser* test
Biden, Joe, 4–5
bilateral monopolies, 205
binarism, 242
Bork, Robert, 147–48, 204
Brandeis, Louis (Supreme Court Justice), 137–40. *See also* neo-Brandeisian movement
  anti-monopoly movement and, opposition to, 137
  "curse of bigness," 139
  on economic competition, 140
  Federal Trade Commission formation and, 137
  on laissez faire capitalism, opposition to, 139
Bresnahan, Timothy, 92
brewing industry
  consolidation of, 112–13
  mergers and acquisitions in, 62, 67–68
Brooke Group test, for predatory pricing, 182–87
Brozen, Yale, 87
bundled discounts, 44
Buttigieg, Pete, 142

capitalism
  antitrust law and, 14, 15
  laissez faire, 139
Carnegie, Andrew, 138
Celler-Kefauver Amendment of 1950, U.S., 60, 82–83, 84, 159
Chamberlin, Edward, 73, 79–80
Chicago School
  as applied economics, 15
  consumer-welfare standard and, 257, 265
  economic restraints and, 89
  efficiency rationales and, 2
  game theory and, reliance on, 90–91
  laissez faire capitalism and, 147–48
  law and economics movement and, 151
  market structure and, 87–90

mischaracterization of, 14
neo-Brandeisian movement in opposition to, 14
neoclassical economics and, 11, 14
  price theory in, 89, 141
political antitrust and, 29–30
pro-competition mandates and, 125–26, 127–28
Structure-Conduct-Performance methodologies, 15
Chopra, Rohit, 150
  Federal Trade Commission and, 155–56, 206–7
  neo-Brandeisian movement and, 20, 142, 146, 155–56
Cicilline, David, 150
City of Mishawaka v. Am. Elec. Power Co., 47
Clark, John, 82, 83–84
classical economic theory, market structure and, 76–79
  duopolistic competition in, 78–79
  marginalism in, 76–77
  monopolies in, 77
  perfect competition models in, 77
Clayton Act, U.S. (1914), 14, 82
  Utah Statement and
    enforcement mechanisms, 212–13
    exemptions from act, 202–3
close call merger decisions, 247
Colgate doctrine, 261–62
collective bargaining, 202–3
competition, economic. *See also* declining economic competition; free markets; Sherman Act; *specific topics*
  ancillary-restraint doctrine and, 9–10
  Brandeis on, 140
  concentrated markets and, 75
  consumer-welfare standard and, 258–59
    anticompetitive effects, 259, 260
    prediction of competitive effects, 259, 264
  Cournot-Nash model of, 94–95, 163
  declining, neo-Brandeisian movement and, 112–16, 120–21
  duopolistic, 78–79
  imperfect competition revolution, 79–80
  innovation strategies and, 11
  interbrand, 18–19
  intrabrand, 18–19
  investment strategies and, 9–10
  market structure and
    fear competition, 76–79
    functions of, 85
    pricing and, 82
    workable competition, 80–82
  natural monopolies and, 11
  perfect competition models, 77
  price theory and, 82

competition, economic (cont.)
    Cournot-Nash competition, 94–95
    non-price based competition, 94
    structuralism in, 18–19
competition law. *See also* antitrust law and policies
    economic progress of, 269–72
    in EU, 149
        predatory pricing in, 185
    history of, 1
    structuralism and, 269–70
competition policy
    anti-monopoly movement and, 4
    with free markets, 6
competitive effects
    free markets and, 274
    prediction, 259, 264
    structuralism and, 97
competitive fragility, for communications technologies, 38–39
concentrated markets. *See also* declining economic competition; deconcentration of industries
    competition policy on, 75
    errors analysis in, 244–46
    in free markets, 10–11
    globalization as influence on, 130–31
    Herfindahl-Hirschman Index, 74
    innovation as influence on, 130
    mandates against, 24
    market power and, 74–75
    neo-Brandeisian movement and, 112–16, 120–21
    neoclassical antitrust and, 24
    price theory and, 88, 90–95
        cost differences as factor in, 94–95
        endogeneity issues and, 91–96
        as indirect relationship, 91–95
        innovation as influence on, 94
        market share and, 93
        New Empirical Industrial Organization, 90–91
    pro-competition mandates and, 125–32
    by sector, from 1997–2012, 118
    structuralist approach to, 74–75
    in Utah Statement, 212–13
consequentialism, 155
Consolidation Prevention and Competition Act of 2019, U.S., 161–62
constrained optimization model, for price theory, 2
consumer harm, 260–65
consumer preferences, neoclassical antitrust and, 26
consumer welfare, 5
consumers, as stakeholders, under antitrust law, 204
consumer-welfare standard, 204, 254–68
    anti-monopolists on, 256
    Chicago School and, 257, 265
    Colgate doctrine, 261–62
    competition and, 258–59
        anticompetitive effects, 259, 260
        prediction of competitive effects, 259, 264
    consumer harm under, 260–65
    deficiencies in, 255–56
    definition of, 254
    descriptive power of, lack of, 256–60
    in EU, 255
    evolution away from, 268
    Federal Trade Commission hearings on, 250–51, 266–67
    Horizontal Merger Guidelines and, 255
    horizontal mergers and, 259
    Lynn's opposition to, 141, 153, 250–51
    mislabeling of, 251–52
    overenforcement issues in, 263–64
    Robinson-Patman Act and, 257
    under Sherman Act, 255
    structuralism and, 265–66
    theoretical approach to, 250–52
    in U.S. antitrust law, centrality of, 255
    Wu on, 148, 250–51
contracts. *See* freedom of contract
coordination
    horizontal, in Utah Statement, 202–3
    in market structure, 86
cost differences, within concentrated markets, prices and, 94–95
Council of Economic Advisers, 61, 117, 119, 123, 158
Cournot-Nash model, of competition, 94–95, 163
    free markets and, 273–74
Crane, Daniel, 30
Credit Suisse case, 180–82, 236, 237
cross-market effects, 213–14
"curse of bigness," 139
The Curse of Bigness (Wu), 147

decision theory. *See also* errors
    Easterbrook and, 237–41
    enforcement and, 248
    outcome improvement, 247–49
    unknown as element of, 234–35
declining economic competition, 111–25
    anti-monopoly movement and, 119
    evidence of, 117–25
        cross-industry, 117–19
        Herfindahl-Hirschman Index, 117
        interpretation of, 119–24
        market power and, 124–25
    exogenous factors for, 122
    from industry consolidation

in airline industry, 112
in brewing industry, in U.S., 112–13
in food industry, 115–16
in healthcare industry, 113–14
of mobile communications, 113
neo-Brandeisian movement and, 112–16, 120–21
in merger context, 121
simultaneity bias and, 122
Structure-Conduct-Performance methodologies and, 121–22
deconcentration of industries
in free markets, 11
Khan and, 149
Demsetz, Harold, 87–88
Department of Justice (DOJ), U.S., 125–29
exclusionary conduct cases, 45–47
merger review by, 229–30
narrow markets and, challenges to, 278–80
dissynergies, 173, 295
diversification, of products, market structure and, 86
diversion ratios, 97–98
DOJ. *See* Department of Justice
duopolistic competition, market structure and, 78–79

Easterbrook, Frank, 229, 238
decision theory and, 237–41
econometrics, 105
economic competition. *See* competition
Economics of Imperfect Competition (Chamberlin and Robinson), 79
The Economist, 5, 118, 119, 124
effect prediction, structuralism and, 96–97
efficiencies, through mergers and acquisitions review, 54–72
acceptance rates for, 56
antitrust policy influenced by, 71–72
in banking industry, 63–65
in brewing industry, in U.S., 62, 67–68
under Celler-Kefauver Amendment of 1950, 60
competition reduction and, 59
criticism of, 65
in electricity industry, in U.S., 69–70
evaluation of, 56–57
in horizontal mergers, 59–60, 66–67, 70
cost savings and benefits from, 72
in hospital industry, 66, 67
mixed evidence of, 58–71
optimal antitrust rules
error-cost analysis and, 57

frequency of merger-driven efficiencies influenced by, 57–58
under Hart-Scott Rodino Act, 58
significance of merger-driven efficiencies influenced by, 57–58
in paper and paperboard industry, 68–69
perpetual monopoly claims and, 55
productivity measures, 65, 68–69
in retail grocery industry, 70–71
standards for, 34
studies, 60–71
by Council of Economic Advisers, 61
endogeneity problems in, 65–66
by Federal Trade Commission, 62
during 1980s, 60–63
during 1990s, 63–66
from 2000 to present, 66–71
substantiated variable-cost savings, 56–57
synergies and, 55–57
revenue, 60
theoretical approach to, 58–71
verification condition, 56
in vertical mergers, 72
efficiency rationales, Chicago School on, 2
E.I. du Pont case, 223–24
electric industry, mergers and acquisitions in, 69–70
empiricism
game theory and, 90–91
New Empirical Industrial Organization, 90–91
structuralism and, 99
Structure-Conduct-Performance methodologies and, validation of market structures through, 83–86
employment. *See* statutory employment status
endogeneity problems
in concentrated markets, for prices, 91–96
in mergers and acquisitions studies, 65–66
for prices, in concentrated markets, 91–96
enforcement mechanisms, for antitrust. *See also* Utah Statement; *specific topics*
decision theory and, 248
through litigation, 136
neo-Brandeisian movement and, 11
overenforcement fears, 236–38
overview of, 135–36
through pro-competition mandates, 132
policy-setting for, 132–35
for Type I errors, 1–2
for Type II errors, 1–2
enterprise resource planning software (ERP software), 276–77
errors
analysis of, 57, 242–47

errors (cont.)
  in concentrated markets, 244–46
  error costs in merger review, 247
  exclusionary conduct by dominant firm, 246–47
  in mergers, 244–46
  preservation-of-competition framework for, 234
  procompetitive effects, 243–44
costs of, 236–38
  in merger review, 247
error-cost analysis, 57, 247
genesis of, 232–38
Type I, 240–41
  enforcement for, 1–2
  self-correction of, 238–39
  social costs of, 166, 243
Type II, 240
  enforcement for, 1–2
  exclusionary conduct and, 44, 246–47
  minimization of, 166
  social costs of, 243
Essential Facilities Doctrine, 189–94
  forced sharing in, 189–90
  property rule in, 191
  transaction costs in, 190
EU. *See* European Union
European Commission, neo-Brandeisian movement and, 149
European Union (EU)
  competition law in, 149
    predatory pricing in, 185
  consumer-welfare standard in, 255
  neo-Brandeisian movement in, 172
exclusionary conduct, 43–47
  below-cost pricing and, 44
  bundled discounts, 44
  Department of Justice cases, 45–47
  exclusive dealing, 44
  Federal Trade Commission cases and, 45–47
  game theory and, 44–45
  predatory pricing and, 44
  product tying, 44
  Type II errors, 44
  U.S. Justice Department cases, 45–47
  vertical integration, 44
  volume rebates, 44
exclusive dealing, 44

fear competition, 76–79
Federal Trade Commission (FTC)
  as activist, 169–71
  on antitrust law, hearings for, 5, 20
  Brandeis role in formation of, 137
  Chopra and, 155–56, 206–7
  consumer-welfare standard hearings, 250–51, 266–67
  exclusionary conduct cases and, 45–47
  Khan's critique of, 150
  mergers and acquisitions studies, 62, 229–30
  narrow markets and, challenges to, 278–81
  Part III litigation mechanism, 224–25
  pro-competition mandates and, 125–29
  structuralist approach to antitrust and, 169–71
  in Utah Statement, 195
financial crisis (2008), 3
First Amendment, U.S. Constitution, 202
food industry, consolidation of, 115–16
forced sharing, in Essential Facilities Doctrine, 189–90
free markets. *See also* concentrated markets; platform markets; self-correction
  competition policy with, 6
  concentrated industries in, 10–11
  Cournot model and, 273–74
  deconcentration of industries in, 11
  definition of, 271–84
    competitive effects and, 274
    of narrow markets, 276–77
    purpose of, 273–76
    as structural inquiry, 282
  natural monopolies, 11
  neo-Brandeisian movement and, 34–35
  per se claims, 273
  relevant markets, 275–76
  segmentation of, by product differentiation, 281–84
  Sherman Act and, 9
freedom of contract, under Sherman Act, 11
FTC. *See* Federal Trade Commission
FTC Act, U.S., 14

game theory
  Chicago School and, reliance on, 90–91
  empiricism and, 90–91
  market structure and, 87–90
  neoclassical economics and, 15
GDP. *See* gross domestic product
global distribution systems (GDSs), 278
globalization, industrial concentration influenced by, 130–31
Google, 25–26, 39
Great Recession, 3–4
gross domestic product (GDP), pro-competition mandates and
  labor share and, 129–32
  market share trends, 125–32
GUPPI, 219, 220

Index

harmful transactions, structuralism and, 104–8
Hart-Scott Rodino Act, U.S. (2019), 58
healthcare industry, consolidation of, 113–14
Herfindahl-Hirschman Index (HHI), 74, 117, 159–60
horizontal coordination, in Utah Statement, 202–3
horizontal equity, 16
Horizontal Merger Guidelines, 71, 127–28
  consumer-welfare standard and, 255
horizontal mergers, 59–60, 66–67, 70, 245
  consumer-welfare standard and, 259
  inhibition of, 86
hospital industry, mergers and acquisitions in, 66, 67

IAPs. *See* Internet Access Providers
IBM, 42–43
idealism, antitrust law and, 2
imperfect competition revolution, 79–80
incrementalism, neo-Brandeisian movement compared to, 2–3
industrial economics, 90
industrial economists, 74
industrial organization, competitive markets and, 73
innovation
  competition and, 11
  in concentrated markets, prices and, 94
  industrial concentration influenced by, 130
  pro-competition mandates and, 130
integration. *See* vertical integration
intellectual property (IP)
  in *Noerr-Pennington* case, 287–92
    immunity and, 289–92
    public action on, 288–89
    scope of, overreach of, 287–88
interbrand competition, 18–19
Internet Access Providers (IAPs), 54
Interstate Commerce Commission, 138
intrabrand competition, 18–19
IP. *See* intellectual property

Justice Department, U.S., exclusionary conduct cases, 45–47

Khan, Lina, 150–51, 175. *See also* Utah Statement
  neo-Brandeisian movement and, 4–5, 141–42, 146, 149–52
  on Amazon, 151–52
  critique of FTC, 150
  deconcentration of industries and, 149
  on mega-platforms, 150
Kingsbury, Nathan, 49
Kodak, 39–40
Krugman, Paul, 120

labor market monopsonies, 210–12
labor unions, bilateral monopolies and, 205
laissez faire capitalism, 139
  Chicago School and, 147–48
law and economics movement, 3–4
  Chicago School and, 151
  monopsonies in, 210–11
  structuralism and, 101–2
Law of Unintended Consequences, 102–4
liability. *See* limitation of liability
limitation of liability, in Utah Statement, 201
The Limits of Antitrust (Easterbrook), 238
linkLine Doctrine, 199–202
Lorain Journal case, 48–49
Lynn, Barry
  neo-Brandeisian movement and, 119–20, 141, 152–54
  opposition to consumer-welfare movement, 153, 250–51
  on super-giant corporations, 153
  New America Foundation, 152

M&A. *See* mergers and acquisitions
marginal revenue product of labor (MRP), 210
marginalism, 76–77
margins. *See also* profit margins
  structuralism and, 97–98
market share, in concentrated markets, prices and, 93
market structure, antitrust policy and, 76–90
  under Celler-Kefauver Amendment of 1950, 60, 82–83, 84
  Chicago School on, 87–90
  classical economic theory and, 76–79
    duopolistic competition in, 78–79
    marginalism in, 76–77
    monopolies in, 77
    perfect competition models in, 77
  under Clayton Act, 82
  competition
    fear, 76–79
    functions of, 85
    pricing and, 82
    workable, 80–82
  coordination in, 86
  development of antitrust policy, 80–82
  excess capacity in, 86
  game theory and, 87–90
  horizontal mergers and, inhibition of, 86
  imperfect competition revolution, 79–80
  under National Industrial Recovery Act, 81
  product diversification in, 86
  under Sherman Act, 77–78

market structure, antitrust policy and (cont.)
  Structure-Conduct-Performance methodologies, 15, 73, 80–82, 87–90
    criticism of, 87
    empirical validation of, 83–86
    Mason and, 80–81
    misspecification of, 88
    supracompetitive pricing and, 86
    vertical integration in, 86
    vertical mergers and, inhibition of, 86
markets. *See* free markets
Marshall, Alfred, 76–77
Mason, Edward, 73, 80–81
maximization approach, to antitrust law, 253–54
mega-platforms, 150
mergers and acquisitions (M&A)
  anticompetitive, 142–43
  in banking industry, 63–65
  in brewing industry, 62, 67–68
  close call, 247
  declining economic competition and, 121
  Department of Justice review of, 229–30
  dissynergies and, 173, 295
  in electric industry, 69–70
  error costs, 247
  errors analysis in, 244–46
  Federal Trade Commission review of, 62, 229–30
  filings for, increase in, 34
  horizontal, 59–60, 66–67, 70, 245
    consumer-welfare standard and, 259
    Horizontal Merger Guidelines, 71, 127–28, 255, 259
    inhibition of, 86
  in hospital industry, 66, 67
  neo-Brandeisian movement and, 71
  in paper and paperboard industry, 68–69
  political antitrust and, 30–31
  Staples-Essendant merger, 30
  vertical, 31
  pro-competition mandates and, 132–33
  in retail grocery industry, 70–71
  review standards for, 34
  SSNIPs, 220, 221, 275
  structuralist review of, 107–8
  in Utah Statement, restoration and review of, 194–99
    enforcement practices for, 222–24
    through Federal Trade Commission, 195
    for natural monopolies, 196–97
    network effects, 196–97
    T-Mobile/Sprint merger, 198–99
  vertical, 72, 177–79
    inhibition of, 86

  zero-efficiency vertical acquisition, 243
Microsoft, 40
  Internet Access Providers and, 54
  Java Virtual Machine and, 52
  Original Equipment Manufacturer restrictions, 51, 53–54
Microsoft case, 50–54
  platform markets and, 51
mobile communications, consolidation of, 113
monopolies. *See also specific topics*
  bilateral, 205
  leveraging of, restoration of, 187–89
  natural, 196–97
  perpetual
    mergers and acquisitions and, 55
    myths about, 36–54
  in railroad industry, 138
  shared monopoly theory, 169
  Standard Oil, 138
monopsonies
  labor market, 210–12
  in law and economics movement, 210–11
Morgan, J. P., 77–78, 138
Morton, Fiona Scott, 143
Moss, Diana, 58
Motorola, 38–39
MRP. *See* marginal revenue product of labor
Murdoch, Rupert, 37

narrow markets, 276–81
  definition of, 276–77
  Department of Justice challenges to, 278–80
  Federal Trade Commission challenges to, 278–81
National Economic Council, 4–5
National Industrial Recovery Act, U.S., 81
natural monopolies, 11, 196–97
NEIO. *See* New Empirical Industrial Organization
neo-Brandeisian movement, 140–56. *See also* consumer-welfare standard; Utah Statement
  Anti-Merger Act and, 146–47
  as antitrust philosophy, 157–62
    structuralist approach to, 157–73
  Chicago School as opposition to, 14
  Chopra and, 20, 142, 146, 155–56
  critique of, 143–56
    preview of, 143–45
  declining economic competition and, 112–16, 120–21
  as economic vision, theoretical approach to, 174–75
  on enforcement mechanisms, 11
  European Commission and, 149

in European Union, 172
free markets and, 34–35
incrementalism compared to, 2–3
industry consolidation and, 112–16, 120–21
Khan and, 4–5, 141–42, 146, 149–52
   on Amazon, 151–52
   critique of FTC, 150
   deconcentration of industries and, 149
   on mega-platforms, 150
Lynn and, 119–20, 141, 152–54
   opposition to consumer-welfare movement, 153
   on super-giant corporations, 153
on merger-driven consolidation, 29
mergers & acquisitions and, 71
Open Markets Institute and, 141, 152–54, 157
overview of, 141–43
political antitrust and, 26–27, 32
pro-competition mandates and, 128
rejection of Chicago School theories, 140
Sagers and, 141, 146, 154–55
   consequentialist approach of, 155
Steinbaum and, 141
structuralist approach to antitrust, 157–73, 270–71
   abandonment of accuracy with, 163
   activist Federal Trade Commission and, 169–71
   under Anti-Merger Act, 158
   burden of proof in, 167–68
   through extreme proposals, 171–73
   moderate versions of, 163–71
   negative critiques of, 162–73
   reforms through, 168
Warren and, 4, 142–43
Wu and, 4–5, 29, 141, 146–49
   on consumer-welfare mandate, 148
   on EU competition law, 149
neoclassical antitrust, 21–26
   anti-concentration mandates and, 24
   competitive market structures and, 23–24
   concentration mandates and, 24
   consumer preferences and, 26
   framework for, 22
   nonprice effects, 26
   price theory and, 24–25
   rationalization goals in, 23
   in Silicon Valley, 24–25
   transparency and, 23
neoclassical economics
   Chicago School and, 11, 14
      price theory and, 89, 141
   game theory and, 15
network effects, 196–97
New America Foundation, 152

New Empirical Industrial Organization (NEIO), 90–91
   price theory and, 91
New York Times, 4–5, 38
Noerr-Pennington case, 272, 284–92
   executive branch lobbying in, 286–87
   intellectual property in, 287–92
      immunity and, 289–92
      public action on, 288–89
      scope of, overreach of, 287–88
   legislative branch lobbying in, 286–87
   in Utah Statement, 202
Nokia, 38–39
non-compete agreements, 179–80
nonprice effects, 26
Northern Securities Company, as railroad monopoly, 138

OEMs. *See* Original Equipment Manufacturer restrictions
Ohlhausen, Maureen, 18
Open Markets Institute, 141, 152–54, 157
Original Equipment Manufacturer restrictions (OEMs), 51, 53–54

paper and paperboard industry, mergers and acquisitions in, 68–69
Part III litigation mechanism, FTC, 224–25
per se claims, 273
perfect competition models, market structure and, 77
perpetual monopoly
   mergers and acquisitions and, 55
   myths about, 36–54
Philadelphia National Bank, 167, 179, 182, 194, 274
Pitofsky, Bob, 26–28
platform markets, *Microsoft* case and, 51
political antitrust, 21–32. *See also* neoclassical antitrust
   anti-monopolists and, 28
   Chicago School and, 29–30
   mergers, 30–31
      Staples-Essendant merger, 30
      vertical, 31
   neo-Brandeisian movement and, 26–27, 32
predatory bidding, *Weyerhaeuser* test for, 182–87
predatory pricing
   below-cost pricing as, 183–84
   Brooke Group test for, 182–87
   in European Union, 185
   Khan on, 186–87
preservation-of-competition framework, for error analysis, 234
price discrimination prohibitions, under Robinson-Patman Acts, 16–17

price fixing
  through below-cost pricing, 44
  predatory pricing and, 44
price squeezes, 199–202
price theory
  antitrust law and, 2
  competition and, 82
    Cournot-Nash, 94–95
    non-price based, 94
  concentrated markets and, 88, 90–95
    cost differences as factor in, 94–95
    endogeneity issues and, 91–96
    as indirect relationship, 91–95
    innovation as influence on, 94
    market share and, 93
    New Empirical Industrial Organization, 90–91
  modeling for, constrained optimization, 2
  neoclassical antitrust and, 24–25
  nonprice effects, 26
  predatory pricing
    below-cost pricing as, 183–84
    Brooke Group test for, 182–87
    Khan on, 186–87
  supracompetitive pricing, 86
pro-competition mandates, 125–32
  antitrust-enforcement mandates, 132
    policy-setting for, 132–35
  in Chicago School ideology, 125–26, 127–28
  Department of Justice errors and, 125–29
  Federal Trade Commission errors and, 125–29
  gross domestic product
    labor share of, 129–32
    market share trends and, 125–32
  industrial concentration and, changes in, 129–32
    globalization factors, 130–31
    innovation as factor in, 130
    superstar firm effect, 131
    technology advancements, 130–31
  mergers and acquisitions and, 132–33
  neo-Brandeisian movement and, 128
  profit margins influenced by, 129–32
procompetitive effects, in error analysis, 243–44
product diversification. *See* diversification
product tying, 44
profit margins, pro-competition mandates and, 125–32
property rule, in Essential Facilities Doctrine, 191
public choice theory, 204
public monopolization cases. *See* self-correction

railroad industry
  Interstate Commerce Commission and, 138
  monopolization of, 138

Northern Securities Company, 138
  Sherman Act and, 138–39
rebates. *See* volume rebates
rents
  supracompetitive, 35
  supranormal, 124–25, 133–34, 229
retail grocery industry, mergers and acquisitions in, 70–71
Robinson, Joan, 79–80
Robinson-Patman Acts, 11, 239, 307
  antitrust law and, 206
  consumer-welfare standard and, 257
  price discrimination prohibitions under, 16–17
Rockefeller, John D., 77–78, 138, 151
Rosch, Thomas, 20
Ross, Diana, 143

Sagers, Chris, neo-Brandeisian movement and, 141, 146, 154–55
  consequentialist approach of, 155
Schor case, 187–88
SCP methodologies. *See* Structure-Conduct-Performance methodologies
segmentation, of free markets, by product differentiation, 281–84
self-correction, of free markets, 35–54
  abuse of dominance cases, 45
  AOL and, 36–37
  competitive fragility and, for communications technologies, 38–39
  perpetual monopoly myths and, 36–54
  public monopolization cases, 41–54
    antitrust limits in, 42–44
    antitrust reform and, 44–47
    AT&T case, 49–50
    exclusionary conduct in, 43–47
    IBM, 42–43
    Lorain Journal case, 48–49
    Microsoft case, 50–54
  for social media platforms, 37–38
    Myspace, 37–38
  suppression of incentives, 35
  supracompetitive rents, 35
shared monopoly theory, 169
Sherman Act, U.S.
  antitrust law under, 9
  consumer-welfare standard under, 255
  free markets and, 9
  freedom of contract under, 11
  market structure under, 77–78
  purpose of, 10, 14
  railroad industry under, 138–39
  in Utah Statement, 203–5

Silicon Valley
  antitrust interventions in, 36
  neoclassical antitrust and, 24–25
  superstar firms in, 133–34
simultaneity bias, 122
Singer, Eugene, 87
Slaughter, Rebecca Kelly, 20
Smith, Adam, 73
social media platforms, 37–38
  Facebook, 25–26
    breakup of, calls for, 33–34
  Myspace, 37–38
social-welfare, antitrust law and, 16
SSNIPs, 220, 221, 275, 283–84
stakeholders, consumers as, under antitrust law, 204
Standard Oil
  break-up of, 77–78
  as monopoly, 138
Staples-Essendant merger, 30
statutory employment status, 202–3
statutory worker protections, 202
Steinbaum, Marshall, 141, 175. *See also* Utah Statement
Stigler, George, 85–86
structuralism, 95–99, 295–97. *See also* market structure; neo-Brandeisian movement
  anticompetitive effects, 105–7
  antitrust interventions and, 102–4
  Chicago School on, 101
  competition law and, 269–70
  competitive effects, 97
  concentrated markets and, 74–75
  consumer-welfare standard and, 265–66
  design of, 101–2
  diversion ratios, 97–98
  in economic competition, 18–19
  economic shift away from, effects of, 99–108
    enforcement limitations, 100–2
    harmful transactions and, 104–8
    Law of Unintended Consequences and, 102–4
    merger review, 107–8
  effect prediction and, 96–97
  empirical work and, 99
  government policy and, 98
  law and economics revolution and, 101–2
  margins and, 97–98
  mergers and, 98
  in relevant markets, 96
  structural ratios, 97
  in Utah Statement, 194–99, 213
Structure-Conduct-Performance methodologies (SCP methodologies)
  declining economic competition and, 121–22

market structure and, 15, 73, 80–82, 87–90
  criticism of, 87
  empirical validation of, 83–86
  Mason and, 80–81
  misspecification of, 88
  Mason and, 80–81
structure-profit hypothesis, 85–86
Stucke, Maurice, 250–51
super-giant corporations, 153
superstar firm effect, 131
  in Silicon Valley, 133–34
supracompetitive pricing, 86
supracompetitive profits, 124–25
supracompetitive rents, 35
supranormal rents, 124–25, 133–34, 229

Telecommunications Act, U.S. (1966), 182, 192
Theory of Monopolistic Competition (Chamberlin and Robinson), 79
Tirole, Jean, 90
T-Mobile/Sprint merger, review of, 198–99
transaction costs, in Essential Facilities Doctrine, 190
transparency, neoclassical antitrust and, 23
Trinko doctrine, 180–82, 189, 191–92, 193–94
Type I errors, 240–41
  enforcement for, 1–2
  self-correction of, 238–39
  social costs of, 166
Type II errors, 240
  enforcement for, 1–2
  exclusionary conduct and, 44, 246–47
  minimization of, 166
  social costs of, 243

Uber, 25–26
United States (U.S.). *See also* Federal Trade Commission; Sherman Act
  Anticompetitive Exclusionary Conduct Prevent Act, 161
  Anti-Merger Act, 158
    in Utah Statement, 212–13
  Celler-Kefauver Amendment of 1950, 60, 82–83, 84, 159
  Clayton Act, 14, 82
    Utah Statement and, 202–3, 212–13
  Consolidation Prevention and Competition Act of 2019, 161–62
  Council of Economic Advisers, 61, 117, 119, 123, 158
  Department of Justice, 125–29
    exclusionary conduct cases, 45–47
    merger review by, 229–30
    narrow markets and, challenges to, 278–80

United States (U.S.) (cont.)
  First Amendment, 202
  FTC Act, 14
  Hart-Scott Rodino Act, 58
  National Economic Council, 4–5
  National Industrial Recovery Act, 81
  Robinson-Patman Acts, 11, 239, 307
    antitrust law and, 206
    consumer-welfare standard and, 257
    price discrimination prohibitions under, 16–17
  Silicon Valley
    antitrust interventions in, 36
    neoclassical antitrust and, 24–25
    superstar firms in, 133–34
  Telecommunications Act, 182, 192
Utah Statement, 175–226
  on anticompetitive conduct, 213–16
    cross-market effects, 213–14
  Anti-Merger Act in, 212–13
  antisteering clauses in, 214–16
  Berkley Photo standard, 187–89
  Clayton Act and
    enforcement of, 212–13
    exemptions from, 202–3
  collective bargaining in, 202–3
  Credit Suisse case and, 180–82
  as doctrine, 176–203
  enforcement practices in, 203–26
    under Clayton Act, 212–13
    costs of, 216
    after evidence of anticompetitive intent, 220–21
    against labor market monopsonies, 210–12
    for mergers, 222–24
    private, 208–10
    public, 208–10
    in states, as laboratories of economic experimentation, 207–8
    through structural remedies, 217–18
  Essential Facilities Doctrine and, 189–94
    forced sharing in, 189–90
    property rule in, 191
    transaction costs in, 190
  excessive industrial concentration in, 212–13
  First Amendment defenses, 202
  horizontal coordination in, 202–3
  limitation of liability in, 201
  linkLine Doctrine, 199–202
  merger review in, restoration of, 194–99
    through Federal Trade Commission, 195
    for natural monopolies, 196–97
    network effects, 196–97
    T-Mobile/Sprint merger, 198–99
  methodology practices in, 203–26
    for mergers, 222–24

for predictions of harm, 218–21
for relevant market definitions, 224–26
monopoly leveraging in, restoration of, 187–89
Noerr-Pennington case and, 202
non-compete agreements under, 179–80
preamble to, 175
predatory pricing in
  below-cost pricing as, 183–84
  Brooke Group test for, 182–87
  Khan on, 186–87
price squeezes in, 199–202
Schor case, 187–88
Sherman Act in, 203–5
statutory employment status in, 202–3
structuralism in, 194–99, 213
Trinko doctrine and, 180–82, 189, 191–92, 193–94
vertical coercion in, 177–79
vertical mergers in, 177–79
vertical restraints in, 177–79
  welfare effects of, 178
Weyerhaeuser test, for predatory bidding, 182–87
worker protections, as statutory, 202

verification condition, 56
vertical coercion, 177–79
vertical integration, 44
  market structure and, 86
vertical mergers, 31, 72, 177–79
  inhibition of, 86
  zero-efficiency vertical acquisition, 243
vertical restraints, 177–79
  welfare effects of, 178
volume rebates, 44

Walras, Léon, 76–77
Warren, Elizabeth, 4, 142–43, 150
  on anticompetitive mergers, 142–43
wealth maximization, antitrust law and, 16
Weimar Republic, in Germany, 30
welfare. *See also* consumer-welfare standard
  social-welfare, 16
  vertical restraints and, 178
Weyerhaeuser test, for predatory bidding, 182–87
workable competition, market structure and, 80–82
worker protections. *See* statutory worker protections
Wu, Timothy, 147, 175, 214–15. *See also* Utah Statement
  neo-Brandeisian movement and, 4–5, 29, 141, 146–49
  on consumer-welfare standard, 148, 250–51
  on EU competition law, 149

zero-efficiency vertical acquisition, 243

Lightning Source UK Ltd.
Milton Keynes UK
UKHW022002021221
394680UK00018B/473